New Zealand – New Caledonia:
Neighbours, Friends, Partners

La Nouvelle-Zélande et la Nouvelle-Calédonie:
Voisins, amis et partenaires

New Zealand – New Caledonia: Neighbours, Friends, Partners

La Nouvelle-Zélande et la Nouvelle-Calédonie: Voisins, amis et partenaires

Edited by
Frédéric Angleviel and Stephen Levine

Victoria University Press

TE WHARE WĀNANGA O TE ŪPOKO O TE IKA A MĀUI
VICTORIA
UNIVERSITY OF WELLINGTON

VICTORIA UNIVERSITY PRESS
Victoria University of Wellington
PO Box 600 Wellington
victoria.ac.nz/vup

First published 2008

National Library of New Zealand Cataloguing-in-Publication Data

New Zealand-New Caledonia : neighbours, friends and partners
= La Nouvelle-Zélande et la Nouvelle-Calédonie : voisins, amis
et partenaires / edited by Frédéric Angleviel, Stephen Levine.
Nouvelle-Zélande et la Nouvelle-Calédonie
ISBN 978-0-86473-582-9
1. New Zealand—Foreign relations—New Caledonia.
2. New Caledonia—Foreign relations—New Zealand.
3. New Caledonia—History. 4. New Zealand—History.
I. Angleviel, Frédéric. II. Levine, Stephen I.
327.9309597

Ouvrage honoré d'une subvention du Fonds de coopération économique, sociale et culturelle pour le Pacifique, Secrétariat permanent pour le Pacifique, Ministère des Affaires Etrangères, République française

Publication supported by the Government and Provinces of New Caledonia, and by France through the Fonds Pacifique

Printed by Printlink, Wellington

Contents

Part Two – the 20th century relationship

Part Three – the 21st century relationship

Foreword

New Caledonia owes its name to one of history's greatest navigators, James Cook, whose memory is closely linked to New Zealand and who in 1774 christened 'la Grande Ile' in reference to his native Scotland.

From the onset, this historical coincidence could have brought the two entities together. However, we have to acknowledge that the two populations have not entered into much contact. Despite the geographical proximity (Noumea is closer to Auckland than Brisbane or Sydney are), exchanges between the two countries have remained limited until relatively recently. Undoubtedly the reasons for this lack of mutual knowledge have been linguistic and cultural in nature. New Caledonia, which has an essentially European and Melanesian culture, feels less closely related to New Zealand, which for its part has a Polynesian culture.

The history of New Caledonia and that of New Zealand have evolved in parallel ways, met similar challenges. Both have had to surmount the tyranny of distance with France and England respectively. Their challenges have been very similar in terms of establishing multicultural and multi-ethnic societies, overcoming conflicts between indigenous populations and European immigrants, as well as in terms of economic diversification.

Yet links did exist during difficult times. During the second world war, New Caledonia was home to a contingent of 18,000 New Zealand soldiers who took part in the Pacific War from a veritable rearguard base on Caledonian territory. The memory of this period is piously kept alive at Bourail, which maintains with great care the cemetery where 32 New Zealanders are laid to rest. For that matter, a commemorative exhibition held in August 2007 at the Museum of Wellington City & Sea, as part of the New Caledonian Season in New Zealand, featured a particularly successful presentation of historical photographs.

New Caledonia is establishing its position in the South Pacific thanks to its new constitutional status after the signing of the Matignon Agreements in 1988, allowing it to enjoy new competencies. From this time on local and provincial governments, elected by the New Caledonian people, have been responsible for economic and social development. This autonomy also applies to fiscal, commercial and legal matters, through control of the budget vote, local tax allocations and the adoption of the territory's own specific laws. In addition, New Caledonia plays an increasing role in regional affairs following its admission to the Pacific Islands Forum as an associate member.

This evolution, accompanied by a significant transfer of funds from the French state, has gone hand in hand with economic development sustained by the high prices of commodities like nickel, of which New Caledonia is an important producer. In political terms, this will offer the inhabitants the possibility to choose, from 2014, the option of acceding to full sovereignty if they so desire.

This economic flourishing and the clarification of the political status warrant a renewed mutual interest between New Zealand and New Caledonia, who share their standard of living as well as common interests. These links were reinforced following the visit in 2003 of Phil Goff, Minister of Foreign Affairs at the time. Subsequently Mme Marie-Noëlle Thémereau made an official visit to New Zealand, in 2005, as President of the New Caledonian government.

The exchanges are not limited to the economy and politics. The richness and diversity of Kanak culture have been discovered by a large number of New Zealanders who participated in cultural events or visited exhibitions organised as part of the New Caledonian Season in New Zealand. The relationships that were formed between partners of the two countries on this occasion will undoubtedly serve to develop future collaborations between artists and administrators of cultural institutions, which we all hope will be fruitful and long lasting.

In terms of scientific exchanges, fruitful links already exist between universities and research insitutes of New Zealand and New Caledonia, which collaborate on numerous research projects, particularly in the fields of geology, marine sciences, horticulture and agriculture as well as the social sciences.

Victoria University of Wellington and the University of New Caledonia have played a major role in bringing together these two very close yet very different neighbours, thanks to their joint initiative in organising a bilingual academic seminar on a broad range of topics. We thank them for this successful effort, on which they are to be warmly congratulated.

Hon. Michel Legras
Ambassador of France
– New Zealand

La Nouvelle-Calédonie doit son nom à l'un des plus grands navigateurs de l'Histoire, James Cook dont le souvenir est étroitement lié à la Nouvelle Zélande et qui baptisa en 1774 la « Grande Île » en référence à son Ecosse natale.

Ce hasard historique aurait pu, dès l'origine, rapprocher les deux entités. Pourtant force est de constater que les deux populations se sont longtemps assez peu fréquentées. Malgré la proximité géographique (Nouméa est plus proche d'Auckland que celle-ci ne l'est de Brisbane ou Sydney), les échanges entre les deux pays sont restés, jusqu'à une date récente, relativement limitée.

Sans doute faut-il rechercher la raison de cette méconnaissance mutuelle dans la dimension linguistique et culturelle. La Nouvelle Calédonie, à la culture essentiellement mélanésienne et européenne, se sent moins proche de la Nouvelle Zélande marquée, quant à elle, par la culture polynésienne.

L'Histoire de la Nouvelle Calédonie et de la Nouvelle Zélande a connu des cheminements parallèles, faits de défis comparables. Toutes deux ont dû surmonter la tyrannie des distances avec, respectivement, la France et l'Angleterre. Les défis ont été fortement similaires, en termes d'établissement de sociétés multi-culturelles et multi-ethniques, de dépassement des conflits entre populations autochtones et immigrants européens, et de diversification économique.

Les liens n'ont cependant pas manqué lorsque les temps furent difficiles. Pendant la Seconde Guerre Mondiale, la Nouvelle Calédonie a abrité un contingent de 18 000 soldats néo-zélandais qui ont participé à la Guerre du Pacifique à partir de cette véritable base arrière qu'a constitué le territoire calédonien. Le souvenir de cette période est pieusement conservé à Bourail qui entretient avec soin le cimetière où reposent 32 Néo-Zélandais. Une exposition commémorative, présentée en août 2007 au City and Sea Museum de Wellington dans le cadre de la Saison de la Nouvelle Calédonie en Nouvelle Zélande, a d'ailleurs connu un remarquable succès pour sa présentation de photographies d'époque.

La Nouvelle Calédonie s'affirme dans le Pacifique Sud, grâce à son statut original en termes institutionnels, qui lui permet, depuis la signature des Accords de Matignon en 1988, de disposer de compétences nouvelles. Le gouvernement local, directement élu par la population de Nouvelle Calédonie, et les Provinces sont désormais responsables du développement économique et social. Cette autonomie s'exerce également dans les domaines fiscaux, commerciaux et légaux, avec la maîtrise du vote du budget, l'affectation des impôts locaux et l'adoption de lois propres au territoire. De surcroît la Nouvelle Calédonie joue un rôle croissant dans les affaires régionales depuis qu'elle a été admise, comme membre associé, au Forum des Îles du Pacifique.

Cette évolution, accompagnée d'un transfert financier important de la part de l'Etat français, s'accompagne d'un développement économique soutenu par le prix élevé des matières premières comme le nickel dont la Nouvelle Calédonie est un important producteur. Au niveau politique, elle ouvre la possibilité aux habitants de choisir, à partir de 2014, la possibilité d'accéder à la pleine souveraineté s'ils le désirent.

Cet essor économique et cette clarification du statut politique justifient un regain d'intérêt mutuel entre la Nouvelle Zélande et la Nouvelle Calédonie qui partagent un niveau de vie et des intérêts communs. Les liens se sont resserrés à partir de la visite de Phil Goff, à l'époque ministre des affaires étrangères, en 2003. Mme Marie-Noëlle Thémereau qui présidait alors le gouvernement de Nouvelle Calédonie, a effectué en 2005 un déplacement officiel en Nouvelle Zélande.

Les échanges ne se limitent pas à l'économie et à la politique. La richesse et la diversité de la culture kanak ont été une découverte pour nombre de Néo-Zélandais qui ont assisté aux manifestations culturelles ou visité les expositions organisées dans le cadre de la Saison de la Nouvelle Calédonie en Nouvelle Zélande. Les relations établies entre les partenaires des deux pays à cette occasion serviront à n'en pas douter aux collaborations futures que chacun espère fructueuses et durables entre artistes et administrateurs d'institutions culturelles.

Sur le plan des échanges scientifiques, il existe déjà des liens fructueux entre les universités et instituts de recherche de la Nouvelle-Zélande et de la Nouvelle-Calédonie qui collaborent à de nombreux projets de recherche, notamment dans les domaines de la géologie, des sciences marines, de l'horticulture et de l'agriculture, ainsi que les sciences humaines et sociales.

L'université Victoria de Wellington et celle de Nouvelle Calédonie ont joué un rôle majeur dans ce rapprochement des deux voisins si différents et si proches, grâce à leur initiative commune d'organiser un colloque académique bilingue sur une variété de sujets. Qu'elles en soient chaleureusement félicitées et remerciées.

Hon. Michel Legras
Ambassadeur de France
à Nouvelle-Zélande

Foreword

The Museum of Wellington's exhibition *War in Paradise – the unofficial story of New Zealand soldiers in New Caledonia 1942-44* opened as the proceedings for the New Zealand-New Caledonia relations conference closed on the afternoon of 31 August 2007. The exhibition depicted through photo and song, text and imagery, the unofficial history of New Zealand soldiers in New Caledonia 1942-44.

Officially opened by Minister of Veterans' Affairs Rick Barker it was attended by members of Parliament, the Wellington City mayor and councillors, and representatives of the Embassy of France as well as a delegation from New Caledonia with representatives of the government of New Caledonia and the township of Bourail.

As the curator of *War in Paradise* my focus was on the relationships between the people depicted in the photographs – New Zealand third division members and the New Caledonian people, whether Kanak, Caldoche, French, Indonesian or Vietnamese. It is this community of people, and their relationships, that is important – both in *War in Paradise*, and in the cross-national conference that we were pleased to host. It is also, inevitably, the principal focus of this book of the conference.

The conference theme complemented the exhibition, highlighting New Zealanders' and New Caledonians' experience of one another. More specifically, the conference agenda provided for discussions of New Zealand soldiers' experiences in New Caledonia during the two world wars.

The exhibition and the conference were supported by the government and provinces of New Caledonia and France through the Fonds Pacifique. And both were communal projects, involving collaborations and partnerships among a variety of people, based in New Zealand, New Caledonia and metropolitan France.

It is hoped that this record will contribute to further the relationship between the peoples of New Zealand and New Caledonia, of the past, to the present and into the future.

Brett Mason
Director
Museum of Wellington

Preface

This book arises out of two conferences held as part of the 'New Caledonia New Zealand Season 2007' – an initiative aimed at raising the profile of New Caledonia in New Zealand – the first in New Caledonia (on ANZAC Day), and the second in New Zealand. These conferences, and other events (including the exhibition of photographs, 'War in Paradise – The unofficial story of New Zealand soldiers in New Caledonia 1942-44', held at the Museum of Wellington City & Sea), draw attention to the relationship between two Pacific Island neighbours, each at different stages of political development but with many shared interests and concerns. While New Zealand is an independent country and New Caledonia is not, from a political standpoint the two entitles nevertheless have a great deal in common, including a commitment to the rule of law, free elections and democratic political processes. Although language differences remain a significant barrier, an increasingly close relationship can nevertheless be expected, arising out of economic and political ties as well as cultural and intellectual contacts such as those that have led to this book.

Cet ouvrage est le résultat de deux conferences qui se sont tenues en 2007 dans le cadre de la saison calédonienne en Nouvelle-Zélande, l'une en Nouvelle-Calédonie lors de l'ANZAC day, l'autre en Nouvelle-Zélande. Ces conferences et d'autres événements culturels, dont l'exposition, 'War in Paradise – The unofficial story of New Zealand soldiers in New Caledonia 1942-44', ont attiré l'attention des Néo-Zélandais sur les relations entre ces deux archipels voisins, qui partagent un certain nombre d'intérêts communs. Alors que la Nouvelle-Zélande est un Etat indépendant et que la Nouvelle-Calédonie ne l'est pas, ces deux entités ont de nombreuses similarités au niveau politique : l'importance des lois, des élections libres et une vie démocratique normale. Bien que la langue reste une barrière importante, des relations de plus en plus amicales et fécondes se développent tant au niveau économique que politique, culturel ou intellectuel, ainsi que cet ouvrage en fait foi.

Introduction

This book is the result of a series of meetings looking at the New Caledonia–New Zealand relationship. The first was held in New Caledonia, at the New Zealand memorial at the cemetery at Bourail, and took place on ANZAC Day – 25 April – in 2007. The second was held in Wellington in August 2007, over two days, at the Museum of Wellington City & Sea, by the city's waterfront.

Each occasion provided an opportunity for a range of perspectives to be offered on the relationship between the two 'new' entities – New Zealand and New Caledonia – including commentaries on economic, security and religious links between the two, as well as presentations drawing attention to literary and cultural aspects. These various perspectives are to be found in this book, with contributors including scholars from a range of disciplines, among them historians, linguists, and anthropologists. Some of the contributors are based in New Zealand and others in New Caledonia; several of the participants in this volume are based in France, with others in Australia. The book itself is alternately bilingual, with some of the chapters appearing in English (with abstracts in French) and others in French (with abstracts in English). The descriptions of the contributors to the book, given at the back, are in both languages.

While the book is not the last word on the New Zealand-New Caledonia relationship – no volume can ever hope to be, so long as that relationship continues to evolve – neither is it the first. In 2006, for instance, an initiative from the French Embassy in New Zealand saw the publication of *60 years ago . . . celebrating the anniversary of diplomatic relations between New Zealand and France*, a work which identified historical, cultural, military and diplomatic connections among France, New Zealand and New Caledonia.

Likewise, this book, with its dual title – *New Zealand – New Caledonia: Neighbours, Friends, Partners*; *La Nouvelle-Zélande et la Nouvelle-Calédonie: Voisins, amis et partenaires* – draws attention to a relationship that has various facets to it – economic, political, military and cultural – and that has developed across a number of recognisable historical periods. A nineteenth century relationship that involved colonial conquest and settlement, and Christian missionary activity, can hardly be compared with the broader dynamics associated with twentieth and twenty-first century interactions. In this latter period a relationship influenced by world war has evolved to be influenced by post-war anti-colonial trends and outlooks. A contemporary look at developments within each entity sees emphasis given to more egalitarian and respectful attitudes towards indigenous peoples, and the emergence of political cultures and outlooks significantly different from those of earlier periods and, of course, from the perspectives of these polities' colonial creators, Britain and France.

The New Caledonia-New Zealand relationship: a political perspective

As a political scientist I am drawn, by inclination, experience and training, to look at the *political* features of relationships. As a result, I want to make just a few observations which introduce that point of view into this publication.

While the two conferences alluded to above point towards a closer attention being paid to the relationship between New Zealand and New Caledonia, historically, the two entities have not tended to look across to each other with any kind of instinctive or natural affinity.

New Zealand, for much of its history, looked to Great Britain, seeing itself as part of the British Empire, with *its* destiny and Britain's joined together. It was as *British* citizens that New Zealanders made their way in the world and it was only with much reluctance that New Zealand, gradually, made its way towards a more distinctive, and separate, identity.

Similarly, for New Caledonia, familiarity and self-interest led to its perspective being towards France, with the territory itself seen constitutionally as an integral component of sovereign French territory.

In summarising matters like this, I am, of course, referring to the history of the two entities since their acquisition by Britain and France during the nineteenth century. Now if matters are looked at in a more contemporary way, it is possible to see a progression of developments which have made New Zealand and New Caledonia more relevant to each other, more salient to each other, than previously has been the case.

For both territories, there has been a gradual shift of perspective away from Europe towards the Pacific region in which they are, of course, actually to be found. While a major difference – perhaps *the* major difference – between New Zealand and New Caledonia is and has been one of language, preventing there from being an ease of communication between peoples from the two territories, the linguistic barrier was accompanied in the past by an historic mistrust, an antagonism, between the two European nations, Britain and France, to which each territory was instinctively aligned from the onset of colonisation.

These once mutually exclusive loyalties have lost a good deal of their power. Britain and France, though still at times given to mutual acrimony and intermittent expressions of national stereotypes, have long since lost any sense of national enmity. They constitute, together, what political scientists term a 'security community': that is, neither need take any precautions against the possibility of an attack by the other. Two hundred years ago this sense of security, this confidence, would have seemed delusional. Now, in this extended post-second world war era, with the two nations being members of NATO and of the European Union, we can characterise Britain and France as allies, partners, even friends – former adversaries, former colonial competitors, now in a sometimes ambiguous relationship, but enemies no longer.

It is possible, therefore, even natural, for entities associated with Britain and France, though geographically distant from them, likewise to regard each other with a greater degree of warmth – to perceive opportunities and to seek to make the most of them.

It is sometimes said that states are more likely to develop closer relations with each other, the more closely they begin to resemble each other. Thus countries that share similar values, goals and political institutions can be expected to recognise more readily the affinity between them than those whose outlook, objectives and systems of government are markedly different.

From this perspective, once the principal divide – i.e., the linguistic barrier and the opposed British and French associations that were associated with colonial acquisition and settlement – between these two nations is put to one side, it seems evident that the two territories have far more in common than is generally appreciated.

Each country brings to its political culture – its basic set of values relating to politics – traditions, habits and customs that are recognisably democratic. The French inheritance inclines New Caledonia's polity towards those famous, and constitutionally embedded, transcendent values – liberté, égalité et fraternité.

Similarly, the British inheritance causes New Zealand's polity, constitutionally casual though it may be, to consider freedom, the rule of law and a sense that people should be treated fairly, behaving towards one another with common decency, to be innate and fundamental to the country's character.

These aspirations, though expressed in different ways, with different motifs and through different languages, *are* fundamentally similar in outlook.

In both New Zealand and New Caledonia, moreover, it is expected that *the rule of law* will be upheld through an independent and professional court system; that the laws themselves will be enacted by an assembly comprised of elected representatives; that the elections will be 'free and fair', their results respected; that the political executive – that is, the government – will be drawn from the assembly. In other words, in both places there is a *parliamentary* system, with a Cabinet and with Ministers responsible to the assembly. Both New Zealand and New Caledonia have elected local governments, too, as well as political party systems, competitive election campaigns, and independent voices heard through the news media.

In each country, too, the hope that women will play a more equal role in government, politics and the law has gained more widespread acceptance, with tangible results. In New Zealand, at the time of publication (2008) women were holding the positions of Prime Minister, Speaker of the House of Representatives, and

Chief Justice of the Supreme Court – being at the head, therefore, of the executive, legislative and judicial branches of government. This is in addition to a woman serving as Head of State – Queen Elizabeth II – who, until only fairly recently (August 2006), was represented in New Zealand by a female Governor-General. Indeed, the 1999 New Zealand election was noticeable for the fact that for the first time each of New Zealand's two major parties (Labour and National) was led by a woman, meaning that whichever party won the election a female prime minister was a certainty.

In New Caledonia, likewise, until recently (July 2007) a woman was the head of the territorial government, with another woman serving as her deputy.

Similarly, in both New Zealand and New Caledonia there have also been strides taken towards greater numbers of indigenous representatives taking up positions in government. In both countries, therefore, there has been an awareness in recent times of the awkwardness for democratic purposes of imbalances in representation when viewed from either a gender or ethnic perspective. As a result, in both polities, with the support of public opinion and with leadership from intellectual and cultural elites, there has been progress made towards reducing these imbalances. In New Zealand, for instance, the number of Maori members of Parliament has increased since the introduction of a new electoral system in 1996; there has also been a growth in the number of Maori members of Cabinet; and, following the 2005 election, for the first time in New Zealand's history the country is represented in its international dealings through a Maori serving in the post of Minister of Foreign Affairs. In New Caledonia, likewise, the woman serving as deputy head of the territorial government was an indigenous Melanesian, and no doubt other examples can also be given of developments in this area, including, of course, the Kanak majorities in several of the provincial governments established as a result of the accords negotiated with the support and active participation of the French government.

A comparative politics perspective can also not fail to note that the major unresolved problem in both societies has to do with a comparable historic legacy, namely, the relationship between the descendants of migrants (largely from Europe, principally Britain in one case and France in the other) and the indigenous population. In each case, matters (at least demographically) have continued to become increasingly complex, with bi-national or bi-cultural arrangements now something of an oversimplification, given the increasingly heterogenous character of their make-up, as residents now come from various Asian countries and other Pacific islands, and with even the European composition of the population no longer exclusively British or French in origin.

So it is not only in their values and democratic institutions that New Zealand and New Caledonia have so much recognisably in common, politically, but also in the challenge facing their political development, with, in a sense, the basic legitimacy of the system still in question as a result of the aforementioned unresolved issue – one whose implications can scarcely be exaggerated.

In both territories, too, there remains, steadily evolving, a transformation of what is generally referred to as 'national identity'. New Zealanders, only a few decades ago, began more confidently to think of themselves as something other than British people who happened to be living in the South Pacific. What has replaced this once common identity is less stable, but seems to involve a sense of distinctiveness in which certain elements have become paramount: the position of New Zealand in the Pacific; the position of Maori as the indigenous people, with a distinctive culture of their own; and a recognisably distinct policy outlook for the country, as an automatic ally of no one – not the British, not the Americans, not the Australians; a country not 'Western', not Asian, not entirely Polynesian either but something else – possessed of an outlook in which pride in a defiant *nuclear-free* and, more recently, *Iraq war-free* stance plays a large role.

In New Caledonia, too, there seems to be a move away from simply being French citizens somehow living in the South Pacific, but otherwise no different from people in Paris or Lyon, Marseille or Aix-en-Provence. Again, there is, instead, an acceptance of the Pacific location; an emerging pride in the Melanesian, or Kanak, culture; and the possibilities of a more positive and productive partnership relationship developing between indigenous peoples and other groups. This represents something of a political, cultural and psychological evolution, one that has combined to produce a new identity, so that all residents of New Caledonia regard the territory as having a separate and viable political identity, whatever that may be, irrespective of what eventual relationship with France may someday be validated and confirmed through subsequent legislative and referendum-related developments.

For New Zealand, the acceptance of a Pacific identity – as at least part of the country's sense of itself – has been expressed, politically, through its membership (as a founding member) in the Pacific Islands Forum, which held its first-ever meeting in the New Zealand capital, Wellington, in 1971.

For New Caledonia, too, recognition that it is, essentially, a Pacific polity – whatever links to France it may possess – has also brought about, fairly recently, an association with the Pacific Islands Forum (admitted in 2006 as an Associate Member). For New Caledonia – as for other French Pacific territories – participation in the affairs of the Forum, as an ongoing element in what might be called the territory's foreign policy, likewise brings it closer to New Zealand, not only through the contacts that will take place between New Zealand and New Caledonia at Forum meetings and under Forum auspices, but because for both entities, almost grudgingly, and certainly gradually, the logic of their location has finally brought each of them to seek a more secure and prosperous existence predicated on at least a partly Pacific identity for each of them, complemented by a determination to preserve, protect and defend the idea of cooperation and shared enterprise in the Pacific region.

Conclusion

From a political point of view a considerable convergence between New Zealand and New Caledonia can be observed, with each increasingly seeking to bring about, within their territories, social, economic, political and cultural relations among all groups that are more in line with the basic values of justice, equity and tolerance to which these societies like to consider themselves dedicated. In their external relations, too, there seems a greater likelihood that each will see in the other a shared outlook, in which Pacific cooperation is seen as desirable, and in which Pacific security – which ultimately embraces human security for Pacific Island inhabitants – is given an increasingly high priority. This reordering of priorities would at least in part reflect a recognition that the Pacific, too, can become exposed to malign purposes if neglected; thus 'benign neglect' in the shared immediate neighbourhood of New Zealand and New Caledonia is not, and never can be, truly 'benign' at all.

Finally, of course, conferences and books such as this one – as well as visits, diverse publications, cultural and educational exchanges, tourism, trade and investment – all have a role to play in overcoming neglect, repairing indifference, and enlarging a relationship between Pacific Island neighbours whose importance from a number of vantage points has for too long been overshadowed. Barring the unforeseen, I believe that we can look forward to a future in which the relationship between New Zealand and New Caledonia, on many levels, will continue to both broaden and deepen – to use the language of the EU – to become ever closer, with consequences that can only be for the mutual benefit of the residents and citizens of both Pacific polities.

Stephen Levine
Professor
Political Science and International Relations
Victoria University of Wellington

Introduction

New Zealand in Perspective – Identity and the Search for Security

Stephen Levine

New Zealand's history as a modern state begins with colonial settlement by British migrants, with a pivotal event being the signing of the Treaty of Waitangi in February 1840. British rule over the territory known as New Zealand led to the establishment of political institutions, with the colony evolving towards full internal self-government over the remainder of the nineteenth and early twentieth century. New Zealand's independence was recognised by its membership in the post-World War I League of Nations and the post-World War II United Nations, with full independence being achieved through the ratification by the New Zealand Parliament of the Statute of Westminster in 1947. New Zealand has become a diverse society – multi-cultural and multi-ethnic – while recognising a special status for the Maori people as the indigenous population. In international affairs New Zealand has adopted an independent foreign policy, diversifying economic, diplomatic and political links with countries in the Asia-Pacific region as well as in Europe, the Middle East and the Americas.

L'histoire de la Nouvelle-Zélande en tant qu'Etat moderne commence lors de la colonisation des deux îles par des immigrants anglais, avec l'événement fondamental que fut la signature du traité de Waitangi en février 1840. L'instauration de la loi anglaise dans un territoire désormais dénommé Nouvelle-Zélande entraina l'établissement d'institutions politiques, la colonie évoluant vers l'autonomie interne dès la fin du dix-neuvième siècle. L'indépendance d'action de la Nouvelle-Zélande fut reconnue lors de sa participation à la

Société des Nations puis lors de la création de l'Organisation des Nations Unies. Son indépendance pleine et entière pris place en 1947 lorsque le parlement de la Nouvelle-Zélande ratifia le statut de Westminster. La Nouvelle-Zélande est devenue une société plurielle – multiculturelle et multiraciale – qui reconnaît un statut particulier à la population autochtone. En ce qui concerne les affaires internationales, la Nouvelle-Zélande a développé une politique autonome, diversifiant ses liens économiques, diplomatiques et politiques avec de nombreux pays, tant dans la région Asie-Pacifique qu'en Europe, tant en Orient qu'avec les Amériques.

A historian of the United States of America can choose to begin that history with the establishment of the country now known by that name – a country with a written constitution, a government in Washington and state governments in 50 states, elections, political and social institutions of various kinds, and – to sum up – a meaningful narrative of national experience arising out of events, ideas and circumstances. There are, of course, many ways to tell that history, but in addition to those choices, of methodology, perspective and interpretation, there is the initial one of starting point – where, precisely, to begin.

For prior to the establishment of the country there was a period of settlement, with migrants arriving from Britain to establish colonies, situated along the eastern seaboard of the north American continent. Of course, prior to that there was a history of European exploration and 'discovery', as sailors encountered a new land, with a distinctive geography and peoples previously unknown to them. Or the story of America – the country as it is today – can be begun with those earlier inhabitants, indigenous peoples, organised into various tribal groups dispersed across an entire continent, already there, 'from sea to shining sea'.

Much the same challenge faces anyone seeking to provide a history of a place – where to begin? It is a challenge especially difficult for historians of communities established by external settlement – by colonial possession and migration – as indigenous and migrant communities together inhabit a new/old land, with a new identity and new institutions.

New Zealand in Perspective

This relatively brief historical overview is not intended as a systematic account of the land on which now is to be found the nation-state of New Zealand. Nor is it intended as a history of the people now to be found living on that land, as residents and citizens. Other histories serve those purposes[1] and this account is provided in any case merely as a brief introduction to New Zealand intended for contextual purposes, as background for the detailed discussions of New Zealand culture, society and development that follow later in this book. New Zealand and New Caledonia are juxtaposed in this volume, chapter by chapter, and it seemed appropriate to the editors to offer at the outset an historical backdrop before readers move on to the more focused expositions given by the book's various other contributors.

The chapter that follows this one, by Frédéric Angleviel, provides a detailed look at the history of the territory known (in English, in any event) as New Caledonia, with an account of the development of the territory under French sovereignty complemented by a narrative emphasising the culture and traditions of indigenous peoples prior to French settlement. The formation and development of the contemporary New Zealand state likewise was preceded by a period of indigenous habitation in which distinctive cultures and lifestyles flourished.[2]

The territory of New Caledonia remains a part of metropolitan France, full sovereignty not yet achieved. It does not, as yet, possess the attributes of a separate, independent nation-state; perhaps it may never do so. Its future, in this respect, is yet to be clarified.

As for New Zealand, it *is* an independent state, and it seems appropriate, given the limited purposes associated with this chapter (and the space available), to confine the background history to an account of the establishment of this state and its development as a self-governing, independent entity, free – although precisely when it became so is difficult to say[3] – from British rule.

There are some key dates in New Zealand's progression towards recognised independent statehood.[4] The most important, for New Zealanders, is 6 February 1840, the day on which a treaty was signed between the chiefs (or representatives) of various Maori tribes and a British naval captain. This document, the Treaty of Waitangi, provided (in British understanding, at least) for British sovereignty over the country, at the same time offering protection for indigenous tribal interests (over land, certainly, but also over other 'taonga' ['treasures'] as well) while granting Maori 'the rights and privileges of British subjects'.[5] Thus a political entity was established – New Zealand, a territorial dependency (or colony) of Great Britain – and at the same time the existence of a distinct indigenous population was affirmed and recognised, to be regarded as a people entitled to certain collective rights as well as the liberties and privileges owed to individuals by virtue of their lawful and equal status as members of the wider British polity.

The Treaty of Waitangi – now considered to be New Zealand's 'founding document' – has its own history, from rather muddled beginnings, through neglect and indifference, on through to its current position as a deeply respected agreement with a nonetheless controversial setting within contemporary New Zealand society. In any case, whatever various views of the treaty's contemporary relevance and meaning may be, New Zealand's history as a British territory may be said to begin with what the British understood to be a treaty of cession.

Under British rule it was not long before various steps were being taken to 'invent' a south seas Britain in miniature. A capital 'city' was established; a ruling Governor (dispatched from, and responsible to, London) was appointed; and a colonial government (with an elected legislature) was brought into being. Settlements of British colonists were established in the two rather prosaically named 'North' and 'South' islands, which began to acquire farms and urban centres along with a rudimentary infrastructure. Conflicts between settlers and the indigenous population led in due course, and perhaps inevitably, to wars that encompassed British soldiers and settler militias. These battles, like the treaty that was intended to forestall them, have also cast a long shadow, with unresolved grievances and memories still.

While New Zealand's overall population numbers grew steadily during the nineteenth century, the indigenous population declined significantly, leading many observers to consider its fate as having been sealed. In the twentieth century, however, the Maori population stabilised and then grew, with intermarriage and economic recovery contributing to population growth. The colony of New Zealand in some ways came to distinguish itself with the innovative character of its politics.[6] In 1867 parliamentary representation for the indigenous population was introduced, with four Maori seats being established. A system of distinct Maori parliamentary representation remains to this day.[7]

International developments

New Zealanders like to consider that the introduction of votes for women in 1893 made New Zealand the first 'country' to introduce women's suffrage.[8] While New Zealand had a degree of autonomy and self-government through its elected House of Representatives, it was not yet considered to be an independent country but rather a colonial dependency within the British Empire. Loyalty was to Britain, in the person of the British monarch, who is still today, by law, the New Zealand Head of State (with a representative in New Zealand known as the Governor-General).

Indeed, it was as a proud and loyal member of the British Empire that New Zealand joined the British campaign in South Africa, known as the Boer war, in 1899. It was, still, as a part of the Empire that New Zealand took part in the first world war. This was, however, an experience that came, in the end, to enlarge the sense of a separate and distinct New Zealand nationhood, although it was a separate identity that New Zealanders in no way saw as being in conflict with loyal membership in the larger Empire. If it was a proud claim, in ancient times, to declare oneself 'civitas romanus' – a citizen of the Roman Empire – then for New Zealanders, in the nineteenth century and for the first decades of the twentieth, it was an equally honoured boast to proclaim oneself a citizen of Britain, a member, by birth and by right, of the greatest empire the world had ever known.

But New Zealand's loyal membership of an Empire was at odds with both its own internal dynamic towards self-government and, in due course, a perhaps inevitable drive towards self-assertion, as well as with internal tensions within the Empire itself among its various constituent members. In 1907 New Zealand's political status was upgraded to that of 'Dominion', an ambiguous term that nevertheless suggested a kind of independent position within a larger Empire entity. The first world war saw New Zealand contribute large numbers of men to that conflict – a significant proportion of the colony's total non-Maori adult male population – suffering severely as a result. While the most famous battle area for New Zealanders (and Australians) was at Gallipoli, in which an utterly doomed struggle was waged against the Turks, many more New Zealanders went on to perish on the Western front, in the trench warfare waged on French battlefields against a strong German adversary.[9]

It was as a 'Dominion' – a part of the British realm – that New Zealand signed the postwar Treaty of Versailles, inscribing its signature to that document in its own right and subsequently joining the newly established League of Nations as a founding member. As the League was open only to independent states, it is clear that New Zealand was, by that stage, by definition, an independent country. Nevertheless, it was as a 'Dominion', still, that New Zealand entered the second world war against Germany, with the country's Anglocentric focus sharply in evidence in the New Zealand prime minister's rationale for doing so. After all, the British decision to declare the existence of a state of war with Nazi Germany stemmed from a rather late expression of British resolve, finally taking shape in the country's determination to honour its commitment to Poland's independence. For New Zealand – far from Poland and with no such commitment at stake – entry into war may seem in retrospect paradoxical, yet it was nonetheless a foregone conclusion, with Prime Minister Michael Joseph Savage declaring, 'where Britain goes, we go; where Britain stands, we stand'. Nothing much more needed to be said by way of rationale for the New Zealanders of 1939 outlook.[10]

New Zealanders fought in Europe, the Middle East and in the

Pacific Islands, a small country not exactly taking on the world but certainly involved, fully, in what had become a world-wide conflict.[11] The postwar settlement saw New Zealand Prime Minister Peter Fraser contributing to the formulation of the United Nations Charter, with New Zealand joining the U.N. as a founding member.[12] Two years later saw New Zealand, at last, ratifying the 1931 British Act of Parliament known as the Statute of Westminster, thus achieving formal, legal 'independence', leaving behind 'Dominion' status to become, rather quietly, a fully independent state.[13] In 1951 New Zealand signed the peace treaty with Japan, at the same time entering into a military alliance (known as ANZUS) with the United States and Australia. It was a security guarantee, initially accepted against the possibility of a resurgent Japan but later repositioned as a hedge against an expansive Asian communist threat. This treaty remained the cornerstone of New Zealand's security thinking, irrespective of which party (National or Labour) governed the country, until July 1984, when a new Labour government, committed to a non-nuclear policy, barred U.S. naval vessels from visiting New Zealand ports (in the absence of explicit guarantees that they were neither nuclear-powered nor nuclear-armed), a step considered by the United States as inconsistent with the alliance relationship.

The post-1984 governments of New Zealand have had, as a result, a significantly different orientation from those that preceded them. In this respect, what political scientists call 'path dependency' can be said to have had a significant impact on developments. Put succinctly, the path taken in mid-1984 established a direction that proved, in the end, too difficult for any political party seeking a place in government to reverse. The momentum towards a non- (or anti-) nuclear status led, in turn, to an act of Parliament enshrining the policy into law. New Zealand also worked, successfully, with Pacific Island countries to introduce a treaty establishing a nuclear-free zone in the South Pacific.[14] More broadly, New Zealand came increasingly to adhere to an independent foreign policy, distancing the country from its traditional allies, Britain, the United States and Australia. The sinking of a Greenpeace protest vessel, the Rainbow Warrior, in the harbour of New Zealand's largest city, Auckland, by French agents (some of whom were apprehended and placed on trial), played its part as well in consolidating the anti-nuclear and 'independent' outlooks,[15] the latter, at times, in effect coming to mean 'anti-Western'.

Internal politics

New Zealand's domestic politics also show evidence of the development of an approach and outlook distinct from British origins. From its earliest days as a colony New Zealand was populated by settlers expecting, where possible, assistance from the state. How else could a new society be established? A happy readiness to accept help led, by steps, to a kind of welfare state, introduced in the 1890s by New Zealand's first formal party government (organised by the Liberals). It was under the Liberals, too, that women acquired the right to vote.[16]

Under the auspices of the Liberal Party, first under John Ballance (1891-93) and then under Richard John Seddon (1893-1905), a series of measures were introduced offering New Zealanders a degree of protection (old age pensions) against adversity. A visitor to New Zealand's parliamentary grounds, today, will see only two statues outside the buildings – monuments to two Liberal premiers, Ballance and Seddon, indicating the respect accorded to them for the contribution made by them and their governments to the welfare of New Zealanders.

In other ways the society that the colonists worked towards established a cultural distance from Britain. The entrenched class consciousness common to Britain was far less important in a far-off colony where industry, self-reliance, hard work and collective effort were necessary if the colony were to establish itself, endure and progress. There was also much less religious prejudice. In the 1870s Julius Vogel, a Jewish immigrant, became the colony's premier, proving to be one of its most energetic, responsible for a visionary programme of infrastructure development. Francis Henry Dillon Bell, a descendant of the founder of the Wellington Jewish community, Abraham Hort, also held high office, serving briefly (in May 1925) as prime minister.

New Zealand today is a country of more than four million

people, with a relatively low population density. The country offers an attractive and varied environment, from warm beaches in the far north and the east of the North Island through to ski fields in the central North Island and the South Island (with its glaciers). There are also intermittently active volcanoes and far from infrequent earth tremors. While the capital city is Wellington, the country's largest city is Auckland (with roughly one-quarter of the New Zealand population).[17] The two largest South Island cities are Christchurch and Dunedin, with Queenstown a major tourist centre.

Contemporary New Zealand politics and society is much more complex than the previous British/Maori dichotomy – itself a simplification, since 'British' immigrants included arrivals from England, Ireland, Wales and Scotland, while 'Maori' have held enduring tribal identities, separate from any all-encompassing ethnic or national label. Immigration has transformed the country into a multi-cultural society.[18] While those identifying as Maori are approximately 15 per cent of the total, the remaining 85 per cent comprise Pacific Islanders (itself a composite category embracing Samoans, Cook Islanders, Tokelauans, Niueans, Tongans and others), Asians (largely people of Indian and Chinese ethnicity and ancestry, but also including Cambodians and Vietnamese among others), Somali refugees, and other ethnic and national groups. The once-common presumption that non-Maori were almost invariably 'European' – i.e., New Zealanders descended from European migrants, largely from Great Britain and Ireland – is certainly no longer true.

The diversity of culture and national origin has its counterpart in a growing political diversity. Where once, in a sense, New Zealand's politics revolved around a two-party rivalry, competing for power and resources, New Zealand politics since the late 1980s has become a more complex multi-party competition. This became institutionalised in 1996 when the country held its first elections under a new, 'mixed member' proportional [MMP] electoral system, first recommended in 1986 by a royal commission and then approved in referendums held in 1992 and 1993.[19] All governments elected since 1996 have been coalition governments, and both the style of government (more consultative, at least among the ruling coalition's constituent parties) and its content have altered over this period.[20] The post-1996 governments have largely ended the surge of deregulation that characterised the 1984 Labour government, which had joined a neo-liberal pro-privatisation agenda to its independent foreign policy to present a hybrid right-left face to the world and to the New Zealand electorate. The New Zealand coalition governments under MMP have been more pragmatic, less ideological, recognising the tenacity of New Zealanders' expectations for government assistance and protection; consequently the role of the state (and the size of taxation) in New Zealand society has continued to be strong.

Identity and security

As with any society – with any person, in fact – New Zealand's history can also be approached as a search for a distinct identity. New Zealanders' sense of themselves – and, it might be said, the 'purpose' of their country – remains incomplete, in a state of becoming / being. For some, the country's identity begins with a treaty that promises a unique 'partnership' between an indigenous population, deeply attached to the land, and migrants with their descendants. For others, the word 'partnership' is nowhere to be seen in that document, so that a distinct New Zealand identity and purpose needs to be fulfilled in some other way. New Zealanders can nevertheless can be defined by who they are not – *not* Australians; *not* British; *not* Americans. Are New Zealanders Pacific Islanders, as some would have it? New Zealand was a founding member of the South Pacific Forum – now Pacific Islands Forum – and has continued to play an active role in that organisation. Is New Zealand's destiny to be part of Asia? At least one New Zealand prime minister, James Bolger, thought so – and said so – and more recently, in 2005, New Zealand took part in the founding East Asian Summit, linking the country's future (or at least its economic wellbeing) to a place in East Asian / Southeast Asian integration, much as an earlier New Zealand government had sought to guarantee the country's economic prospects through assurances of a place in the European Economic Community [subsequently European Union], with guarantees of continued (and generous) trade access.

In broad terms, put into perspective, the history of New Zealand is, in its own way, much the same as for many another country. A small country searches for security – physical, economic, even cultural – and finds it, at least for a time, through adjustments that are political and diplomatic, strategic and tactical, involving both the state and its citizens in processes and manoeuvres at times liberating and at other times painful. This is the New Zealand past; it is its present; and, inescapably, it is sure to be its future as well.

Notes

1 There is an increasingly varied and authoritative New Zealand historical literature. Probably the most respected histories of the country are those by: Keith Sinclair, *A History of New Zealand* (Harmondsworth: Penguin, 1969; Auckland: 2000); Jamie Belich, *Making Peoples: A History of the New Zealanders – From Polynesian Settlement to the Nineteenth Century* (Auckland: Penguin, 1996); Jamie Belich, *Paradise Reforged: A History of the New Zealanders from the 1880s to the Year 2000* (Auckland: Penguin, 2001); and Michael King, *The Penguin History of New Zealand* (Auckland: Penguin, 2003). To these should be added *The Oxford History of New Zealand* – first edition, edited by W. H. Oliver, with B. R. Williams (Oxford: Clarendon Press, 1981); and second edition, edited by Geoffrey W. Rice (Auckland: Oxford University Press, 1992). A third edition, under the editorship of Giselle Byrnes, is anticipated.

2 The effects of European settlement and state-building on the indigenous population – on its land, culture and way of life – has continued to preoccupy not only historians, but also Maori claimants, government policy-makers and others involved in the consideration and settlement of grievances related to the promises, purposes and provisions of the Treaty of Waitangi. Some New Zealand historical research, with important political and legal ramifications, thus centres on investigations into claims filed with New Zealand's Waitangi Tribunal. Analyses of the work of the Tribunal include: Giselle Byrnes, *The Waitangi Tribunal and New Zealand History* (Melbourne: Oxford University Press, 2004); Paul McHugh, *The Maori Magna Carta: New Zealand Law and the Treaty of Waitangi* (Auckland: Oxford University Press, 1991); Andrew Sharp, *Justice and the Maori: The Philosophy and Practice of Maori Claims in New Zealand since the 1970s* (Auckland: Oxford University Press, 1997); and Paul Temm, *The Waitangi Tribunal: The Conscience of the Nation* (Auckland: Random Century New Zealand, 1990).

3 See W. David McIntyre, *Dominion of New Zealand: Statesmen and Status, 1907-1945* (Wellington: New Zealand Institute of International Affairs, 2007), for a witty and well-documented account exploring New Zealand's status as a self-governing Dominion.

4 W. David McIntyre offers twelve of them – potential holidays each – in his article on New Zealand's path to independence, 'Why we don't need a fourth of July', *Political Science*, vol. 60, no. 2, 2008.

5 Not surprisingly, given its status as 'founding document', the Treaty of Waitangi has become the subject of a substantial and, at times, controversial scholarly literature. Evolving interpretations of the document's intent, meaning and legal status have contributed to an evolving Treaty jurisprudence as well. The following are only a few of the many important (and interesting) publications focusing on the Treaty: Claudia Orange, *The Treaty of Waitangi* (Wellington: Bridget Williams Books, 1992); Claudia Orange, *An Illustrated History of The Treaty of Waitangi* (Wellington: Bridget Williams Books, 2004); Paul Moon and Peter Biggs, *The Treaty and its Times: the illustrated history* (Auckland: Resource Books, 2004); and I. H. Kawharu (ed.), *Waitangi: Maori and Pakeha Perspectives of the Treaty of Waitangi* (Auckland: Oxford University Press, 1989). Another perspective on the Treaty, looking at what might have happened had it not been signed, is the subject of a 'counterfactual' chapter by Giselle Byrnes, 'What if the Treaty of Waitangi had not been signed on 6 February 1840?', in Stephen Levine (ed.), *New Zealand as it might have been* (Wellington: Victoria University Press, 2006), while Janine Hayward considers alternative ways in which New Zealand might have developed had the Treaty of Waitangi not conferred upon Maori the rights and status of British subjects (see Janine Hayward, 'What if Maori had not been made British subjects in 1840?', in Levine (ed.), *New Zealand as it might have been*).

6 Early studies of these developments include those by André Siegfried, *Democracy in New Zealand* (London: Bell, 1914; Wellington: Victoria University Press, 1982) and William Pember Reeves, *State Experiments in Australia and New Zealand* (London: Grant Richards, 1902). A now classic post-second world war overview of New Zealand's democracy is by the first Professor of Political Science in New Zealand, Leslie Lipson: *The Politics of Equality: New Zealand's Adventures in Democracy* (Chicago: University of Chicago Press, 1948).

7 The history of Maori parliamentary representation is set forth in an Appendix to the report of the Royal Commission on the Electoral System (which submitted its report in December 1986, recommending a change to the system and the introduction of MMP): see M. P. K. Sorrenson, 'A History of Maori Representation in Parliament', in Electoral Commission, *Report of the Royal Commission on the Electoral System: 'Towards a Better Democracy'*, Wellington: Government Printer, 1986. The subject is also among those covered in the history of New Zealand's electoral system produced to mark the 150th anniversary of elections to the country's first legislative assembly: see Neill Atkinson, *Adventures in Democracy: A History of the Vote in New Zealand* (Dunedin: University of Otago Press, 2003).

8 As a U.S. territory (prior to attaining statehood), Wyoming introduced women's suffrage in 1869 – 51 years before an amendment was added to the

U.S. constitution providing voting rights for women throughout the country.

9 New Zealand's first world war experience, commemorated annually on ANZAC Day, is the subject of a still growing body of historical writing. Three battles on the Western front, in which New Zealand soldiers took part at a heavy price, are the subject of Glyn Harper, *Dark Journey* (Auckland: HarperCollins, 2007). How New Zealand came to be at Gallipoli is the subject of Ian McGibbon's *The path to Gallipoli: defending New Zealand 1840-1915* (Wellington: GP Books, 1991). New Zealand's participation in World War I is the subject of John Crawford and Ian McGibbon (eds.), *New Zealand's great war: New Zealand, the Allies and the First World War* (Auckland: Exisle, 2007).

10 Denis McLean's counterfactual chapter, 'What if New Zealand had not gone to war in 1939?', in Levine (ed.), *New Zealand as it might have been*, arose out of the sense that New Zealand, today, would never consent to follow Britain – or any other country – with that same sense of instinctive and unconditional loyalty and mutual identification of identity and purpose, reflecting profound changes in the country's outlook and orientation.

11 For a recent work on New Zealand's participation in World War II, see Ian McGibbon, *New Zealand and the Second World War* (Auckland: Hodder Moa Beckett, 2004).

12 Regarded as perhaps New Zealand's premier international statesman – and as one of its finest prime ministers – Peter Fraser has been the subject of two relatively recent studies: Margaret Clark (ed.), *Peter Fraser: master politician* (Palmerston North: Dunmore, 1998); and Michael Bassett with Michael King, *Tomorrow comes the song: a life of Peter Fraser* (Auckland: Penguin, 2000).

13 See McIntyre, *Dominion of New Zealand*, chapter 8 and epilogue.

14 The nuclear-free policies were among the topics covered in a 2004 conference examining the record of the government that introduced them. See Margaret Clark (ed.), *For the Record: Lange and the fourth Labour government* (Wellington: Dunmore, 2005), particularly the chapters by Denis McLean ('A serious non-meeting of minds'), Merwyn Norrish ('The Lange Government's Foreign Policy'), and Bruce Brown ('The great debate at the Oxford Union').

15 A documentary record of New Zealand's conflict with France over nuclear matters – including cases brought before the International Court of Justice, beginning with atmospheric testing, through to underground testing; as well as matters pertaining to the Rainbow Warrior incident (and its aftermath) – is found in Paul Harris and Stephen Levine (eds.), *The New Zealand Politics Source Book*, second edition (Palmerston North: Dunmore, 1994); and Stephen Levine with Paul Harris (eds.), *The New Zealand Politics Source Book*, third edition (Palmerston North: Dunmore, 1999). The texts of New Zealand's nuclear-free legislation and of the South Pacific Nuclear Free Zone Treaty are also reprinted in these publications.

16 New Zealand distinguished itself further by enacting legislation in 1919 giving women the right to become members of Parliament – a step taken under a

Reform government, the Liberals' successors. The first woman was elected to the New Zealand Parliament in 1933.

17 Auckland's position as New Zealand's capital lasted from 1841, when Captain William Hobson (who signed the Treaty of Waitangi on behalf of the British) moved his residence there from a site in the Bay of Islands named Russell, until 1865, when the colony's General Assembly moved its deliberations from Auckland to Wellington.

18 This diversity is recorded in *Settler and Migrant Peoples of New Zealand*, organised and produced through New Zealand's Ministry for Culture and Heritage (Te Ara – the Encyclopedia of New Zealand, Auckland: David Bateman, 2006): see http://www.teara.govt.nz/NewZealanders/NewZealandPeoples/en.

19 For analysis of the background and basis to MMP, see Jonathan Boston, Stephen Levine, Elizabeth McLeay and Nigel S. Roberts, *New Zealand Under MMP: A New Politics?* (Auckland: Auckland University Press, 1996); and Keith Jackson and Alan McRobie, *New Zealand Adopts Proportional Representation: Accident? Design? Evolution?* (Aldershot: Ashgate, 1998). The introduction and implementation of the new voting system, with its many consequences across the political system, is documented in Jonathan Boston, Stephen Levine, Elizabeth McLeay and Nigel S. Roberts (eds.), *Electoral and Constitutional Change in New Zealand: An MMP Source Book* (Palmerston North: Dunmore, 1999).

20 The introduction of coalition governments, in multi-party parliaments in which no single party was able to obtain a majority, began with the 1996 election. The four MMP elections – their campaigns and their consequences – are analysed and documented in: Jonathan Boston, Stephen Levine, Elizabeth McLeay and Nigel S. Roberts (eds.), *From Campaign to Coalition: New Zealand's First General Election Under Proportional Representation* (Palmerston North: Dunmore, 1997); Jonathan Boston, Stephen Church, Stephen Levine, Elizabeth McLeay and Nigel S. Roberts (eds.), *Left Turn: The New Zealand General Election of 1999* (Wellington: Victoria University Press, 2000); Jonathan Boston, Stephen Church, Stephen Levine, Elizabeth McLeay and Nigel S. Roberts (eds.), *New Zealand Votes: The General Election of 2002* (Wellington: Victoria University Press, 2003); and Stephen Levine and Nigel S. Roberts (eds.), *The Baubles of Office: The New Zealand General Election of 2005* (Wellington: Victoria University Press, 2007).

A history of New Caledonia: a chronological approach and contemporary issues[1]

Frédéric Angleviel

This contribution provides an overview of New Caledonian history in a chronological perspective, as background for the other chapters which deal more specifically with different aspects of New Caledonian history. The archipelago of New Caledonia, a French overseas territory, is inhabited by a people who first arrived there over three thousand years ago. It was a colony between 1853 and 1946 and then gained the status of an official French Overseas Territory from 1946 to 1998. A period of decolonisation, with many changes in the territory's legal statutes, was followed by the Noumea Accord, signed in 1997, which turned New Caledonia into a unique entity recognised by the French constitution – an entity which must choose its future status in a referendum on self-determination set to take place between 2014 and 2018.

Cette contribution nous offre une vision générale de l'histoire calédonienne dans une perspective chronologique afin de donner aux autres contributeurs le large "background" nécessaire pour développer comparaisons historiques et théories de l'approche comparative. La Nouvelle-Calédonie, archipel doté d'un people premier arrive il y a plus de trois mille ans, est aujourd'hui un territoire français. Elle fut une colonie de peuplement de 1853 à 1946. Devenue Territoire d'Outre-Mer de 1946 à 1998, elle traversa la période de la colonisation grâce à de multiples evolutions statutaires. En 1998, l'Accord de Nouméa en a fait une entité unique reconnue par la Constitution française, entité qui a vocation à choisir son avenir lors d'un reférendum d'autodétermination qui interviendra entre 2014 et 2018.

'What is the hottest time of the year?'
Voices cry out.
'December, Miss!
—January, Miss!'
—'Wrong, children . . . summer isn't in December or January but from June 21st to September 21st. July and August are the hottest months in the year. July and . . .' François politely stands up and stubbornly says, 'Miss, I'm sorry but it's cold in July and August. Papa says that the bananas don't ripen well then and the sun isn't as strong, so it's winter.'
—*'François,' Mrs. Bounignan said calmly . . .'Open your book and read it! This is a geography book. When I talk about the seasons I mean the REAL seasons, not what the weather is like here! December is when there's snow and July is when there's sun . . .'*
The children listen in amazement, swept away by a fairy tale about a wonderful country – the one, the only . . .
And yet, deep inside lurked a feeling of shame and humiliation, of not belonging to the world people wrote about in every text book, the REAL world! Not a single text book mentioned the season or time of year when you harvested coffee, pigeon peas and vanilla, yet they all talked about the 'yellow harvest'.

Jean Mariotti, *A bord de l'Incertaine*, 1942

The archipelago of New Caledonia, a French overseas territory, is inhabited by a people who first arrived there over three thousand years ago. It was a colony between 1853 and 1946 and then gained the status of an official French Overseas Territory from 1946 to 1998. There was a period of decolonisation following many changes in its legal statutes, and then the Noumea Accord was signed in 1997 which turned New Caledonia into a unique entity recognised by the French constitution – an entity which must choose its future status in a referendum on self-determination set to take place between 2014 and 2018.

New Caledonia is still waiting for someone to paint its full historical picture so it can finally be completely understood.[2] This is why we have decided to focus on writing a general history using a chronological approach and highlighting new perspectives and questions.[3]

Recent history has taught us that it isn't enough to just present historical facts as objectively as possible.[4] It's also important to continually push back the limits of historical research by looking at what has not been said and/or forgotten over time while discussing them in a new way.

We will therefore discuss Kanak society by looking at it through its social organisation, then we will address the touchy question of the ancient practice of anthropophagy (i.e., cannibalism). After that we will look at the colonial period of New Caledonia, taking into consideration the perceptions of the 'men and women' involved, many of whom came at the French State's initiative in the nineteenth and twentieth centuries. The 'native population' became marginalised at that time, which is why we now have the responsibility of presenting the 'impact of colonisation' and 'recognising the darker aspects of the colonial period' (Appendix I).

It has never been easy to write the history of New Caledonia and in the introduction to her thesis Christiane Terrier stated that, '*History, which is at the heart of political issues, got bad publicity. . . up until the Matignon Accords (1988). Mindsets have evolved since then towards a common interest and openness, but the interpretation of historical events is still a fundamental issue due to its direct impact on our perception of the present*'.[5]

New Caledonian pre-history (-1100 to 1774)

The presentation of New Caledonian pre-history from the 1970s until the 1992[6] history book was organised around ceramic discoveries[7] and technical evolutions (or regressions). Debate still continues today over changes in ways of life and the name to give to the prehistoric era.

The ceramic era

The Kone period: a coastal population (1100 B.C. to +200 A.D.)

The oldest incontestable signs of a human presence in New Caledonia date back to around 1100 B.C. with the arrival of the Austronesians and their ceramics. The most original pottery brought here by these navigators is called Lapita pottery. The name comes from a site in the region of Kone and this type of pottery is decorated with many dotted or cut geometric designs. Podtanean pottery also existed at this time which was decorated with long designs made with a wooden beater and used for cooking. Most of the sites that have been discovered to date are located by the sea. Traditional houses were also discovered during the digs but very little remains. What is left are mainly *cases rondes (*traditional round houses*)*, sometimes surrounded by palisades. The stone ovens that were used for cooking brought about the end of the Kone period and Lapita pottery stopped being made altogether in approximately 200 A.D.

The Naia-Oundjo era: an inland population (200 A.D. to 1800 A.D.)

A cultural separation occurred around 200 A.D. The old wooden beater pottery technique continued to be used in the north and this type of pottery came to be called Oundjo. It has also been given the nickname 'Kanak cookpot'. In the south, however, cut designs replaced dots and handles began to appear.

The most important feature of the Naia-Oundjo period is the definitive migration of part of the New Caledonian main island's population inland. Clans settled in the fertile valley plains, clearing the trees on the hills and the mountains to make horticultural gardens and irrigated tarot root fields on the mountain slopes.

Setting the date for the first signs of Kanak culture

This new approach is based on the very first research ever done which has turned out to be very logical and plausible. However, due to a lack of documentary evidence, it is still understandably under debate by archaeologists.

Ancient pre-history or the Austronesian period corresponds to a settling phase that started along the coastlines between 1100 B.C. and +1000 A.D. with wide-spread fire-stick agriculture and very little social hierarchy.

The roots of Kanak culture started appearing after that along with the major characteristics of Kanak society[8] as discovered by James Cook in 1774. This included such things as full land occupation, intensive agriculture (tarot root fields and yam beds) and its organisation in powerful chiefdoms (+1000 A.D. to 1774 A.D.).

Austronesians can thus be said to be the ancestors of the Kanaks, just as the Gauls are the ancestors of the French. All Kanaks are therefore Austronesians, but not all Austronesians are Kanaks.

According to Christophe Sand, however, it is also necessary to study an hypothesis stating that when New Caledonia came in contact with the West 'the appearance of epidemics caused a dramatic decrease in population, much greater than what has been supposed to date, thereby resulting in a major upheaval in Kanak society, leading to wars, group migrations and the partial collapse of political hierarchies'.[9]

Caledonian pre-history or ancient society?

Today there is an important academic debate going on over whether or not to use the term 'New Caledonian pre-history'. Some prefer the term 'ancient society' to match what has been included in school curricula in places like French Polynesia.[10] The main argument some elementary school teachers have for getting rid of the term 'pre-history' is due to the legitimate concern that students could potentially confuse New Caledonian pre-history with world pre-history. In other words there is a risk that students would immediately think of the stereotypical, sexist and Darwinian point of view with the Neanderthal carrying a club in one hand and dragging his companion by the hair in the other when asked about New Caledonia.

Yes, there is a real risk of this, just as for any historical period and subject. The problem can be resolved in the comments and additional material section of the programmes. A teacher's role is to (among other things) prevent these falsehoods from being perpetuated throughout the years and to put the caricature's importance back into perspective, as simply the price to pay for humour based on the interest any society has in its history.

The term 'New Caledonian pre-history' appears to be essential for technical reasons. If on one hand we group 2,800 years of pre-European Kanak history (pre-history being of course part of History written with a Capital H, meaning preceding history as it is commonly accepted) into an 'ancient' or a 'traditional' period, there is a tendency to play down the importance of certain evolutions that completely transformed this society. The original fisher-gatherers became farmers, first using fire-stick farming methods and later planting big tarot root fields. They went from an 'anarchistic' society to a juxtaposition of chiefdoms, then to a hierarchy of these existing groups. This becomes even more important when the 'big virus outbreak' occurs, which eradicated anywhere from 40 to 90 per cent of the Kanak population. The state of society prior to this event is essential to understanding the slow structural changes and brutal upheavals that prevailed in Kanak society during these initial contacts.

At the same time the idea of 'leveling things out', which was first put forth in the Matignon Accords and then the Noumea Accord, makes it necessary to rethink the place of the actors involved in the discussion on New Caledonian history.[11] The first people to arrive must have been treated at least as well as the men and women who came in larger numbers later on . . . .The most appropriate methodological response to this legitimate evolution would be for Melanesians to be given a more important place in text books.

Emmanuel Kasarherou further explains how important this is when he regretfully states that due to a lack of publications on the subject 'Kanak history too often has to be read as the negative aspect of colonialism'.[12]

There is therefore much work left to be done by historians, not only in studying the oral traditions already transcribed by ethnologists and linguists but also in going out in the field themselves and recording the many different oral traditions that still exist in the tribes today (Appendix II).

New Caledonian protohistory (1774-1853)

Protohistory, a recent concept for New Caledonia, is a combination of the period of mutual discovery and initial contact with the traditional approaches distinguishing them. The classical period known as the 'Discovery of the Pacific' had, in fact, the effect of causing everyone to believe that the newly discovered lands were free of all human life prior to the arrival of the Europeans. It minimised the role of the natives in the discovery of 'the Other' and the indigenous people were seen as objects, not participants.

At the same time the history of a few hundred sailors over three hundred years took on enormous proportions, compared to the study of cosmogonic and demographic changes resulting from the sudden appearance of western differences and 'modernity' in an insular area populated with anywhere from 60,000 to 200,000 Melanesians.[13]

It was therefore necessary to wait until the late arrival of the first beachcombers followed by the missionaries for real human relationships to appear. Yet the Kanak way of life would be profoundly affected by these coastal intrusions, which included technological revolutions (iron, firearms, glass, cloth), the introduction of new animal species (dogs and pigs, followed by goats and cows), cosmogonic upheavals (Europeans who were pale like their ancestors and Christian missionaries), and especially the big virus outbreak (a long period of isolation, diseases that were unheard of in Oceania).

From a demographic perspective, it is possible that this virus outbreak caused the death of between 40 to 80 per cent of the original population, leading to a serious economic and political crisis prior to colonialism. There were no longer enough people to work the tarot root fields while Kanak social organisation, founded on little chiefdoms governed by larger chiefdoms, collapsed on the main island.

The Kanaks prior to the Europeans

Daily life

Yam and tarot root cultivation took up most of their time. The men cleared and plowed the land, dug irrigation ditches for the tarot fields and harvested the first yams, while the women broke up the clumps of dirt, planted and made the fields more attractive.

Work was divided up so when *cases* (traditional houses) needed to be built the men would cut down tree trunks and make the frames while the women would gather straw for the roofs and weave mats for the interior.[14]

Clans often went to war for many reasons (breakdowns in alliances, the conquest of new lands and profanation of taboo areas). They would circulate 'Kanak money'[15] to warn their allies, call on their ancestors for protection, and prepare their weapons (assegai spears, slings, maces, etc.). Battles also included the ritual practice of anthropophagy.

Anthropophagy, myths and reality

This is not the time to draw conclusions on a subject which requires much more research and study, but we can at least affirm three things. Firstly, anthropophagy was definitely a New Caledonian practice during the pre-European and protohistory era. Secondly, it was first and foremost ritualised warrior cannibalism, with very few variations, feared and criticised by the Melanesians themselves and related to the lack of animal proteins. Thirdly, the Europeans spoke about cannibalism in a greatly exaggerated and derogatory way while colonising the area, even though the practice itself had already disappeared as a socially acceptable practice by the 1860s.

This paradox is related to the change in relations between the existing communities. The colonists needed to speak about the 'savagery' of the Melanesians while at the same time these people were unilaterally losing their freedom and falling under colonised status. Anthropophagy can therefore be seen as real physical violence in the ancient past, but speaking about imaginary cannibalism became an example of verbal violence in a country where 'political correctness' has not yet become the standard.

At the same time the lack of transversal university research to date[16] on such an important subject, to try to understand 'the Other' and go beyond the language referring to the imaginary division between savages and civilised people, each community having its own savage and humane behavior, is a significant indication of the continuing violence in a 'young country' made up of a patchwork of communities. Isn't it about time to level everything out (as stated in the preface to the Noumea Accord) concerning colonisation in regards to the darker and brighter aspects of pre-European Kanak civilisation?

Social and religious organisation

Exchanges took place during customary law ceremonies like weddings, adoptions and births for the purpose of creating, strengthening or extending alliances between different clans. The exchanges were always equivalent in nature with a gift and a counter-gift.

The gods were the clans' founding ancestors, the spirits those of the dead. Their descendants called on them after they died to make the rain fall, the crops grow and to protect them during times of war . . . Their skulls were usually placed on a rock set aside for this purpose, which is where the clan went to call on them.

Political organisation

A Kanak chiefdom is made up of several clans located in a given geographic area, each with specific complementary functions and statutes to maintain social balance. A chief's authority can be seen in the respect and consideration he inspires but he is also responsible for presiding over important traditional ceremonies like the yam festival, wakes, weddings and burials. There is no outer sign to distinguish a chief, or older brother, from the rest of the group. He is simply the one who ensures continued respect for tradition, important moral and social values and is the moderator for customary law and land conflicts in Kanak society.[17] There are also many different linguistic variations still alive today in New Caledonia as seen in the 28 languages or dialects spoken in the territory.

The discovery of New Caledonia by the Europeans (1774-1840)

Cook, La Pérouse and Entrecasteaux reveal Grande Terre (the main island)

After exploring the New Hebrides archipelago (Vanuatu), British captain James Cook[18] was sailing towards New Zealand during his second voyage in the Pacific when Midshipman Colnett saw new land. The date was 04 September 1774 and Cook called this island New Caledonia.

As he sailed south down the east coast he came in sight of the island called Kunie on 23 September 1774 which he named the Isle of Pines because of its many *araucarias* (columnar pines). Later on, Bruni d'Entrecasteaux spent time in New Caledonian waters baptizing many maritime areas (Huon, Surprise, Beautemps-Beaupré . . .) and drafting the first map of the west coast while searching for the unfortunate La Pérouse between 1792 and 1793.

Dumont d'Urville discovers the Loyalty Islands

While English ships often sailed through the Loyalty channel, these islands were only shown very vaguely on maps at the beginning of the nineteenth century. Dumont d'Urville rediscovered Mare, Lifou and Ouvea in 1827[19] and drafted a definitive map of the Loyalty Islands during his second voyage in the Pacific in 1840.

The pre-colonial era of adventurers and missionaries

The first adventurers (originally passing through, then settling down: 1820-1860)

At the beginning of the nineteenth century, whale and sperm whale hunters discovered the rich variety of South Pacific *cetacea* and began to spend time in New Caledonian waters as of 1820. Boats would drop anchor in the Loyalty Islands and the north to stock up on water and food supplies and a whale oil extraction centre was set up in Lifou. This activity ended in 1860 when whale oil was replaced by petrol and whale pods had virtually disappeared.

At the same time the development of the first Australian centres contributed to the development of Oceanian trading routes and soon certain goods helped make big profits. The opening of the Chinese market, a big tea producer but not very interested in European manufactured goods, let these traders sell sandalwood and sea cucumbers at the highest price.

Sandalwood commerce is what led to the first exchanges between the New Caledonian Melanesians and the modern European world. These relations – which were sometimes very rocky – lasted from its discovery in 1840 until the late 1850s.[20]

The first Europeans began settling in New Caledonia in 1840 and the New Caledonian coast lines began seeing more and more beachcombers, shipwrecked Westerners, deserters, mutineers, or those who had escaped Oceanian wrath. While history has forgotten the names of this pre-colonial generation, mainly Anglo-Saxon in origin, it has retained the names of their descendants (Streeter, Forest, etc.).

Arms dealers Townes and Paddon built permanent work stations, first on the Isle of Pines in 1848 and a second on the Isle of Pines with another on Isle Nou in 1854. They would sometimes drop off sailors to run their temporary trading posts as well. These men would trade bits of iron, fabric, glass, pearls, tobacco and soon a few rifles and bullets, for sandalwood and Melanesian labor (cutting, cleaning and transporting the wood to the beach). The traders were also interested in other products like mother of pearl, coconut oil and sea cucumbers.

Sea cucumber fishermen were very important during this period of initial contact since they spent several months on land in the tribes and their activity required the active protection and participation of the Kanaks.

The arrival and acceptance of the missionaries (1840-1851)

English missionaries from the London Missionary Society (L.M.S.) decided to Christianise the Pacific in 1797. The New Caledonian archipelago was reached in 1840 and the protestant missions were based on a few courageous Oceanian pastors (teachers) from Samoa or Rarotonga. After several unsuccessful attempts on *Grande Terre* and the Isle of Pines, the conversion of chiefs Nidoish Naisseline in Mare (1848) and Boula in Lifou (1851) enabled teachers Tataio and Fao to settle there definitively. European pastors would settle there later on, as well as in Ouvea in 1856.

This success, which was the greatest encountered in Melanesia, explains why the Loyalty Islands are still primarily protestant today and many religious, culinary and sociological traditions still exist. English origin words have become part of the island languages and the game of cricket is very popular.

The protestant church recognised the key role played by important Melanesians,[21] thanks to its ecclesiastical structure, and the importance of their free will in accepting and promulgating Protestantism. Kerry Howe further developed this idea in his work, rightly stating that 'cultural change is not necessarily the result of some kind of social displacement'.[22]

The first Oceanian conversions to the Protestant faith encouraged priests from the Society of Mary to settle in Melanesia and a French warship brought a bishop (Mgr Douarre) and four Marist missionaries to Balade via Wallis[23] at the end of 1843.

The Marist missionaries, like the Protestants, condemned anthropophagy and disapproved of women being burdened with so much work. They also fought against polygamy and the practice of abandoning the sick. Then in 1847 the Kanaks attacked the mission in Balade, where brother Balise Mamoiton became a martyr. After several years in exile, the missionaries came back to Balade in 1851.

The fact that New Caledonia was taken over by France, a mostly Catholic country, also explains why only Catholic missionaries were authorised to settle on *Grande Terre* throughout the nineteenth century. This is the main reason why the country is still primarily Catholic today.

The colonial era (1853-1945)

The colonial era is the period where New Caledonia was given legal status as a colony of the French Empire, from the time it was claimed in 1853 to when it obtained the status of Overseas Territory in 1946. There wasn't a colonial war when the country was claimed by France as Kanak society didn't have any kind of statehood. Its very basic technological level encouraged it to welcome this new migration, but incidents began to occur when the French state began colonising *Grande Terre* after unilaterally laying claim to all the land in 1855.

New Caledonia was a special kind of colony in that it was not only a penal colony; it was also one of only two countries colonised by metropolitan France (the other being Algeria). This period corresponds to European expansion, with its darker and brighter aspects, in a period of excessive domination: that of managers over workers (who were forbidden to form trade unions); husbands over their legally minor wives; and pioneers over colonised people, who lost both their sovereignty and most of their land.

This is why a large part of contemporary New Caledonian history can only be seen through the prism of Kanak demographic collapse in the protohistory period and the subordination of Kanak lands to pioneering and penal colony interests during the colonial era. The new country was also affected by the settling of freedmen and indentured workers from Vanuatu, Malabar and Asia. These unintentional colonists and victims of history were far from being conquering pioneers and their sweat and hard work contributed to the construction of what is present day New Caledonia (Appendix III).

New Caledonia becomes part of the French Empire (1853-1880)

France claims New Caledonia

France under Napoleon III was looking for new land free of European occupation to found a penal colony. It also wanted to strengthen its presence in the Pacific and as England already had Australia and New Zealand (and was thinking about claiming New Caledonia)

France decided it 'had' to protect and support French missionaries and trading ships.

Rear admiral Febvrier-Despointes organised an official claiming ceremony in front of the missionaries and local chiefs at Balade on 24 September 1853 on his way back from Tahiti. The ceremony was repeated at the Isle of Pines on 29 September in front of Chief Vendegou who signed the official act.

The beginning of the colony (1853-1860)

From 1853 to 1860, New Caledonia was part of the *Établissements Français d'Océanie (Tahiti)*. Since this new colony needed a capital Tardy de Montravel chose Noumea because of the many advantages offered by its location. It had a large and deep bay that was well-protected from the wind and was also easy to defend. Fort Constantine was quickly built to strengthen its defense and the first urban zones were allocated along with the first rural land concessions around the capital.[24]

Colonial expansion in 1855 caused certain Kanak chiefs to rebel due to being slowly but surely pushed off their land.[25] The rebels on the east coast were mainly chiefs Bouarate (Hienghene) and Boueone (Balade) while the opposition was led by chief Kuindo[26] in the Port-de-France region.

The decisiveness of Guillain, the first governer (1862-1870)

New Caledonia began to develop as an autonomous colony in 1862. Everything needed to be done, including organising transportation, both penal and free colonisation. Charles Guillain,[27] the first governor, had to create an administration, organise the economy and establish indigenous policy. He encouraged agriculture and animal husbandry using (among other things) a model farm set up in Yahoue, while engineer Jules Garnier explored the mining resources on the main island between 1863 and 1866.

Guillain, a staunch Saint-Simonian, was a strong believer in both assimilation and colonisation. Assimilation – from the point of view of a colonist – must encourage peaceful and tolerant encounters between both cultures. Tribes were then created in 1867 with tribal lands the following year divided into 'reservations' and declared 'inalienable and non-commutable'. The reservations freed up land for the colonial pioneers and the penal colony while protecting traditional society from the excesses of dual colonisation at the same time.

Guillain attracted many immigrants by encouraging small property concessions (the sale of plots of land varying between 5 to 500 ha). As of 1870 there were 1,300 Europeans settled in Noumea, Mont Dore and Saint Vincent.

The penitentiary in New Caledonia

New Caledonia was designated a penal colony in 1863 for those sentenced to forced labour. These people were known as *les forçats*, *les transportés* or more commonly *les bagnards*. The first 250 prisoners arrived in 1864 on the *Iphigenie* and were responsible for building their own cells.[28] Over 22,000 men and 250 women[29] were sent to New Caledonia. Deportation reached its peak in 1886, which is when the penal administration had close to 700 agents overseeing the work of 7,600 prisoners and 1,900 freedmen. Most of the prisoners served their sentences at the *Isle Nou* penitentiary.

Deportation was a political solution which enabled the government to distance its opponents and rebels. 4,300 people were deported to New Caledonia between 1872 and 1880 following the sentences pronounced against the Paris Commune in 1871. These prisoners were mainly kept on the Isle of Pines until 1880, when a new law granted them amnesty and gave them permission to leave. Less than 40 families decided to stay and settle in Noumea.

Several hundred Kabylians were deported to the region of Bourail in 1871[30] following the uprising led by Sheik El Mokrani in Algeria. They were given amnesty in 1895 but many of them stayed and founded New Caledonian families.

In 1885 a new law stated that all repeat offenders would be 'relegated' overseas and a total of over 4,000 men and 457 women were shipped to New Caledonia. These prisoners were sent to the Isle of Pines (to the former deportation communities) and Prony (to operate a sawmill).

Governor Feillet began preparing public opinion for the end of deportation on Paris' orders in 1894. The colony's economy basically ran on the penitentiaries at that time which performed major construction projects, salary redistribution, supplied meat and other goods (beans, corn) as well as 'human flesh contracts' for the mining companies. The freedmen and missionaries were, however, more open to the idea of closing the prisons. The last convoy arrived in 1897, the last penitentiaries closed in 1922 and by 1931 New Caledonia was no longer a penal colony.

These seventy years as a penal colony resulted in penal colonisation as well since the 1854 law stated that 'prisoners who have proven themselves through good behavior, hard work and penance, may obtain a land concession.' The most deserving were given land concessions in the penitentiary areas primarily located around Bourail, La Foa, le Diahot, Pouembout[31] and Prony.

Land concessions could be urban or rural; as the latter were more common it was necessary to create a large penitentiary domain. This represented 110,000 hectares of the best land in the country, often taken away to the detriment of the tribes, which was one of the reasons for the 1878 uprising.

Deportation also laid the groundwork for major infrastructures (buildings, roads and bridges) and the appearance of the first New Caledonian farmers, as well as the arrival of many technicians who were either prisoners or penitentiary employees. Their expertise and hard work greatly contributed to shaping the country.

The 1878 Kanak uprising

Many Kanaks were unhappy because colonisation was taking their land, profaning their sacred places and treating them more and more like inferiors. The image of the 'good savage' gave way more and more often to 'savage'[32] and incidents occurred on a more regular basis. In 1877 cattle destroyed indigenous crops on lands near the penitentiary grounds and sometimes within the tribes because of drought. December saw the beginning of boundaries being set on the tribes around La Foa and on 19 June 1878 freedman Chene, his Melanesian wife and their son were assassinated. This led to the arrest of all the chiefs in the region.

Atai and his warriors attacked La Foa and Bouloupari on 25 and 26 June, freeing the chiefs. They massacred approximately one hundred Europeans and destroyed everything on their way. On 27 June Ship-of-the-Line Lieutenant Servan gained the support of warchief Nondo from Canala, who seized this chance to fight his hereditary enemies. From this point on the Kanaks chose sides according to their traditional allegiances and a majority of the tribes joined the French. Widespread battles continued even after Atai's death on 01 September.

Other areas of revolt sprang up on the west coast because many tribes were afraid of reprisals if they didn't act. In February 1879, Governor Olry promised to pardon the rebels who surrendered and on 03 June, the siege between Bouloupari and Bourail was lifted. There were heavy casualties[33] with more than 1,000 dead, of which 200 were European and between 800 to 1,000 Kanak. More than 1,500 of these rebels were deported, some to Tahiti, while many of the colonists were ruined and the colonial authorities worried about the future of the colony.

The colony takes off (1880 - 1918)

Noumea, a trading centre

Trade was the key activity in New Caledonia and was monopolised by the capital of the archipelago, which became a trading outpost as soon as it was created. Ships transporting merchandise to and from metropolitan France and other countries could be found in the harbour along with those that sailed throughout the archipelago. At the end of the nineteenth century the city had 7,000 inhabitants (about 14 per cent of the total population) with 137 registered businessmen in 1903. The harbour was modernised and a new dock was inaugurated in 1879. Noumean trading establishments did business with French and foreign companies and then retailed these products throughout New Caledonia.

One of these trading establishments, *les Etablissements Ballande*, soon gained a special position. They opened their first business premises on Alma street in 1883 and then retailed products inland. These trading establishments helped encouraged economic development[34] by offering easy payment terms to the colonists.

New Caledonia, mining territory

Australian prospectors found gold in Pouebo in 1863. The only worthwhile vein was mined for almost seven years at the Fern Hill Mine. Copper was found in the region of Ouegoa in 1872 and chrome began to be mined in the Lucky Hit Mine near Plum in 1880. It was also mined later on in the Tiebaghi mountains.

New Caledonia ranked third in world chrome production from 1896 to 1912 and in 1883 requests for cobalt extraction land concessions started to multiply. These mines were located in Moneo, Koumac, Mont-Dore and Canala. Cobalt production didn't have any competition until 1905 and later collapsed in 1910. Many other minerals were also mined, including iron in Prony and manganese near Voh.

Nickel was discovered by J. Garnier in 1864[35] and the discovery of a rich vein of this green-colored mineral at Mont-Dore in 1873 led to a big rush. Before this time world nickel use barely equaled 400 tons per year. In 1874 many land concession requests were made to mine the New Caledonian type of nickel called garnierite. Mines opened all over the colony, including the Boa Kaine in Canala, Bel Air in Houailou and other mines in Thio. The very first mining operations were carried out with picks and pickaxes in underground galleries and later on in quarries.

The first processing factory was built at Chaleix point by Higginson, Hanckar and Company but it stopped operating in 1885, while in 1880 Jules Garnier and John Higginson founded the *Société Le Nickel*. The *Société des Hauts Fourneaux de Nouméa* (which belonged to *Etablissements Ballande*) was built in 1910 on what is now the SLN site in Doniambo. This is the only factory that is still in operation today.

Governor Feillet's touch (1894-1903)

There were very few free colonists at the end of the nineteenth century and the trouble caused by the 1878 uprising caused some of the herders who had settled out in the countryside to leave. The only people left were mainly a few freedmen to whom the penitentiary administration had allocated a plot of land. Paul Feillet arrived in 1894 and, surprised by the low number of free colonists, took steps to try to populate the territory by recruiting people from metropolitan France.

The French administration published a request for volunteers, preferably farmers, with a minimum capital of 5,000 gold francs intended to support a family while they waited for their first harvests. Soon three hundred families had replied and when they arrived the administration gave them land concessions varying from 10 to 25 hectares on which governor Feillet recommended growing coffee. Some problems developed, however, due to the isolation, mediocre soil, the inexperience some colonists had in working the land and, most of all, the collapse of coffee prices in 1900 which led to the virtual failure of the Feillet Plan.[36]

Feillet's government also set up a definitive system of reservations while land colonisation continued to develop, putting drastic boundaries on tribal land. At the same time indigenous law laying out the status of native populations throughout the French empire became generalised as of 1887.

World War I (1914-1918)

The first contingent of volunteer New Caledonians embarked on the *Sontay* in April 1915. The volunteers in the second contingent's indigenous rifle battalion left in June 1916 to join the *Bataillon Mixte du Pacifique*, which grouped New Caledonians and Tahitians together. A total of four contingents sailed to metropolitan France between 1915 and 1917.

The Pacific soldiers participated in many battles between 1916 and 1918, including Barleux near Soissons, the Chemin des Dames, Champagne, the second battle of the Marne, Vesles-et-Caumont and Verdun. 2,113 men left to join the 177 New Caledonians already mobilised in metropolitan France, for a total of 1,006 soldiers of European descent and 1,107 soldiers of Kanak descent. 456 New Caledonians fell on the battlefield.[37]

This war allowed colonised populations throughout the French empire to express their discontent, often violently. A lack of understanding between the communities in New Caledonia led to the Kanak uprising of 1917.

The Kanaks saw that they were growing further and further away from their traditions and the indigenous population statute and land boundary measures had made them bitter and suspicious. From 1896 on problems arose occasionally that affected the region of Kone. In 1914, the chiefs from Mueo, Temala, Hienghene and Tiwaka were convened by chief Poindet Apengou and witchdoctor Pateou to a big war *pilou* (traditional dance). The refusal of some Melanesians to leave for the front and the decrease in the number of soldiers caused these chiefs to draft a schedule of hostilities during a meeting at Tiendanite at the end of 1916. On 17 February 1917, the pro-French tribes from Koniambo were attacked by Noel, the little-chief of Tiamou, and insecurity reigned from this time on. Attacks on outposts in Pouembout, the upper Amoa Valley, and the Tipindje valley multiplied.

The uprising was limited to the rectangular area of Hienghene, Poindimie, Mueo and Voh, and Noel's last action was to attack the Voh military outpost on 09 September. This 'peace expedition', assisted by Caledonian and Tahitian soldiers on leave, continued until Noel's death in January 1918 (killed by an Arab acquaintance).

Sleeping Beauty (1919-1939)

Between the wars

New Caledonia went through a severe economic crisis after the first world war due to a decrease in nickel sales which Governor Guyon tried to correct upon his arrival in 1925.[38]

The last attempt at the agricultural colonisation of New Caledonia took place in 1926 with 219 people from the north of France. They mainly settled in the region of Gouaro (Bourail) to grow cotton, but this attempt failed due to their lack of means and organisation.[39]

New Caledonia didn't escape the world crisis either and some New Caledonians lived in extreme poverty. Coffee wasn't selling anymore and the Yate centre closed.

In 1937 the first measures enacted by the Popular Front (40 hour work week and paid vacation) were applied to the territory. New horizons were about to open for New Caledonia in 1939 as well as it was about to receive its first deputy seat.

Changes in the indigenous people's way of life

Change continued to occur at a growing rate in Kanak society. Encouraged by the national police (indigenous unions), traditional round homes virtually disappeared, giving way to rectangular houses with straw roofs and cob walls.[40] The French administration created new districts and made big chiefs responsible for them while little chiefs were responsible for the tribes. In some regions, the French administration appointed chiefs to replace those who were already there and it should be noted in passing that the Kanaks continue to distinguish between the two to this day.

New crops such as manioc, coffee and fruit trees (mango, orange and mandarin) joined the traditional crops of yams and tarot root. The Kanaks also made coprah, and worked outside as handymen, sowers, herders, watchmen, nurses, etc.

The Kanaks were completely Christianised by the Protestant and Catholic[41] missionaries and the demographic renewal[42] shows how they integrated these different outside influences (not without some difficulty) into their culture while maintaining the essential parts of their traditions, including using violence to resolve major internal land conflicts.[43]

Life in the countryside

Life was hard for the colonists. Housing was rustic and merchandise very expensive and often lacking. Only extreme hard work and considerable ingenuity provided basic comforts.[44] Electricity was only available in Noumea and gas ovens and irons were considered luxuries.

Communication was difficult and families were often isolated because of the island's geography. The only source of written local information was a daily paper called *France Australe* and a twice-weekly paper called *Le Bulletin du Commerce*. Unfortunately it took a week for them to arrive at the other end of the island. The first Radio-Noumea shows didn't start broadcasting until 1937. Paradoxically, contact with the 'first arrivals' became more and more spaced out at this time. Racial blending[45] decreased and tended to be kept secret by the *Niaouli* community (a nickname given to whites born in the archipelago between the wars, followed by *Caldoche,* a pejorative nickname that appeared in the 1970s). Land despoilment, the reservation system and depopulation in the second half of the nineteenth century caused Kanak society to close in on itself.[46]

At the same time people came from Vanuatu[47] throughout the nineteenth century and Asia at the end of the nineteenth century to meet the need for labour. A first shipment of contractual Japanese laborers arrived at the S.L.N. on 18 January 1892[48] and at the end of their contract many of them chose to take advantage of their right to settle in New Caledonia and become traders, fishermen or farmers. Two other colonies, French and Dutch Indochina, replied favorably to the contractual immigration policy with the first people from Indochina arriving in 1891 and the first Javanese arriving on 16 February 1896.

By 1929 three out of four workers were Asian and after the war (in 1945) governor Tallec gave free residence to all immigrants who had entered with a work contract. Their children were granted French citizenship and integrated New Caledonian society.[49]

New Caledonia and World War II (1940-1945)

In support of Free France (1940-1944)

Despite the Petainists a De Gaulle committee was created by New Caledonians who supported the ideas of Free France. General De Gaulle sent Henri Sautot, who had just obtained Vanuatu's support, to New Caledonia where he officially proclaimed the colony's support of Free France on 19 September 1940.

Many volunteers joined the Pacific Expeditionary Corps and the

New Caledonians, Tahitians and Ni-Vanuatu made up the Pacific Battalion. They gained fame in the desert sand (Bir-Hakeim) and in Italy (Monte-Cassino), then participated in liberating France. Others fought in commandos and were part of the D-Day debarkation on 06 June 1944. Many New Caledonians also served in the Free France Naval Forces.

The Americans in New Caledonia (1942-1946)

The Americans, assisted by New Zealand and preceded by an Australian commando, made New Caledonia the cornerstone of the allied defense against the Japanese advance in the Pacific and for their counter-attack.[50] On 12 March 1942, a big convoy of 17,000 men under General Patch's orders debarked in Noumea which then became the Pacific headquarters. Airports were built (at Tontouta, Plaine des Gaïacs . . .) and ammunition and fuel depots occupied all the available docks. Hospitals were built in Anse-Vata, La Conception, Dumbea, north of Bourail, on the east coast and in the far north.

The Americans introduced mechanical farming methods, clearing the ground with bulldozers and using planting machines. They also made contact with the tribes, who received salaries in dollar amounts unheard of until then. Operations began to take place farther away from New Caledonia in 1944 and in 1946 the last GIs left while the New Caledonian volunteers came home.

Modern-day New Caledonia (1945 to present day)

While the real modern-day political history of New Caledonia can't be written until at a later date in the future, it has been included in New Caledonian school curricula from elementary history lessons through to high school due to its importance in understanding both the present and the future. This is why it is essential to have a first draft now[51] despite all the difficulties involved in writing present-day history (no archives for the last thirty years, language that is more political than historical and a lack of historical perspective in the interpretation of events),

Towards greater autonomy (1945-1958)

In 1945 the indigenous people statute was abolished and all the inhabitants of New Caledonia became French citizens. The Melanesians were progressively given the right to vote[52] and New Caledonia changed status under the Fourth Republic's constitution on 02 October 1946. It was no longer a colony but rather a French overseas territory (TOM), represented in Paris by Deputy Roger Gervolino and Counselor of the Republic Henri Lafleur elected in 1947.

A vast gathering of 'the little against the big' took the name *Union Calédonienne* (UC) in the 1953 elections. This party, led by Maurice Lenormand who has been a deputy since 1951, dominated the political scene for 20 years.[53] Its logo is: 'Two colors, one people'.

In 1956, the Deferre Law gave New Caledonia much greater autonomy with the creation of a Territorial Assembly and a Government Executive Council made up of eight ministers. The momentum generated by the war continued to grow, with many big construction projects, like the dams in Yate and Dumbea, and villages being wired for electricity and road improvement. Many Caldoches and Kanaks began to leave the countryside to work on these projects and many Polynesians, Wallisians and Tahitians were also hired.

The creation of a strong currency (the Pacific franc (XPF)) supported by metropolitan France helped boost the economy along with the opening up of the territory through the creation of regular maritime lanes and air routes.

The peak followed by the decline of autonomy (1958-1974)

In 1963 the Jacquinot Law abolished the ministries and the Government Executive Council was reduced to five members. It no longer had any authority except to advise the governor. The government later held an election on the Billotte Laws in 1969 which reduced territorial jurisdiction in the mining sector. During this same period, the New Caledonian level of living greatly increased with the creation of government assistance and the beginning of the mining boom in 1967. Television came along in 1965 after radio.

Nickel prices kept going up after 1962 and New Caledonian nickel production quickly increased, reaching 7.5 million tons at the end of 1971. The world's biggest conveyor belt was assembled in Nepoui (13 km long) along with a mineral preparation factory in Poro. Major construction work was undertaken to renovate the city of Noumea, which housed most of the new immigrants.

This increase in capital led to an increase in the population of Noumea, which boasted 5,000 Europeans, 3,000 Tahitians and 2,000 Wallisians. However, the end of the Vietnam War and the drop in the value of the dollar put an end to this euphoric period. Many Melanesians did not benefit from this prosperity and wondered about the speculation on and distribution of mining resources. At the same time the recession led to the appearance of a demand for independence.

In July 1969 a political association called *les Foulards Rouges* (the Red Bandanas) disputed metropolitan France's authority over New Caledonia. The recession deepened in 1974 leading to bankruptcies and unemployment and in 1975, a committee for independence was created that included youth groups, elected representatives from *Union Multiraciale* and Melanesian elected representatives from *Union Calédonienne* including deputy Roch Pidjot.[54]

From nationalism to the Matignon Accords (1975-1988)

In 1975, the Melanesia 2000 Festival led by Jean-Marie Tjibaou[55] reaffirmed Kanak cultural identity and in 1977 *Union Caledonienne* took sides for independence at a rally in Bourail. The French government tried to appease the growing sense of discontent by offering a new statute and development plan favoring Melanesians and land reform. Jacques Lafleur in the meantime gathered the vast majority of people who wanted New Caledonia to stay in the French Republic into the *Rassemblement Pour la Calédonie dans la République (RPCR)* party in 1978. In 1979 most of the Kanak parties joined together to create *Front Independantiste* which grouped together approximately 30 per cent of the voters for the next elections.

Positions became more entrenched and tension increased after the failure of the attempted reconciliation in Nainville-les-Roches in 1983. Those in favor of independence created the *Front de Libération Nationale Kanak Socialiste (FLNKS)* party in 1984 and serious problems occurred between 1984 and 1988 (blockages, confrontations, property destruction, assassinations) which sent New Caledonia into a period of mourning. This period has come to be known as *Les Evenements.*[56] Prime Minister Michel Rocard called for delegates from the RPCR and FLNKS to meet together in Paris to sign an historic agreement on 26 June 1988, which was accepted by referendum on 06 November 1988.

From reconstruction to the vision of a common destiny (1988-2005)

The Matignon Accords and equal distribution

After one year of direct State administration, the Matignon Accords set up a new three province system, each with its own legal jurisdiction giving them a certain amount of autonomy. The Oudinot Accord signed on 20 August 1988 introduced the idea of leveling things out between the Kanaks and other communities, doing the same between Noumea and the rest of the archipelago and lastly between the three provinces. A vote on self-determination was set for 1998.

The assassination of Jean-Marie Tjibaou and Yeiwene Yeiwene by a militant independentist in Ouvea on 04 May 1989 did not prevent the Rocard statute from being put in place, nor several projects intended to develop New Caledonia and improve its economy from being carried through (in particular the construction of the Kone-Tiwaka road and the deep water harbour in Nepoui). Consideration for specific Melanesian needs, necessary to appease tensions, appeared in the form of different actions like the creation of the *Agence de Développement de la Culture Kanak (ADCK),* the *400 Cadres* plan and the building of the Tjibaou Cultural Center.[57]

Well before 1998, the year the self-determination referendum was set to take place, Jacques Lafleur suggested the idea of finding a 'consensual solution' to avoid a 'hatchet referendum' whose results in favour of keeping New Caledonia in the French Republic risked bringing back a troubled climate. This idea was accepted by the FLNKS as a 'negotiated solution' and met with success once the 'mining pre-agreement' was resolved. The result was the Noumea Accord, signed on 5 May 1998 by French Prime Minister Lionel Jospin, RPCR representative Jacques Lafleur and FLNKS representative Rock Wamytan.

The Noumea Accord founded on the changing status of New Caledonia

In the preface to the Noumea Accord, France made a strong public gesture by recognising 'the darker and brighter aspects' of the colonial period and the suffering inflicted on the Kanaks, while honouring the different communities who participated in the construction of New Caledonia. The Noumea Accord gave a new status to New Caledonia, which since 1999 is no longer an overseas territory but a specific collectivity of the French Republic, waiting to become a 'country' whose autonomy is gradually increasing through transfers of power from the Republic of France to New Caledonia.[58] At the end of a period of twenty years, with the possibility of anticipation up until 2014, a referendum is scheduled to take place in which a limited number of electors will vote on eventual total emancipation (political independence).

The autonomy acquired by the provinces through the Matignon Accords has been recognised by New Caledonia, which has a collegial government[59] responsible for running the executive branch while the congress is responsible for the 'country's' laws. The customary law senate made up of representatives from the eight customary law districts must be consulted on all things related to Kanak identity. Then there is the question of 'New Caledonian citizenship' which led to the creation of a limited body of electors to vote for members of the provincial assemblies and referendums on self-determination. Priority has also been given to local employment.

The Noumea Accord became applicable through a constitutional revision voted by Parliament on 20 July 1998. It was ratified by referendum on 08 November 1998 with the 'yes' greatly outdistancing the 'no' compared to 1988. While the three historical partners to the Accord found a consensual solution, it quickly became apparent that the two Caledonian partners had (to say the very least) differing viewpoints on the developing country's future over the next twelve years. The daily local paper *Les Nouvelles Calédoniennes* published the words of the two men who allowed this second peace agreement to take place on 05 May 1998: '*Deputy (J. Lafleur) has repeatedly stated his hopes that the vote set to place place in twenty years will be in favor of keeping New Caledonia in the Republic . . . For us (R. Wamytan) it's clear, we have now begun the evolutionary process at the end of which the Territory will gain its political emancipation*'. It is therefore possible to interpret the text of the Accords in three different ways in the future: full, complete internal autonomy; total independence; or emancipation within the French Republic.

It is clear that during the signature of the Matignon Accords, and then the Noumea Accord, an agreement was only able to be reached when the main question – whether or not to become independent – was postponed, first for ten then twenty years. No one can predict who the parties or the politicians will be in 2018, if they will once again postpone the danger hanging over them from any referendum on self-determination, or if they will put their trust in the ballot boxes.

Betting on intelligence again

It appears that any reflection on the New Caledonian political situation involves not a single answer but a chain of elements, each giving part of the answer. Three years after the start of the second of the four specified five-year mandates, it is clearly too early to predict the failure or the success of the Noumea Accord on a local scale. Some journalists would like to consider this Accord to be a 'peaceful decolonisation process', taking the subject today and discussing it from a 'historical perspective'. Others see it as a 'masterful semantic balancing act' intended to collapse at the first sign of conflict.

However it is perceived, this political agreement can be modified as the situation changes, as stated by Alain Christnacht in 2003: '*Legally speaking, the transfer of power to New Caledonia was declared "irreversible" in the Noumea Accord and recognised as such in the Constitution, but a constitutional revision did take place and another revision could undo it'*. The Noumea Accord furthermore cannot result in a 'hatchet referendum' if both major Caledonian political parties come to an agreement again in 2018 and sign a new framework agreement. This could for example be called the Kone Accord in the name of balancing out mining resources.

Lastly, all the statutes and agreements bear the signature of the third partner, the French State, whose behaviour has never been neutral and which acts according to what it considers to be the greater interest of the Republic of France. The reasons laid out for the Fabius-Pisani statute remind us of this unavoidable fact: '*No solution is possible without meeting these two principles: ensuring order and dialogue, and taking into consideration both the interests of the various communities and the interests of France*'.

Green gold (nickel) at the heart of New Caledonia's future

On a global scale, international mining companies have begun investing billions of dollars locally due to the fairly optimistic perception of current New Caledonian political realities and a metallurgical market that has been growing for at least a decade. Economists are already talking about a new economic deal with the development of one or even possibly two mining projects.

If this came to happen, wouldn't New Caledonian economics, society and therefore politics be profoundly affected in another ten years by the unavoidable societal changes that would result, just as during the 1969-1972 mining boom?

Appendix I
Preface to the Noumea Accord, Noumea 05 May 1998

'1. *When France laid claim to Grande Terre, called 'New Caledonia' by James Cook, on 24 September 1853, it took possession of the territory in accordance with international legal conditions recognized by Europe and America at that time. It did not establish any legal relations with the indigenous population. The treaties signed with the customary law authorities were not fair agreements but in fact unilateral acts.*

This country, however, was not uninhabited.

Grande Terre and the Loyalty Islands were inhabited by men and women now known as Kanaks. They had developed their own civilisation, their own traditions, languages and customary law governing political and social life. Their culture and spiritual life were expressed in a variety of creative ways.

The Kanak identity was based on a special relationship with the land. Each individual and clan identified itself in relation to a specific valley, hill, sea or river estuary and kept alive in its memory the acceptance of other families on its land. The traditional names given to everything around them, the taboos associated with certain things and their customary ways shaped their environment and exchanges.

2. *The colonisation of New Caledonia was part of a vast historical movement where European countries imposed their dominion on the rest of the world.*

A large number of men and women came to New Caledonia in the 19th and 20th centuries, convinced they were bringing progress, motivated by their religious faith, forced against their will or looking for a second chance. They settled here and multiplied, bringing their ideals, knowledge, hopes, ambitions, illusions and contradictions with them.

Some of them, in particular those with a certain level of education like priests or pastors, doctors and engineers, administrators, soldiers and politicians, looked differently at the indigenous people, showing greater understanding and genuine compassion.

The new arrivals with their scientific and technical knowledge participated in mining and agricultural activities, often under difficult conditions. With state assistance they helped shape New Caledonia and their determination and creativity made it possible to use the resources available and lay the groundwork for development . . .

3. The time has come to recognise the darker aspects of the colonial era, even though it wasn't devoid of light.

The impact of colonisation has caused lasting pain and suffering on the indigenous population . . .

4. Decolonisation is the means to rebuild lasting social bonds between the communities currently living in New Caledonia, allowing the Kanak people to establish new relations with France reflecting current realities . . .

It is now necessary to start laying the groundwork for New Caledonian citizenship which will allow the indigenous people to create a humane community with the men and women who live there affirming their common destiny . . .

The past was a time of colonisation. The present is a time of sharing through the achievement of new balance. The future must be a time of identification in a common destiny.

5. The signatories of the Matignon Accords have therefore decided to come to a negotiated agreement, based on consensus, which they will ask the inhabitants of New Caledonia to endorse.

At the end of a period of twenty years the transfer to New Caledonia of the reserved powers, its achievement of, full international responsibility status and the conversion of citizenship into nationality will be voted upon by the people concerned.

Their approval would mean full sovereignity for New Caledonia'.

In order of signature: Lionel Jospin, Jean-Jack Queyranne, Jacques Lafleur for the RPCR, Pierre Frogier, Simon Loueckhote, Harold Martin Jean Leques, Bernard Deladrière, Rock Wamytan for the FLNKS, Paul Neaoutyine, Charles Pidjot and Victor Tutugoro.

Appendix II
The old man. . . storyteller and historian.
Sénès Jacqueline, Terre et hommes de Nouvelle-Calédonie, Ed. du Cagou, Nouméa, 1976, 166 p, p. 128.

'I plugged my tape recorder in with shaking hands, waiting in the traditional round house with its blackened beams. Hippolyte began to speak. . . . I would have liked to disappear, to let the child and the old man have a real discussion. I was going to ruin everything just by being there. I had heard so much in Noumea about how the young people were being brainwashed by the schools and various propaganda, how they wouldn't listen to their elders anymore. They could care less about traditional stories and protocol! They passed too quickly now from customary law marriages to erotic rage, from assagai spear tips to bic razor blades, from pilou – pilous dances to pop rhythms. They paraded around Noumea, their foreheads wrapped in red, defying their Ancestors as much as the white government.

The tide always rises after the yam leaves fall. Its rage can go far beyond the sacred rocks at the equinox. But the adolescent's eyes shone brightly as if he were hanging at the edge of the reef, and my conviction deepened that the power of the spell rock is still vast and strong. It's the power of the hearthstone. The past is like the yam, always noble when it is planted in the heart of man.'

Appendix III
« Manifeste pour que vive la mémoire collective », C.S. (Christophe Sand), *Les Nouvelles Calédoniennes,* 18 avril 2001, p. 47.

For an old woman from the land of suffering. My grandmother died today. She was the daughter of a deported Kabylian from Tisi Ousou, who was sentenced to prison for refusing to let his Algerian mountains be colonized. As the child of a 'chapeau de paille' (straw hat), a 'bicot' (goat), who wasn't baptized until she was an adult and was refused the right to go to the Catholic school because her father was Muslim, my Granny bore the burden of her origins all her life, in the violent childhood she experienced growing up in an unfair and inegalitarian colonial society. Her entire life was one of deep suffering, a life that was too hard, a life where being different was a heavy weight. She put all her effort into trying to 'fit in', into trying to make people forget where she came from, into trying to make the tangible signs of a difficult past disappear: Kabyle, Nouville, Nessadiou, Boghen, la Vallee du Tir.

This generation, the last of the prisoners' children, never told its story. It has been swallowed by time and change. It has seen the established order change along with its certitudes, as well as demands appear that it only rarely understood.

How can one understand the Caldoche attachment to this land, this land where the freedmen were given concessions, if you don't know what they had to pay the administration for the lands they were forced to live and work on? How can one admit to violent speech and even acts if you don't know the routine violence that existed in this colony three generations ago?

And what about the attachment that many of these descendants (often of mixed blood with pariahs) have to France? Isn't it just a way to 'rehabilitate' New Caledonian society which bore the burden of being 'at fault' for such a long time? The children weren't guilty of anything. They were simply born into a closed, segmented and hierarchical colonial society. A society in which the thoughtful administration had created castes based on origin.

Today our pleasure in living in New Caledonia is founded on the difficult lives of these people, on their hopes (often dashed) of a better society. The reason I'm giving away your secret Granny, despite everything it represents, is because your story is where we came from. Our fragile happiness is a legacy, it's a gift that has been built progressively by the prisoners' descendants, along with Kanak forced labor, volunteer Asian workers, the little colonists who were abandoned far away from everything, and all those who suffered under the dominating system.

The departure of these last witnesses of the past (though greatly responsible for recent conflicts) with the acceleration of historical events and the country changing more in the past thirty years than it did for the previous one hundred, has left a void in our collective memory. Walled in by their silence until the end, they have now deprived us of a part of our past.

History books will always be able to describe the penitentiary in New Caledonia in detail, but the lives of the children of freedmen often fade away. By joining the half-slave Javanese and Tonkinese minors, the old people from the penitentiary's past were finally able to 'fit in' and changed their real history into a hagiography of colonisation.

Faced with the gradual disappearance of past cultural landmarks, our 'duty to remember' can only be that of thanking our predecessors for all the horizons they opened in their suffering which built the foundations of our happiness.

New Caledonians from every background, Kanaks, Javanese, Ni-Vanuatu, those who suffered from the injustice of the 'colonial system', be merciful with the memory of these people who deserve your forgiveness. And you children, grandchildren and great-grandchildren of history, don't attempt to judge the past violence but rather work to be deserving of their legacy. Don't miss out on the key part of their message: work to create a better land.

There is a date palm tree in Nessadiou, a living symbol of Kabylian roots in New Caledonia today. The Bourail lizard has come home. He doesn't need to look at skin color to see that all these children belong to this land and have the same history.

Thanks for everything Granny.

Notes

1 This chapter is available in a French language version: see Frédéric Angleviel : 'L'histoire de la Nouvelle-Calédonie. Approche chronologique et enjeux contemporains', *Tsingy: Revue de l'association des professeurs d'histoire et de géographie de Madagascar*, N°6, Tamatave, 2007, 146 p., p. 119 à 146.

2 Please refer to the following for lack of a single work giving an overall picture of New Caledonian history: F. Angleviel (dir.), *101 mots pour comprendre l'histoire de la Nouvelle-Calédonie*, Ed. Ile de Lumière, Nouméa, 1997, 224 p.; Alban Bensa, *Nouvelle-Calédonie vers l'émancipation*, Gallimard, Paris, 198 p.; Alain Christnacht, *La Nouvelle-Calédonie*, La Documentation Française, n°5184-5185, Paris, 2003, 174 p.; Anne Pitoiset, *Nouvelle-Calédonie. Horizons pacifiques*, Autrement, N°114, Paris, 1999, 280 p.

3 Isabelle Amiot & Christiane Terrier (dir.), *Histoire, Cycle 3, Nouvelle-Calédonie,* Centre de Documentation Pédagogique, Nouméa, 2007, 178 p. Cf. aussi F. Angleviel, *Histoire de la Nouvelle-Calédonie. Nouvelles approches, nouveaux objets*, L'Harmattan, Paris, 2006, 350 p.; ibid, *Les fondements de l'histoire de la Nouvelle-Calédonie. Définition, périodisation, sources*, Centre de Documentation Pédagogique, Collection Université, Nouméa, 2004, 201 p.

4 Additional works available which are essential to understanding the many facets of New Caledonian history include: Patrick O'Reilly, *Bibliographie de la Nouvelle-Calédonie*, Publication de la Société des Océanistes N°4, Paris, 1955, 361 p.; Georges Pisier, *Bibliographie de la Nouvelle Calédonie 1955-1982*, Publication N°34, Société d'Etudes Historiques de la Nouvelle Calédonie (S.E.H.N.C.), Nouméa, 1983, 350 p.; Frédéric Angleviel, « La Nouvelle-Calédonie : Droit et sciences économiques, Sciences humaines et sociales, bibliographie 1999-2002 » dans *Revue juridique, politique et économique de Nouvelle-Calédonie*, recension semestrielle, Nouméa, 2003-2007 ; Ibid, « Bouquet de paroles kanaks. Première bibliographie des écrits kanaks » dans *Chroniques du pays kanak, tome 3*, Planète Mémo, Nouméa, 1999, 356 p., p. 342 à 347 ; Ibid, « Etat des connaissances sur le monde kanak. Bibliographie générale et historique » dans *Chroniques du pays kanak, tome 4*, Planète memo, Nouméa, 1999, p. 360 à 372.

5 Christiane Terrier, *La colonisation de peuplement libre en Nouvelle-Calédonie (1889-1909)*, thèse d'histoire, Université de la Nouvelle-Calédonie, Nouméa, 2000, 863 p.

6 F. Angleviel, Bernard Capecchi & Christiane Douyère (dir.), *La Nouvelle-Calédonie. Histoire CM*, CTRDP, Nouméa, 1992, 96 p.

7 Jean-Christophe Galipaud, *La poterie préhistorique néo-calédonienne et ses implications dans l'étude du processus de peuplement du Pacifique occidental*, thèse d'archéologie, université de Paris I, 1988, 2 tomes.

8 For a long time I refused to harmonise the writing of the terms canaque-kanak because *canaque* currently suggests someone against independence, while the

unvarying term *kanak* suggests someone who is for independence. The name kanak(e)(s) retained by many scientists was furthermore perceived as being too moderate by some and too innovative by others. I, however, eventually came to agree with my literary colleagues that some kind of harmonisation was technically necessary and chose to write the term *kanak(e)(s)* in French. This seems to be most appropriate and the most logical according to the rules of French language. For more information concerning the etymological evolution of the word 'kanak', please refer to the following article: F. Angleviel, « De kanaka à Kanak : l'appropriation d'un terme générique au profit de la revendication identitaire » dans *Hermes, Cognition. Communication. Politique*, N°32-33, Editions du CNRS, Paris, 2002, 634 p., p. 191 à 196.

9 Christophe Sand, Jacques Bole & André Ouetcho, « Les sociétés préeuropéennes de Nouvelle-Calédonie et leur transformation historique. L'apport de l'archéologie » dans *En pays kanak*, Edition de la maison des Sciences de l'Homme, Mission du Patrimoine ethnologique, Collection Ethnologie de la France, Cahier 14, Paris, 2000, 366 p., p. 171 à 194. Cf. aussi C. Sand, *"Le temps d'avant". La préhistoire de la Nouvelle-Calédonie*, L'Harmattan, Paris, 1995, 356 p., p. 172.

10 Collectif : *Histoire CE2-CM1-CM2*, Ministère de l'éducation-CTRDP, Papeete, 1998, 174 p. « chapitre 12. Le peuplement de l'espace polynésien jusqu'au Xè siècle ; chapitre 14. La Polynésie aux temps anciens ». Cf. aussi Christiane Terrier, « Problèmes et perspectives pédagogiques liés aux questions de la périodisation de l'histoire océanienne à travers l'exemple néo-calédonien » dans *Histoire de la Nouvelle-Calédonie. Regards croisés*, Les indes savantes, Paris, 2007, 300 p, sous presse.

11 The preface to the Noumea accord putting history in the centre. François Garde, « Le préambule de l'Accord de Nouméa, prologue d'une histoire officielle ? » dans *Les Kanaks et l'histoire*, numéro spécial de la revue *Annales d'Histoire Calédonienne*, N°2, Les indes savantes, Paris, 2007, 560 p., sous presse.

12 Emmanuel Kasarhérou, « Introduction » to *Portraits kanak. Paroles kanak*, Agence de Développement de la Culture Kanak, Nouméa, 1995, 85 p., p. 9. Alban Bensa wrote a similar work, « L'histoire des avatars locaux du colonialisme français dessine, le plus souvent en creux, les formes de la résistance politique et culturelle kanak ». Alban Bensa, Jean Marie Kohler, Alain Saussol & Jean Tissier, *Comprendre l'identité kanak*, l'Abresle, Centre Thomas More, 1990, 75 p. Several works attempt to rebalance historical research. Collectif, *Sous la grande case de l'histoire*, numéro spécial de *Mwà Véé, revue culturelle kanak*, Agence de Développement de la culture Kanak, Nouméa, 2004, 62 p.; F. Angleviel, Luther Voudjo & Eddy Wadrawane (dir.), *Les Kanaks et l'histoire*, Les indes savantes, Paris, 2007, 560 p., sous presse.

13 F. Angleviel, « Un nouveau regard sur la démographie kanak » dans *Chroniques du pays kanak, Tome 1*, Planete Mémo, Nouméa, 1999, 293 p., p. 32 à 37.

14 Roger Boulay, *La maison kanak*, Parenthèses-ADCK-Orstom, Marseille, 1990, 165 p.

15 H. Marchal (dir.), *De jade et de nacre. Patrimoine artistique kanak*, Réunion des musées nationaux, Paris, 1990, 246 p.
16 We published the first article on this subject in 2004, which is still taboo in the scientific world today even though all New Caledonian oral traditions speak about this practice and are sometimes proud of it. F. Angleviel, « L'anthropophagie en Nouvelle-Calédonie. Réalité ou violence imaginaire » dans *Violences océaniennes*, L'Harmattan & IMOA, Paris, 2004, 234 p., p. 189 à 216.
17 Jean Guiart, *Structure de la chefferie en Mélanésie du Sud (N.C.)*, Institut d'ethnologie, Paris, 1992, 462 p. Collectif, *Chroniques du pays kanak, Tome 1 à 4*, Planète Mémo, Nouméa, 1999, 1200 p.
18 James Cook, *Relations de voyage autour du monde*, La découverte, coll. poche N°50, Paris, 1998, 456 p.; Pisier Georges, *La découverte de la Nouvelle-Calédonie*, Société d'Etudes Historiques de la Nouvelle-Calédonie N°5, Nouméa, 1983, 195 p.
19 Numa Broc, *Dictionnaire illustré des explorateurs et grands voyageurs français du XIXè siècle, Tome 4. Océanie*, Comité des travaux historiques et scientifiques, Paris, 2003, 407 p.
20 Dorothy Shineberg, *Ils étaient venus chercher du santal*, SEHNC N°3, Nouméa, 1973, 452 p.
21 Philippe Rey Lescure (ancien missionnaire en Nouvelle-Calédonie, 1922-1933), *Vos racines.. Essai d'histoire des débuts de l'Evangélisation de la Nouvelle-Calédonie*, à compte d'auteur, 1967, 183 p.
22 Kerry Howe, *Les îles Loyauté, histoire des contacts culturels de 1840 à 1900*, SEHNC publication N°19, Nouméa, 1978, 251 p.
23 Claude Rozier, *La calédonie ancienne*, Fayard, Paris, 1991, 322 p.
24 Joël Dauphiné, *Les débuts d'une colonisation laborieuse. Le sud calédonien (1853-1860)*, L'Harmattan, Paris, 1995, 185 p.
25 Alain Saussol, *L'héritage, essai sur le problème foncier mélanésien en Nouvelle-Calédonie*, Société des Océanistes, N°40, Paris, 1979, 493 p. ; Joël Dauphiné, *Les spoliation foncières en Nouvelle-Calédonie (1853-1913)*, L'Harmattan, Paris, 1989, 346 p.
26 Jean Guiart, *Heurs et Malheurs du pays de Numea ou du péché originel*, Le Rocher-à-la-voile, Nouméa, 2000, 160 p.
27 Michel Reuillard, *Les Saint-simoniens et la tentation coloniale. Les explorations africaines et le gouvernement néo-calédonien de Charles Guillain, (1808-1875)*, L'Harmattan, Paris 1995, 580 p.
28 José Barbançon, *Histoire du bagne en Nouvelle-Calédonie (1863-1931)*, Septentrion, Lille, 2003, 447 p.
29 Odile Krakovitch, *Les femmes bagnardes*, O. Orban, Paris, 1990, 296 p.
30 Mehdi Lallaoui, *Kabyles du Pacifique*, Au nom de la mémoire, Paris, 1994, 135 p.; Gisèle Chauvet, *Les déportés kabyles et arabes en Nouvelle-Calédonie*, DEA Espaces, temps et sociétés dans le Pacifique insulaire, Université Française du Pacifique, Nouméa, 1994, 108 p.

31 Cynthia Debien, *La colonisation pénale en Nouvelle-Calédonie. L'exemple des concessionnaires de Pouembout, 1883-1895*, maîtrise d'histoire, Université de Toulouse, 1990, 183 p.

32 Roger Boulay, *Kannibals et Vahinés. Imagerie des mers du Sud*, Editions de l'aube, Paris, 2000, 130 p., p. 117. ; Bruno Corre, *Histoire du service des affaires indigènes de Nouvelle-Calédonie : affaires indigènes, indigénat et politiques indigènes de 1856 à 1954 assimilation ou ségrégation ?*, DEA Sociétés et cultures dans le Pacifique insulaire. Dynamiques et mutations, Université Française du Pacifique, Nouméa, 1997, 108 p.

33 Roselène Dousset-Leenhardt, *Colonialisme et contradictions, étude sur les causes socio-historiques de 1878 en Nouvelle-Calédonie*, L'Harmattan, Paris, 1970, 208 p. ; Jean Guiart, *La terre qui s'enfuit. Les pays canaques anciens, de La Foa à Moindou, Bourail et Kouaoua, Le Rocher-à-la-voile*, Nouméa, 1998, 168 p.

34 Catherine Buttet, *Histoire d'un échec ? mise en valeur et pouvoirs publics en Nouvelle-Calédonie de 1870 à 1914*, Septentrion presses universitaires, Lille, 1999, 581 p.

35 Yann Bencivengo (Dir.), *101 mots pour comprendre la mine en Nouvelle-Calédonie*, Ile de Lumière, Coll. 101 mots pour, N°2, Nouméa, 1999, 268 p. ; Yann Bencivengo, *La Société Le Nickel : une grande entreprise industrielle en Nouvelle-Calédonie (1880-1960)*, DEA Sociétés et cultures dans le Pacifique insulaire. Dynamiques et mutations, Université Française du Pacifique, Nouméa, 1995.

36 Christiane Terrier, *La colonisation de peuplement libre en Nouvelle-Calédonie (1889-1909)*, thèse d'histoire, Université de la Nouvelle-Calédonie, Nouméa, 2000, 863 p. ; Nathalie Lemetayer, *Paul Feillet (1857-1903). Le parcours d'un fonctionnaire colonial sous la IIIème République*, DEA d'histoire coloniale, Université de Paris IV, 1995, 118 p.

37 Sylvette Boyer-Boubin, *De la première guerre mondiale en Océanie. Les guerres de tous les Calédoniens, 1914-1918*, thèse d'histoire, Université de la Nouvelle-Calédonie, 2001, 760 p.

38 Bernard Brou, *Espoirs et réalités. La Nouvelle-Calédonie de 1925 à 1945*, SEHNC N°9, 1975, 315 p.

39 Benoît Delvinquier, *L'épopée des colons nordistes en Nouvelle-Calédonie*, La découvrance, coll. L'Amateur averti, Rennes, 1998, 198 p.

40 Jean-Marie Lambert, *La nouvelle politique indigène en Nouvelle-Calédonie. Le capitaine Meunier et ses gendarmes, 1918-1954*, L'Harmattan, Mondes Océaniens, Paris, 1999, 240 p.

41 Jean-François Zorn, *Le Grand Siècle d'une mission protestante. La Mission de Paris de 1822 à 1914*, Karthala, Paris, 1993, 792 p.; Georges Delbos, *L'église catholique en Nouvelle-Calédonie. Un siècle et demi d'histoire*, Desclée, Paris, 1993, 450 p.

42 Christiane Kasarherou-Leurquin, *L'histoire démographique de la population mélanésienne de la Nouvelle-Calédonie entre 1840 et 1950*, thèse NR

d'histoire, Université de Paris I, 1992.

43 Michel Naepels, *Histoires de terres kanakes. Conflits fonciers et rapports sociaux dans la région de Houaïlou (Nouvelle-Calédonie)*, Belin, Paris, 1998, 380 p.

44 Isabelle Merle, *Expériences coloniales. La Nouvelle-Calédonie (1853-1920)*, Belin, Paris, 1996, 478 p.

45 F. Angleviel (dir.), *La Nouvelle-Calédonie, terre de métissages*, Annales d'histoire calédonienne, N°2, Les indes savantes, Paris, 2004, 274 p.

46 Cf. le témoignage d'un colon : Bernard Papin, *Vie et mort de Ludovic Papin chez les Canaques*, L'Harmattan, Paris, 1999, 130 p.

47 Dorothy Shineberg, *La main d'œuvre néo-hébridaise en Nouvelle-Calédonie (1865-1930)*, SEHNC, N° 61, Nouméa, 2003, 438 p.

48 Philippe Palombo, *La présence japonaise en Nouvelle-Calédonie. (1890-1960)*, ANRT, thèse à la carte, Lille, 2003, 581 p.

49 F. Angleviel, « La quadruple diaspora asiatique en Nouvelle-Calédonie. Histoire et enjeux contemporains », actes du colloque IMASIE, Paris, 2007, à paraître.

50 Henry Daly, *Nouvelle-Calédonie. Porte-avion américain dans les mers du Sud*, A compte d'auteur et SEHNC, publication N°60, Nouméa, 2002, 321 p.

51 F. Angleviel, *Brève histoire de la Nouvelle-Calédonie contemporaine, (1946-2005)*, Les éditions du G.R.H.O.C., Nouméa, 2006, 313 p.

52 Ismet Kurtovitch, *La vie politique en Nouvelle-Calédonie : 1940-1953*, Septentrion presses universitaires, Lille, 2000, 690 p.

53 Jean Le Borgne, *Nouvelle-Calédonie 1945-1968. La confiance trahie*, L'Harmattan, Paris, 2005, 600 p.

54 Frédéric Angleviel (dir.), *Une histoire en cent histoires. L'histoire calédonienne à travers 100 destins hors du commun*, Bambou editions, 2004, Nouméa, 110 p.

55 Jean-Marie Tjibaou, *La présence kanak*, O. Jacob, Paris, 1996, 324 p.; Hamid Mokaddem, *Ce souffle venu des ancêtres... L'œuvre politique de Jean-Marie Tjibaou (1936-1989)*, Expressions, Nouméa, 2005, 411 p.

56 Pierre Maresca, « La Caillou à feu et à sang » dans *Le mémorial calédonien, 1981-1988, tome IX*, Pacifique presse communication, Nouméa, 1993, 670 p. ; Cédric Michalski, *L'assaut de la grotte d'Ouvéa. Analyse juridique*, L'Harmattan, Paris, 2004, 320 p.

57 Daniel Dommel, *La crise calédonienne. Rémission ou guérison ?*, L'Harmattan, Paris, 1993, 254 p.

58 Jean-Yves Faberon & Jean-Raymond Postic, *L'accord de Nouméa. La loi organique et autres documents juridiques et politiques de la Nouvelle-Calédonie*, île de lumière, Nouméa, 2004, 188 p.; François Garde, *Les institutions de la Nouvelle-Calédonie*, L'Harmattan, collection Mondes Océaniens, Paris, 2001, 350 p.

59 Robert Bertram, *Le gouvernement de la Nouvelle-Calédonie dirigé par Jean Lèques : 1999-2001*, DEA Sociétés et cultures dans le Pacifique, Université de la Nouvelle-Calédonie, Nouméa, 2004, 158 p.

Part One

The 19th century relationship

Avant-hier

L'évangélisation en Nouvelle-Calédonie et en Nouvelle-Zélande: Étude Comparative de Deux Phases Pionnières entre 1838 et 1853

Yannick Essertel

Deux vicaires apostoliques Maristes évangélisent au cours de la même époque les deux grandes îles du Pacifiques : la Nouvelle-Zélande par Mgr Pompallier et la Nouvelle-Calédonie par Mgr Douarre. Si la rencontre avec les Maoris en Nouvelle-Zélande provoque un choc culturel positif qui évolue vers une acculturation réussie, il en va tout autrement en Nouvelle-Calédonie où les Canaques et les missionnaires ont des difficultés à se rejoindre sur le plan culturel. A part quelques sujets qui se convertissent, l'acculturation est bloquée avec bon nombres de tribus canaques. Quant à l'inculturation, si Mgr Pompallier arrive à développer une pastorale cohérente et respectueuse des coutumes maories, Mgr Douarre, malgré son désir, a bien du mal à mettre en place une pastorale adaptée et à inculturer le christianisme.

Two Marist vicars were engaged in evangelical activity during the same period on the two great islands of the Pacific – Bishop Pompallier, in New Zealand, and Bishop Douarre, in New Caledonia. If the encounter with Maori in New Zealand provoked a positive cultural shock which led towards a successful acculturation, it was quite different in New Caledonia, where Kanaks and missionaries had difficulties meeting on a cultural level. Apart from some individuals who converted, acculturation was blocked by a good many Kanak tribes. As for enculturation – the process of learning another group's culture, by observation and experience – while Bishop Pompallier was able to develop a coherent and respectful pastoral approach to Maori custom, Bishop Douarre, in spite of his wishes, found it very difficult to put in place a pastoral approach adapted to his circumstances, or to inculcate Christianity among the Kanak peoples.

Les travaux des historiens, et notamment de Frédéric Angleviel[1] et Claude Rozier,[2] ont fait connaître les aléas de la mission mariste en Nouvelle-Calédonie dirigée par Mgr Guillaume Douarre[3] de 1843 à 1853. De son côté, Mgr Jean-Baptiste Pompallier[4] évangélise la Nouvelle-Zélande de 1838 à 1868. Il reste un personnalité controversée malgré l'ouvrage de Ernest Simmons[5] qui donne une vision plus équilibrée en partant des archives. Ainsi, en ce début du XIX° siècle, deux vagues de Maristes, parties de Lyon, évangélisent les peuples de Mélanésie et Polynésie. Les deux vicaires apostoliques sont en phase pionnière au cours d'une période quasi identique. Si la carrière de Mgr Douarre s'achève en 1853, celle de Mgr Pompallier s'arrête en 1868. Mais, pour ce dernier, la première phase d'évangélisation prend fin vers 1856. Donc, la comparaison entre ces deux expériences pionnières est possible entre 1838 et 1856, car celle de Mgr Douarre s'inscrit dans ce laps de temps.

La comparaison porte sur les trois phases que comprend une période pionnière : le choc culturel, l'acculturation et l'inculturation. Il est pour le moins curieux, mais plein d'enseignement, de constater à quel point ces trois étapes du processus d'évangélisation ont été radicalement différentes dans les deux cas que nous étudions. Notre approche ne veut pas reconstituer une histoire événementielle plus ou moins connue, mais plutôt de tenter un parallèle entre ces deux évangélisateurs maristes. Dans un premier temps nous comparons la rencontre, le contact ou l'acculturation, ensuite nous analysons les pratiques pastorales ou l'inculturation.

Choc Culturel et Acculturation

Mgr Pompallier Face aux Maoris

L'arrivée, en janvier 1838 à Hokianga, de Mgr Pompallier et ses missionnaires est marquée par un incident. Le Révérend Nathanaël Turner, pasteur wesleyen qui habite à Mangungu sur le Hokianga, s'empresse de déverser son opinion sur les catholiques romains parmi ses fidèles : les catholiques apportent des dieux de bois, ils veulent s'emparer du pays, les égorger, brûler leurs wharées et prêcher une doctrine d'erreurs. Le 22 janvier 1838, des fidèles maoris du pasteur viennent menacer les Maristes. Mgr Pompallier s'adresse à la foule :

Nous avons quitté nos parents, nos amis, notre patrie en Europe, leur dit-il, pour venir à la Nouvelle-Zélande. Nous n'avons en vue que de faire le bien, en vous laissant, aux chefs et au peuple, votre autorité et tout ce qui vous appartient. Nous sommes les ministres du vrai Dieu et de son Eglise. Nous venons instruire les peuples qui voudraient nous écouter, et laisser en paix ceux qui ne voudraient point de notre doctrine. Nous ne sommes nullement venus pour amasser des biens de ce monde, mais pour donner ceux du ciel. Enfin, nous n'avons ni femmes, ni enfants, et nos coeurs et nos corps sont consacrés à Dieu, pour n'avoir d'autre sollicitude que celle de son service et du salut des peuples.[6]

La découverte du célibat sacerdotal a un effet immédiat sur les Maoris : comment peut-on se passer de femme ? Cet aspect du catholicisme joue un rôle essentiel dans l'adhésion à l'Epikopo. Son effet sur les Maoris s'est répété dans de très nombreux cas. Premier choc culturel en faveur des missionnaires chez un peuple qui ne peut imaginer qu'on puisse avoir de femme.

Le lendemain, 23 janvier, Mgr Pompallier décide de faire sa première visite pastorale chez les Irlandais catholiques du bassin d'Hokianga et espère rencontrer les tribus riveraines encore païennes. Avec quelques catholiques européens, un prêtre et un frère, il décide de rendre visite à celle de Wirinaki. Aussitôt on lui explique de n'en rien faire : ceux de Wirinaki sont méchants, intraitables et ils ont toujours refusé les Wesleyens. Or, à Wirinaki, ils reçoivent un accueil chaleureux et enthousiaste. Puis, un des chefs déclare à tout le peuple assemblé :

Ces deux étrangers n'ont ni femmes, ni enfants ; ils ne paraissent pas faire bonne chère ; voilà les ministres du vrai Dieu.[7]

Personne parmi les Européens ne comprend ce retournement. C'est Mgr Pompallier, qui donne la raison de cette attitude après s'être renseigné :

Il est bon de remarquer ici que cette tribu et plusieurs autres d'Hokianga et de la Baie des îles, avaient appris depuis plusieurs années que les ministres de la vraie Eglise n'étaient pas mariés ; qu'ils viendraient à la Nouvelle-Zélande ; et qu'on pourrait les reconnaître facilement au célibat qu'ils observaient.[8]

Il s'agirait d'un esprit qui aurait prophétisé du temps de leurs pères.

Étrange 'prophétie' qui fait basculer spontanément plusieurs tribus riveraines de l'Hokianga. Lors de la soirée, la tribu entonne autour d'un grand feu un chant d'éloge aux 'vrais envoyés du ciel' (sic). Le matin suivant, Mgr Pompallier se prépare pour la messe et revêt ses ornements. L'émerveillement se lit sur les visages devant les ornements liturgiques et surtout la chasuble brodée. Avant son départ, l'évêque est supplié de dire quelques paroles ainsi que la prière catholique. Alors, tous les Européens présents et l'évêque se mettent à genoux, puis montent en latin les accents du Pater, de l'Ave et du Credo. Devant ces visages sérieux et levés au ciel, les indigènes s'écrient : 'Kapaï, Kapaï', c'est-à-dire, 'Que c'est bon ! Que c'est bon !'. Au moment de se séparer, c'est l'heure des grandes promesses : les Naturels jurent qu'ils attendront l'évêque, voulant absolument suivre son enseignement et celui de l'Eglise catholique.[9] Deuxième choc culturel ou plutôt choc spirituel : l'évêque est celui annoncé par la prophétie.

Ces événements vont agir comme une onde de choc et se propager très vite dans l'ensemble des tribus maories : ceux qui sont attendus sont là et ils n'ont pas de femme. Pour couronner le tout, Mgr Pompallier guérit la fille du grand chef Rewa, de la Baie des îles. Ce dernier devient catéchumène et se fait baptiser. Chef de renom, il devient le plus fidèle ami de l'évêque et sincère chrétien. Le plus fascinant reste le degré d'insertion de Mgr Pompallier dans la culture maorie et la manière dont les Maoris l'ont à ce point adopté. Epicopo est devenu l'un des leurs, leur Père sur qui ils comptent et qu'ils admirent comme le rapporte le Père Viard :

> *Je m'édifie au spectacle des vertus de notre premier pasteur. Quelle douceur admirable il conserve au milieu d'un peuple qui l'importune à toute heure. Ces insulaires sont de véritables enfants, dont l'indiscrétion n'a d'égale que la patience du saint prélat. Quand ils sont auprès de Sa Grandeur, ils ne savent plus s'en séparer. Epicopo, j'ai faim, disent-ils, sans plus de façon en se mettant à table, et Epicopo leur donne à manger ce qu'il a, sans que sa condescendance s'épuise et que son zèle connaisse jamais la fatigue.*[10]

Il était devenu Maori parmi les Maoris.

Ses nombreuses visites, ses voyages jusqu'en 1846, lui permettent d'étendre son champ de mission. Pour apprécier cette progression, nous avons les rapports officiels de Mgr Pompallier, du père Forest et les lettres des missionnaires en postes. Dans son rapport à Rome, du 14 septembre 1841, alors qu'il visite son vicariat, et envoyé le 15 novembre suivant, l'évêque mentionne l'existence de douze stations en Nouvelle-Zélande et de deux dans les Tropiques. Un rapport précis du Père Forest, alors Visiteur de la mission de Nouvelle-Zélande pour le Père Colin, révèle que fin 1843 le nombre de stations a progressé[11] de douze à seize. En 1846, au moment du voyage de Mgr Pompallier en Europe, Mgr Viard[12] dresse un état global du nombre de Maoris baptisés : 5044 inscrits sur les registres ecclésiastiques en avril 1846. A côté, il y a 100 000 Maoris non convertis favorables ou pas à l'évêque. Tel était le résultat d'une dizaine d'années d'apostolat au moment où l'évêque fait son premier voyage en Europe.

Mgr Douarre Face aux Canaques

Du côté de la Nouvelle-Calédonie, la done était toute autre. Le 21 décembre 1843, le *Bucéphale* commandé par Julien-Laferrière, dépose Mgr Douarre, les pères Piere Rougeyron et Philippe Viard et les frères à Balade en Nouvelle-Calédonie. L'évêque qui croyait trouver des Protestants constate qu'ils sont absents et même qu'ils ont abandonné des postes après avoir tenté une implantation. Ils débarquent dans un secteur resté à l'écart de tout contact. Néanmoins, les premières rencontres sont rassurantes. Accompagné du Père Viard qui l'initie aux langues locales, Mgr Douarre visite l'intérieur de son vicariat entouré de Naturels au milieu des quels il dit être en parfaite tranquillité et sûreté. Il reçoit partout un accueil chaleureux et visiblement spontané. Les missionnaires comme le père Rougeyron sont très impressionnés par le respect qu'ils inspirent aux chefs et aux populations. Partout où ils passent, les habitants les prennent pour des hommes extraordinaires :

> *Comme leur île n'avait presque pas été visitée par les Européens,* explique le Père, *ils ont encore une grande idée des Blancs. Ils nous attribuent la puissance sur le vent et la pluie. Le ciel, selon eux, est la terre que nous habitons, et ils l'ont conclu parce qu'ils voyaient nos navires à l'horizon toucher le ciel [. . .] La vue de nos navires, à*

l'horizon, tombant presque des nues, leur a, sans doute, fait penser que c'était notre demeure. Aussi ne sont-ils pas touchés, quand nous leur disons que Dieu règne dans les Cieux. Pour eux, le Ciel est une belle terre, dans le genre de la leur, seulement plus riche.[13]

Le ciel est le lieu des Blancs et non celui des dieux ou des âmes de leurs ancêtres. Nous voilà en plein choc culturel : les missionnaires blancs sont des êtres supérieurs descendus du ciel chez les Canaques. Ces Blancs ne sont-ils pas en réalité les âmes de leurs ancêtres qui reviennent ? Au Père Rougeyron qui pose la question à quelques vieillards de Balade, ceux-ci lui font cette réponse :

'Vous, nous vous considérions comme les âmes de nos parents, qui, de noirs, étaient devenues blanches et plus belles dans l'autre monde. Nous vous aimions beaucoup, car vous nous rappeliez de touchants souvenirs'.

Dans son journal, Mgr Douarre confirme qu'ils ont une idée de l'immortalité de l'âme. Âmes qui peuvent faire du bien ou du mal. Elles possèdent un indéniable pouvoir sur les vivants comme de guérir des maladies si on leur fait des offrandes. Les missionnaires se voient donc attribuer un réel pouvoir de commandement sur les éléments de la nature. Pouvoir bienfaisant ou malfaisant. Le 31 janvier 1844, les missionnaires reçoivent des projectiles et deviennent victimes de diverses tracasseries. Les naturels pensaient que les récents orages et coups de tonnerre étaient une manifestation hostile des Blancs à leur égard. Le Père Rougeyron rapporte l'apostrophe suivante d'un Canaque :

Tu ne nous fais pas donner de pluie ; tes compatriotes, les Blancs, la gardent toute. Tiens, viens voir nos plantations, elles meurent !' Partout où je vais, on ne cesse de me demander de la pluie et de les empêcher de mourir ; ils croient qu'il est en notre pouvoir d'accéder à leur demande.[14]

Cette vision des habitants est porteuse de dangers pour la mission. Le Blanc commande à la nature et devient donc responsable de ses effets sur le monde des Canaques. Terrible méprise qui débouche sur un drame. Alors que Mgr Douarre est reparti en Europe demander de l'aide, l'établissement de Poubéo bâti par le Père Rougeyron est attaqué et incendié.b Le Frère Blaise est massacré et les biens pillés. C'est le résultat d'une coalition de Bayao, Bouélate, Mamate et Ouonbone qui avaient réussi à convaincre ceux de Pouébo. L'ensemble de la mission n'est que ruine. C'était le 18 juillet 1847. Cet événement dramatique puise ses racines dans le choc culturel/spirituel :

> *Une épidémie épouvantable a eu lieu. Nous devions tous périr ; mais non, Marie nous a sauvés, notre bétail seul a été enlevé. L'Esprit malin a ensuite suggéré aux naturels que c'était nous qui faisions mourir les autres, pendant que nous restions debout. Des missionnaires étaient promis à Bouarat, chef de Hienguène. Ces missionnaires n'arrivant pas, Bouarat, furieux contre nous, a soufflé aux gens de Bayao, par suggestion du démon, de nous massacrer.*[15]

La convoitise des biens, une promesse qui ne se réalise pas et le 'choc microbien', telles sont les causes de ce gâchis. Quelle a été la part de chacune de ces causes ? Peu importe de le savoir, le choc culturel place les habitants dans une situation de méprise et aussi d'insatisfaction. Or, le chef blanc, celui qui en impose aux autres chefs, est absent. Un instant, les instincts traditionnels reprennent le dessus montrant la fragilité de l'oeuvre.

Du côté des missionnaires le choc culturel n'avait pas été moins fort. On découvrait ceux envers lesquels le discours européen de l'époque était chargé de préjugés, tour à tour 'bon sauvage' paré de toutes les vertus ou 'bête féroce' vivant au fond des forêts. Le contact direct provoque une prise de conscience comme celle du père Rougeyron :

> *Vous ne vous étiez peut-être jamais imaginé que des sauvages aimassent la société ; je m'étais figuré, moi, que les sauvages vivaient dans les bois, comme des bêtes féroces, qu'ils vivaient chacun dans leur gîte sans se fréquenter. Hélas, comme j'étais dans l'erreur ! Ces hommes sont parfaitement des hommes semblables à nous, à quelques différences près, non essentielles. Ils vivent en société. Leurs cases ne sont point bâties dans les forêts mais bien dans les plaines ou les vallées.*[16]

Longue lettre remarquable sur le plan ethnographique. Il décrit le climat, le milieu naturel, les habitants, leurs coutumes, moeurs guerrières, rites, pratiques diverses. Pour Rougeyron c'est le fruit de son observation :

> *Voilà trois ans que nous sommes sur cette terre, que nous étudions les moeurs et les usages, et cependant nous sommes loin de les connaître entièrement.*[17]

Le premier contact, on l'a vu est sympathique, bienveillant des deux côtés, mais fondé sur une erreur de jugement. Assez rapidement, face à l'anthropophagie, aux massacres dues aux vengeances, aux vols et mille tracasseries, les missionnaires en viennent à penser que ces peuples ont perdu les principes de la loi naturelle. Attristé par toutes ces pratiques, Mgr Douarre, sans se décourager et modifier son opinion sur ces hommes et femmes qu'il aime, tente d'intervenir, souvent en pure perte :

> *Lorsque nous leur disons qu'il est mal d'attaquer et de massacrer de pauvres femmes sans défense, explique l'évêque, ils nous répondent que ce sont leurs usages.*[18]

L'incompréhension de Mgr Douarre demeure face à l'anthropophagie, à la coutume d'enterrer quasi vivant les veillards infirmes, les malades et tout autre membre de la tribu qui deviennent une charge. Lorsqu'il en fait la remarque aux Canaques, il s'attire cette réponse : "c'est comme cela, c'est la coutume !" Cette différence de l'autre, l'évêque la perçoit mal, alors que lui, il raisonne selon ses principes en termes d'égalité et de respect de la personne devant Dieu. Mgr Douarre butte sur ces pratiques et les perçoit comme un obstacle à la progression de l'évangélisation. La condition de la femme aussi le choque :

> *Les femmes surtout ont besoin que la religion vienne les arracher à leur esclavage et à leur avilissement. Comme chez toutes les nations que l'évangile n'a pas civilisées, elles rampent aux pieds de l'homme qui les tyrannise. A elles est dévolue la charge de porter les fardeaux, d'aller chercher la nourriture, d'avoir soin des champs une fois qu'ils sont défrichés. Elles ont la plus grande part aux travaux et la plus petite aux douceurs du ménage. Y a-t-il un bon morceau à manger ? Aussitôt le mari le fait tapou et il est permis à l'épouse d'être témoin du dîner de son mari mais sans y toucher, autrement elle serait punie de mort. Si elle tombe malade, elle est à l'instant*

séquestrée; elle couche à la belle étoile ou sous quelques branches plus ou moins bien entrelacées. Il faut qu'elle reste là exposée aux injures de l'air et de la pluie. Si une femme était infidèle, si même elle osait désobéir à son mari, celui-ci entre en fureur et la traite avec une barbarie incroyable. Il lui brise le crâne avec une pierre.[19]

Afin de capter leur attention, Mgr Douarre a essayé de faire jouer la corde de la sensibilité :

Lorsque nous leur disons, raconte-il, que nous avons tout quitté pour venir leur apprendre à prier et à faire le bien, ils en sont peu touchés, mais lorsque nous ajoutons que nous pleurions, ainsi que nos parents, ils en paraissent affectés. Ils ne comprennent pas que nous n'ayons pas de femmes et nous demandent souvent pourquoi nous n'en prenons pas.[20]

Ici, le célibat, tout quitter pour l'amour et le salut du prochain, reste culturellement difficile à saisir par le plus grand nombre. Les baptêmes d'enfants et de malades sont une source d'incompréhension mutuelle. Des Canaques y ont vu un remède :

Ils ajoutent [Les Naturels], quand nous allons voir les malades, que nous pouvons les empêcher de mourir en leur donnant une certaine eau que nous connaissons et qui a beaucoup de vertu.[21]

D'autres pensent que le baptême fait mourir. Pour de nombreux Canaques le baptême relève de la médecine ou du maléfice. En décembre 1846, une épidémie ravage les tribus du Nord. Les pères interrompent les baptêmes des enfants qui mouraient : les habitants pensaient que le baptême en était responsable. Au cours de l'été 1847, Alexis, grand chef de Tiavoite et fervent chrétien, meurt. Son père et son entourage en accusent le Père Rougeyron : Alexis est mort parce qu'il est chrétien.

Le choc culturel n'est donc pas résolu en 1847, plus de trois ans et demi après leur arrivée. Cependant, tous les écrits des missionnaires, jusqu'en 1847, notent des avancées : le vol régresse et plusieurs commencent à avoir honte de l'anthropophagie. Ni désespoir, ni amertume donc chez Mgr Douarre. Pourtant, trois ans et demi après l'installation de la mission, le premier poste est détruit. Les missionnaires partent avec un groupe de chrétiens que le Père Rougeyron destine à Wallis. La première étape et tentative d'évangélisation de la Nouvelle-Calédonie est close. Pourtant, Mgr Douarre revient et jusqu'à sa mort en 1853, il n'abandonne pas l'idée de convertir ses chers 'Canaques'. Entre 1849 et 1853, il a tenté quatre fois de reprendre son apostolat, mais chaque fois il a buté sur les mêmes obstacles. Même son groupe de chrétiens était persécuté par des chefs qui ne supportaient pas de voir certains des leurs abandonner les coutumes ancestrales guerrières, la polygamie ou l'anthropophagie.[22] De surcroît, en avril 1853, une deuxième vague d'épidémie s'abat sur le pays. Les missionnaires 'venus du ciel' en sont encore rendus responsables.[23]

Pastorale et Inculturation

Une Pastorale Adaptée en Nouvelle-Zélande

> *Rien n'était plus expédient pour la mission,* explique Mgr Pompallier, *que d'aller en commencer les travaux par l'étude des langues* [. . .] *Il est important dès le début de ne pas enseigner la Religion, ni de se faire connaître comme ayant l'intention de changer celle du pays : on ne peut réussir dans le ministère de l'enseignement que quand on possède suffisamment la langue des peuples. Il suffit au commencement qu'on soit reçu chez eux en hospitalité.*[24]

C'est avec l'aide des Irlandais présents que les missionnaires ont appris la langue, c'est-à-dire avec des populations qui avaient déjà une expérience du maori. Comme l'importance de la langue lui apparaît avec une forte évidence, Mgr Pompallier entreprend un travail sur le néo-zélandais. Il ne l'achève qu'en 1841 et le livre à l'imprimeur pour 'être utile aux missionnaires catholiques afin que cela puisse l'être aussi à la colonie européenne'.[25]

L'âme maorie lui offre des perspectives intéressantes pour l'évangélisation. Frappé de leur extrême sensibilité face à toutes les formes d'expression artistique, il commence à inculturer l'évangile en passant par une pastorale du sensible. Constatant l'effet produit par les images, Mgr Pompallier utilise ce moyen comme première approche :

> *Une prédication muette mais très sensible et fort salutaire pour nos insulaires, ce sont des images des principaux mystères de la vie de*

notre Seigneur et de la très sainte Vierge, de notre saint père le pape et de l'arbre chronologique de l'Église [. . .] On est venu ici de plus de 50 lieues pour voir un tableau à couleur grossière, qui représente le mystère de la naissance de notre Seigneur et de l'adoration des bergers. Tous les naturels qui le voyaient en étaient émerveillés. Les explications qu'on leur donne en même temps ne s'effacent plus de leur mémoire.[26]

Il en est de même pour le chant. Les premières messes chantées par l'évêque et ses missionnaires attirent les Maoris :

'Sa Grandeur avait établi l'usage de chanter le Miserere, le Domine non secundum, le Parce Domine ; ces chants qui sont si attendrissants par eux-mêmes ont fait une heureuse impression sur les sauvages.'[27]

Les prières essentielles sont traduites en maori, publiées et diffusées auprès des tribus grâce à l'imprimerie de la mission mise en place en 1842. Mgr Pompallier des chants simples à portée doctrinale.

Sur les regards qu'il a portés sur la religion des Maoris et sur sa méthode personnelle d'évangélisation, le vicaire apostolique nous a laissé un texte capital.[28] A l'égard de la culture maorie, il adopte une attitude paulinienne et xavierenne. Ayant lu et médité la vie apostolique de saint François-Xavier, il la met en pratique et sa vision positive le porte à l'optimisme. Loin d'être un novateur, il se situe dans la ligne définie par la Propaganda Fide, depuis le XVII° siècle, de ne pas européaniser. Il adopte la conception de l'acculturation jésuite qui englobe l'ensemble des composantes d'une culture. Mgr Pompallier constate que la religion maorie n'est pas faite de grossières traditions. En effet, ils ne possèdent pas d'idoles et de temples. Ils croient 'à l'existence d'esprits supérieurs bienfaisants ou malfaisants, et à la transmigration des âmes de leurs parents; ils avaient la croyance à un enfer, lieu de ténèbres qu'ils appelaient Reinga ; et à un paradis, lieu de délices et de lumières, qu'ils nommaient Aotéa.' Les Maoris confessent donc une religion nettement spirituelle. Ce qui frappe Mgr Pompallier c'est leur 'Genèse' :

Tout l'univers se bornait à la Nouvelle Zélande et à une autre île, qu'ils appellent Awaihi, et dont ils ne savent pas le lieu. C'est de cette île que selon quelques-uns de leurs savants, des hommes

> *divins seraient venus peupler leurs terres. L'un de leurs ancêtres qu'ils vénèrent le plus, porte le nom de Mawi. C'est à lui qu'ils attribuent la création même de la Nouvelle Zélande. D'après leurs superstitions, un jour Mawi étant à la pêche sur la mer en ces parages, tira du fond de l'eau un poisson énorme et immense, lequel arrivé à la surface de l'eau, devint une terre productive, et forma tout le grand Archipel qu'ils habitent. Mawi avait une femme appelée Hina, dont d'abord il eut deux fils; l'aîné tua le second; il encourut par ce fratricide la juste colère de son père, qui le proscrivit de son habitation, et il fut errant sur les terres de l'Archipel, où il devint le père de plusieurs tribus. Il est rapporté encore que les ancêtres de Mawi n'avaient point de femmes; et que la mort n'existait pas dans le monde; ce n'est que lorsque la première femme fut créée, que les hommes ont commencé à mourir.*[29]

Mgr Pompallier établit tout de suite un parallèle avec l'Ancien Testament et particulièrement la Genèse :

> *Qui ne voit ici, commente-t-il, des rapprochements frappants entre les traditions des Maoris et quelques faits principaux cités dans la Genèse, pour le commencement du monde ? Mawi et Hina ne figurent-ils pas Adam et Eve ? Le fils aîné de Mawi, qui tue son frère ne représente-t-il pas Caïn qui tua Abel ? Le fils aîné de Mawi qui est proscrit par son père, ne rappelle-t-il pas la proscription de Caïn ? Enfin la mort, qui est entrée dans le monde, après que la première femme fut créée, n'indique-t-elle pas le fruit défendu qui fut mangé par Eve et par Adam, c'est-à-dire, le péché originel qui a été la source de tous les maux, et dont le châtiment a été la mort pour tous les hommes ? Or d'après toutes ces traditions ne pourrait-on pas conclure que dans l'antiquité, les pères des Maoris, n'étaient pas privés de toutes connaissances sur les traditions divines, rapportées dans la Genèse ?*[30]

En les instruisant, Mgr Pompallier note que les Maoris font eux-mêmes le rapprochement :

> *Ils écoutaient avec intérêt et avec docilité ce que la raison et la foi enseignent sur l'unité, la simplicité et l'éternité de Dieu, sur la création du monde, d'un premier homme et d'une première femme; sur leur péché, cause de tous les maux; sur le meurtre d'Abel, commis par Caïn; sur la rédemption des hommes opérée par le fils de Dieu fait chair. Les indigènes en foule remarquaient certain*

> *rapprochement entre ces vérités et leurs traditions, et s'écriaient, oh ! Nos pères, desquels nous descendons avaient eu certainement connaissance de ces choses; ils vivaient dans la lumière; mais c'est nous, leur postérité infortunée et ignorante, qui les avons oubliées et altérées. Tu es envoyé, Evêque, ajoutaient-ils, pour dissiper l'obscurité de notre intelligence et nous replacer dans la voie que nous avons perdue.*[31]

Ainsi, loin de considérer le christianisme comme une intrusion dans leur cosmogonie, les Maoris le voient comme un accomplissement, une révélation. Epikopo est bien l'envoyé annoncé par la prophétie pour les remettre dans la foi droite.

Cependant, c'est dans un document exceptionnel et inédit que se trouve l'essentiel de la pensée et de la pédagogie de l'évêque. Daté du 29 janvier 1841 et comprenant 89 pages, il est intitulé *Instructions pour les travaux de la mission.*[32] Mgr Pompallier jette là les bases de l'action missionnaire auprès des Maoris. Ce corpus est destiné à l'instruction des missionnaires afin d'asseoir sur des bases cohérentes l'évangélisation des Maoris. Nous pouvons distinguer trois volets : des conseils de conduite pour les missionnaires à l'égard des populations à évangéliser et de leurs coutumes, un exposé sur la manière de catéchiser les Maoris, et pour finir, une réfutation du protestantisme. L'essentiel réside dans son approche de l'âme maorie. L'évêque propose une démarche pastorale progressive pour amener les Maoris au christianisme. Il faut respecter le plus possible la fierté et la dignité des Maoris. Tout ce qui relève des relations et des aspects matériels doit s'insérer parfaitement dans la culture et les coutumes locales. Il ne s'agit pas d'une tactique, mais bien d'une pédagogie construite à partir d'une expérience de trois ans entre janvier 1838 et janvier 1841. La prudence et le discernement doivent être appliqués à tout ce qui relève des us et coutumes et des croyances :

> *Leur faire quitter leurs superstitions par la persuasion et successivement, mais après avoir bien étudié leurs usages et comparé que telle ou telle de leurs pratiques est vraiment superstitieuse.*[33]

Surtout, Mgr Pompallier demande au missionnaire ne de pas faire de remarque dans les débuts, de fermer les yeux sur certaines pratiques et même de ne pas répondre aux questions, de ne pas commettre d'erreur et de ne pas choquer les Maoris. Simplement répondre

> *que dans la suite ils comprendront tout ce qui est vrai, tout ce qui est bon. . . Dire aussi quelquefois que nous examinerons bien leurs coutumes et quand nous les comprendrons parfaitement alors nous leur dirons ce qui est bien ou ce qui est mal.*[34]

Après les conseils de prudence à l'égard des moeurs et de la manière de les aborder, Mgr Pompallier propose un catéchisme progressif pour leur faire assimiler les mystères catholiques et les données de la Foi. Pour le baptême des adultes il suggère de leur apprendre quelques 'Vérités religieuses élémentaires' qui se composent des éléments suivants : l'unité de Dieu en trois personnes, la spiritualité et l'infinité de Dieu. Toutes les étapes sont soigneusement décrites avec des exemples ou des conseils de présentation très pédagogiques. Il passe en revue les principaux dogmes, les Commandements, les Sacrements, les questions de morale. Sur ce dernier point, il établit une gradation pour répondre aux cas de conscience que les Maoris se posent.

Plusieurs lettres pastorales jalonnent ces années d'apostolat. Leur but principal : garder l'unité dans les pratiques cultuelles et pastorales afin d'éviter la confusion dans l'esprit des Maoris. Elles nous montrent comment Mgr Pompallier, depuis son instruction de 1841, a construit, affiné sa pastorale évangélisatrice. De celle-ci et de son application nous pouvons distinguer quatre niveaux d'adhésion :

1) Les tribus qui tournent au christianisme : celles qui sympathisent, se déclarent du côté de l'Epikopo.
2) Les catéchumènes : les convertis qui se préparent au baptême.
3) Les néophytes : les baptisés, chrétiens de fraîche date.
4) Les catéchistes : ceux dont les qualités de piété, d'intelligence de la doctrine permettaient de les associer à l'évangélisation de leur propre milieu culturel.

La pastorale de Mgr Pompallier était réfléchie et ne procédait pas d'une improvisation au coup par coup. Le catéchuménat s'adaptait parfaitement à un catéchisme progressif, respectueux de la mentalité et des coutumes maories. Mgr Pompallier laissait les Maoris progresser par une lente prise de conscience, ne voulant en rien les bousculer et les forcer. Chacun se déterminait librement.

Tentatives et Tâtonnements en Nouvelle-Calédonie

Le premier événement important qui marque le début de la mission, est la célébration de la messe de Noël au village de Balade avec les officiers et marins du *Bucéphale* et les habitants du village. Cérémonie en grande pompe. Le commandant Julien-Laferrière note dans son rapport la forte impression ressentie par les naturels. Fin janvier, Mgr Douarre achète une propriété au chef Païma de Balade. L'évêque demande au chef de définir lui-même les contours du domaine. La première station missionnaire de Maamate est née. La mission avance lentement, tant les missionnaires sont occupés à bâtir une station correcte. Les journées harassantes se suivent et la nourriture reste insuffisante pour maintenir les corps.[35] De surcroît, les habitants de tel ou tel village, soutenus par un chef, inventent mille tracasseries, agrémentées de vols, à l'encontre des missionnaires.

Pendant ce temps, le seul qui peut réellement débuter l'évangélisation c'est le Père Viard. Il a été prêté par Mgr Pompallier, à la demande de Mgr Douarre, en raison de ses quatre ans d'expérience à Wallis et de ses connaissances linguistiques. Grâce au wallisien parlé par certains indigènes migrants, il arrive à accéder à la langue canaque. Aidé par un Naturel qui connaît les deux langues, il peut traduire le Pater et l'Ave Maria et faire quelques cantiques.[36] Sa connaissance du wallisien devient son meilleur allié, car beaucoup d'habitants, étant des Naturels de Wallis qui ont migré en Nouvelle-Calédonie, le considèrent comme un ami. Néanmoins le Père Rougeyron explique que l'accès à la langue des habitants est difficile :

> *La langue des Calédoniens m'a semblé fort difficile, tant à cause de son génie tout différent de nos langues d'Europe qu'à cause de sa prononciation. Seuls Européens dans cette île, sans interprète, sans grammaire, sans vocabulaire [. . .] nous avons eu d'énormes difficultés à vaincre. Depuis trois mois nous commençons à balbutier en calédonien et à faire quelques petites instructions.*[37]

Donc, plus à l'aise avec la langue que Mgr Douarre et le Père Rougeyron, le Père Viard débute l'évangélisation en s'occupant des malades des alentours du poste Maamate. Au mois de mars 1844, il soigne et convertit la femme du chef de Coco, qui prend le nom de baptême de Marie. La maladie n'ayant pu être enrayée, Marie, épouse de Pakilipouma décède le 13 mars. Pour Mgr Douarre c'est la première chrétienne qui, du Ciel, peut intercéder et prier pour la mission. Le Père Viard s'emploie aussi à former un catéchiste à la station de Balade au cours des premiers mois de 1844. A partir du 1er novembre 1844, il a commencé à réunir soir et matin, dans une maison du chef de Ballade, un certain nombre de naturels à qui il a pu apprendre dans l'espace de trois mois et demi le pater, l'ave Maria et le symbole des apôtres, le décalogue et plusieurs cantiques en l'honneur de Marie.[38] Méthode employée par Mgr Bataillon à Wallis et par Mgr Pompallier en Nouvelle-Zélande.

En juin 1844, la résidence de Bayao achevée, le père Viard part visiter la tribu de Yenguene où il reçoit un bel accueil par le chef. Arrivée opportune qui empêche une guerre. Il baptise le fils du chef en expliquant son geste au chef qui parle le wallisien et qui transmet les explications à son peuple. Ensuite, on lui demande de chanter les cantiques qu'il a appris à ses néophytes de Balade. Comme ils sont Intrigués par le crucifix que porte le père à la ceinture, et à leur interrogation, il leur raconte ce que le Christ a fait et souffert pour eux. Le lendemain au moment de se séparer, le chef demande au Père de revenir les instruire.[39] Il poursuit sa visite des villages et à son retour à Bayao, il fait le bilan : 270 baptêmes, surtout de petits enfants, dont plusieurs sont morts. Selon, la conception missionnaire de l'époque, cette pratique faisait de 'petits anges' qui intercédaient ensuite pour la mission.

A son tour, Mgr Douarre, sachant se débrouiller dans la langue, peut commencer à instruire les habitants du secteur de Bayao. C'était le 1er juillet 1845, soit dix-huit mois après son arrivée. Il débute par Paravouat où il constate que ses efforts donnent de maigres résultats : 'Si on nous écoutait, encore, avec attention, se plaint Mgr Douarre, les fatigues ne seraient rien ; mais les uns rient, d'autres font des grimaces ; quelques-uns nous écoutent et nous demandent ensuite une récompense pour avoir prié.[40] Cependant, la mission commence à porter quelques fruits. En effet, le 15 août 1844, Mgr Douarre célèbre la messe de l'Assomption à laquelle assistent 16 néophytes préparés par le Père Viard.

Le départ du Père Viard, le 5 octobre 1845, achève la première étape de l'apostolat et laisse Mgr Douarre et le Père Rougeyron un peu démunis. Pourtant, en dépit des vexations, de la rudesse du milieu, le Père Viard note au moment de son départ qu'il s'est opéré déjà parmi les naturels un très grand changement en mieux. A partir de cet instant, Mgr Douarre et le Père Rougeyron prennent en main l'apostolat des Canaques. Le Père Rougeyron poursuit la rédaction de son dictionnaire canaque. Très tôt, les missionnaires tentent d'obtenir tel ou tel enfant de chef à former, alphabétiser. En 1847, le Père Rougeyron écrit qu'il instruit cinq petits enfants qu'il souhaite pousser le plus loin possible.[41]

Au bout de trois ans et demi, le résultat restait maigre. D'abord, pour arriver à bien parler la langue et se faire comprendre cela a duré presque une année. Ensuite les données abstraites de la doctrine chrétienne avaient du mal à se frayer un passage dans l'intelligence concrète des Canaques. Certaines notions comme le Ciel et l'âme n'avaient pas la même signification dans les deux religions. L'Enfer choquait et provoquait des réactions ambiguës. La question était donc de savoir comment leur faire saisir les 'Vérités' de la Foi ? Les sources ne montrent pas que les missionnaires aient eu le loisir de résoudre cette question. Et pourquoi pas recourir au miracle ? Pour Mgr Douarre, 'Des miracles ne convertiraient pas nos sauvages, ils croiraient que c'est une chose que nous savons faire, rien de plus.'[42]

Après un voyage en Europe, Mgr Douarre retourne dans sa mission, malgré la destruction des premiers postes. Durant la période de 1850 à 1853, il tente, avec ses missionnaires de bâtir pour leur groupe de chrétiens, revenus de Futuna, une Réduction. L'expérience s'achève sur un nouvel échec, face à l'opposition de certains chefs qui voient la nouvelle religion comme une concurrente de leurs coutumes.

Conclusion

Au-delà des personnalités, le milieu culturel semble bien l'élément déterminant de la réussite ou des échecs rencontrés par les deux vicaires apostoliques. Lorsque Mgr Pompallier débarque en Nouvelle-Zélande, il y trouve des appuis et un peuple qui connaît les Blancs, qui échange avec eux. L'antériorité de la présence protestante, même si nombre de pasteurs sont malveillants, est loin de leur avoir nui. La comparaison par les Maoris entre la méthode d'européanisation des méthodistes et l'acculturation catholique a joué en faveur de l'évêque. En Nouvelle-Calédonie le milieu était vierge de présence européenne. Le Blanc n'y est pas connu à quelques exceptions près. Or, quelle que soit la situation, dans les deux cas il s'est produit un choc culturel aux conséquences radicalement différentes.

En Nouvelle-Calédonie, le choc culturel a été extrêmement violent et a quasiment bloqué le processus d'acculturation. Les missionnaires ont été assimilés aux âmes des ancêtres venant du ciel. Ensuite, la pratique du baptême a pris une signification ambivalente : il empêche la mort ou la provoque. C'est cette dernière interprétation qui a pris le dessus en raison des baptêmes administrés *in articulo mortis* ou durant les épidémies. Les missionnaires n'ont trouvé au début aucun élément de la cosmogonie des Néo-Calédoniens à relier au christianisme pour faciliter la compréhension de sa doctrine. Enfin, le choc culturel et le choc microbien ont débouché sur un drame. Scénario connu et qui a fonctionné en Amérique latine aux XVI° et XVII° siècle comme un piège sournois et imprévisible. En Nouvelle-Zélande, bien des points de la religion maorie pouvaient trouver une correspondance avec la religion des missionnaires. Mgr Pompallier en a profité pour montrer que le christianisme venait clarifier et ordonner leurs traditions religieuses. Autre aspect favorable, la prophétie transmise dans la tribu de Wirinaki qui voit Mgr Pompallier comme celui annoncé. Elle crée une situation qui offre une légitimité à l'évangélisation dès l'arrivée de l'évêque. Le célibat sacerdotal, qui n'évoquait rien chez les Néo-Calédoniens, était une preuve pour les Maoris de la véracité de la mission de Mgr Pompallier. Il était devenu un Maori parmi les Maoris. Du côté de Mgr Douarre, malgré ses efforts il n'a pu vraiment devenir un des leurs, un Canaque parmi les Canaques. Ceci nous révèle non seulement l'importance du milieu, mais la capacité de celui-ci à réagir négativement s'il le veut à l'évangélisation. En Nouvelle-Zélande les chefs ont adopté le christianisme librement ; en Nouvelle-Calédonie, du moins sous Mgr Douarre et à part un groupe solide, la majorité l'a rejeté librement au nom de ses coutumes ancestrales. Il devient évident qu'il existe une réelle réflexion chez les peuples évangélisés à partir de laquelle ils évaluent, discutent de l'intérêt d'adopter ou pas la nouvelle religion.

Mgr Douarre était perçu comme venant contrecarrer les coutumes ancestrales alors que Mgr Pompallier réalisait, à son insu, une prophétie. Il ne représentait pas une réelle rupture dans la religion maorie, contrairement à Mgr Douarre face au milieu canaque. Le malentendu s'est produit au niveau cosmogonique. Les habitants intègrent et interprètent les missionnaires dans leur cosmogonie. Alors, devons-nous encore parler, dans le cas de la rencontre du christianisme et d'autres cultures, de choc culturel ? Le mot culturel comprend le religieux et le spirituel qui forment une composante, parmi d'autres de ce choc. N'est-il pas plus juste de parler de choc religieux ou de choc cosmogonique dans ces deux cas précis ? C'est bien le rapport au divin qui est bouleversé, même si celui-ci englobe un certain nombre de rites qui ont des ramifications dans la culture.

Les pastorales d'évangélisation ont-elles joué un rôle dans ces réussites et ces échecs ? Elles peuvent aider à résoudre le choc culturel et/ou spirituel, mais leur rôle étant plutôt d'enraciner l'Evangile et de bâtir une Eglise locale. Le Père Viard a de l'expérience ; sa méthode est fondée sur la connaissance de la langue, le chant, et l'apprentissage des prières essentielles. Les résultats restent modestes car les missionnaires ont du mal à se faire comprendre. Et, malgré leur intention, une pastorale adaptée a été impossible à construire car le choc culturel/spirituel n'a pas été résolu. En revanche, c'est parce que le milieu a été favorable, accueillant, que Mgr Pompallier a réussi à mettre en place une pastorale adaptée, synthèse des principes de la Propaganda Fide et des doctrines paulinienne et xaviérenne.

Notes

1 Frédéric Angleviel, *La mission mariste en Nouvelle-Calédonie, 1843-1903.* Revue d'Histoire de l'Eglise de France, Tome LXXIX, N°202, Paris, 1993, p. 115 à 137.

2 Claude Rozier, *La Nouvelle-Calédonie ancienne.* Fayard, 1990.

3 Né le 16 décembre 1810 à La Forie (Puy-de-Dôme). Nommé coadjuteur du vicaire apostolique d'Océanie centrale le 23 août 1842 et vicaire apostolique de Nouvelle-Calédonie en 1847. Il sacre son supérieur, Mgr Bataillon le 3

décembre 1843. Il meurt le 27 avril 1853.

4 Né le 11 décembre 1801 à Lyon. Le 30 avril 1836, il est sacré vicaire apostolique de l'Océanie centrale. Le 3 juillet 1860, Pie IX l'élève au rang d'évêque d'Auckland. Démissionnaire en 1868, il meurt dans la banlieue de Paris le 21 décembre 1871.

5 Ernest Simmons, *Pompallier, Prince of bishops*. Auckland, 1984.

6 Jean-Baptiste Pompallier, *Notice historique et statistique de la mission de la Nouvelle-Zélande*. Anvers, 1850. p. 78.

7 Ibid, p. 80.

8 Ibid.

9 Ibid, p. 79 à 81.

10 Philippe Viard, *Lettre à Jean- Marie Noailly, curé de la Guillotière, Baie des îles, 6 janvier 1840*. Archives des Pères Maristes Z 208.

11 Jean Forest, *Lettre à Jean-Claude Colin, Baie des îles, le 4 novembre 1843*. APM, Z 208.

12 Ernest Simmons, *Pompallier, Prince of bishops. . .*, chapitre 7.

13 Pierre Rougeyron, *Lettre à Jean-Claude Colin, Nouvelle-Calédonie, 1er octobre 1845*. Archives des Pères maristes, ONC 208 Rougeyron.

14 Pierre Rougeyron, *Lettre à Jean-Claude, Balade le 3 septembre 1846*. Archives des pères maristes.

15 Pierre Rougeyron, *Lettre à Jean-Claude Colin, à bord de la Brillante, le 28 août 1847*. Archives des pères maristes.

16 Pierre Rougeyron, *Lettre à Jean-Claude Colin, Balade le 3 septembre 1846. . .*

17 Ibidem.

18 Guillaume Douarre, *Journal 1er cahier, décembre 1843 à novembre 1846 (Balade)*. Version dactylographiée. Archives des Pères Maristes. p. 65.

19 Pierre Rougeyron, *Lettre à Jean-Claude Colin, Nouvelle-Calédonie le 1er octobre 1845. . .*

20 Guillaume Douarre, *Journal 1er cahier, décembre 1843 à novembre 1846. . .*

21 Pierre Rougeyron, *Lettre à Jean-Claude Colin, Balade le 3 septembre 1846. . .*

22 Claude Rozier, *La Nouvelle-Calédonie ancienne. . .*

23 Guillaume Douarre, *Journal terminé par le Père Montrouzier, IVème cahier, du 28 novembre 1852 au 20 octobre 185*, p. 12.

24 Jean-Baptiste Pompallier, *Notice historique. . .*, p. 27.

25 Jean-Baptiste Pompallier, Journal du 23 juillet 1841 jusqu'au 24 août 1842. Archives des OPM, Dossier H 34, H01177, p. 10.

26 Jean-Baptiste Pompallier, *Lettre à Jean-Claude Colin, de la Baie des îles, 14 mai 1838*. Archives des Pères Maristes OOc 418.1.

27 Catherin Servant, *Lettre à Antoine-Adolphe Thiollière du Treuil, curé de Saint-Pierre à Saint-Chamond, Hokianga le 22 mai 1838*.

28 Jean-Baptiste Pompallier, *Notice historique et statistique de la mission de la Nouvelle-Zélande. . .*, p. 103 à 110.

29 Ibidem.
30 Ibid.
31 Jean-Baptiste Pompallier, *Notice historique et statistique de la mission de la Nouvelle-Zélande. . .*, p. 106.
32 Jean-Baptiste Pompallier, *'Instructions pour les travaux de la mission du 29 janvier 1841'*. Auckland Catholic Diocesan Archives, POM 14-3.
33 Ibidem, p. 31-32.
34 Ibid, p. 32.
35 Guillaume Douarre, *Journal 1er cahier, décembre 1843 à novembre 1846. . .*
36 Philippe Viard, Lettre à Jean-Claude Colin, à bord du Rhin, le 27 octobre 1845. Archives des Pères maristes, ONC 208 Viard.
37 Pierre Rougeyron, *Lettre à Jean-Claude Colin, Nouvelle-Calédonie le 1er octobre 1845. . .*
38 Philippe Viard, Lettre à Jean-Claude Colin, à bord du Rhin, le 27 octobre 1845. . .
39 Ibidem.
40 Guillaume Douarre, *Journal 1er cahier, décembre 1843 à novembre 1846. . .* p. 65.
41 Pierre Rougeyron, *Lettre à Victor Poupinel, Sydney, le 30 novembre 1847.* Archives des Pères Maristes, *OP 458.2.*
42 Guillaume Douarre, *Journal II1ème cahier, du 15 avril 1851 au 26 novembre 1852. Archives des Pères maristes,* p. 65.

Missionary contacts between New Zealand and New Caledonia in the nineteenth century

Peter Tremewan

(1) French warships stationed in Akaroa, New Zealand, regularly visited French mission stations in the Pacific islands, including New Caledonia, providing them with logistic and military support. (2) The Society of Mary, a French religious order, founded the Catholic missions in New Caledonia and New Zealand. This explains how some French Catholic priests played significant roles in both countries. (3) Protestant missionaries were there too. The Anglican Bishop of New Zealand, after visiting New Caledonia on a British warship, worked actively there, sending missionaries and bringing young kanaks back to Auckland to be educated.

(1) Des navires de guerre français stationnés à Akaroa, Nouvelle-Zélande, se rendaient régulièrement aux stations de mission françaises dans les îles du Pacifique, dont la Nouvelle-Calédonie, leur donnant un appui logistique et militaire. (2) La Société de Marie, ordre religieux français, a fondé les missions catholiques en Nouvelle-Calédonie et en Nouvelle-Zélande. C'est ainsi que certains prêtres catholiques français ont joué un rôle important dans les deux pays. (3) On y trouvait aussi des missionnaires protestants. L'évêque anglican de la Nouvelle-Zélande, suite à un voyage sur un navire de guerre britannique, a travaillé activement en Nouvelle-Calédonie, en y envoyant des missionnaires mais surtout en ramenant des jeunes kanaks à son école d'Auckland.

Introduction

French warships stationed in Akaroa, New Zealand, regularly visited French mission stations in the Pacific islands, including New Caledonia, providing them with logistic and military support. A French religious order, the Marists, founded the Catholic missions in New Caledonia and New Zealand in the nineteenth century. This explains how some French Catholic priests played significant roles in both countries. But it was not just Catholics. The Anglican Bishop of New Zealand, after visiting New Caledonia on a British warship, worked actively there as an extension of his work in New Zealand, sending missionaries and bringing young Kanaks back to Auckland to be educated.

The French naval base at Akaroa

To protect its commerce, France established a naval base in Valparaiso, Chile, in 1824.[1] This was its sole military base in the South Pacific for many years. Then, in the late 1830s, a French warship was stationed in New Zealand waters to keep an eye on the French whaling fleet at a time when New Zealand was a major focus for the world's whaling industry. This developed into a fixed, on-shore French naval base at Akaroa, where a succession of warships were stationed in the 1840s: the *Aube*, *Allier*, *Héroïne*, *Rhin* and *Seine*. From this base they often made very long voyages to various South Pacific destinations, including Tahiti, the Marquesas, Tonga, Wallis, Futuna and New Caledonia. On shore at Akaroa there were a naval farm, a garden and a number of naval buildings, including a house for the commander.

The Akaroa ships' captains were instructed, among other things, to protect the interests of the French missionaries in the Pacific. For example, the Minister of the Navy and Colonies told one captain that, 'Wherever [. . .] French missionaries are established, you will realise how important it is to support their influence and encourage the natives to see them in a positive light through the respect that you yourself show them.'[2] The missionaries could see the advantages of this policy:

> One of the effective ways of preventing the native peoples of Oceania from causing grievous harm to my missionaries who, by working for their salvation are bringing them civilisation and happiness, is to show these people from time to time the greatness and might of France through the appearance of some naval warship.[3]

Missionaries, politicians and naval captains were aware of the possible links between religious conversion, displays of military might and political sovereignty. As a leading French priest put it: 'if they become Catholic, they will become French.'[4] Even so, the French naval ships were seen as a weapon against the Protestant propaganda which claimed that French Catholic missionaries were just trying to acquire colonies for France:

> Their presence intimidates and suppresses intolerance and bad feeling towards our missionaries, and gives people a favourable impression of our country and of true religion.[5]

If the French missionaries often felt lost in a region dominated by the British[6], a small number of French warships not only showed Pacific peoples the military power that France could bring to bear to protect its citizens but also helped to transport the French missionaries, their correspondence and their provisions. Here, for example, is what a French priest in New Zealand wrote in his diary:

> The natives [. . .] told me that the warship that had taken a Bishop to New Caledonia [. . .] has arrived [. . .] and brought many letters. [. . .] I started reading the letters I got from France via the warship [. . .] I had 7 letters to read, it took me until 2 in the morning.[7]

(a) Captain Lavaud

The first commander at Akaroa, Captain Charles Lavaud, had the status of a King's Commissary[8] as he was sent as the official representative of the Government in an attempt to declare French sovereignty over New Zealand's South Island. At a time when it had, as yet, no colonies in the Pacific and was looking to establish strategic bases around the world, the French Government backed a private project to buy southern New Zealand from the Maori as a prelude to annexation and gave Lavaud extensive powers that were intended to last until a governor was sent out.[9]

When Father Pierre Chanel was killed on Futuna in 1841, the news reached Captain Lavaud in Akaroa. He instructed Captain Du Bouzet to sail to Futuna on the *Allier* to sort the situation out, which he did without any bloodshed, visiting and helping the mission on nearby Wallis at the same time. This naval intervention was crucial to the success of the Catholic missions on both these islands.

(b) Captain Bérard

Lavaud was replaced as commander at Akaroa by Captain Auguste Bérard who methodically visited the French Catholic mission stations in Tonga, Wallis, Futuna and New Caledonia on his ship, the *Rhin*, providing much needed assistance wherever he went and writing a detailed nautical guide for future captains who would follow him there. Approaching Balade in New Caledonia, all the crew of the *Rhin* felt 'a great joy' at the sight of a French flag flying from the mission house. During the short time they were there in 1845 they discharged the flour, wine and seventeen cases of hardware, tools and clothes that had been sent for the mission, to which the officers and crew added their own substantial personal contributions, which included sheep, goats and a large fierce bulldog that greatly impressed the Kanaks; timber and garden seeds from Akaroa; grape vines from the Bay of Islands; orange, lemon and banana trees from Tonga; basic text books and some carpentry tools. (They had intended to leave a cow and bull there as well, but Bérard was so worried that they would not last the journey that he gave them to the missionaries on Wallis.)

Bérard felt that the ship's visit to Balade had 'a wonderful effect on the chiefs and natives' who had 'the highest opinion of a nation that could build such enormous canoes', and he concluded that 'the people of this part of New Caledonia have been won over to our nation'. The chief of Poebo 'offered me all the fertile land in his tribal area and beseeched me to settle there with Father Viard'. While vehemently rejecting the British rumours that the French were trying to take over the indigenous people's land, Bérard constantly linked France's political and religious interests in his comments on the missions.[10]

(c) Captain Leconte

The third commander of the Akaroa naval station was Captain François Leconte of the *Seine*. He was a very experienced officer and had thought very carefully about the relationship between the navy and French missionaries. He told missionaries explicitly that he was not there to take part in evangelisation or in religious wars between Catholics and Protestants but to protect any French people who were threatened with possible violence: France's interests, he said, did not necessarily coincide with those of Rome. Even so, he would not prevent the missionaries from using the threat of naval intervention to control their flock: they could do this up to a certain point, he said, but he would not himself say anything to back up such a view, but merely indicate when his ship or another ship would be calling again. Like Lavaud, who was a freemason, Leconte comes over as an independent-minded, pragmatic man.[11]

When Leconte arrived in Akaroa in 1846, he expected to be stationed there for four years and he had already planned a number of voyages around the Pacific to protect the interests of French missionaries and French whalers. After very successful visits to the French Catholic mission stations in Tonga and Wallis, the *Seine* headed for New Caledonia where Leconte had secret instructions to remove the French flag from flying over the mission in case it caused trouble with the British. He also intended to spend a month charting the coastline but, before he could do any of these things, the corvette was wrecked on a reef off the coast of Balade. This time the mission came to the aid of the French navy, providing the sailors with food and shelter until they were able to return, via Sydney, to France. There were some positive consequences for the mission: three sailors volunteered to stay to help with manual work, the mission acquired some of the ship's boats and, for two months, the *Seine*'s senior doctor impressed the local Kanaks by accompanying the missionaries on their visits and providing medical expertise. The Kanaks gave him the nickname of one of their own respected healers, which translates as House-Burner (Brûle-Maison).[12]

However, Leconte was very aware of the negative influence his crew could have on the work of the missionaries if they stayed too long and showed the Kanaks, through their behaviour, that the values of ordinary French people were not necessarily the same as those preached by the French missionaries.[13] It has also been suggested that the Kanaks, who led a precarious and difficult existence, resented having a very large number of sailors in their midst for two months and that this was one factor that led to looting and violence against the mission station the following year when one missionary was killed.[14] Certainly, the boats and stores left by the *Seine* were prime targets of the Kanak attacks.[15] The arrival of another warship, the *Brillante*, at the height of this violence allowed the missionaries to withdraw to the safety of Sydney.[16] The captain of the *Brillante* was the same Du Bouzet who had earlier been sent from Akaroa to Futuna when Father Chanel was killed, but his new ship had come from Tahiti. When it called in to Akaroa later that year it was not to stay there but to pick up the members of the crew of the *Seine* and the *Rhin* who had been left in charge of the naval station with its farm and garden. It was the wreck of the *Seine* in New Caledonia that put an end to the French naval station in Akaroa. Tahiti replaced it.

Du Bouzet, then, reported back to Tahiti, to the Governor of the French Settlements in Oceania, who was none other than Lavaud, the former commander of the French naval base in New Zealand.[17] A few years later Du Bouzet himself became governor in Tahiti, and by that time New Caledonia had become part of his territory and, in his official capacity, he again visited the mission stations there.[18] French warships had been based at Akaroa in the 1840s while London and Paris sorted out the question of South Island sovereignty and, during that time, French and British law operated side by side there.[19] But, by the time the *Brillante* called to remove the last sailors from Akaroa in 1847, Tahiti was providing an alternative French naval base. The failure to annex the South Island had led France to move into its second choice for a South Pacific colony, the Marquesas, and then the Society Islands. Even so, in the Archives Nationales in Paris it is in the records of the French navy's New

Zealand station that one still finds the documents, some written from Tahiti, that were categorised under the heading 'Oceania. General file. Protection given to French missionaries in the various archipelagos of Oceania'.[20]

Catholic missions

When the Catholic Church decided to send missionaries to convert the inhabitants of the islands of the Pacific, it placed Western Oceania in the hands of the Society of Mary, the Marists. New Zealand and New Caledonia found themselves in the same 'vicariate'. The Society of Mary had recently been founded in the Lyon region by a small group of priests and brothers. Eight of them, under Bishop Pompallier, left France in 1836 and headed for their new territory, unsure where they would establish their first stations. It was largely chance which led to some of them being left on the little islands of Wallis and Futuna, while they established their headquarters in New Zealand. Other Marists followed and, gradually they set up stations in other islands. As the number of missionaries increased, the Western Oceania vicariate was subdivided and soon there was a bishop of Central Oceania, of New Caledonia, of Auckland, of Wellington, and so on. The missionaries naturally learned as they went along and those who moved into new tropical islands were anxious to avoid the mistakes that had been made earlier. One Marist wrote: 'Already there is concern that what is called the New Zealand system will operate here, a system whereby all assistance is centralised around the bishop while those who work in distant mission stations have to go without.'[21] The New Zealand system, whereby Bishop Pompallier imposed his will with little regard for the views of his Marist priests and brothers and the Marist hierarchy, was duplicated at first in the islands under Bishop Bataillon, which is why the Marists were anxious to make New Caledonia a separate vicariate, a status which was authorised by the Pope in 1847.

Because of the hierarchical structure of the Catholic Church and the Society of Mary, there were few direct links between the Marist missionaries in New Zealand and New Caledonia. Rather, when writing outside their vicariate, they would communicate on financial and logistic matters with the regional Marist procure house in Sydney, and on spiritual matters and matters of mission policy with the Marist Father Superior or other leaders of the order in France. They would, however, read each other's letters when they appeared in various missionary publications.[22] Despite the limited direct links between the two countries, three Marist priests who worked among the Maori of New Zealand did contribute in quite significant ways to the work of the Catholic Church in New Caledonia.

(a) Philippe Viard

When Father Chanel was killed on the island of Futuna, Father Viard left his work among the New Zealand Maori and went on the expedition to Futuna to sort the matter out and ended up spending two years on Wallis. When a new group of Marists called in to Wallis on their way to start a new mission in New Caledonia, Viard boarded their ship in order to return to New Zealand on it.[23]

The ship went first to Balade in New Caledonia. The Marists found that there were some people there from the Loyalty Islands who spoke a language that was very close to the language of Wallis, which in turn was quite close to New Zealand Maori. Thanks to his knowledge of Maori and Wallisian, Viard was able to communicate immediately with the people of Balade and quickly acquire the local Kanak language.[24] This is why Bishop Douarre, who led the New Caledonian mission, asked him to stay on and help him: 'he agreed to stay with me for six or seven months until I could handle things on my own'.[25] Viard's presence was appreciated by his colleagues, not only for his linguistic skills but also because he was a nice man and because he had already learnt a great deal from working with other South Pacific peoples.

> The good Father Viard (wrote Father Rougeyron) rivalled Bishop Douarre in his devotion. But as his experience and his knowledge of the language of some foreigners living here allowed him to get straight into missionary work, he was the one who more often visited the various tribes, and not without success. He set out enthusiastically to study the Caledonian language and was a great help to us as we tried to learn it.[26]

While the others, with his help, were learning the language of Balade, Viard visited the sick, taught the basic tenets of Catholicism, baptised nearly 300 children, translated prayers, hymns and the ten commandments, and taught a little group of children to sing hymns. When a hostile tribe approached to burn down the mission and kill the missionaries, Viard went out to meet them, got his children's choir to sing and gained the confidence of the would-be attackers.[27] When a Kanak stole an axe from the mission, Viard went to see the relevant chief and acted with such firmness that, to the utter amazement of other Kanaks, the axe was returned. 'From that moment,' wrote Viard, 'I acquired a considerable reputation. I was regarded as all-powerful.'[28] Little examples like these show that this man, who, according to Douarre, acted 'with the utmost kindness and prudence',[29] knew how to be accepted and respected by people from another culture. If Viard had remained longer in New Caledonia, it is easy to imagine that the Marist mission would have avoided the disasters that occurred soon after he left.

Viard had to spend nearly two years in New Caledonia before a warship arrived from Akaroa to take him back to New Zealand. 'The *Rhin* is about to leave,' wrote Father Rougeyron, 'and will take away our beloved colleague who has been called back by Bishop Pompallier. We shall really miss him!'[30] The captain of the *Rhin* felt that Viard was the man who 'more or less formed the mission' in New Caledonia because his linguistic ability had allowed him to get so much done.[31] Viard was arguably the key figure in the beginnings of the Catholic mission in New Caledonia.

(b) Jean Simon Bernard

As a result of a fundamental policy disagreement between Bishop Pompallier and the Society of Mary, a second vicariate was created in New Zealand and all the New Zealand Marists were instructed to leave Pompallier's northern vicariate of Auckland and found a southern vicariate which would be based in Wellington under a new Marist bishop, who was none other than Viard. This was the very moment, in 1850, when Bishop Douarre was obliged to withdraw his missionaries from New Caledonia for the second time in the face of

Kanak hostility. Douarre told his missionaries that they were free to go and work in another vicariate or to stay with him in Sydney while they awaited orders from Europe. They refused to work in other tropical islands or in New Zealand: 'We don't really know the part of New Zealand where Bishop Viard is, but we know enough not to accept this position unless we receive a positive order from you, which we hope won't happen.'[32] This opinion can be understood if one looks at what the Marist missionaries in New Zealand were saying.

Feeling isolated in some little Maori village, they often dreamed of missionary life in more densely populated tropical islands like New Caledonia where they would not have to walk vast distances through forests, across swollen rivers and over mountain ranges. The rather grumpy Father Jean Simon Bernard, for example, explained that the Maori were

> scattered all over the place in tiny villages. This is what disconcerted me. However, I've made my sacrifice to God; I'm resigned to the Lord's will; He has sent me to this part of the globe to remain more or less inactive when there are so many populous tropical islands without priests.[33]

The situation got worse in 1850 when the Marists left Pompallier and moved to southern New Zealand where there were hardly any Maori and where they were generally parish priests among a small number of Catholic settlers who were mostly Irish. They often felt discouraged and thought that they should be replaced by English-speaking priests. 'Our new mission [. . .] has only a sprinkling of Catholics, and some of us would like to move on to other missions, while others would like to return to France.'[34]

Indeed, Father Bernard left New Zealand to work in the islands.[35] He had arrived in New Zealand in 1843, and, after a short period in Northland, spent six years working among the Maori of Tauranga where, despite a somewhat dispirited start, he soon had very large congregations, five chapels, and was instrumental in bringing about peace between warring tribes. A visitor in 1847 wrote: 'The site worth seeing most at Tauranga is the interior of the Roman Catholic chapel [which] as an exquisite piece of workmanship reflects the greatest credit on the natives who I am told did it all without any remuneration and even supplied themselves at their own expense food during their carrying on the work.'[36] When New Zealand was divided into two vicariates, Bernard had to leave Tauranga and work for several years under trying conditions in the south.[37] So he left New Zealand and went briefly to Samoa and Wallis before going on to New Caledonia.[38]

Because of his knowledge of the Maori and Wallisian languages, he was sent in 1857 to Uvea in the Loyalty Islands off New Caledonia's east coast, where he founded the Catholic mission, aided by a Wallisian catechist, and gave it the same name, St Joseph, that he had given his church in Tauranga. Bernard is now known as the Apostle of Uvea and has a very special status on the island. He stayed there for more than thirteen years, despite advancing age and poor health, creating a parish with a church and five chapels in the north of the island, a gentle, kind man who was devoted to his people. His immediate superior said of him, 'On his own he has converted the whole of this large parish. [. . .] As a priest, as a religious, he is exemplary. His major fault [. . .] is that he is always complaining and asking for things, thinking only of his parish, the rest of the world having no importance to him.'[39] One thing that he constantly complained about was that experience had taught him the importance of having books in the language of his parishioners and yet, although he had spent a lot of time translating a number of works into Uvean, he could never get permission to have them published. When he finally left this station, 'All of Uvea was in tears.'[40] Bernard's successor found himself 'among a people who are quite numerous and nearly all baptised. Doubtless the spirit of Christianity has not yet penetrated very deeply, but they faithfully observe its main duties; our people are particularly keen on going frequently to confession.'[41]

Bernard spent the rest of his life in New Caledonia, where he died at sea in 1876 when his boat capsized off the Belep Islands. In addition to his many long letters, he has left important detailed notes on Uvean traditions and on mission life.[42] This has led to a rather mixed modern judgement on him: 'A precious observer of Uvean society at the time of its initial contact with the West, Father Bernard was also the main instrument of the disappearance of whole sections of the culture of this tiny archipelago.'[43] However, this opinion reflects a 'fatal impact' approach which makes indigenous people passive recipients of European ideas and actions: another historian has convincingly shown how the Uveans used Bernard and other Catholic and Protestant missionaries to advance their own traditional agendas.[44] Agency on both sides must be acknowledged.

(c) Antoine Garin and Pierre Janin

Four years before Father Bernard died, a new Marist priest, Pierre Janin, arrived from France to work in New Caledonia. Many years earlier he had been the pupil of Father Antoine Garin in a minor seminary near Lyon. Like Father Garin, Janin got on very well with other people and was musically very gifted: he saw himself as the minstrel of Our Lady of La Salette and composed, among other works, the hymn 'I will go to see her one day'.[45] After leaving France in 1840 to be a missionary in New Zealand, Garin wrote some extremely long letters for all his former pupils to read.[46] So Janin knew him through his letters as well as through his teaching at the seminary. Inspired by Garin's character and work, Janin eventually decided to go to New Caledonia. From the moment he arrived there, he wrote to Garin regularly to tell him what he was doing and constantly praised his former teacher to the latter's embarrassment: 'you saturate me with my own glory and I feel very humble when I hear the story of the little that I have accomplished'.[47] In Garin's letter register, one reads, 'Reply to his letter. He was my pupil at Meximieux. I give him details of the Nelson station.'[48] And thirteen years later, after many other letters, 'It is with great pleasure that I receive news about you and the places you live in.'[49]

Janin was responsible first of all for the political deportees on the Isle of Pines, before the general amnesty which he had asked for and which was finally granted. He tried to get close to the people whom he called 'my wolf-like sheep' through humour and jollity: 'I try to treat the horrendous things they say as jokes. I laugh so as to make them laugh. When I leave them, I want them to say, "Well! He's a good sort of priest, he makes people laugh. He's broadminded. He's a tolerant sort of guy."'[50] All the same, he had very limited success with the political deportees who were generally anticlerical and anti-Christian and did not want to be seen by their friends conversing with a priest.[51] Another Marist, Father Binsfeld, who worked for Garin in New Zealand, also spent a short time with the political deportees before returning to New Zealand: 'Surprised to see you are in New Caledonia. Those Communists must be tricky to handle,' wrote Garin.[52] After the Communards returned to France, Janin worked much more successfully with the convicts on the island of Nou. Like Garin, he wrote at length about his experiences as a Catholic priest in the South Pacific, including a detailed report on the life of the political deportees.[53]

The Anglicans

However, there were not just French Catholic missionaries and French warships in the two countries. George Selwyn arrived in New Zealand in 1842 as New Zealand's first Anglican Bishop. Six years later he visited a number of tropical islands on a British warship and began to put in place what he would eventually call the Melanesian Mission, which would operate in New Caledonia, the New Hebrides and the Solomon Islands. He gained some financial support from the Anglican Church in Australia, but was anxious to have the mission based in New Zealand, not Australia, because he saw Australian settler society and its political leaders as harbouring negative views about non-white races.[54] Anglicans and Catholics had been preceded in New Caledonia by the London Missionary Society, which had sent Polynesian catechists there, especially Samoans, from the early 1840s. A friendly agreement between this society and Selwyn in 1848 assigned the Loyalty Islands to the Anglican bishop of New Zealand. The LMS assumed that Selwyn would send missionaries from the Church Missionary Society to his new mission. However, like Pompallier, the Catholic Bishop of New Zealand, who wanted exclusive control over the men sent to him by the Society of Mary, Selwyn followed his own missionary philosophy which was at odds with that of the Church Missionary Society in England. Both bishops were dynamic and impressive in their personal dealings with indigenous peoples, but both were difficult for priests to work for.

In 1849, Guillaume Douarre, the Catholic Bishop of New Caledonia, met George Selwyn, the Anglican Bishop of New Zealand. The latter is quite positive about his Catholic homologue—'He is the first of his order whom I ever met in society, and we had much friendly conversation.'[55]—while giving a negative judgement on the Catholic missions:

> After witnessing many Romanist missions in these seas, I have not seen one which had any sign of vitality. So far as I have conversed with the Romanist missionaries they have not impressed me with any idea that they have any love for the races among whom they serve.[56]

Selwyn was very aware of the high death-rate from violence and disease among Catholic missionaries in Melanesia. The method he adopted to combat this problem was well-known to the Marists:

> The zeal of the Anglican church for these sorts of missions has just surfaced this year through the influence of their Bishop of Auckland [. . .] The first theatre of their influence will be New Caledonia and the neighbouring islands. Their avowed aim is not to leave missionaries in places where they would fear for their lives and property, but to sail to the islands during the months when the weather is favourable, taking as many young men as they can back to their Auckland college to make catechists out of them.[57]

During his 1849 voyage, Selwyn found five boys, three from Maré and one from Lifu on the Loyalty Islands and one from Hienghène on the mainland, to go back with him to Auckland. The chief of Hienghène, Bouarate, asked Selwyn for a permanent English missionary, but Selwyn could find no one to fulfil this role. An Anglican minister, William Nihill, spent three months on Maré in 1852 with a Maori assistant, Henare Taratoa. He returned the following year with his wife to work there, but soon died of tuberculosis, but not before he had set up a small press, translated and distributed prayers and scripture, taught local people how to use the press as well as how to read, and then helped set up a larger press.[58]

The Auckland school of what Selwyn called his Melanesian Mission made a great deal of progress in the 1850s and, over a period of ten years, some 120 boys attended it, including thirty-nine from the Loyalty Islands. But the unanimous judgement of historians is that Selwyn's system did not work because the boys, when they returned home, reverted to the traditional life they had led earlier.[59] Another Anglican minister from New Zealand, Patteson, who would become the first Anglican Bishop of Melanesia, spent four months on Lifu in 1858 teaching boys from the Solomons and Banks Islands, but that marked the end of the Anglican mission in New Caledonia. Recognising the 'priority of occupation' of the London Missionary Society, the Anglican Melanesian Mission was restricted after that to the Solomon Islands and the New Hebrides.

Conclusion

We have seen, then, that, without setting foot in New Caledonia himself, a New Zealand Marist, Father Garin, inspired Father Janin to work for twenty-six years among the political deportees and convicts of New Caledonia. After working among the Maori of New Zealand, two other Marist priests, Bernard and Viard, made significant contributions to the Catholic mission in New Caledonia, Viard on the mainland in Balade and Bernard on Uvea among the Loyalty Islands. French warships stationed in Akaroa, New Zealand, provided considerable help in the early years of the Catholic mission to Western Oceania, which included New Caledonia, Wallis and Futuna. For ten years the schooner of the Anglican bishop of New Zealand was seen in New Caledonia, looking for boys to take back to his school in Auckland. Separated by distance and differences in language and culture, these two countries had some quite significant missionary contacts in the nineteenth century, thanks especially to the Society of Mary but also to the French Navy and the New Zealand Anglican Church's Melanesian Mission.

Notes

1 Jean-Paul Faivre, *L'Expansion française dans le Pacifique, 1800-1842*, Paris: Nouvelles Éditions Latines, 1953, pp. 315-23.

2 Minister of the Navy and Colonies to Lavaud. Instructions. 14 January 1840 (Archives Nationales, Paris: Marine BB^4 1010).

3 Pompallier to Lavaud, 6 November 1841 (Archives Nationales, Paris: Marine

BB^{4} 1011).

4 Father Colin to Bishop Pompallier, 9 November 1839 (Marist Archives, Wellington: HD3, ff 13-15). Colin was the Father Superior of the Marist order.

5 Pompallier to Rear-Admiral Du Petit-Thouars, 15 February 1843 (Archives Nationales, Paris: Marine BB^{4} 1012).

6 The English 'are everywhere, their ships, their nearby colonies, they are at home, so to speak, while we seem like abandoned strangers, with no obvious power behind us.' Gilbert Roudaire to Victor Poupinel, 11 June 1851 (Charles Girard, *Lettres reçues d'Océanie par l'administration générale des Pères Maristes pendant le généralat de Jean-Claude Colin*, to be published, letter 1015. Father Girard has kindly sent a CD with a preliminary version, dated March 2008, of his 11-volume work).

7 Antoine Marie Garin, Notes sur la mission, 13-14 February 1844 (Marist Fathers' Archives, Rome). See Hélène Serabian's PhD thesis : 'Le journal du père Antoine Garin, 1844-1846. Édition critique présentée avec commentaire, transcription et annotations', University of Canterbury, 2006, pp. 416-7, 419.

8 Commissaire du roi.

9 For a full account of the French settlement at Akaroa, see Peter Tremewan, *French Akaroa. An Attempt to Colonise Southern New Zealand* (Christchurch: University of Canterbury Press, 1990).

10 Bérard to the Minister of the Navy and Colonies, 1 August 1846, 'Tournée dans les missions de l'Océanie occidentale' (Archives Nationales, Paris: Marine BB^{4} 1011); François Leconte, *Mémoires pittoresques d'un officier de marine*, Brest: Le Pontois, II, 562.

11 Leconte, II, 427, 586.

12 Leconte, II, 574-5.

13 Leconte, II, 586.

14 Georges Delbos, *The Catholic Church in New Caledonia*. Suva: CEPAC, 2000, p.67.

15 Pierre Rougeyron: Procès-verbal des vivres laissés en dépôt à la Nouvelle-Calédonie par la corvette la *Seine*, 20 July 1847 (Girard, letter 645); Xavier Montrouzier à Gabriel Montrouzier, 13 October 1847 (Girard, letter 674).

16 Delbos, pp. 62-74.

17 Lavaud to the Minister of the Navy, 24 November 1847 (Archives Nationales: Marine BB^{4} 1012), refers to Dubouzet's report and to the 'destruction of the mission station in Port Ballade'.

18 Lavaud was governor 1847-49; Du Bouzet 1854-1858.

19 Richard M. Hill, *Policing the Colonial Frontier*, Wellington: Government Printer, 1986, 2 vols., I, pp. 142-5.

20 Archives Nationales, Paris. Marine BB^{4} 1012. Océanie. Dossier commun. Protection accordée aux missionnaires français dans les divers archipels de l'Océanie.

21 Calinon to Colin, Tonga, 27 July 1844 (Girard, letter 344).

22 *Annales des missions de la Société de Marie* (1853-1886), *Annales des missions*

d'Océanie (1886-1921), *Annales de la Propagation de la foi* (1822-1948).

23 The *Allier*, under Captain Du Bouzet, went from Akaroa to Futuna and Wallis; the *Bucéphale* transported the first missionaries to New Caledonia.

24 Delbos, p. 33.

25 Douarre to Colin, 10 January 1844 (Girard, letter 304).

26 Pierre Rougeyron to Colin, 1 October 1845 (Girard, letter 407). When Viard died in 1872, aged 61, the newspapers ascribed his illness to the privations and rigours of the time he had spent in New Caledonia (*Colonist*, 4 June 1872, p. 3).

27 Viard, Mémoires, no. 2, p. 19 (APM; photocopy in the Wellington Archdiocesan Archives) ; Lillian Keys, *Philip Viard, Bishop of Wellington*. Christchurch: Pegasus Press, 1968, p. 41. One should probably be wary of the rather too perfect self-portrait in Viard's memoirs.

28 Viard, Mémoires, no. 2, pp. 20-2; Keys, *Philip Viard*, pp. 41-2.

29 Douarre to Colin, 10 January 1844 (Girard, letter 304).

30 Pierre Rougeyron to Colin, 1 October 1845 (Girard, letter 407).

31 Bérard to the Minister of the Navy and Colonies, 1 August 1846 (Archives Nationales, Paris: Marine BB^4 1011).

32 New Caledonian priests and brothers to Colin, 6-10 January 1850 (Girard, letter 863).

33 Jean-Simon Bernard to Colin, 5 October 1843 (Girard, letter 272).

34 Jean Forest, quoted in Jean-Louis Rocher to Colin, 23 August 1851 (Girard, letter 1046).

35 Bernard was born in 1807 in Chantenay in the diocese of Nantes. His early life is recounted in the Francis Trochu's biography of Bernard's sister: *La Mère Marie-Thérèse, fondatrice des Sœurs franciscaines de Saint-Philibert-de-Grand-Lieu, au diocèse de Nantes (1804-1884)*. Saint-Philibert-de-Grand-Lieu: Maison-Mère des Religieuses franciscaines, 1933. This work also quotes a number of letters he wrote to his sister from the Pacific.

36 See Patricia Brooks. *By the Name of Mary: Tauranga Catholic Church, 1840-2000*. Tauranga: 2000, especially chapter 4.

37 Notably in Akaroa, Otaki and Wanganui.

38 In Samoa, where he was known as Patele Pelenato, Bernard created a station at Lufilufi on the island of Upolo in 1853, the first step in the founding of the parish of Falefa (Joseph Heslin, *A History of the Roman Catholic Church in Samoa 1845-1995*. Apia: the author, 1995, p. 34).

39 Father Rougeyron, Annual report to Father Favre, 12 December 1868 (APM: ONC 418).

40 Father Roussel to Father Poupinel, October 1870 (APM: ONC 208).

41 Father Pionnier to Father Marcellin Gay, 13 June 1871 (*Annales des missions de la Société de Marie*, III, 255).

42 Notice historique sur l'île Ouvéa et les îles Beaupré, ms, 70pp. (Archives de l'archevêché de Nouméa: 67.1). There are plans to publish this work in the near future.

43 Jacques Izoulet. *Ouvéa. Histoire d'une mission catholique dans le Pacifique sud au XIXe siècle.* Paris: L'Harmattan, 2005, p. 319.
44 K.R. Howe, *The Loyalty Islands: a History of Culture Contacts, 1840-1900*, Canberra: Australian University Press, 1977.
45 J'irai la voir un jour.
46 See, for example, his very long letter, dated 12 June - 17 July 1841 (which was printed in the *Annales des missions de l'Océanie* in 1895 and will appear as letter 99 in Girard's collection). Other letters to the pupils of Meximieux were dated 29 November 1841, 16 January 1843, 23 October 1843, 19 March 1845.
47 Garin, Letter Register, 17 June 1885 (St Mary's Parish, Nelson: DNM 2/33).
48 Garin, Letter Register, 25 February 1872 (DNM 2/32).
49 Garin, Letter Register, 17 June 1885 (DNM 2/33).
50 Janin to M. Scipion Gouchon, 19 October 1872 (*Annales des missions de la Société de Marie*, III, 185).
51 See, for example, Théodore Ozeré. *Carnets et lettres d'un déporté de la Commune à l'île des Pins (1871-1879).* Nouméa: Société d'Études Historiques de Nouvelle-Calédonie, 1993, with its frequent negative references to Janin: pp. 101, 122, 125, 148, 152, 153, 154, 155, 169, 178, 180, 181, 182, 197, 198, 199, 205, 206, 225, 233, 243, 246.
52 Garin to Binsfeld, 1 March 1876 (Garin, Letter Register, DNM 2/33). Among other New Zealand priests who had passing contacts with New Caledonia, one could include Father Jérome Grange who spent a little time in New Zealand before going first to Tonga and then to New Caledonia; Father Léopold Verguet who made some interesting sketches in both countries, and Father Claude Baty, whose name Douarre put forward as his successor but who died on the Isle of Pines in 1851 soon after arriving there.
53 Report, 6 October 1875. (See Delbos, p. 206.)
54 Selwyn to Gladstone, 17 Nov. 1850 (Alexander Turnbull Library, Wellington: Micro MS 426), quoted in H. Laracy, 'Selwyn in Pacific Perspective', in *Bishop Selwyn in New Zealand 1841-68*. Palmerston North: Dunmore Press, 1983, p.126; H.W. Tucker. *Memoir of the Life and Experience of George Augustus Selwyn*. London: William Wells Gardner, 1879, I, 313.
55 Tucker, I, 314.
56 Selwyn to Gladstone, 2 December 1850.
57 Gilbert Roudaire to Victor Poupinel, 11 June 1851 (Girard, letter 1016). Selwyn's system was adopted in the face of explicit opposition from the Church Missionary Society.
58 Howe, pp. 125-6. This, of course, is what Father Bernard wanted to do on nearby Uvea.
59 David Hilliard. *God's Gentlemen. A History of the Melanesian Mission, 1849-1942*. St Lucia: University of Queensland Press, 1978, pp. 17-23; H. Laracy, p. 130; Allan Davidson, 'An Interesting Experiment—The Founding of the Melanesian Mission', in *The Church of Melanesia 1849-1999*. Auckland:

Les modèles coloniaux anglais et français comparés : Le regard des voyageurs français sur le « cas » néo-zélandais (1860 – 1914)

Christian Huetz de Lemps

La Nouvelle-Zélande, « aux antipodes » de la France, a vivement intéressé nombre de voyageurs et d'observateurs français dans la période 1860 – 1914, d'autant plus qu'elle apparaissait comme une sorte de modèle réussi d'une colonisation « à l'anglaise » que l'on opposait volontiers aux méthodes françaises de colonisation qui s'appliquent alors de la Nouvelle-Calédonie à Tahiti. Ces visiteurs français, qui nous ont laissé des récits imprimés à l'époque de leurs voyages, étaient soit de simples touristes de passage, soit des « résidents » séjournant plus longtemps, soit de véritables « chercheurs » attirés par les multiples originalités physiques et humaines du « cas » néo-zélandais. Tous se sont intéressés, à des degrés divers et aussi une profondeur très variable, aux thèmes essentiels, de la splendeur et de la spécificité de la nature néo-zélandaise, de l'identité culturelle menacée de la « race indigène » maorie, et enfin de la naissance et du développement d'une société coloniale à la fois profondément britannique et pionnière tant sur le plan de la condition des travailleurs que sur celui du rôle et de la place des femmes.

New Zealand, at the antipodes of France, was a subject of lively interest for many French travellers and observers during the 1860–1914 period, especially as it seemed to be a successful example of 'English' colonisation, contrary to the French model developing in New Caledonia and Tahiti. These French visitors, who left us published accounts of their trips, were simply ordinary tourists going through, or residents for a longer stay, or real 'searchers' attracted by the many unique physical and human features of 'the New Zealand case'. All of them, in different ways and with varying degrees of profoundness, displayed a strong interest in several essential themes, including the splendour and originality of New Zealand nature, the threatened cultural identity of the 'indigenous race' (the Maori), and finally the birth and development of a colonial society at the time profoundly British and yet also a pioneer, very much in advance on matters of workers' welfare and the role and place of women in society.

Malgré l'éloignement, la Nouvelle-Zélande intéresse les Français à la fin du XIXe et au début du XXe siècle, même dans cette période 1860-1914 qui voit d'une part s'atténuer leurs regrets d'avoir raté de si peu la chance de coloniser eux-même le grand archipel, et précède d'autre part la première guerre mondiale durant laquelle vont s'établir de nouveaux liens de frères d'armes sur les champs de bataille. Nombre de voyageurs français passent ou séjournent en Nouvelle-Zélande, étape souvent d'un « tour du monde » puisque l'archipel est exactement « aux antipodes », et ils jugent le « cas » néo-zélandais assez intéressant pour lui consacrer une part appréciable de leurs observations et du récit de leurs pérégrinations. Entendons nous bien : nous sommes loin encore du temps des déplacements de masse, et l'immensité des distances, la longueur et les difficultés du voyage limitent ces audacieux à quelques dizaines ou centaines de gens fortunés et disponibles, ou alors ayant un intérêt professionnel ou scientifique à l'accomplissement de leur périple. Il n'empêche, la Nouvelle-Zélande fait partie de ces noms qui attirent, voire fascinent. A cela, plusieurs raisons. Laissons de côté pour le moment la beauté et l'originalité de la nature néo-zélandaise, ou encore « l'exotisme » des populations maories, thèmes récurrents mais souvent présentés de façon peu originale et superficielle. Pour l'observateur français, la Nouvelle-Zélande est perçue aussi en général comme une sorte de modèle réussi de la colonisation « à l'anglaise », avec ses qualités et ses défauts spécifiques. Et ce « modèle réussi » affirme dans ces lointaines colonies de peuplement que sont la Nouvelle-Zélande et l'Australie, à la fois une étroite filiation culturelle avec la mère patrie et des caractères extrêmement novateurs sur le plan social, qui sont source d'étonnement, d'ironie et parfois de critique acerbes de la part des voyageurs venus de la « vieille Europe ». Les Français en particulier s'intéressent à ce cas néo-zélandais qui s'oppose assez nettement à la façon de coloniser « à la française » qui s'applique au même moment pas très loin, en Nouvelle Calédonie notamment. Cette idée d'une opposition des « façons de coloniser » est récurrente dans tous les milieux, y compris chez les agents de la colonisation, militaires, marins, fonctionnaires et colons eux mêmes.

Malgré les différences de taille, de climat, de peuplement, elle se retrouve dans une comparaison explicite ou implicite entre Nouvelle-Zélande et Nouvelle Calédonie, qui présentent de fait un certain nombre d'analogies au départ ; toutes deux ont été ou ont voulu être, des colonies de peuplement européen malgré l'existence d'une population autochtone relativement nombreuse mais affaiblie par un fort recul démographique. Cela ouvrait la voie à d'éventuels conflits comme à d'éventuels traités, à la différence du cas de l'Australie où le peuplement aborigène était si lâche qu'a pu s'imposer dès l'origine l'idée d'une « terra nulluns », c'est à dire d'un espace ouvert à prendre librement par les colons sans qu'il y ait besoin de traités.

En tout cas, la Nouvelle-Zélande souvent associée à l'Australie est perçue en quelque sorte comme l'archétype de la réussite coloniale britannique, même pour des Français qui n'y ont jamais séjourné et qui jugent de la colonisation française à l'aune de ce cliché. On peut trouver un bon exemple de cette admiration pour le système colonial britannique dans les mémoires en cours d'édition d'un grand colonial français, le général Emmanuel Ruault.[1] Polytechnicien ayant opté pour l'artillerie de marine, E. Ruault reçoit sa première affectation en 1878 pour Tahiti, mais du fait de l'insurrection canaque, son navire est détourné sur Nouméa, et c'est en Nouvelle Calédonie qu'il fait sa première expérience du système colonial français, expérience qu'il complétera lors d'un second séjour en 1894 – 1896. Son jugement comparatif est sans appel, quoique un peu sommaire !

« La Nouvelle Calédonie », nous dit-il « est un fort beau pays, accidenté, boisé, doté d'immenses richesses naturelles . . .ainsi dotée par la nature, la Calédonie devrait être la plus riche colonie du monde et elle le serait, si elle était tombée aux mains des Anglais. La

France, hélas, n'a pas su en tirer parti . . . Comme il arrive toujours dans nos colonies, la Nouvelle Calédonie fut envahie, aussitôt après son annexion, par un tas de fainéants, ignorants et paresseux, s'imaginant que les alouettes allaient leur tomber toutes rôties dans le bec, et qu'ils n'auraient qu'à se tourner les pouces ; en regardant travailler les nègres pour faire fortune . . . » et de poursuivre : « notre conception coloniale est celle de la charrue avant les bœufs, surtout depuis qu'on a créé l'administration civile des colonies pour servir de refuge à tous les ratés et déclassés de la métropole et offrir de riches prébendes aux politiciens » (on reconnaît le militaire dans cette critique féroce de l'administration civile). Et Emmanuel Ruault continue : « La France s'annexe-t-elle quelque îlot, couvert de rares cocotiers et habité par des autropophages ? Immédiatement, on y envoie un gouverneur et un secrétaire général, avec leurs maisons civiles et militaires. On y organise les services de la justice, du trésor, des contributions, de l'enregistrement, du domaine, de l'instruction publique, des douanes . . . Bref, on peuple la Nouvelle Calédonie de fonctionnaires dont l'unique occupation est de toucher leurs appointements. Et si quelque malheureux a la malencontreuse idée de venir s'installer dans un si charmant pays, aussitôt tous ces budgetivores se précipitent sur lui, comme des araignées sur une mouche pour lui réclamer des droits de toute espèce. Et notre administration satisfaite rentre dans son repos : elle a achevé la colonisation de notre nouvelle possession ».

Ce qui est intéressant, c'est que pour E. Ruault, les références de la réussite coloniale sont la Nouvelle-Zélande qu'il mentionne pour se désoler que la France y ait été devancée par les Anglais, et l'Australie, qui lui permet d'opposer aux « magnifiques résultats » que la colonisation pénale y a obtenus l'échec de celle de Nouvelle Calédonie. Pour les voyageurs français en Nouvelle-Zélande, voir comment y fonctionne la colonisation britannique est donc un objectif tout naturel, même si l'idée d'une comparaison directe avec les méthodes françaises n'est pas toujours explicitée.

Les auteurs et ouvrages français sur la Nouvelle-Zélande ont tous été publiés à l'époque, souvent par de grands éditeurs, ce qui témoigne de l'intérêt porté par le public aux voyages en général et plus particulièrement à ces terres lointaines. Certains même, comme le

Comte de Courte ont été intégrés également dans la série périodique à gros tirage « le Tour du Monde ». La consultation directe de ces ouvrages est bien sûr une source essentielle, à laquelle s'ajoutent les excellents travaux (maîtrise et DEA) d'une étudiante de l'université de Paris IV Sorbonne, Mlle Anne-Lise DEJENNE sur ces voyageurs entre 1870 et 1940, et l'incontournable dictionnaire illustré des explorateurs Français de Numa Broc.[2]

Naturellement, la qualité, la densité, l'intérêt des témoignages de ces voyageurs est fonction de leur ouverture d'esprit, de leur culture, de leurs qualités littéraires, mais aussi de la motivation de leur périple et des thématiques abordées. On peut distinguer schématiquement trois catégories essentielles, les « touristes » de passage, les « résidents » faisant de longs séjours et les « chercheurs » venus spécialement pour étudier les spécificités néo-zélandaises, physiques et humaines.

Les auteurs de loin les plus nombreux sont ceux que nous qualifions de « touristes ». Ils rapportent, sans prétentions scientifiques, ils le disent eux-mêmes en général, ce qu'ils ont vu et ressenti dans des séjours plus ou moins courts en Nouvelle-Zélande, intégrés dans de vastes itinéraires souvent autour du monde. Dans cette catégorie, citons, parmi d'autres, Jean LEVACON, Gaston de SEGUR, Charles de VITIS, mais aussi Ernest MICHEL et Eugène GALLOIS, même si ces derniers intègrent déjà des réflexions de portée plus large que celles des simples visiteurs.

Jean LEVACON est le type même de ces « touristes » qui, à la fin du XIXe siècle et au début du XXe, prennent un temps dans leur carrière professionnelle et dans leur vie personnelle pour « découvrir le monde ». Avocat à la cour d'appel de Paris, il réalise en 8 mois en 1910-11 un tour du monde par l'Ouest (Amérique – Tahiti – Nouvelle-Zélande – Australie – Timor – Manille – Hong Kong – Singapour – Colombo – Port-Saïd – Paris). Il est très fier d'avoir accompli ce périple qu'il présente plaisamment dans l'ouvrage qu'il publie en 1912 (« Chez les Maoris. Tahiti et Nouvelle-Zélande, notes de voyage » Paris, E.Larose) comme une excursion « de la gare Saint Lazare à la gare de Lyon en passant par Tahiti ». Malgré le titre accrocheur laissant espérer une approche polynésienne et comparative du récit, c'est un simple survol. Jean LEVACON d'ailleurs n'est resté en Nouvelle-Zélande que du 17 au 31 Décembre 1910, il n'a visité que l'île Nord, où il s'est intéressé avant tout aux merveilles naturelles, notamment aux formes et manifestations volcaniques. Ses observations humaines restent limitées et ne vont guère au delà du constat descriptif (Auckland, « ville jeune et pimpante », est « absolument anglaise ») et des stéréotypes classiques. Il s'extasie ainsi sur les Maoris qu'il côtoie dans sa descente de la Wanganui : « qui dirait que ces indigènes souriants qui crient de la rive Ia Ora na (Bonjour) sont les descendants des féroces maoris, hideux sous leurs tatouages, entre les mains ou plutôt les dents desquels il ne faisait pas bon de tomber il y a 40 ans . . . » On reconnaît là le cliché traditionnel sur l'anthropophagie. Il entrevoit le déclin puis la lente renaissance numérique des Maoris, sans y apporter beaucoup d'explications, et s'extasie devant la beauté des sculptures maories : « je ne crois pas que dans aucune peuplade sauvage l'art natif ait atteint ce degré de perfection ».

Gaston de Ségur est lui aussi un « touriste », mais qui a séjourné plus longtemps que Jean LEVACON, plusieurs mois en 1900. Lui non plus n'a pas, il le dit clairement, de prétention scientifique. Son récit (« au bout du monde. Une saison en Nouvelle-Zélande » Paris, Plon 1901), couronné par l'Académie Française, également publié en petite partie dans la série du Tour du Monde, est avant tout descriptif, œuvre d'un observateur attentif et intelligent. Bien sûr, il est fasciné par la nature néo-zélandaise, dans l'île Nord volcanique mais aussi dans l'île Sud où la splendeur des paysages des Alpes néo-zélandaises le ravit. Mais il se passionne aussi pour les Maoris dont il déplore, nous le verrons, la perte d'identité culturelle. Charles de Vitis, un romancier a visité lui aussi la Nouvelle-Zélande au cours d'un Tour du Monde, qu'il nous raconte dans un ouvrage publié en 1908 par l'éditeur religieux Alfred MAME et fils à Tours : « A travers le globe, impressions de partout ». Il intègre dans son texte assez court (une vingtaine de pages sur la Nouvelle-Zélande) des extraits de lettres de missionnaires des débuts de l'évangélisation, et quelques réflexions sur la richesse agricole, la condition des domestiques et le déclin des Maoris.

De tout autre calibre est l'ouvrage d'Ernest Michel « A travers, l'hémisphère Sud ou mon second voyage autour du monde »Paris, V.

Palme, 1888. L'auteur, un juriste, engagé dans les œuvres catholiques à l'étranger, exécute en un an en 1883 – 84 son second tour du monde par lequel il entend montrer l'importance culturelle des voyages et la nécessité de prendre en compte ces puissances émergentes de l'hémisphère Sud. Il s'intéresse aussi bien à la condition des ouvriers néo-zélandais, qu'il trouve bien supérieure à celle des ouvriers européens, qu'aux école, aux hôpitaux et aux prisons qu'il visite. C'est un bilan important pour un séjour d'un mois à peine.

Eugène Gallois est selon l'expression de Numa Broc, un véritable globe trotter passionné de géographie, membre de plusieurs sociétés de géographe, et qui a bénéficié de missions données par divers ministères. Sa vision de la Nouvelle-Zélande (une quinzaine de pages seulement dans son ouvrage « Voyage autour du monde par l'Océanie » Paris, Librairie africaine et coloniale, 1903) n'est pas plus tendre pour la politique néo-zélandaise que pour les Maoris. Mais l'intérêt de son témoignage est malgré tout limité par la relative brièveté de son séjour.

Naturellement, les « résidents » c'est à dire ceux qui ont résidé en Nouvelle-Zélande des années et non pas quelques semaines ou mois comme les « touristes » apportent des témoignages en général plus riches et des réflexions plus approfondies. Dans cette catégorie figurent bien sur au premier rang, comme partout en Océanie , les missionnaires, dans le prolongement de l'action et dans l'entourage de Mgrs Pompannier et Viard. La longueur de leur séjour, leur volonté d'apprendre la langue des populations indigènes en font des observateurs de premier plan, dans la mesure où ils nous ont laissé des lettres et des récits. Je n'y insisterai pas car d'autres ont évoqué déjà l'intérêt de ces témoignages missionnaires.[3] En revanche, un diplomate, le comte de Courte, nous a livré un ouvrage de qualité. Après divers postes à Zurich, Aden, Batoum, il devint en 1898 Consul de France à Wellington où il resta 5 ans. Il tira de cette expérience une belle monographie intitulée « La Nouvelle-Zélande », publiée à Paris par Hachette en 1904, avec une version pré originale dans le premier semestre de 1904 du Tour du Monde (pp. 61 à 132), illustrée de très belles photos souvent en grand format. Il embrasse aussi bien une description régionale (le comte de Courte a beaucoup voyagé en Nouvelle-Zélande) que des approches thématiques sur la société, les modes et les rythmes de vie, les us et coutumes présentés de façon concrète sous la forme de « petits croquis de la vie publique et privée ». Globalement, il ne dissimule pas son « admiration sincère » pour la façon dont progresse ce pays, dont par ailleurs il vante l'extraordinaire beauté de la nature et des paysages.

La troisième catégorie de voyageurs français en Nouvelle-Zélande correspond à des « chercheurs » qui viennent y faire des études sur des thèmes spécifiques. Leurs analyses plus ciblées dépassent en précision bien sûr le niveau des simples descriptions et réflexions générales, même de qualité comme celles du Comte de Courte. Deux noms s'imposent plus particulièrement dans cette catégorie. Le premier, Paul Leroy-Beaulieu, brillant journaliste économiste à la Revue des Deux Mondes puis au Journal des Débats, fondateur en 1873 du journal « l'économiste français », professeur aux Sciences Politiques puis au collège de France (1880), mena une enquête de terrain en Nouvelle-Zélande en 1895 et 1896, comme il l'avait fait précédemment en Afrique du Sud et en Australie. Il en tira en 1897 un ouvrage comparatif important sur « les nouvelles sociétés anglo-saxonnes Australie, Nouvelle-Zélande, Afrique Australe » (Paris, A. Colin). Les chapitres consacrés à la Nouvelle-Zélande soulignent l'originalité de celle-ci tant sur le plan de la législation sociale que des mœurs, avec des hardiesses qui la placent très en avance par rapport à la « vieille Europe ». C'est le thème qu'est venu étudier aussi pour sa thèse le second « chercheur » célèbre, le jeune (23 ans) André Siegfried, qui a fait un long séjour en Nouvelle-Zélande au cours duquel il a été en contact avec le Comte de Courte qui évoqua par la suite « ce jeune français qui a visité la colonie en 1898 et en a décrit fort exactement l'organisation politique et sociale ». Cette description, publiée en 1904 (Paris, A. Colin) sous le titre « la démocratie en Nouvelle-Zélande » est certainement à l'époque l'ouvrage le plus complet sur le plan de l'analyse politique, économique et sociale. Il reste une base très utile (encore étudiée en Nouvelle-Zélande même) pour la compréhension des fondements et de la construction de la société néo-zélandaise actuelle, même si son approche parfois critique est établie, nous le verrons, à l' aune des valeurs, des traditions voire des préjugés de la vieille Europe.

Ces trois catégories de voyageurs que nous venons d'évoquer

à travers quelques noms caractéristiques ont en fait traité, avec plus ou moins de qualités d'observation et de profondeur suivant leur formation, le motif et la longueur de leur séjour, trois thèmes fondamentaux que l'on retrouve à des degrés divers dans leurs ouvrages.

Le premier thème bien sur, c'est celui de la splendeur et de l'originalité de la nature néo-zélandaise, qui constitue souvent l'essentiel des descriptions dans les récits de ceux que j'ai appelés les touristes. Les manifestations volcaniques de l'île Nord, la beauté des Alpes néo-zélandaises de l'île Sud sont traités soit dans leur spécificité, soit souvent aussi par référence à des paysages connus de l'Europe. Le comte de Courte par exemple s'extasie sur la diversité de l'archipel : « il n'est sans doute sur aucun point du globe, un pays comparable à la Nouvelle-Zélande. Dans lequel en effet trouverait-on réunis tous les spectacles de la nature, depuis la végétation et la mer bleue des tropiques au Nord jusqu'aux neiges éternelles et aux fjords de Norvège au Sud, en passant par les paysages de pays tempérés ? ».

L'endemisme de la flore (les majestueux Kauris) et de la faune (Kiwis) a frappé aussi bon nombre de voyageurs. Nous n'insisterons pas sur cette approche descriptive et pittoresque qui n'a rien de bien original. Les itinéraires comme les émerveillements des visiteurs se recoupent et se répètent plus ou moins.

Le deuxième thème, présent dans tous les ouvrages, mais à des degrés et sous des formes différents, c'est celui de la population maorie. La place qui lui est accordée dépend bien sur du type de voyageur. Elle est souvent considérable dans les récits des « touristes » car les « indigènes » constituent un élément essentiel du pittoresque et de l'exotisme néo-zélandais. En revanche, dans les études à dominante économique et sociale de ceux que nous avons appelés les « chercheurs », leur présence est plus secondaire dans la mesure où les Maoris étaient en déclin démographique et restaient marginaux tant sur le plan économique qu'au sein d'une société anglo-saxonne qui se construisait en dehors et peut on dire, au dessus d'eux. Mais l'image aussi des Maoris a sensiblement varié, cette fois ci avec le temps. Jusqu'à la fin des années 1860, voire 1870, c'est le cliché du maori sauvage et anthropophage, celui qui avait tué Marion Dufresne et avait combattu férocement les Anglais qui reste dominant. Même Jules Verne par exemple, dans « les Enfants du Capitaine Grant » publié en 1868 insiste lourdement sur le thème du cannibalisme, il est vrai très porteur dans un roman d'aventures. Jules Verne en fait n'est pas allé en Nouvelle-Zélande, mais s'est appuyé notamment sur le récit d'un géologue allemand, Ferdinand de Hochstetter qui, traduit en français, avait été publie dans le premier semestre 1860 du Tour du Monde.[4] Par la voix du géographe de l'équipe des naufragés Paganel, Jules Verne relativise un peu son jugement sur la férocité des Maoris en remarquant d'une part que « le cannibalisme a longtemps régné chez les ancêtres des peuples civilisés » et que d'autre part les indigènes associent « une étrange réunion d'affections si tendres avec les mœurs les plus féroces ». Mais par la suite, à la fin du XIXe et au début du XXe siècle, le cliché de la sauvagerie va largement s'estomper au profit de celui d'une fière et belle race déchue et perdant peu à peu les signes de son identité.

Nombreux sont les voyageurs qui insistent d'abord sur la beauté des Maoris. Pour le Comte de Courte par exemple, ils constituent « l'une des plus belles et nobles races polynésiennes, à bien des degrés dans l 'échelle de l'espèce humaine au dessus des misérables aborigènes australiens ». Ce jugement, je dirai classiquement raciste pour l'époque, marque la réhabilitation d'une certaine façon des Maoris dont les pratiques anthropophages, naguère mises continuellement en exergue, sont ramenées en quelque sorte à une tradition culturelle parmi d'autres. L'accent est mis désormais de plus en plus sur les qualités originelles du peuple maori et sur sa dégénérescence au contact de la « civilisation ». Les traditions comme le tatouage sont peu à peu abandonnées, les vieilles coutumes comme la danse de guerre, le fameux hakka, se folklorisent. Gaston de Ségur s'en désole :

« hélas, la génération actuelle n'est pas sensible à ces choses : elle délaisse le moko (tatouage) comme elle a négligé la sculpture. Le moko effraie les Maoris de nos jours : ils reculent devant les douleurs de l'opération. A Ohinemutu, à Whakarewarewa, on voit de jeunes dégénérés, en costume européen, dont la figure, lisse et intacte d'un côté, porte sur l'autre tout au plus une légère empreinte. Demandez leur pourquoi ce demi-tatouage, ce honteux compromis J'en ai eu assez du premier coup, vous répondront-ils. Cela fait trop souffrir.

tempora mutantur ». Même le trophée guerrier par excellence, la tête tatouée de l'ennemi, est devenu objet de commerce et de collection pour les visiteurs. « Une tête tatouée a beaucoup de valeur nous dit Paul Privat Deschanel. . . Il y a même des maoris qu'ont profité de l'acharnement des amateurs pour réaliser une bonne opération. Ils vendent leur tête à forfait, pour tant par an. Avec cet argent, ils se grisent. C'est ce qu'on appelle la bas « boire sa tête » !

Cette version romantique du déclin démographique et de la déchéance sociale et même artistique[5] des « beaux sauvages » maoris, présente chez tant de voyageurs, trouve peut être sa meilleure expression dans le très long (164 vers) poème de Leconte de Lisle qu'il consacre en 1889 dans ses Poèmes Tragiques, au « dernier des Maourys », dont les derniers vers expriment bien cette mélancolie.

Et le vieux mangeur d'homme, alors grinça des dents,
nous mordit d'un regard de haine et de famine,
et brusque, redressant les jarrets et l'échine,
s'en alla, tête basse et les deux bras pendants.
Fantôme du passé, silencieux image
D'un peuple mort, fauché par la faim et le fer,
Il s'enfonça dans l'ombre où soupirait la mer
Et disparut le long de la côte sauvage.

Pour bon nombre de voyageurs français, cet effondrement de la race maorie n'est pas sans causes ni responsables. Le constat en fait débouche sur une critique de la colonisation anglaise, et dans une comparaison explicite ou implicite avec la colonisation française, dans la ligne par exemple de ce qu'écrivait André Ballande en Nouvelle Calédonie dans une lettre à Mgr Fraysse (16 Mai 1897) « Le génie français, en opposition avec le patricisme anglais, avait essayé de respecter et d'améliorer la situation des habitants du pays . . . » Gaston de Segur par exemple porte un jugement sans appel sur les résultats de la colonisation britannique sur les Maoris :

« Mais ces fruits de la colonisation (anglaise) tant vantés, je les ai vainement cherchés : je n'ai trouvé qu'alcoolisme, corruption et hypocrisie. Peu des anciens vices furent extirpés, beaucoup de nouveaux ont été acquis. Calcul ou non, le fait semble incontestable :

l'anglo-saxon ne peut coexister avec l'indigène. Colonisateur merveilleux, il est civilisateur médiocre, il détruit les sauvages ou les abrutit ».[6]

Il fait ainsi une distinction fondamentale entre d'un côté la « merveilleuse » réussite de la colonisation britannique tant sur le plan du peuplement que sur celui de l'économie et de la cohésion sociale interne, et de l'autre les effets catastrophiques sur les populations indigènes. Cette dichotomie a frappé nombre d'observateurs, qui se sont particulièrement tournés vers la spécificité de cette société coloniale du bout du monde. C'est le troisième thème qui a le plus vivement intéressé ces « chercheurs » que nous avons déjà mentionnés, comme Paul Leroy-Beaulieu et André Siegfried, mais d'autres aussi comme Albert Metin,[7] Louis Vigouroux,[8] ou encore Paul Privat-Deschanel.[9]

La société néo-zélandaise en effet apparaît comme un cas remarquable, à la fois culturellement très proche de la mère patrie mais en même temps très en avance sur celle-ci et très pionnière dans le domaine des rapports sociaux. Pour des observateurs français de plus, le contraste, notamment politique avec la colonisation « à la française » est particulièrement saisissant, comme le remarque le comte de Courte : « ces possessions anglaises du Pacifique sont de véritables Etats, si différents avec leur self government de nos colonies françaises ». Ce qui les frappe le plus cependant, c'est l'approche très « moderne » des questions sociales et en particulier de la condition ouvrière que nombre de voyageurs jugent meilleure qu'en France. Plusieurs auteurs s'interrogent sur le « socialisme » néo-zélandais, et sur la législation qui se met en place à la fin du XIXe siècle, avec la loi sur l'arbitrage obligatoire entre patrons et ouvriers (1894) visent à assurer la paix sociale ou encore celle créant un système de pensions de retraite (1898). Il n'y a pratiquement pas d'équivalant en Europe, et ce « laboratoire » d'expérimentation sociale que constitue la Nouvelle-Zélande intéresse et parfois irrité un peu certains qui soulignent que cela ne peut être un modèle transposable en Europe. Mais ce qui suscite le plus d'étonnement chez les voyageurs français, ce sont les conséquences concrètes de cet « égalitarisme » néo-zélandais, comme l'abandon par exemple des normes classiques régissant en Europe les rapports entre maîtres et domestiques. Le comte de Courte n'est naturellement pas le dernier à marquer sa désapprobation : « La plupart des domestiques, en Nouvelle-Zélande, parlent avec un sans-gêne, un laisser-aller dont on ne peut se faire une idée : oui, non, si vous voulez ; jamais Monsieur ou Madame ». Charles de Vitis lui aussi évoque la désinvolture voire l'arrogance du petit personnel : « Le cocher vous parle avec une familiarité rare ; le domestique, le batelier, la femme de chambre reçoivent un pourboire avec répugnance . . . ».

Le plus étonnant, le plus irritant même pour certains voyageurs, c'est l'ensemble des dispositions en faveur de la condition féminine, en particulier la loi sur le vote des femmes de 1893 qui a cristallisé l'incompréhension des chercheurs français comme Paul Leroy-Beaulieu et André Siegfried, qui n'y voient qu'une sorte de coup publicitaire et démagogique destiné à faire parler de la Nouvelle-Zélande. La femme néo-zélandaise, dans ses aspects pionniers, sportif et revendicatifs est bien loin de l'image voire de l'idéal de la femme mineure, inactive et soumise qui imprègne encore largement la société française de la fin du XIXe siècle. Cela lui vaut des attaques que l'on qualifierait aujourd'hui de sexistes ou machistes. Même le comte de Courte juge les néo-zélandaises « pas très jolies » car elles font du sport, s'habillent comme les hommes, ont de la couperose à cause de la vie au grand air et gâtent leurs dents en mangeant trop de sucre et de viande ! Paul Privat-Deschanel persifle à la fois sur le sport et les femmes (mais notons qu'aucun voyageur français ne remarque l'importance de l'émergence d'un nouveau sport, le rugby) : « Comme les courses améliorent, dit-on, la race chevaline, le sport fortifie, à ce que l'on assure, et embellit l'humanité. On répète cet aphorisme à qui mieux en Nouvelle-Zélande, mais on ne le prouve guère. La race n'a pas gagné à ces exercices violents. Si le sport a développé quelque chose, ce sont les mains et les pieds des néo-zélandais. Quelles mains ! Ce sont des rames ! Quels pieds ! Ce sont des paquebots ! A voir s'avancer, dans une figure de bal, une ligne de jeunes néo-zélandaises, on se croit en présence des flottes de sa majesté britannique ».

Ce genre de plaisanterie, reflet d'une certaine incompréhension du nouveau monde par l'ancien, ne doit pas masquer une évidente admiration de la part des visiteurs français. Même Paul Privat-

Deschanel, pourtant assez caustique vis à vis de la Nouvelle-Zélande, conclut de façon lyrique :

> Il nous faut épier avec attention, avec anxiété peut être, l'éveil à la vie de l'hémisphère Sud, qui surgit tout armé des flots de l'océan. L'avenir appartiendra aux peuples qui ne se laisseront pas surprendre quand brillera dans le ciel austral, l'aurore des temps futurs.

Le comte de Courte, lui, fait de la Nouvelle-Zélande le symbole de la réussite coloniale britannique : « en voyant ce qu'est devenu, dans l'espace de 50 ans, un pays comme celui-ci, il est impossible de méconnaître la puissance colonisatrice de l'anglo-saxon ». On est loin ici du ton critique du général Emmanuel Ruault sur la colonisation « à la française ».

Notes

1 Les mémoires du général Emmanuel Ruault doivent paraître à l'automne 2007 aux Presses Universitaires de Bordeaux, sous la direction de Paul Butel, avec des notices de C. Huetz de Lemps (Campagnes dans le Pacifique, Nouvelle Calédonie, Tahiti, Marquises) et de A. Huetz de Lemps (Sénégal, Soudan).

2 Tome IV Océanie, Editions du CTHS 2003. Anne-Lise DEJENNE : La Nouvelle-Zélande vue par les voyageurs français entre 1870 et 1914. Maîtrise sous la direction de JP Poussou, 2000 idem, entre 1914 et 1940. Mémoire de DEA 2001. Univ. Paris IV Sorbonne.

3 dont certains d'ailleurs se rattacheraient plutôt à la catégorie « touristes », comme Mgr Henri Pasquier, qui visita la Nouvelle-Zélande au cours d'une tournée des couvents du bon Pasteur disseminés autour du monde, et en tira des « Notes d'un voyage autour du monde : Les Indes, Ceylan, l'Australie, la Nouvelle-Zélande, les Etats-Unis ». Angers, Siraudeau 1902.

4 pp. 273-320.

5 Gaston de Ségur par exemple remarque que « le maori de nos jours se contente d'admirer les œuvres que lui ont léguées ses ancêtres industrieux : son esprit inactif, ses mains oisives ne savent plus diriger ni manier le ciseau . . . ».

6 Au bout du monde : une raison en Nouvelle-Zélande, 1901, p. 213.

7 Metin Albert : Le socialisme sans doctrines, la question agraire et la question ouvrière en Australie et en Nouvelle-Zélande. Paris, F. Alcan 1901, 281 p.

8 Vigouroux Louis, L'évolution sociale en Australie. Paris, A.Colin 1902, 441 p.

9 Privat-Deschanel Paul, professeur agrégé de géographie a beaucoup travaillé sur l'Australie et la Nouvelle-Zélande (il avait même commencé une thèse sur l'eau en Australie). Ses réflexions sur la Nouvelle-Zélande, solidement documentées, ont été éditées en 1908 (Rouen, L.Gy) et lui ont ouvert la voie de la direction du volume de l'Océanie de la géographie universelle de Vidal de la Blache en 1930.

New Caledonia and New Zealand: A Linguistic Connection

Darrell Tryon

The New Zealand and Australian connection with New Caledonia goes back well over a century. This article focuses mainly on the contribution of Australasian and New Zealand English to Pacific French, particularly that of New Caledonia, particularly in the nineteenth century. At the same time it traces the other influences on the lexicon of New Caledonian French, especially Kanak languages. This article also briefly documents the linguistic legacy of New Caledonia's inter-colonial contacts. It pays tribute to the lifetime commitment of New Zealand linguists such as Hollyman, Butler, Corne et al, and the establishment of the Observatoire du Français dans le Pacifique at the University of Auckland in 1979.

Les liens de la Nouvelle-Zélande et de l'Australie avec la Nouvelle-Calédonie remontent à plus d'un siècle. Cette contribution insiste surtout sur la contribution de l'anglais australasien et néo-zélandais à la langue française du Pacifique, et plus particulièrement au français utilisé en Nouvelle-Calédonie au dix-neuvième siècle. Dans le même temps, cette contribution étudie les emprunts de ce parler français aux langues kanak tout en montrant l'importance de la recherche néo-zélandais dans ce domaine, avec la création en 1979 d'un observatoire du français dans le Pacifique à l'université d'Auckland ainsi que les travaux remarquables de messieurs Hollyman, Butler et Corne.

Preamble

The New Zealand and Australian connection with New Caledonia goes back well over a century. This paper focuses mainly on the Australasian contribution to Pacific French, particularly that of New Caledonia, while briefly documenting the linguistic legacy of New Caledonia's inter-colonial contacts. It pays tribute to the lifetime commitment of New Zealand linguists such as Hollyman, Butler, Corne et al, and the establishment of the Observatoire du Français dans le Pacifique at the University of Auckland in 1979. The paper concludes with an account of current Australasian research on Pacific French, with particular reference to New Caledonia.

Introduction

New Caledonia has a rich cultural and linguistic heritage in that it has 28 indigenous Austronesian languages (also known as Malayo-Polynesian) as well as a French-based creole, known as Tayo, spoken at Saint-Louis near Noumea. New Caledonia also has a rich and diverse colonial history, apart from its history as a former penal colony. Indeed, New Caledonian French reflects its extensive history of linguistic contacts around the region.

English has made a contribution to New Caledonian French since the earliest days of its European settlement in 1853, and even earlier, and has been a major external influence. In the 1840s and 50s New Caledonia and the Loyalty Islands were visited by English-speaking sandalwooders, whalers, bêche-de-mer fishermen, blackbirders and trochus divers. These people used a variety of pidgin English known as Beach-la-mar, or Sandalwood English, which, because of its Polynesian elements, found ready acceptance as a lingua franca between them and the Pacific Islanders. These English speakers were Americans, Australians, English and New Zealanders.[1]

In spite of the fact that from 1863 onwards French was the only language of instruction countenanced by the administration, O'Reilly (1953:211) reports that:

> 'On parlait autant anglais que français à Port-de-France – le futur Nouméa – vers 1860. . . ..des mineurs, des marins, des commercants

> néo-zélandais, des éleveurs australiens. . . .propagent leur langue et font de Nouméa à cette époque une ville pratiquement bilingue'.

As described below, the influence of English in New Caledonia lessened considerably by the end of the nineteenth century, although it was to have a further period of significant impact there during World War II, with the stationing there of hundreds of thousands of English-speaking Allied troops.

Apart from the English-speaking world, other inputs to the rich tapestry that is New Caledonian French come from Reunion in the Indian Ocean, North Africa (in particular Algeria), from Indonesia, Japan and Vietnam (the source of labour for the mining industry), China, Wallis and Futuna, Tahiti, and the French Caribbean (Guadeloupe and Martinique).

The New Zealand Connection

In 1979 the late Professor K. J. (Jim) Hollyman founded the *Observatoire du Français dans le Pacifique* at the University of Auckland in New Zealand, after becoming interested in Pacific French when he was on active service in New Caledonia with the NZ forces in World War II. He worked on and published extensively on New Caledonian and other Pacific French varieties from about 1960. His publications were mainly focussed on the phonology and lexicon of French spoken in the Pacific, with a heavy concentration on New Caledonia. In fact it was K. J. Hollyman who was co-supervisor and examiner of my own Masters thesis, *Le Français Parlé aux Iles Loyauté* (University of Canterbury, 1963). Hollyman worked in close collaboration with the French linguist André-Georges Haudricourt of the Centre National de la Recherche Scientifique (CNRS), mainly on the indigenous languages of north-east New Caledonia. After Jim Hollyman's retirement it was another of his students, Chris Corne, who took up the baton and maintained the tradition of New Zealand engagement with Pacific French. Corne, before his untimely death in a road accident, also pioneered the study of Tayo, the French creole spoken at Saint-Louis, near Noumea. It is not without a sense of history, then, that in the last few years I have been engaged in a study of Pacific French varieties (with Peter

Brown, Australian National University and two doctoral students), looking particularly at the evolution of Pacific French (especially in New Caledonia) and questions of identity as New Caledonia takes on greater autonomy, especially since the Noumea Accord (1998).

The *Observatoire du Français dans le Pacifique* had its centre at the Department of Romance Languages at the University of Auckland. Team members included A. S. G.Butler, J. C. Corne, J. L. Glasgow, K. J. Hollyman, B. D. McKay and P. A. Petit. Other members who joined subsequently included Paul De Deckker (later to become President of the University of New Caledonia, but then lecturer in Sociology), and E. D. Jones of the University of Canterbury.

In 1981 the *Observatoire du Français dans le Pacifique* became an associate research unit of the Institut National de la Langue Française, itself a part of CNRS, the French national centre for research. Between 1983 and 1996, twelve volumes of the *Observatoire du Français dans le Pacifique* appeared, all published in Paris by Didier-Érudition. A listing of the volumes and their contents gives some idea of the scope of the *Observatoire*, as follows:

1983	Vol 1:	1. Documentation Lexicographique (JH)[2] 2. Vocabulaire des Noms d'Oiseaux en Nouvelle-Calédonie (JH) 3. Identité d'Emprunt, Identification de Repère (JH) 4. Bibliographie des Études sur le Français dans le Pacifique(JH)
1984	Vol 2:	1. Documentation Lexicographique (JH) 2. Vocabulaire des Noms des Arthropodes en Nouvelle-Calédonie (JH) 3. L'Occlusion Glottale dans le Français Tahitien (CC) 4. Bibliographie des Études sur le Français dans le Pacifique (JH)
1985	Vol 3:	1. Documentation Lexicographique (JH) 2. Vocabulaire des Noms de Batraciens et de Reptiles (JH) et Vocabulaire des Zoophytes et des Vers (JH) 3. Vocabulaires Français et Tahitien dans le Noanoa de Gauguin (PP) 4. Bibliographie des Études sur le Français dans le Pacifique (JH)

1988	Vol 4:	1. Documentation Lexicographique (JH) 2. Vocabulaire des Noms de Poissons en Nouvelle-Calédonie (JH) 3. Vocabulaire des Mammifères Marins en Nouvelle-Calédonie (JH) 4. Bibliographie des Études sur le Français dans le Pacifique (JH)
1990	Vol 5:	1. Documentation Lexicographique (JH) 2. Vocabulaire des Noms de Coquillages en Nouvelle-Calédonie (JH) 3. Bibliographie des Dictionnaires des Langues Océaniennes (JH) 4. Bibliographie des Études sur le Français dans le Pacifique (JH)
1991	Vol 6:	1. Documentation Lexicographique (JH) 2. Vocabulaire des Mammifères Terrestres Sauvages en Nouvelle-Calédonie. (JH) 3. Vocabulaire des Langues Calédoniennes (JH) 4. Pour une Description de la Langue Créole Parlée à Saint-Louis (CC) 5. Bibliographie des Études sur le Français dans le Pacifique (JH)
1993	Vol 7:	1. Ethnobotanique franco-calédonienne et noms des plantes (JH) 2. Lexique des Noms Français Locaux des Plantes Indigènes et Introduites de la Nouvelle-Calédonie (JH) 3. Classement taxonomique (JH) 4. Structuration linguistique. (JH)
1994	Vol 8:	1. Documentation Lexicographique (JH) 2. Le Lexique du Bagne à la Nouvelle (JH & ASGB) 3. De l'enculé à l'onkilé (CC) 4. Bibliographie des Études sur le Français dans le Pacifique (JH)
1995	Vol 9-10:	1. Présentation 2. Lexiques des Noms Français des Animaux Indigènes et Introduits de la Nouvelle-Calédonie (JH) 3. Classement taxonomique (JH) 4. Structuration linguistique (JH) 5. Conclusions
1996	Vols 11-12:	1. Le Lexique de l'Élevage du Bétail (JG & JH)

2. Les Caldoches et les Autres: le lexique inter-ethnique calédonien (JH)
3. La Formation de Deux Nouvelles Langues Vernaculaires en Nouvelle-Calédonie: le français calédonien et le tayo (CC)
4. Index Lexicographique des Tomes 1-12 d'OFPED (JH)

The contribution of Austral English

As mentioned above, in the 1840s and 50s New Caledonia and the Loyalties were visited by English-speaking sandalwooders, whalers, bêche-de-mer fishermen, blackbirders and trochus divers. Apart from the Sandalwood English or Beach-la-mar which was used as a lingua franca across the Pacific with the islanders, the English spoken in this region between Europeans should perhaps better be described as Pacific English, or as Morris (1898) called it, 'Austral English', since it is very difficult to distinguish between Australian, English expatriate and New Zealand English, in the mid-1800s.

Hollyman (1963:215) reports that during the early period of settlement, the dominant role in New Caledonia was at times played by English speakers such as James Paddon, one of the first to introduce cattle and sheep. Also important were the New Zealand farmers who came in the 1860s.[3] Mrs Caporn records in her journal:

> The English consul Cruickshank was very much pleased with New Caledonia. He brought numbers of farmers from New Zealand and the Governor gave him a vessel to visit the island and choose the settlement he deemed fit for his colony. He chose Bouloupari. . . ..he ran a boat for years to Bouloupari. . . . . ..planted cotton which was a failure owing to rust. . . .the Cruickshank colony wended their way back to New Zealand save two or three after some ten years. A good class of people.
>
> Sydney and New Zealand had numerous vessels, some twenty sailing vessels principally here and to Fiji. . .there were 400 English in New Caledonia, principally coasters'. (Caporn ms Mitchell Library).

Also important were the Australian miners who came both before and after the discovery of gold at the Fern Hill goldmine in 1870.

There was no direct shipping, other than naval vessels, from France to New Caledonia until 1882. Colonists and visitors came on British ships to Sydney, and normally had to wait there before completing their journey, as there was only a monthly voyage from Sydney to Noumea, and this often involved going via New Zealand. 'Even the local coastal trade was long in the hands of English speakers' (Hollyman 1963:215).

It is not surprising, then, that the new colony became home to the many Franco-British (mainly Franco-Irish) families which were founded by marriages in Australia. As a result of this population pattern, English was as common as French in colonists' usage up to the turn of the century. Newspaper advertisments of the period in particular contain a great deal of English.

The demographic make-up of the population on 1 July 1866 is telling, as New Caledonia then had a total European of 2,340 of whom 1,060 were free settlers, as follows:

Nationality		*Location*	
French	770	Noumea, Mont Dore, Saint Vincent	843
Australian	202	Yaté	22
German	52	Ile des Pins	11
Italian	10	Loyalty Islands	38
Swiss	6	Canala	41
Spanish	6	Wagap	30
Dutch	5	Pouébo	71
American	4	North-West	4
Swedish	2	TOTAL	1,060
Chilean	2	(these figures only cover the free population)	
Belgian	1		
Troops	706		
Transportés	239		
Others	335[4]		
TOTAL	2,340	(Source: Clovis Savoie 1922:53)	

By 1870 the colony had a population of 1,300 European immigrants (Savoie 1922:53). Between 1879 and 1883 there were still more English speakers than French among the newly arriving settlers. By 1887 the European population had grown to 4,165 civilians, 3,015 military, and 11,358 convicts (Hollyman 1971:918)[5].

In the economic development of the new country, a major role was played by Australia as the principal source area for animals, plants and technical knowledge. This was so not only because of shipping arrangements and geographical proximity, but also because Australia had to face up to many similar developmental problems (Hollyman 1963:215).

From the turn of the century English fell off quickly in use, although it survived much longer in Franco-British families than in the community generally. The only major renewal of close contact occurred through the presence of Australian, American and New Zealand troops during World War II.

Borrowings in New Caledonian French from Austral English

Hollyman (1963:216) warns that before considering English words and expressions in New Caledonian French as direct borrowings, it is important to distinguish them from words already borrowed from English into metropolitan French before their use in New Caledonia, or English words borrowed into another overseas dialect of French and subsequently introduced as intercolonial borrowings.

The borrowings generally reflect major fields of social activity or interest, in the immediate post-colonisation period in New Caledonia, agricultural and pastoral enterprises and the mining industry. There are three types: full borrowing, loan extension of meaning and loan translation.

a) Full borrowing:

This occurs especially where new technology or a new industry is introduced.

Thus: *paddock, creek, stockman, stockwhip*

b) Loan extension of meaning: (=meaning borrowing)

This occurs by the process of analogy, as in the following:

Language 1	Language 2
Word *a* has meaning *x*	Word *b* has meaning *x*
Word *a* has meaning *y*	Word *b* borrows meaning *y*

The loan extension of meaning may involve the same semantic field as the common meaning.

Thus: *drove* means 'to drive cattle over a distance for purposes of sale etc'. *conduire* (1925) has had its meaning extended in New Caledonian French to cover the concept of *drove*;

bat in Austral English may mean either a flying marsupial or a fish species (sea-bat). In metropolitan French *roussette* means only a flying marsupial, while in New Caledonian French it has taken on both of the meanings of *bat* in Austral English.

station in New Caledonian French has taken on the additional meaning 'farm, ranch', unknown in metropolitan French with this meaning, following Austral English.

c) Loan translation:

Loan translations fall into two groups: reproductions and renditions. In reproductions, the expression is analysed and its parts reproduced in translation. In renditions the translation is only partial.

Thus:	stock-horse	> *cheval de stock*
	bush-fire	> *feu de brousse*[6]
	paper mulberry	> *mûrier-papier*
	banana passionfruit	> *pomme-liane banane*
	parrot-fish	> *poisson perroquet; Labridae*
	night heron	> *héron de nuit*
Also:	corkwood	> *arbre à bouchons*
	spearwood	> *arbre-sagaïe*

As mentioned previously, the major area of influence from English was in the pastoral and mining industries in New Caledonia in the nineteenth century. While many of the borrowings have retained their currency today, quite a number have fallen into disuse and in some cases are no longer remembered except by a few people still involved in these industries. On the other hand, numerous new

English borrowings have entered New Caledonian French in recent years.

Some examples[7] of lexical borrowings:

Geographical:

Creek	*1892*[8] 'The American English *creek* 'stream' which spread to French Guiana, Australia and New Zealand, also appears (1892) in New Caledonia, in a variety of spellings: *creek*, *cric*, even *crique*, but the normal English spelling is the commonest'. (Hollyman 1963: 219).
Brousse	*1871* 'bush, outback, country area' (see Hollyman 1962:33-34)

Pastoral:

Station or *Station d'élevage*	*1865* 'farm, agricultural or grazing property' *(CP 1995)*[9]
Squatter	*1869* 'farm owner' (no longer used)*[10]; but *vide infra.*
Boy	*1910* 'native station worker, domestic'*
Stock	*1910*[11] 'cattle/horse farm, horse race' *(CP 1995:130)*
Stockman	*1871* 'stockman' pl. stockmen, stockmans (*CP 1995)*
Stockwhip	*1871* 'stock whip' *(CP1995)*
Run	*1871* 'the land is generally known as the 'run' [Rɔn]; also means 'paddock' (*CP1995)*
Paddock	1871 'paddock' *(CP1995)*
Mob	*1871* 'herd of cattle'*
Stockyard	1871 'stockyard' [stokjaR] *(CP 1995)*
Dip	1961 'cattle/sheep dip'*
Fence	*1866* 'fence'* (replaced by *barrière*)
Campement	*1905* 'mustering camp'*(from Australian '*camp*')
Bagrite	*1961* (used by stockmen!)*
Cheval de stock	*1910* 'stock-horse, non-descript breed' *(CP 1995)*
Quater-horse	*1983* 'quarter-horse' *(CP 1995)*
Mustang	*1953* 'mustang' *
Cob	*1961* 'crossbreed'*
Yearling	*1961* 'yearling'*
Piebald	*1961* 'piebald'*

Buck, beuquer *Buker, boquer,bucker*	*1953* 'to buck, bucker' *(CP1995)*
Hereford	*1867* 'Hereford cattle'*
Devon	*1867* 'Devon cattle'*
Angus	*1900* 'Angus cattle'*
Norfolk	*1905* 'Norfolk cattle'*
Pollé	*1961* 'poll' as in *pollé angus**
Stag	*1961* 'castrated bull'*
Billy	*1961* 'bad-tempered bull'*
Dingo rouge[12]	*1961* 'standard working dog'* BUT *chien bleu (CP1995)*
Dingo bleu	*1961* 'standard working dog'* BUT *chien bleu (CP 1995)*
Nani	*1871* 'nanny-goat' (from Bislama)*
Billy	*1961* 'billy-goat' (from Bislama)*

Trees and Grasses:

There were many borrowings related to pastures, grasses, horticulture and forestry:

Kaori	*1858* 'kauri tree', originally NZE, from Maori *kauri, (CP1995)*
Montgoméry	*1961* 'Montgomery red clover' (from NZE)*
Buffalo[13]	*1932* 'buffalo grass' *(CP 1995)*
Paspalum	*1905* 'paspalum grass'[14] *
Mimosa	*1935* 'mimosa' *(CP 1995)*
Lantana	*1884* 'lantana'[15] *(CP 1995)*
Gum-tree	*1859* 'Native-born Australian'*
Niaouli	n.d. 'Native-born New Caledonian'*

Mining:

Prospecteur	*1869*, *1873* 'prospector' *
Nugget	*1873* 'nugget'*
Dish	*1878* 'panning dish'*
Slousse	n.d. 'sluice' *
Tellings	*1900* 'tailings' *
Shaft	n.d. 'shaft' [Shaf]*
Store	*1873* 'general store, but now used only in mining

	camps'.*
Belay	n.d. 'billy-can'. Cf. *Belly, bélé, bélet, billy (CP1995)*

Transport (US Army):

Benzine	*1953* 'petrol'[16]*
Bulldozer	*1945* 'bulldozer' *(CP1995)*
Bus	*1945* 'bus' *
Grader	*1945* 'grader, bulldozer' *(CP1995)*
Jeep	*1945* 'Jeep' *
Motor Pool	*1941* 'Motor Pool, suburb of Noumea'
Receiving	*1941* 'Receiving, suburb of Noumea'
Poken	*1947* 'English-speaker' from 'English spoken' *(CP 1995)*

More Recent Borrowings:

Carport	'carport' *(CP1995)*
Bull-bar	'bull-bar'*
Aérogard	'Aerogard insect spray' *(CP1995)*
Babaille	'Bye bye' *(CP1995)*
Dungaree	'dungarees' *(CP1995)*
Néo	'New Zealander' *(CP 2007)*
Kiwi	'New Zealander' *(CP1995)*
Mummy	'mum' *(CP1995)*
See you	'good-bye' *(CP1995)*
Shop center	'shopping centre' *(CP1995)*
Stone fish	'stone-fish' *(CP1995)*

Borrowings from Bislama:

Tamioc	BIS 'tomahawk' *(CP1995)*
Kaikai	BIS 'eat' *(CP1995)*
Paniken	BIS 'pannikin' *
Pikinini	BIS 'child'*
Takata	BIS 'doctor'*
Boulouk	BIS 'cattle' *(CP1995)*
Poka[17]	BIS 'pig' *(CP1995)*
Tata	BIS 'good-bye' *(CP1995)*
Man	BIS 'man!' *(CP1995)*
Nani	BIS *'nanny-goat' (CP1995)*

Borrowings from Sources other than English

From Melanesian languages in New Caledonia:

There are numerous borrowings from a range of New Caledonian vernaculars, in particular major languages such as Drehu (Lifou, Loyalty Islands) and Ajië (Houailou). For example:

bougna	'traditional vegetable and meat/fish pudding' (Kumak, Drehu)
cagou	'flightless bird, *Rhynochetos jubatus*' (Drumbéa)
dawa	'fish, *Naso unicornis*' (Ajië, Xârâcùù)
houp	'tree, *Montrouziera cauliflora*' (languages of Northern New Caledonia)
kakoune	'bump, collision, accident'
kalolo	'beautiful, nice' (Drehu *ka lolo*)
kanéka	'local Kanak music'
notou	'large pigeon, *Ducula goliath*'(Numèè)
ouapipi	'honey-eater, *Gerygone flavolateralis*' (Paicî)
pilou,	'native dance' (Caaac, Yâlayu)
poingo (banane poingo)	'variety of cooking banana' (Hienghène region)
popinée	'native woman' [from West Uvea *fafine*, through Melanesian]; (*vide* JH 1959:375)[18]
popwaalé	'European' (Paicî)
toghi	'evil spirit, devil' (Ajië, Xârâcùù)

From Tahitian French:

bourao	'hibiscus tiliaceus, yellow hibiscus' (Tahitian *purau*);
tamanou	'tree, Calophyllum inophyllum' (Tahitian *tāmanu*)
maïoré	'breadfruit, breadfruit tree' (Tahitian *maiore*)

From Javanese (Indonesian):

bami	'Indonesian-style vermicelli, Indonesian'
bayou	'Indonesian woman'
kakane, cacane	'Indonesian; Javanese, gardener'

From Vietnamese:

congaï,	'Vietnamese woman'
naï	'Asian'

From Algerian French:

gourbi	'untidy or tumbledown place'*
dis, disque, dixe	'tall grass, *Ampelodesmos*'*

From Reunion French:

aloës	'plant, *Agave sisilana*'.
ambrevade	'pigeon-pea'
bois noir	'tree, *Albizzia lebbek*'
brède	'plant with edible leaves, *Amaranthus interruptus*'
chouchoute	'choko, *Sechium edule*'
pipengaye	'plant, *Luffa cylindrica*'

From West Indian French:

barbardine	'vine, *Passiflora quadrangularis*'
bécune	'fish, *Sphyraena sp*'
crocro	'fish, '*Haemulon plumieri*'
pomme-liane	'vine, *Passiflora laurifolia*'

Referential readjustment of metropolitan French terms:

acajou	'tree, *Semecarpus atra*'.
astiquer	'beat, hit, reprimand'
chêne	'tree with sinuous branches and medium heavy timber' (22 compond names)
fromager	'dye-producing tree, *Morinda citrifolia*'

French regionalisms:

pistache	'peanut, *Arachis hypogaea*'
criquet	'locust, *Locusta migratoria*'.

New Caledonian French neologisms:

Where items of New Caledonian flora and fauna, especially, have no name in metropolitan French as they do not exist in that part of the world, they were often given a name related to the closest European term. These terms often involve an adjective or descriptive phrase. Thus:

amande amère	'tree with edible fruit, *Ximenia ellipitica*'
bois barre à mine	'tree with timber dificult to bend, *Syzygium wagapense*'
groseiller kanak	'shrub, *Physalis peruviana*'
chou kanak	'native spinach, *hibiscus manihot*'
pois collant	'sticky-seeded plant, *Desmodium heterocarpum*'
long cou	'héron, *Dimigretta sacra albolineata*'
lunette	'white-eye, *Zosterops sp*'

Other current items are recent neologisms, which are well established, for example:

bibiche,	'sling-shot' (*contra* metropolitan French *lance-pierres*)
mobilis	'portable telephone'
nordiste	'someone from the Northern Province'
squat	'slum dwelling, usually in the bush or on undeveloped land'

Slang and informal speech is the source of many new words and colourful expressions in New Caledonian French. While many are common to all Caledonian communities, quite a number tend to be limited to a particular age or ethnic group.

For example, the following expressions are seemingly limited to Kanak French:

Araïeu!	expresses surprise (Drehu *axaiö*) (vulg.)
Babane	bald, idiotic
Babao	ghost
Doghi	devil, evil spirit (Ajië)
Ekoloini	surprise! (Nengone *koloini* 'poor me!')
Kaïkaï	eat, food
Kalolo	pretty, good (Drehu *ka lolo* 'beautiful')
Kaya fou	bohemian (Jamaican Creole *kaya* 'marijuana')
Lin nien	good-bye (Drehu *elahnyë*)
Pe a keu	none, no more (Drehu *pëkö*, 'zero', none')
Popwaalé	European
Wanamatcha	Expresses surprise (Drehu)

Polynesian French (Tahitians and Wallisians), also in use by Kanaks:

Brown, and two post-graduate researchers Peter Myers, and Rowena Dickens Morrison (all from the Australian National University). This four-year project, in collaboration with the Ministère de la Culture in New Caledonia, has as its aim to analyse and document in monographs, critical editions, doctoral theses and other forms the evolution of linguistic and cultural change in the French Pacific through a comprehensive case study of the contemporary literature and press of New Caledonia, together with an analysis of spoken New Caledonian French, on radio and in rural and urban areas in all three provinces of the country.

Conclusion

The variety of French spoken in New Caledonia, like that in metropolitan France, is not adequately represented by a single label. New Caledonian French is distinguishable from metropolitan French by a number of phonological, morpho-syntactic and lexical criterea, a sample of which has been presented above.

However, while a single label may suffice to distinguish New Caledonian French from metropolitan French, it is important to observe that there is a whole range of speech varieties or registers covered by this label, whose main function is to proclaim one's New Caledonian identity as opposed to any other identity. In the same way, New Zealand English may be distinguished from Australian or Canadian English for example.

Within New Caledonian French it is not difficult to identify varieties spoken by the Kanak population which differ in some ways from the variety spoken by Caldoche residents engaged in pastoral and agricultural pursuits on the west coast of the mainland. Even within Kanak French there are notable differences between the speech of urban and rural dwellers on the mainland, and between them and their neighbours in the Loyalty Islands. And even within Caldoche speech, there are recognisable Javanese and Tonkinese varieties.

More important than the identifiable speech varieties within New Caledonian French is the fact that nearly all speakers have a number of registers or varieties at their disposal. These registers or codes may be invoked depending on the identity/background of one's interlocutor, normally to express in-group solidarity/ membership. It is this complex set of code-switching scenarios and the multiple identities so encoded which lies at the heart of our current research.

References

Barnèche, Sophie. *Gens de Nouméa, gens des îles, gens d'ailleurs. . .Langues et identités en Nouvelle-Calédonie.* Paris: L'Harmattan, 2005.

Caporn, Mrs A. *Notes on New Caledonia 1859.* manuscript. Mitchell Library, Sydney.

Cordier-Rossiaud, G. *Relations économiques entre Sydney et la Nouvelle-Calédonie.* Nouméa: Imprimerie du Gouvernement, 1957.

Corne, Chris & Jim Hollyman. 'French in the South Pacific', in Stephen A.Wurm, Peter Mühlhäusler and Darrell T. Tryon, eds., *Atlas of Languages of Intercultural Communication in the Pacific, Asia and the Americas.* Berlin: Mouton de Gruyter, 1996, pp. 251-263.

Darot, Mireille. 'Les noms de minerai: particularités du français calédonien et histoire industrielle', in *Du Caillou au Nickel.* Nouméa: UFP-CDP, 1996, pp. 51-56.

—. Calédonie, Kanaky ou Caillou. Implicites identitaires dans la désignation de la Nouvelle-Calédonie, *Mots, les langages du politique*, 1996, No. 53, pp. 8-25.

—. Les petits mineurs du Caillou, le français et la mine en Nouvelle-Calédonie, *Le français en Afrique,* 1997, No. 12, pp. 105-116.

— and Christine Pauleau. 'Tabou et français calédonien; un exemple de variation en francophonie', *Langage et Société*, 62, septembre 1992, pp. 27-53.

Hollyman, K.J. 'Polynesian Influence in New Caledonia: the linguistic aspect', *Journal of the Polynesian Society*, 68, 1959, pp. 356-389.

—. 'Intercolonial Borrowings with Special reference to New Caledonian French', *AUMLA* 17, 1962, pp. 31-44.

—. 'Anglo-French language contact in New Caledonia', *AUMLA* 20, 1963, pp. 213-240.

—. *Le français régional de l'Indo-Pacifique. Essais de phonologie.* Auckland: Linguistic Society of New Zealand, 1964.

—. 'French in the Pacific', in T. Sebeok ed., *Current Trends in Linguistics*, vol. 8, Linguistics in Oceania. Berlin:Mouton de Gruyter, 1971, pp. 903-937.

— et al. *Observatoire du Français dans le Pacifique* (12 vols). Paris: Didier Érudition, 1983-96.

Morris, E. E. *Austral English*. London: Macmillan, 1898.

O'Reilly, Patrick. 'Le français parlé en Nouvelle-Calédonie. Apports étrangers et vocables nouveaux. Archaïsmes et expressions familières'. *Journal de la Société des Océanistes* 9, 1953, pp. 203-228.

Pauleau, Christine. *Le Français de Nouvelle-Calédonie: contribution à un inventaire des particularités lexicales*. Paris: EDICEF-AUPELF, 1995.

—. *Mots de Nouvelle-Calédonie: éléments de recherche sociolinguistique sur le français calédonien: inventaire lexicographique polylectal*. Nouméa: CDPNC, 2007.

Savoie, Clovis. *Histoire de la Nouvelle-Calédonie et de ses Dépendances*. Nouméa: Imprimerie Nationale, 1922.

Tryon, Darrell. *Le Français Parlé aux Iles Loyauté*. Unpublished M.A. Thesis, University of Canterbury, 1963.

—. 'The French Language in the Pacific', *Journal of Pacific History*, vol. 26, no. 2, 1991, pp. 273-287.

Notes

1 There is a record of a New Zealander from Auckland, named Fitzgerald, who was engaged in bêche-de-mer fishing off the NW tip of New Caledonia (see G. Cordier-Rossiaud *Relations Économiques entre Sydney et la Nouvelle-Calédonie* 1844-1860. Paris 1957, p. 50).

2 JH, Jim Hollyman; CC, Chris Corne; PP, Pierre Petit; ASGB, Alex Butler; JG, Jeanette Glasgow.

3 This group was brought over by the English Consul, Cruickshank. It is mentioned in a manuscript by Mrs A. Caporn, *Notes of New Caledonia 1859*, Mitchell Library, Sydney.

4 Asian, African & Pacific Island migrants.

5 In comparison, the Melanesian population was about 27,000 in 1860, but fell to less than 19,000 by 1887.

6 *Feu de brousse* appears in 1910, replacing the earlier *incendie de prairie* (1858) (Hollyman 1963:219).

7 The examples presented in this paper represent only a small fraction of lexical borrowings in New Caledonian French. For an extensive listing, see the Index Lexicographique in the *Observatoire du Français dans le Pacifique*, Vol.12: 129-322 (1996).

8 The dates indicate the first recorded written use of the term in New Caledonian French: Source Hollyman OFP.

9 In Christine Pauleau *Le français calédonien* (1995)

10 * indicates not found in Pauleau 1995, an indication that the item has lost currency or disappeared.

11 Certainly used earlier than 1910.

12 Pronounced [diŋgo], unlike the metropolitan French pronunciation.
13 Although this is an American grass, the name is Australian, since it was discovered in Australia near Buffalo Creek, NSW.
14 Also known as '*herbe d'Australie*'.
15 Introduced from Australia before 1868 (Hollyman 1963:225).
16 Recorded by O'Reilly 1953, but disputed by Hollyman (1963:228).
17 *Poka* is old Beach-la-mar, replaced in modern Bislama by *pig*.
18 'Of particular interest is the French word *popinée* "native woman". The Uvean name for 'woman' is *fafine*. The consonant *f* is missing from the phonemic systems of a number of NC languages, including several along the northern coast of the mainland. It is clear that *fafine* underwent a transformation in the mouths of these speakers before being adopted as *popinée* by the French settlers. In view of the habit among north-coast chiefs of obtaining wives from Uvea, it seems that the word was commonly used by them before European visits were frequent' (Hollyman 1959: 375).
19 Usually pronounced *l'ongin* /lõʒæ̃/
20 In metropolitan French there is a four-way distinction in nasal vowels /æ̃ – œ̃ –õ – ã/ while in New Caledonian French there is a two-way distinction /æ̃ – õ/ (Hollyman 1971:926).

Part Two

The 20th century relationship

Hier

De Nouméa à Apia . . . vers un nouvel ordre colonial dans le Pacifique Sud

Sylvette Boubin-Boyer

Dès le début de la Première Guerre mondiale, l'océan Pacifique est au cœur d'une guerre maritime dont les événements seront déterminants pour l'avenir de certaines puissances montantes et un nouvel ordre colonial océanien. Le 31 juillet 1914, les réseaux d'alliances et de traités sont en place entre les alliés que sont la Grande-Bretagne, la France et le Japon. D'août à janvier 1915, les marines française et britannique puis japonaise entreprennent des opérations conjointes de prise de possession des colonies allemandes de Mélanésie et de Polynésie. Une expédition franco-britannique se met en place. Le cuirassé français MONTCALM retrouve la flotte australasienne à Nouméa le 20 août. Les objectifs visés par l'escadre sont avant tout de défendre les colonies françaises et britanniques contre une éventuelle attaque des navires allemands, de mener une guerre de course contre les navires ennemis pour favoriser la circulation des convois vers l'Europe mais surtout de détruire les réseaux allemands de communications et de s'emparer des possessions allemandes océaniennes.

Les premières instructions en possession des amiraux français et britanniques leur enjoignent de partir ensemble pour une expédition contre le Samoa allemand. La colonie allemande est prise sans résistance le 30 août. La Nouvelle-Zélande en devient l'administrateur pour la durée de la guerre avant d'être officiellement mandatée en 1920 par la Société des Nations. L'escadre se rend ensuite vers la Nouvelle-Guinée allemande. Le 24 septembre 1914, le gouverneur fait complète soumission et remet toutes les possessions allemandes de Nouvelle-Guinée et des îles voisines au représentant de l'Australie. L'occupation des archipels allemands se poursuit jusqu'en janvier 1915, le Japon s'étant emparé des archipels micronésiens et de la base de Tsing-Tao en Chine.

Conformément aux ordres de l'amirauté britannique, le navire-amiral français tout comme la division australienne n'ont donc eu qu'un rôle d'assistance à la flotte néo-zélandaise pour la prise des Samoa. Puis, le même rôle échoit à la France pour la prise de la Nouvelle-Guinée allemande. Néanmoins, l'impréparation à la collaboration maritime de guerre est manifeste et les Français remarquent que leur présence n'est jamais citée aux côtés des navires australasiens alors que la collaboration française a été effective. Ce refus d'associer la France à la prise de possession conjointe des colonies allemandes du Pacifique, montre, outre le désintérêt de la France pour ses colonies océaniennes, à quel point l'Océanie semble alors devenue « un lac australasien ». Par ailleurs, l'occupation du Samoa allemand préfigure la naissance de la conscience nationale néo-zélandaise.

From the beginning of the first world war the Pacific Ocean was at the heart of a maritime war, one whose events would be crucial for the future of certain rising powers and for a new colonial oceanic order. On 31 July 1914, alliance networks and treaties were settled among the allies – Great Britain, France and Japan. From August to January 1915, concerted operations by the French and British navies, soon followed by the Japanese, led to the take-over of German colonies in Melanesia and Polynesia. A Franco-British expedition was put in place, and the French ironclad 'Montcalm' rejoined the Australasian fleet in Nouméa on 20 August. First of all, the squadron had as its objective the defense of the French and British colonies against a possible attack by German warships. The war being waged against the enemy was also intended to protect convoys sailing to Europe; but above all it was intended to destroy German communication networks, and to allow the allies to take over Germany's Pacific possessions.

The first instructions received by the French and British admirals ordered them to leave together for an expedition against German Samoa. The German colony was taken without resistance on 30 August. New Zealand became the administrator of Samoa for the duration of the war, before receiving an official Mandate from the newly established League of Nations in 1920. The squadron sailed afterwards to German New Guinea. On 24 September 1914 the Governor surrendered all German possessions in New Guinea and nearby islands to representatives of Australia. The occupation of the German archipelagos lasted until January 1915, while Japan took over Micronesian archipelagos and a base at Tsingtao in China.

In accordance with orders from the British Admiralty, the role of French warships and the Australian division was only to assist the New Zealand fleet in its seizure of Samoa. France had the same role afterwards in the capture of German New Guinea. Nevertheless, the lack of preparation for wartime maritime collaboration was evident; the French notice that their presence is never cited, although the collaboration between the Australasian and French navies proved effective. This refusal to associate France with the takeover of German colonies in the Pacific shows the lack of interest of France in its Oceanic colonies, and also how much Oceania seems to have become at that point 'an Australasian lake'. In addition, the occupation of German Samoa foreshadowed a rising national awareness in New Zealand.

Le partage colonial exclusif du Pacifique est terminé en 1913. La Grande-Bretagne y détient les passages vers les trois océans du globe, l'Allemagne possède les trois archipels-clés des routes maritimes. Les flottes de guerre en présence dans le Pacifique-sud sont britannique (australasienne), française, allemande et japonaise. Il en découle un certain équilibre grâce aux systèmes d'alliances entre la France et la Grande-Bretagne, rejointes le Japon. Malgré une volonté encore discrète d'émancipation, l'Australasie reste liée à la Grande-Bretagne. Le fil directeur de cette étude va montrer en quoi un fait presque anecdotique du début de la Grande Guerre (la prise de possession du Samoa allemand) confronte les Français, les Australiens et les Néo-Zélandais avec « l'épreuve de la guerre moderne » et préfigure une nouvelle répartition coloniale dans l'après-guerre. Le récit de l'événement et son analyse restituent des aspects mal connus des situations et des comportements et rectifient la vision australasienne en donnant, à partir des rapports du contre-amiral français Huguet et de ceux de l'amiral anglais Patey, quelques points d'éclairage sur la collaboration de la France. A-t-on pris la mesure de tous les enjeux immédiats ou « à retardement » des premiers mois de guerre en 1914-1915 en Océanie ? L'investigation complète n'est pas encore achevée du côté des historiens français.

Au début du XXe siècle, l'Américain Alfred Mahan (1840-1914), dans son livre *L'influence de la puissance navale dans l'histoire*, publié en 1890, tend à prouver que le pays qui contrôle les mers peut se prévaloir d'une suprématie économique et politique mondiale. D'après lui, la puissance maritime constituerait un instrument de politique destiné à accroître la puissance et le prestige de la nation. Suivant cette théorie, les États-Unis et le Japon développent alors leur flotte de guerre, la Grande-Bretagne reste déterminée à garder son rang de grande puissance maritime et l'Allemagne place « son avenir sur l'eau ». Une logique d'interdépendance, de compétition, de coopération se met en place, concrétisée par différents traités d'alliances[1] puis, durant la guerre, par l'appel aux populations d'outre-mer[2]. Cuirassés puis *dreadnought* sont construits, les premiers sous-marins voient le jour, et la vapeur remplace définitivement les voiles. De nouveaux armements navals apparaissent (canons, torpilles, mines). Ébauchée durant le XIXe siècle, une notion nouvelle de guerre navale apparaît. Par ailleurs, la nécessité de transmettre des informations et de communiquer entre continents conduit les puissances en place dans le Pacifique à poser des câbles sous-marins nécessaires aux télégrammes et au téléphone. En Océanie, le réseau allemand est le plus perfectionné.

Le Pacifique insulaire en 1914 : une mosaïque de colonies

Les États-Unis sont présents dans la partie nord et centre du Pacifique ; différents statuts gèrent leurs territoires : Hawaii, Philippines, Micronésie (Guam, au sud de l'archipel des Mariannes, Wake, au nord des Marshall à mi-distance entre Guam et Hawaii). Aux Samoa, gérées depuis 1878 par un gouvernement conjoint des États-Unis, Grande-Bretagne et Allemagne, les EU disposent de Pago-Pago dans l'île de Tutuila, de Swains et Manua. Ils sont propriétaires de la zone du canal de Panama qui représente un grand espoir pour la rapidité et la fiabilité des communications entre l'Atlantique et le Pacifique. Leur objectif est principalement d'établir des relations avec le marché de la Chine et du Japon qui s'ouvre alors. La marine de guerre américaine n'est pas présente sous forme de flotte dans le Pacifique. Le Japon a poursuivi avant-guerre son objectif d'installer « un glacis protecteur, complément économique » autour de son archipel dans le Pacifique nord. Sa flotte, en construction, doit devenir l'une des plus modernes du Pacifique. Le Japon détient Formose et les Pescadores, la moitié sud de la presqu'île de Sakhaline, le sud de la Mandchourie, Ryu-kyu, l'archipel des Bonins et assure la libre circulation des biens et des personnes en Corée. Le Japon s'est allié à la Russie (1910) et à la Grande-Bretagne (1911). Avant-guerre déjà, l'état des relations entre le Japon et les États-Unis conduit l'attention des hommes d'État australasiens à prendre des mesures sur la défense des colonies anglaises du Pacifique et des grandes voies de communication océaniennes qui relient entre elles l'Australie, la Nouvelle-Zélande et le Canada.

La Grande-Bretagne est omniprésente dans le sud-ouest et le centre du Pacifique par l'intermédiaire de l'Australie et de la Nouvelle-Zélande (réunies sous le terme d'Australasie) ainsi que dans les archipels mélanésien et polynésien (Tonga, Fidji, Salomon, Nouvelles-Hébrides, Tokelau, Gilbert et Ellice, Pitcairn). La marine australienne, autonome depuis 1907, s'est créée de 1911 à 1913. La base britannique installée à Sydney a été transférée en 1913 à Picton Harbor, face à Wellington, capitale de la Nouvelle-Zélande. En cas de guerre, la marine néo-zélandaise, dirigée par un amiral anglais, se met immédiatement aux ordres de l'Amirauté britannique. La France, présente sur une ligne qui suit approximativement le tropique du Capricorne en Mélanésie et en Polynésie, possède la Nouvelle-Calédonie, l'îlot de Clipperton, les Établissements Français d'Océanie, un protectorat sur Wallis et Futuna et les Nouvelles-Hébrides sous forme de condominium avec l'Angleterre. La flotte française d'Extrême-Orient répond aux besoins de la politique de la France dans la mer de Chine, dans l'Océan Pacifique et sur les côtes de l'Amérique. Elle dispose pour défendre ses colonies, de navires de guerre vieillissants, dont le remplacement ne se fait pas faute de moyens et aussi de désintérêt de l'État. En Océanie, les objectifs de la France et de l'Angleterre, outre l'évangélisation des indigènes, ont été surtout de créer des bagnes et de s'assurer des sources de matières premières et des débouchés.

Dès l'avènement du IIe Reich, en janvier 1871, l'Allemagne peut rejoindre les grandes puissances dans la course coloniale. Elle constitue son empire colonial avec des intentions impériales délibérées, surtout par des achats ou annexions et peu avec des guerres de conquête, les premières grandes puissances ne lui ayant guère laissé de place. L'implantation de ses colonies océaniennes, en 1914, malgré une position définitive ne date que d'une quinzaine d'années, et concrétise néanmoins le dernier partage colonial du Pacifique sud-ouest de la phase colonisatrice du XIXe siècle. Au nord du Pacifique sud-ouest, l'Allemagne possède la partie nord-est de la Nouvelle-Guinée et les archipels Bismarck, Bougainville et Buka. En Micronésie, elle a négocié les archipels des Mariannes, des Carolines, des Marshall, de Palau, de Nauru, et aux Samoa, les îles Upolu et Savai'i[3]. Un maillage du Pacifique est réalisé par les colonies allemandes et la flotte commerciale allemande, souvent agressive, fonctionnant parfois à perte, transporte les produits agricoles et cultures spéculatives comme le coprah et aussi le nickel de Nouvelle-Calédonie. Les colonies allemandes océaniennes sont exploitées pour le plus grand profit de l'industrie métropolitaine ; en dépit d'une implantation très modeste de colons germaniques. Pourtant, les capitalistes allemands ne réinvestissent pas leurs bénéfices dans les colonies. Les possessions allemandes n'ont pas de système de défense par mer ou par terre, pas de troupes militaires ni de bases de marine installées, hormis l'enclave de Kiao Tchéou en Chine qui sert son objectif de créer un puissant empire colonial en direction d'un

Extrême-Orient riche en marchés potentiels. La base navale de Tsing Tao y a été créée pour accueillir la moderne flotte de guerre allemande du Pacifique. Le réseau de TSF déjà réalisé ou en projet en 1914 fait la force des Allemands dans cette partie du monde ; la plupart des navires de guerre et marchands en sont équipés, l'équipement de leurs possessions insulaires est en bonne voie. Aucun autre État européen que l'Allemagne n'a connu un développement économique et scientifique aussi important dans le dernier tiers du XIXe siècle. Mise en présence de deux systèmes d'alliances ordonnés autour de la puissance financière et maritime, l'Allemagne se heurte, dans le Pacifique aux alliances Japon - Grande-Bretagne - France. Ainsi, la coalition de 1914 va-t-elle s'effectuer contre la puissance centrale européenne qui a émergé dans le dernier tiers du 19e siècle et qui est en passe de conquérir une place déterminante parmi les grandes puissances mondiales de l'époque.

C'est dans ce cadre, qu'à partir d'avril 1914, s'est poursuivie la dernière croisière avant-guerre du navire-amiral français *MONTCALM* dans les archipels du Pacifique-sud et sur les côtes de l'Amérique. Les visites protocolaires du vice-amiral Huguet n'ont pas montré d'antagonismes flagrants entre les représentants des puissances européennes. S'il n'évoque pas l'attentat de Sarajevo du 28 juin 1914, dans ses rapports, le contre-amiral explique combien la flotte française dans le Pacifique, vieillissante et n'est pas en mesure de mener une véritable guerre maritime. A cela s'ajoute sa remarque, un mois avant la déclaration de guerre, selon laquelle la Nouvelle-Zélande et l'Australie se sont entendues pour occuper les possessions allemandes du Pacifique. D'après lui, seuls l'Allemagne, le Japon et la Grande-Bretagne par ses dominions, avec leurs navires de guerre modernes, sont de taille à livrer bataille.

Déclarations de guerre et instructions : la mise en œuvre des alliances

Néanmoins, de fin juin au début du mois d'août 1914, les réseaux d'alliances et de traités se sont mis en place. La guerre est immédiatement mondiale, comme le montrent les opérations navales et militaires dans le Pacifique, mais il s'agit avant tout d'une guerre européenne, les nationaux doivent donc rentrer dans leur métropole. L'amiral Von Spee, commandant la flotte allemande d'Extrême-Orient, alors à Ponape en Micronésie, est averti le 31 juillet du « danger de guerre menaçant ». Le 2 août, lui parvient l'ordre de mobilisation contre la Russie et la France et celui de regagner l'Allemagne au plus tôt avec ses navires. Si l'Australie et la Nouvelle-Zélande sont prévenues dès le jour de la déclaration de guerre de l'Allemagne à la France, le 3 août 1914, puis de l'Angleterre à l'Allemagne, le 5 août 1914, la Nouvelle-Calédonie ne l'est officiellement que le 5 août, en même temps que lui parvient l'ordre de mobilisation, les EFO apprennent la nouvelle le 9 août. Le Japon déclare la guerre à l'Allemagne le 24 août. Une guerre navale courte va alors opposer les forces de l'Entente à l'Allemagne. Les opérations de prise de possession des colonies allemandes se déroulent selon un processus défini à l'avance entre la Grande-Bretagne, la France et le Japon et confirmé en janvier 1914. Lorsque le *MONTCALM* reçoit la nouvelle de la déclaration de guerre entre la France et l'Allemagne, le 7 août 1914 dans la nuit, le contre-amiral Huguet est contraint d'obéir aux « instructions en cas de guerre » édictées en 1912, qu'il a en sa possession. Il se met donc dans les dispositions de combat et se rend directement aux îles Fidji pour y recevoir les instructions britanniques. L'expédition franco-britannique se met en place avec trois objectifs : défendre les colonies françaises et britanniques contre une éventuelle attaque des navires allemands, poursuivre les navires ennemis, nuire aux possessions allemandes océaniennes et si possible en prendre possession. L'escadre a l'ordre de s'emparer des possessions allemandes du Samoa puis de Nouvelle-Guinée puis de rechercher la flotte de Von Spee aux Marshall et aux Carolines afin d'enlever aux Allemands toute base et tout moyen d'action dans le Pacifique. Elle doit aussi couler ou s'emparer du plus grand nombre possible de navires allemands qui présentent une menace de taille contre les convois alliés qui transportent les troupes et le ravitaillement vers l'Angleterre ou la France.

Le *MONTCALM* arrive à Nouméa le 20 août 1914 ; il fait la jonction avec la division néo-zélandaise dirigée par le colonel Logan arrivée le même jour, constituée des croiseurs *PSYCHÉ*, *PYRAMUS* et *PHILOMEL* et des deux transports de troupes

MONOWAÏ et *MOERONI* transportant 1383 volontaires néo-zélandais. Le lendemain, la division australienne du contre-amiral Patey composée des croiseurs *AUSTRALIA* et *MELBOURNE*, les rejoint. Cette division rentre d'une tournée d'opérations dans les possessions allemandes de Nouvelle-Guinée où elle a tenté sans succès de détruire le poste de T.S.F. de Rabaul en Nouvelle-Bretagne. Deux vapeurs charbonniers venus tout exprès de Nouvelle-Zélande, via l'Australie, ravitaillent les navires.

La prise de possession du Samoa allemand

Le 23 août, la division franco-australasienne part pour Suva, après avoir fait des tirs d'accord sur l'îlot Tareti et reçu le livret des signaux pour les flottes alliées. Retardés de vingt-quatre heures par l'échouage du *MONOWAÏ*, les navires arrivent à Suva le 26 août au matin. Les petits bâtiments néo-zélandais vont y charbonner. La flotte repart le lendemain et arrive en vue d'Apia le 30 août[4]. A l'aube, craignant d'être attaqués par les Allemands, tous les bâtiments se mettent en position de combat tous feux allumés. A 6 heures, ils sont devant Apia, la *PSYCHÉ* les a devancés en battant pavillon parlementaire. Le contre-amiral Huguet signale à l'amiral Patey l'importance de procéder au dragage de la passe par crainte de mines sous-marines, avant d'y faire entrer la *PSYCHÉ* qui peut alors partir en avant en battant pavillon parlementaire. Elle peut ainsi avertir de l'absence de tout navire ennemi dès 7 heures 45. A 8 heures 20, une embarcation se détache pour porter au gouverneur d'Apia une lettre de sommation demandant la reddition des Samoa. Aucun mouvement n'est signalé sur la plage. Sur une hauteur à l'ouest du port s'élève une fumée d'incendie laissant penser qu'il pourrait s'agir d'une destruction volontaire de la station de T.S.F. par les Allemands. A 10 heures, le parlementaire est de retour pour signaler l'absence du gouverneur des Samoa dont le représentant n'approuve pas la reddition mais ne s'oppose pas au débarquement des Alliés. Il confirme également l'absence de mines dans le chenal et dans le port d'Apia. Malgré cette assurance, l'amiral Patey continue de faire draguer les eaux de la passe et du port. A 10 heures 40, deux embarcations de l'*AUSTRALIA* accompagnées de la *PSYCHE* entrent dans le port. Elles sont ensuite suivies par les transports, les charbonniers et deux petits croiseurs. De 12 heures 45 à 14 heures 45, les troupes néo-zélandaises débarquent sans incident notable tandis que les croiseurs *AUSTRALIA*, *MELBOURNE* et *MONTCALM* demeurent en observation devant Apia durant la journée du 30 et la matinée du 31, tenant la mer à petite vitesse pendant la nuit. Le 31 août au matin, le contre-amiral Huguet descend à terre en compagnie de quelques officiers. Il fait visiter au colonel Logan le club anglais et la mission catholique, vide des pères maristes français dont il avait apprécié l'hospitalité lors de son passage pour rejoindre Nouméa quelques jours auparavant. La bonne entente entre résidents étrangers du Samoa est confirmée par une pétition reçue par le nouveau gouverneur. Le contre-amiral Huguet raconte ces moments au ministre de la Marine : « *Je dois vous signaler l'ordre et la propreté parfaite que j'ai remarqués à terre, preuve de la bonne administration allemande ;- du large on voit de magnifiques plantations de cocotiers ;- enfin le Colonel Logan m'a montré une pétition en faveur du docteur Schulz, ancien Gouverneur allemand, son prédécesseur le remerciant de la protection accordée à tous les étrangers sans distinction.- cette pétition était signée de tous les résidents étrangers, anglais et français compris.*[5] »

L'occupation de l'île par les Néo-Zélandais se passe sans difficultés majeures et sans coups de feu. Il y a près de 200 Allemands qui ne disposent que d'environ 80 fusils. Ils se sont enfuis dans l'intérieur de l'île en abandonnant leurs emplois et leurs maisons dès que les navires de la division alliée ont été en vue. Dans le but de nuire, ils ont ouvert les portes de la prison à de dangereux condamnés chinois. Les marins néo-zélandais forcent les portes des bureaux et des édifices fermés mais la poste ne livre que 400 marks en timbres. La ville d'Apia et ses environs sont occupés par les Néo-Zélandais du colonel Logan qui prend les fonctions de gouverneur du Samoa. Il fait afficher la proclamation confirmant la prise de possession du Samoa allemand par les Britanniques et les règles d'occupation qui débutent par : « *The New Zealand Government of His Britanic Majesty King George Fifth now occupy for His Majesty all the German Territories situated in the Islands of the Samoa Group.*[6] » Il se montre inquiet de la libération des Chinois et surtout du manque de vivres et de possibilités d'approvisionnement car les travailleurs chinois immigrés dont le contrat stipule la fourniture de riz régulière, risquent de se révolter. Le contre-amiral Huguet offre alors dix tonnes de farine qui sont refusées par l'amiral Patey, pressé de repartir pour Fidji le jour même. Les croiseurs *PSYCHE*, *PYRAMUS*, *PHILOMEL* et les deux transports restent pour achever le débarquement du matériel et des vivres destinés au corps expéditionnaire néo-zélandais qui restera à Apia.

La poursuite des opérations conjointes

Le 31 août à midi, la division composée de l'*AUSTRALIA*, du *MONTCALM* et du *MELBOURNE* quitte Apia pour faire route sur Suva, où elle arrive le 2 septembre. Puis, le *MONTCALM* rejoint Nouméa où il rejoint l'escadre australasienne, du 5 au 10 septembre. Les navires allemands de Von Spee ayant été signalés, les alliés quittent Nouméa pour rejoindre à nouveau Apia le 14 septembre. Devant l'absence de danger, l'escadre est déroutée pour aller s'emparer de Friedrich-Wilhelmshafen, chef-lieu de la colonie allemande de la terre de l'empereur Guillaume (Madang) au nord-est de la grande île de Papouasie. L'expédition appareille de Rabaul le 22 septembre et fait route sur la Nouvelle-Guinée, où elle séjourne du 26 septembre au 1er octobre. Le *MONTCALM*, joint à la division d'Australie, séjourne à Rabaul. Pendant ce temps, le *SYDNEY* est en opérations à Angaur, aux îles Palau, pour y détruire le poste de TSF allemand. La division reprend alors la route de Rabaul qu'elle rejoint le 26 septembre. Le 1er octobre, le *MONTCALM* se joint de nouveau à l'*AUSTRALIA*, l'*ENCOUNTER* et le *SYDNEY* en vue de pousser jusqu'aux Carolines et aux Marshall à la recherche des navires allemands de l'amiral Von Spee. Ils font route par l'ouest de la Nouvelle-Irlande, mais devant l'annonce du bombardement de Papeete le 22 septembre, et de la concentration supposée de la flotte allemande en Amérique du Sud, l'opération est annulée après avoir appris des Japonais que ceux-ci n'ont rien trouvé. La division franco australienne rentre alors à Rabaul le 2 octobre. Les Japonais confirment ces informations et annoncent qu'une division nippone est passée à Jaluit, le principal atoll des îles Marshall, sans trouver trace de navire ennemi. Le 3 octobre, les navires de guerre vont reconnaître les passages entre les archipels de Samoa et de Fidji.

L'escadre franco-australienne a rejoint Suva le 12 octobre, après que l'amirauté anglaise ait décidé d'en faire le centre d'opérations navales du Pacifique en lieu et place de Rabaul qui deviendra centre d'opérations japonais. La division d'Australie et le *MONTCALM* couvriront l'Australie, la Nouvelle-Zélande et la Nouvelle-Calédonie. Des Fidji, la division va partir à la recherche des navires allemands de Von Spee. Du 17 au 23 octobre, le *MONTCALM*, l'*AUSTRALIA* et l'*ENCOUNTER* se rendent sur la côte nord-ouest de Savaï au Samoa occidental puis aux îles Wallis et Futuna. Le reste de l'escadre australienne occupe successivement les centres de colonisation allemands, le 17 octobre, de Käwieng à la pointe nord-ouest de l'île principale du Nouveau-Mecklenbourg, le 27 octobre de Namatanaï, au centre de la même île et de Manus le 22 novembre. Les forces australiennes se retrouvent de nouveau au Kaiser Wilhelsland. Elles occupent Eitape, le 4 décembre, Angoram, le 12 décembre, et enfin Morobe le 11 janvier 1915. Par ailleurs, la grande île de Bougainville a été occupée le 9 décembre. En pratique, la plupart de ces opérations maritimes sont exécutées par des navires appartenant aux différentes escadres, qui se rejoignent ou se dispersent selon l'objectif. Toutefois, ces dernières opérations se font alors que le *MONTCALM* n'y participe plus. En effet, à la fin du mois d'octobre, la division alliée du Pacifique a éclaté : le croiseur anglais *PYRAMUS* a quitté l'Australie pour rejoindre Singapour d'où il escortera les transports français jusqu'au canal de Suez. Après un dernier séjour à Papeete où le contre-amiral Huguet enquête, fin novembre et début décembre 1914, au sujet d'un conflit entre le commandant des troupes à terre, le lieutenant de vaisseau Destremau et le gouverneur Fawtier, le navire français regagne son port d'attache. Rattaché à la 3ème escadre, le *MONTCALM* termine la guerre à la surveillance du canal de Suez[7].

L'expédition franco-britannique a eu besoin de l'aide japonaise pour assurer la défense navale contre l'escadre de Von Spee et la protection de ses transports de troupes indiens et australiens ainsi que pour la prise de possession des archipels allemands du Pacifique qui a nécessité, elle aussi, la surveillance et l'aide effective de la marine japonaise. De son côté, le Japon, conformément aux instructions en cas de guerre, s'est emparé de Jaluit aux Marshall le 3 octobre, et, dans les Carolines, de Ponape et de Yap le 7 octobre, de Palau le 8 octobre, d'Angor le 9, des îles Truk le 12, de Saïpan le 14, de Erota le 21, de Nauru le 6 novembre. Dès la fin de l'année 1914, les Allemands ne présentent plus aucun danger dans le Pacifique, leurs colonies océaniennes sont toutes passées aux mains des Australasiens ou des Japonais. Par ailleurs, le 7 décembre, les Japonais ont pris possession de la base navale de Tsing Tao et de la ville de Kiao Tchéou, situées à l'extrémité de la pointe de la péninsule de la province du Shantoung, en Chine. Ils peuvent alors, le long de la ligne de chemin de fer construite par les Allemands, entamer leur progression vers l'intérieur de la Chine. Pour la coalition britannique, française et japonaise en Océanie, les objectifs sont atteints, la prise de possession des colonies allemandes dans le Pacifique est terminée. Dans ces opérations, il est à noter que la ligne de l'équateur semble avoir été fixée comme limite sud à l'expansion japonaise puisque les navires nippons ne s'aventurent guère au-delà, tout comme l'escadre franco-britannique ne franchit pas sa limite nord. En outre, l'ampleur des conquêtes nippones dépasse le contenu des accords entre les deux puissances, au profit du Japon.

Conclusions : l'Océanie depuis 1915, un « lac australasien » ?

Le 4 septembre 1914, l'amiral Patey fait parvenir à l'amirauté britannique un rapport de quatre pages intitulé « *EXPEDITION TO SAMOA* [8] ». On constate que le rôle du *MONTCALM* y est défini dès le départ de Suva où le navire amiral prend sa place sur la même ligne que le *MELBOURNE*. En cas d'engagement avec l'ennemi, le navire français combat sur la même ligne et en même temps que ce dernier et que l'*AUSTRALIA*. Mais lors de l'attaque d'Apia, il n'est qu'un simple observateur. Ainsi se justifie la phrase de l'amiral Patey qui utilise l'expression « *Assisted by Rear Admiral A.L.M. HUGUEST of* « *MONTCALM*. »[9] Le commandement de l'opération de prise de possession du Samoa allemand a été effectué par le colonel Logan, à la tête de la division néo-zélandaise.

Ses croiseurs sont portés en avant, suivis du *MONTCALM* et des croiseurs australiens *AUSTRALIA* et *MELBOURNE* fermant la file selon l'ordre protocolaire. Lors du débarquement à Apia, les troupes néo-zélandaises débarquent, alors que les Français et les Australiens demeurent en observation devant Apia. La reddition allemande est remise au colonel Logan, représentant la Nouvelle-Zélande, qui restera résident des Samoa (l'administrateur pour la durée de la guerre, conformément aux instructions) jusqu'à la décision du traité de Versailles. Conformément aux ordres de l'Amirauté à Londres, mais aussi à l'entente d'avant guerre, le navire-amiral français tout comme la division australienne n'ont donc eu qu'un rôle d'assistance à la flotte néo-zélandaise pour la prise des Samoa.

Mais une certaine ambiguïté de l'attitude australasienne est relevée par la France : « J'ai l'honneur de vous informer que j'ai reçu votre lettre n° 22 du 1er février 1915 dans laquelle vous me transmettez une lettre de remerciements de l'Amirauté anglaise. Je suis très sensible à ces remerciements et je n'ai eu de mon côté qu'à me louer de mes rapports avec l'Amiral Patey ainsi que des facilités de toutes sortes que je trouvais auprès de lui, je vous en ai rendu compte en temps convenable. Cependant, je remarque que l'Amiral ne parle aucunement de la présence du MONTCALM à APIA au moment du débarquement des Néo-Zélandais, pas plus que de son séjour en Nouvelle-Guinée soit à Rabaul au moment où se discutait entre les deux gouvernements Australien et Allemand la question de remise de la souveraineté, soit à la prise de possession de Frederich Wilhem Wielhenshafen. Si je soulève cette question c'est que j'ai cru remarquer une tendance chez les Australiens à faire le silence le plus absolu sur la coopération française. En résumé, le MONTCALM a pris part à l'occupation d'APIA les 30 et 31 août 1914. A séjourné à Rabaul (Nouvelle-Bretagne) notamment du 15 au 22 septembre 1914 pendant que se discutait à Herbertshohe (près de Rabaul, Nouvelle-Bretagne) avec le Gouvernement Allemand la question de la remise de la souveraineté des possessions allemandes. La soumission du Gouverneur est du 17 septembre 1914. Enfin, il a pris part à l'expédition de Frederich Wilhemshafen et à la prise de cette localité de 24 septembre 1914. »[10] Le commandant du MONTCALM, en stigmatisant le refus permanent de l'amiral anglais d'associer la

France à la prise de possession conjointe des colonies allemandes du Pacifique a montré à quel point l'hégémonie australasienne est en train de grandir dans le Pacifique Sud. Lorsqu'il s'agit de répartir ces prises de guerre, la France est d'office exclue du partage. C'est bien le manque de réaction des autorités françaises aux avertissements du contre-amiral Huguet qui permet aux Néo-Zélandais et aux Australiens de considérer que le Pacifique Sud est, depuis la fin de l'année 1914, une zone australasienne, tout comme les Japonais ont la certitude d'avoir renforcé leur « glacis protecteur » autour de leur archipel. Les zones d'influence des nouvelles puissances du Pacifique Sud sont en place dès la fin de l'année 1914, et ne sont pas modifiées par les traités à la fin de la guerre.

Durant les opérations conjointes de prise de possession des colonies allemandes et lors de la recherche de la flotte de l'amiral Von Spee, Français et Britanniques, Australiens et Néo-Zélandais ont coopéré sur le plan militaire. La collaboration avec les Japonais n'a pas été de même nature car ceux-ci n'ont pas toujours fourni les renseignements en leur possession et ils ont mené des actions isolées à leur propre avantage. Il est certain que les forces en présence étaient difficilement comparables mais les traités passés dix ans plus tôt n'ont pas toujours été respectés et certains en tirent profit. Ainsi, lorsque Rabaul devient leur centre d'opérations, les Japonais se trouvent singulièrement rapprochés d'Honolulu. De la même façon, la prise de Jaluit leur donne une excellente base d'opération en Micronésie. Le Pacifique est déjà sous influence anglo-saxonne et le Japon, s'il semble avoir un rôle mineur, a atteint ses objectifs sur sa façade Est qui est désormais à l'abri. Il peut donc consacrer l'ensemble de ses forces à l'Asie, la Chine, plus particulièrement.

Les quatre mois de guerre maritime contre les Allemands ont forgé entre Français et Australasiens une culture de guerre dans laquelle l'effort d'aide, d'assistance et d'amitié va bien au-delà des signatures au bas d'un traité d'alliance. Ainsi, au retour des opérations conjointes, lors du passage du MONTCALM à Singapour, les Anglais ont mis à disposition des Français à terre, des hommes, du matériel et des vivres qui ont fait l'admiration des marins français qui venaient de subir d'importantes restrictions au cours des mois écoulés. L'arrière-plan reste l'efficacité de l'assistance que les Français attendent des Britanniques dans les relations entre puissances coloniales pour surveiller les abords des îles et de la côte malaise jusqu'en Cochinchine et mettre au pas d'éventuelles révoltes indigènes dans les colonies françaises, ce qu'ils ne manqueront pas de faire dans le condominium franco-britannique des Nouvelles-Hébrides en 1917. Les amiraux Patey et Huguet reçoivent leurs ordres, l'un de l'Amirauté britannique, le second du ministère français de la Marine. Ils ont tous deux une latitude d'action, dans la limite des « instructions en cas de guerre » qu'ils détiennent avant le conflit et qui ont été confirmées et complétées dès les premières semaines de la guerre. Beaucoup de ces opérations montrent le peu de préparation effective et surtout le manque de renseignements des flottes alliées vouées à coopérer. En effet, si les marins ont une culture de géostratèges dont la vision prime pour eux, ce sont les gouvernements, avec les états-majors métropolitains qui imposent leur politique. L'impréparation à la collaboration maritime de guerre est manifeste. Par exemple, les marins français, néo-zélandais et australiens ignorent la quantité de navires allemands dans le Pacifique, qu'ils détruisent au lieu de les capturer pour les militariser à leur profit. Et surtout, leurs objectifs sont différents : ainsi, « Dès le 30 septembre, le vice-amiral Huguet informe le consul général de France à Sydney à titre confidentiel que les Anglais ont l'intention de cesser de faire de Rabaul une base d'opération, lieu pourtant particulièrement bien choisi en raison de son emplacement stratégique. »[11] Les Australasiens tiennent à marquer leur suprématie vis à vis des Français car, pour eux, l'Océanie est un « lac anglo-saxon » depuis les années 1840. Tout en étant devenus alliés, Anglais et Français restent imprégnés de leurs conflits politiques anciens. Ainsi, pendant le séjour de l'escadre britannique à Nouméa, fin août 1914, alors qu'en ville, les volontaires néo-zélandais sont fêtés et choyés par les Nouméens, l'amiral Patey et les commandants de croiseurs, le chef d'état-major de l'amiral et son aide de camp sont « retenus pour des raisons de service » et ne se rendent pas à l'invitation du gouverneur Repiquet qui a organisé une réception en leur honneur : volontairement, ils font savoir qu'ils occultent la France. Ce geste de grande défiance, de portée diplomatique évidente, est-il en rapport avec la situation aux Nouvelles-Hébrides ? En effet, le 6 août 1914, la France et l'Angleterre ont passé un accord figeant la situation pour toute la durée de la guerre.

Le contre-amiral Huguet, plus âgé que l'amiral Patey, a dénoncé « la nervosité » de celui-ci. Il lui a surtout reproché d'avoir perdu du temps et de s'être dispersé dans la poursuite d'objectifs secondaires : « . . .en particulier, si des Samoa, au début de septembre, nous avions été faire un tour aux Marshall, nous y aurions trouvé les Allemands et que ce serait une affaire réglée qui eût prévenu le coup de Tahiti et rendu la liberté à tout le monde. » Pour lui, la politique de la métropole anglaise prime dans le Pacifique : « l'Amiral Patey a été tenu en bride par l'Amirauté de Londres et celle-ci est des plus attentionnée et prévenante vis-à-vis de l'opinion publique australienne. » [12] Ce souci de l'opinion publique australienne a sans doute prévalu lorsque l'Amirauté a retenu les Fidji comme centre d'opération. Nouméa, choisi au tout début de la guerre, est pourtant bien plus central en Océanie que Suva, assez excentré par rapport à Sydney ou Auckland. De Nouvelle-Calédonie, toute division navale aurait été mieux placée pour faire face aux événements, Nouméa ayant comme atouts supplémentaires un port mieux abrité que celui des Fidji et un climat plus sain. Mais au plus haut niveau, il importe de ne pas mécontenter les dominions du Pacifique qui envoient des troupes en renfort de l'armée britannique en Europe et du ravitaillement pour les Alliés.

Si les Français et les Anglais ont appris pour la première fois à se connaître et à s'apprécier, le contre-amiral Huguet ne manque cependant pas de noter que l'amiral anglais Patey a occupé la Nouvelle-Guinée « au compte des Australiens et par les gens de l'Australie », que « le gouvernement de Nouvelle-Zélande au moyen des volontaires néo-zélandais » a pris possession des Samoa. Il ajoute « Je me demande si les Australiens et les Néo-Zélandais n'y verront pas un modèle ». Le commandant du MONTCALM, en stigmatisant le refus permanent de l'amiral anglais d'associer la France à la prise de possession conjointe, même si elle est restée modeste, des colonies allemandes du Pacifique montre à quel point l'hégémonie australasienne est en train de grandir dans le Pacifique sud. Ce que le capitaine de frégate Henry de Villeneuve, commandant le KERSAINT note également en 1917 : « J'ai appris que certains de nos alliés faisaient courir le bruit que l'absence de nos navires en Océanie n'était que le prologue de l'abandon de nos colonies dans le Pacifique. » Pour les Australasiens, ce qui se passe en Océanie n'a pas le même impact que ce qui se passe en métropole. Pour eux, la Nouvelle-Calédonie est un avant-poste de l'Australie, la France peut la perdre, mais pas l'Australasie, ce qui est encore vrai aujourd'hui. La Grande-Bretagne est d'ores et déjà dans une dimension de géopolitique mondiale et les Britanniques tiennent à montrer qu'ils attachent beaucoup d'importance à leur zone d'influence. De nos jours encore, les manuels français d'histoire ne citent pas la participation de la France à la prise de possession des colonies allemandes d'Océanie en 1914, ni le nom du contre-amiral Huguet et de son navire, alors que les Australiens et les Néo-Zélandais ont utilisé cet épisode de la Grande Guerre pour renforcer leurs liens nationaux.

Pendant la campagne de prise de possession des colonies allemandes du Pacifique, les traités d'alliance ont été respectés, la France y a joué un rôle de soutien et d'assistance, la Nouvelle-Calédonie a bien été le relais de l'État français dans le Pacifique. Nouméa a été, pour un temps très court, le centre des opérations interalliées en Océanie. La présence de la flotte australasienne en août 1914 et de la flotte japonaise à Nouméa en décembre 1914 montre aux Calédoniens que leur île a une importance réelle auprès des forces de l'Entente. Même s'il faut reconnaître que, sans la France, les colonies allemandes auraient été prises, les Calédoniens se sont donc imprégné dès le début, d'une culture de guerre qui ne cessera que quatre années plus tard. En raison de la position géographique favorable de la Nouvelle-Calédonie, cette situation, si peu de temps qu'elle ait duré, préfigure ainsi ce qui se passera lors de la Seconde Guerre mondiale. Les colonies européennes d'Océanie découvrent que la notion de guerre totale exige la mobilisation de tous les moyens en hommes en argent et en matériel et recouvre des réalités différentes. Toutefois, Samoa comme les autres archipels océaniens, sauf l'Australasie et la Nouvelle-Calédonie, reste une zone éloignée de l'Europe, en dehors des préoccupations du siècle et des réseaux mondiaux comme en témoigne le temps mis à connaître la guerre. Il est possible d'ajouter que, si les États sont déjà dans la guerre globale, tous n'ont pas encore la volonté politique d'anéantir l'adversaire. La prise de possession conjointe des colonies allemandes du Grand Océan a surtout démontré la suprématie de la marine de guerre britannique et les insuffisances, voire l'indifférence de la France. C'est aussi pour elle un échec parmi ceux du début de la guerre, aux conséquences mesurables dès 1915 et lors de la signature des traités de paix. Après cet épisode d'à peine trois mois en 1914, la France et la Grande-Bretagne conservent des forces navales modestes dans le Pacifique sud-ouest, juste nécessaires à l'accompagnement des convois. L'essentiel est ailleurs, sur le nord du Pacifique, en Extrême-Orient, en Chine et sur la côte ouest des États-Unis. La prise de Samoa n'aura été que la préfiguration du choc entre États-nations par le désir de domination et d'occupation. La « justice » du vainqueur s'impose : les mandats donnés à la Nouvelle-Zélande lui permettent déjà de s'affirmer comme puissance indépendante de la Grande-Bretagne. Pour les Néo-Zélandais, l'épisode de la prise de possession du Samoa allemand, quelques mois avant la défaite transcendée de Gallipoli contribue à la naissance d'une conscience nationale.

Bibliographie

Beaumont, Joan. *Australian War 1914-18*. Sydney: Allen & Unwin, 1995.

Boubin-Boyer, Sylvette. *De la Première Guerre mondiale en Océanie – Les guerres de tous les Calédoniens 1914-1919*. Lille : Diffusion Septentrion, Presses Universitaires, Thèse à la carte, 2 tomes, 2003.

Dufour, Jean-Louis et VAÏSSE, Maurice. *La guerre au XXe siècle*. Paris : Hachette Supérieur, 1993.

Fremeaux, Jacques. *Les colonies dans la Grande Guerre Combats et épreuves des peuples d'Outre-Mer*. Paris : Soteca 14-18 éditions, 2006.

Hiery, Hermann Joseph. *The Neglected War*. Honolulu: University of Hawaii Press, 1995.

Keegan, John. *La Première Guerre mondiale* (1998). Londres : Perrin éditions, 2003.

Notes

1 « L'Entente Cordiale » entre la Grande-Bretagne et la France : conventions franco-britanniques de 1904 (Terre-Neuve, Siam, Nouvelles-Hébrides), conférence d'Algésiras en 1906, affaire d'Agadir en 1911; accord militaire anglo-japonais de neutralité réciproque en 1902, reconduit en 1911 ; traité commercial anglo-américain de 1911.
2 D'après Dufour Jean-Louis et Vaïsse Maurice, *La guerre au XXe siècle*, Hachette supérieur, 1993, p. 20.
3 Depuis 1899, l'archipel est divisé entre l'Allemagne et les États-Unis qui conservent la partie orientale ou Samoa Américaines.
4 Ou le 31 selon que l'on considère la date par rapport au méridien de changement de date.
5 Service historique de la Défense (SHD), SHM/SS ED 132, Contre-amiral Huguet au ministre de la Marine à Paris, *Opération sur les Samoa*, n°89M, 04/09/1914.
6 SHD-SHM/ SS ED 132, *Proclamation*, signée par le colonel Robert Logan, Commanding the Occupying Force.
7 SHD-SHM/SS ED 130. Chemise '*Correspondance expédiée*' 1914 - 1920.
8 SHD-SHM/SS ED 132, *EXPEDITION TO SAMOA : I. FORCE AVAILABLE : Enemy ships, Intentions, cruising order, Speed of convoy, Alternation of course, Time to be kept, Lights, Signals at sea and in harbour, Enemy sighted, II. APPROACH TO AND ATTACK ON SAMOA : Enemy-Men-of-War at APIA, Arrival off APIA, Attack on APIA, Disembarkation of troups*, Rapport du 04/09/1914.
9 SHD-SHM/SS ED 132, *EXPEDITION TO SAMOA, op. cit.*
10 SHD-SHM/SS ED 130, Ministre de la Marine au ministre des Affaires Étrangères, 30/03/1917.
11 SHD-SHM/SS ED 132, n°88A, secret *MONTCALM* à Consul général de France à Sydney du 30 Septembre 1914.
12 SHD-SHM/SS ED 132, n°99M, Contre-amiral Huguet au ministre de la Marine, *Mouvements du MONTCALM joint à la division d'Australie du 26 Septembre au 10 Octobre*, 13/10/1914.

Prochaine page:

Chronologie de la prise de possession des colonies allemandes du Pacifique par les flottes australasienne / française / japonaise

7 août 1914 : le *MONTCALM* est informé par TSF de la déclaration de guerre

24 août 1914 : le Japon déclare la guerre à l'Allemagne

Date	*Prise (ville – colonie allemande)*	*Flottes*	*Attribution puis mandat*
30/31 août 1914	Apia (Samoa)	Franco-australasienne	Nouvelle-Zélande
11 septembre 1914	Herbertshohe (Nouvelle-Poméranie	Franco-australasienne	Australie
13 septembre 1914	Rabaul (Nlle-Poméranie)	Franco-australasienne	Australie
22 septembre 1914	bombardement de Papeete	Allemande	Australie
24 septembre 1914	Friedrich-Wilhemshaffen (Nouvelle-Guinée)	Franco-australasienne	Japon
3 octobre 1914	Jaluit (Carolines)	Japonaise	Japon
7 octobre 1914	Yap (Carolines)	Nippo-australasienne	Japon
7 octobre 1914	Ponape (Carolines)	Japonaise	Japon
8 octobre 1914	Koror (Palau – Carolines)	Japonaise	Japon
9 octobre 1914	Angaur (Palau – Carolines)	Nippo-australasienne	Japon
12 octobre 1914	Truk (Carolines)	Australasienne	Japon
14 octobre 1914	Saipan (Mariannes)	Japonaise	Japon
17 octobre 1914	Käwieng (New Mecklenburg)	Australasienne	Australie
24 octobre 1914	Rota (Mariannes)	Japonaise	Japon
27 octobre 1914	Namatanaï (New Mecklenburg)	Australasienne	Australie
10 novembre 1914	Tsing-Tao (Chine)	Japonaise	
22 novembre 1914	Manus (Nouvelle-Bretagne)	Franco-australasienne	Australie
9 décembre 1914	Kieta (Bougainville-Salomon)	Australasienne	Australie
12 décembre 1914	Angoram (Nouvelle-Guinée)	Australasienne	Australie
11 janvier 1915	Morobe (Nouvelle- Guinée)	Japonaise	Australie

The Poems of Private William E. Scott

Dominique Lataste

Private William E. Scott served in the New Zealand armed forces during the second world war, being based in New Caledonia before going on to fight in the Solomon Islands campaign. While in New Caledonia Private Scott wrote a number of poems about his experience, poems which reflect his perceptions of New Caledonia and, more broadly, of his army experience. This chapter's analysis of Private Scott's poems, and what they reveal about his perceptions and experience, is followed by three of the poems themselves.

Durant la Seconde guerre mondiale, le soldat William E. Scott a fait parti des forces armées néo-zélandaises basées en Nouvelle-Calédonie avant les combats aux îles Salomon. Au cours de son séjour en Nouvelle-Calédonie, le soldat Scott a rédigé quelques poèmes relatant son expérience. Ces poèmes reflètent ses sentiments à propos de la Nouvelle-Calédonie et d'une manière plus générale son expérience dans l'armée. Ce texte tente une analyse de ces poèmes, suivie de la publication de trois d'entre eux.

Introduction

After William Scott's death in 1999, his daughter, Rewa Clough, sold his poems at a garage sale. The poems were purchased by Mr Auckram, who, realising their historical value, donated them to the Hocken Library with a copy to Dr Tom Brooking, of the Department of History, at the University of Otago, in Dunedin.

In December 2006 Professor Frédéric Angleviel – of the Department of History, University of New Caledonia, in Noumea – having a look through the archives of the Hocken Library, found poems describing the poet's stay in New Caledonia while stationed there as a soldier. Professor Angleviel thought the poems were worth publishing. As a result, the poems were translated and a bilingual edition (English and French)[1] was published in commemoration of Anzac Day (2007), in partial tribute to the Kiwis who protected the Caledonian shores and gave their blood to regain control of the Solomon Islands from the Japanese.

The poet

We do not know a very great deal about the life of Private William Scott. Some research that has been carried out indicates that his occupation was that of a 'boilermaker'.

The context of the poems

During World War II, Private Scott belonged to the second NZEFIP: that is, the Second New Zealand Expeditionary Force, based in the Pacific with forces from the United States. Private Scott's poems relate to his stay in Fiji, New Caledonia and the Solomon Islands. In the archives, the poems come with an itinerary and the translation of a captured enemy diary, belonging to a Japanese soldier who was one of a group of ten men killed on Stirling Island (in the Solomons) on 8 November 1943.

A detailed itinerary, as given below, shows where Private Scott stayed while serving in the military overseas.

Military itinerary

43380 Private W. E. Scott 2nd NZEFIP	16.4.41
Entered Camp Trentham, NZ	17.4.41
1ST Final leave	7.5.41-17.5.41
2ND Final leave	5.8.41-13.8.41
Departed Trentham	17.8.41
Embarked S.S. 'Rangitira', Auckland NZ	18.8.41
Arrived Suva, Fiji	21.8.41
Arrived Namaka Camp (29th Bw.D. support boy)	21.8.41
Duty at Momi Bay (coast guard)	4.9.41-18.9.41

Arrived Samabula Camp training centre	18.9.41
Arrived Ballantyne's school, Lami	5.1.42
Arrived Dilkusha Mission, Nausori	19.1.42
Arrived Nasese Camp	31.3.42
Embarked US A.T. 'President Coolidge'	30.6.42
Departed Suva, Fiji	3.7.42
Arrived Papakura Camp, NZ	6.7.42
Furlough	9.7.42-29.7.42
Arrived Hunua Falls	25.9.42
Arrived Karapiro public works camp	7.10.42
Kaimai Range (manoeuvres)	19.10.42-27.10.42
Leave	3.11.42-12.11.42
Departed Karapiro 0350Hrs	28.12.42
Embarked U.S.S. 'West Point', Auckland	28.12.42
Departed Auckland, NZ 1000	29.12.42
Arrived New Caledonia	31.12.42
Disembarked U.S.S. 'West Point' 0430	4.1.43
Arrived Nepoui Valley 1600	4.1.43
Arrived Ouameni Camp 1630	11.2.43
52nd Evacuation Hospital (American)	12.2.43-26.2.43
Ouameni Camp	26.2.43-19.3.43
Tontouta aerodrome (Guard Betty)	19.3.43-29.3.43
Ouameni Camp	29.3.43-27.4.43
Camp Mebrae, Noumea (wharfers)	27.4.43-11.5.43
H Q Boy	June 1943
B Boy	July 1943
8th B de H Q Boulouparis p. et M.A.C.	30.7.43
Thio (holiday), Canala, Nakety	4.8.43-11.8.43
Embarked (PH18) U.S.S. 'President Jackson'	2.8.43
Departed Noumea, New Caledonia	4.9.43
Arrived Vila, New Hebrides	6.9.43
Departed Vila	12.9.43
Arrived Guadalcanal, Solomon Islands	14.9.43
Departed Guadalcanal LC1 61	25.10.43
Arrived Blanche Harbour, Treasury Islands	27.10 43
Hospital, 7th Field (Stirling Island; Mono Island)	25.11.43-14.12.43
HQ Boy 29th (Mono Island)	15.12.43
Embarked U.S.S. 'President Monroe'	25.4.44
Departed Blanche Harbour, Treasury Islands	26.4.44

Arrived Noumea, New Caledonia	29.4.44
Base Training Depot	30.4.44
Arrived Dumbea Transit Camp	5.6.44
Embarked P.H.I. U.S.S. 'Tryon', Noumea	6.6.44
Arrived Papakura Camp N.Z.	9.6.44
Arrived Dunedin 1630	17.6.44

Private Scott's war

Private Scott left New Zealand in 1941 and returned in 1944. He stayed for less than a year in New Caledonia on his first visit – from 31 December 1942 until 4 September 1943. He made a second visit to New Caledonia, returning for a month – from 29 April 1944 until 6 June 1944 ('D Day' in Europe) – before returning to New Zealand. The rest of the war Private Scott was in Fiji and the Solomon Islands, as well as New Zealand.

New Caledonia was used as a 'land-based aircraft carrier' by the Allies during World War II. Along with American and Australian soldiers, 13383 New Zealanders protected the north of New Caledonia. The New Zealand Division was motorised, with 3377 vehicles. Officers took part in TWETs – Technical Exercises Without Troops – while the men trained intensively to prepare for battle.

Life in the camps was far from idyllic as propaganda described it. Facilities (for sport competitions, swimming-pools, picnics, and so on) existed everywhere. The main source of entertainment was to go down to Noumea in a truck on bad roads. The 'Kiwi News newspaper' was far from being neutral on different aspects of the soldiers' life. In that respect, Private Scott's poems give us detailed pieces related to the soldiers' daily life.

The New Zealand presence in New Caledonia comprised a substantial proportion of New Zealand's war effort. Later on, the third Division took 'a more active combat role', leaving New Caledonia for the Solomons campaign. The objectives were to attack from secure air bases all the enemy's strategic points; to prevent enemy ships from approaching; and to carry out an amphibious landing primarily aimed at areas where airfields could be built. The 3rd Division was mainly concerned with three operations, two in the Solomon Islands – Vella Lavella and the Treasury Islands, and the Green Islands (part of the then Australian territory of New Guinea, located between Bougainville and New Ireland). Private Scott evokes it all in his poem *We were there*: 'Rather weak from the tinned food . . . We cut in and out from the jungle'; 'Then, lean, tanned and hard we moved forward' – all this, 'in the Solomon dreary', for '"Glory" . . .'.

In late April 1944 the New Zealanders returned to Noumea, before being transferred back home to New Zealand. Some of the men, however, were sent to Europe to take part in the Italian campaign.

The poems of Private Scott

Eleven poems were written in New Caledonia. Three of them are lyrics, with conventional and nostalgic feelings. Two involve love for a woman – *For honour and her*, and *Alas!* – while the third reflects feelings of love and nostalgia for the homeland, New Zealand – *The other view.*

Three poems complain about New Caledonia – *On Caledonia, stern and wild*; *Lament in New Caledonia*; and *After all that.* The five other poems are on Private Scott's feelings about the army.

Over all, the poems do have a literary value even if it is rather slight. The poet uses rhymes in most of the poems: 'glory/gory; faction/action; New Zealand/free land' in *Legion of the lost*; 'night/light; ease/please; down/brown; prey/day' in *Lament in New Caledonia.* He also uses onomatopoeia : 'The night was bright with theatrical light'; 'And jokes were pokes at officer blokes'; 'With chaffs and laughs from lugubrious staffs' in *Command Performance.*

But what mainly characterises the poems, and Private Scott's outlook, is a sense of humour and, as well, feelings of disillusionment. As for style and setting, he uses the chorus in *After all that*, and he may well have sung or read some of his poems among some of his roommates. No doubt the writing of the poems was partial therapy for all the unhappiness of his army sojourn.

The poems of Private Scott have an historical value, having been written by a New Zealand serviceman posted to the Pacific during the war. Their publication allows readers to understand and appreciate some of the feelings of New Zealand soldiers about their everyday life during the second world war.

The poet's complaints are about different subjects . . .

He is longing for his wife and children: 'Somewhere a woman, thrusting fear aside,/ Faces the future bravely for your sake,' he writes, in *For honour and her.* In this poem he evokes the love for a woman at large: 'woman, mother, sweetheart, wife.' In *Alas!* he writes, of his wife, 'And now must long in vain for you/Across eternity.' In *The other view* he writes, with feeling, 'I sigh for my wife and children . . . and the boy I haven't seen'.

Private Scott's poems evoke love and the possibility of comfort recovered: 'To think when we are one again/When war's alarms are over'. He is longing, too, for his homeland and home: 'To think the winds of Wellington/Were ever cold to me'; 'To think . . .That I shall read my book again' (*Alas!*). 'I sigh for the meadowed paddock,/For the pastures rich and green . . . I sigh for the gantry'd housetop . . . I sigh for my cosy armchair/For my paper and my pipe' (*The other view*). Fed up with army routine, he longs for the 'scones . . . all baked in the oven', his 'armchair, a book and a wireless', his 'feet on the drawing room-mat' (*After all that*). This is the elegiac part of his poems.

New Caledonia is far from being a welcome land to him. He makes this clear at the very end of two of his poems: 'Farewell Caledonia: Foul isle of the sea,/If there's any place worse – Not interested, me' (*Lament in New Caledonia*). And in *Legion of the lost* he concludes: 'if I had a farm in New Caledonia/And a home in Hell, I go home right now'.

The New Zealand soldiers found themselves in a hostile and unusual environment. They came from a cold, rainy country and were confronted by a hot and humid climate. The New Zealanders were living in a tropical countryside, with insects of the kind usually found in the bush: mosquitoes, bull-ants, weevils, blowflies, sandflies, and sea-snakes. In *On Caledonia, stern and wild* the rains are 'endless', bringing humidity and swarms of mosquitoes. The soldiers walk in the mud, while 'Deep in the kitbag the mildew goes . . .'. This moist misery is related in Private Scott's well-titled *Lament in New Caledonia.*

The big entertainment for the New Zealanders is a trip into

Noumea, but the poems show disappointment as what the soldiers find fails to meet their desires and expectations. There is no beer, and 'New Zealand prime rabbit' instead of oranges and oysters. The soldiers found the cost of living quite high, and the girls not so easy after all (*After all that*). Beer seems very important, more even than food. The beer serves a social function. When Private Scott thinks about his own country, he says: 'Where there's a "Speight's brand", let us roam' (*NZEFIP*).

The poet also suffers from lack of privacy. 'Tent-mates annoy and you wish them in hell' (*Lament in New Caledonia*). He doesn't enjoy the atmosphere of the bar, speaking of the 'lugubrious staffs' in *Command Performance*. There is a lack of entertainment: 'We wandered for hours in the streets' (*After all that*). Private Scott also has difficulty with the canned rations. It seems those rations were distributed mostly during the New Zealanders' stay in the Solomon Islands.

The worst complaints are not so much about the soldiers' everyday life, but rather about the meaning of their stay – the goal and importance of their participation in the war. They are the *Legion of the lost* – the title of one of the poems. They are 'but a minor fraction of the USA'. They consider themselves poor relations to the Americans. They are poorly dressed: 'our shirts grow older/ Torn across the shoulder' (*Legion of the lost*). The New Zealand politicians' view of their situation contrasts with the reality: 'We're sure you have heaps and heaps of clothes/And nice new shorts we've heard', say the visiting Members of Parliament (*Two Awfully bright MPs*). Their representatives – the MPs – do nothing to help them. Private Scott describes the MPs' own journey, including their venue and sojourn among the soldiers, with irony. The MPs fly overhead, not confined to a tossed ship on the sea like the troops. The MPs taste all the dishes at the Officer's mess, not sampling the food the ordinary soldiers have to eat. The soldiers' mail is censored and their newspaper 'Kiwi'. Private Scott views the politicians as parasites, embarked on a touring party at the nation's expense. In this sense the New Zealanders in the Pacific – based in New Caledonia, awaiting action – are men virtually abandoned by their country, mired in meaningless (and uncomfortable) inactivity.

In this sense the aim and outlook of Private Scott's poems is to show the New Zealand soldiers as anti-heroes. There is, in these poems, no action, no glory:

> 'Hail New Zealand's Third Division,
> Victims of doubt and indecision,
> Sent upon a labourer's mission,
> To Pacific shore' (*Legion of the lost*).

'We were there!', he says, but it's a strange sort of war. They mainly spend their time waiting. They long for a real war: 'We want nothing more than action' (*Legion of the lost*). His tone may be humorous – 'There were some who got shot on the beer' (*We were there*) – but at times the irony is also bitter: 'Heark unto our tragic story/Ours is not the path to glory' (*Legion of the lost*).

Conclusion

The discovery of Private William Scott's poems, and their publication more than 60 years after he had written them, may not be of major interest to literature. Even so, they are a welcome contribution, providing interesting testimony about New Zealand soldiers' conditions and outlook while based in New Caledonia. Private Scott's tone of disillusionment and his sense of humour demonstrate his feelings at the time. What they contained – the humour and the sadness – were in contrast with what was being said in the official war pronouncements of the time.

Notes

1 See *Caledonian poems of the soldier William E. Scott, 3rd div., 2 NZEF*; *Poèmes calédoniens du soldat William E. Scott, 3e division, 2 NZEF*, tr. by Dominique Lataste, with a preface, and with historical background and bibliography by Frédéric Angleviel, Noumea: Editions du GRHOC, 2007. This publication includes 11 poems (in their original English and with a translation into French), as well the supplementary material from Professor Angleviel and introductory material – about the poet and his poems – by Dominique Lataste. These additional materials, like the poems themselves, are in both English and French [eds.].

Three poems

William E. Scott

Alas!

To think the winds of Wellington
Were ever cold to me
Or that her darkling waters
Could ever sullen be.

To think that I could sit and read
When you were close to me,
And now must long in vain for you
Across eternity.

To think when we are one again
When war's alarms are over
That I shall read my book again,
And winds be cold once more.

Two Awfully bright MPs

We'd better introduce ourselves,
We're a couple of bright MPs
We've come to see you soldier boys
And look into your needs
We don't say we'll fulfil them
But our Cabinet we'll tell
That the 3rd Division live in luxury
And think the Island swell.

We're awfully bright MPs
Touring the southern seas
Taking note of the troops' elation
Charging expenses to the Nation
We've staffs of ten or twelve
We're busy as the bees
With shaking hands and talking tosh
We're awfully bright MPs.

We really sympathise now
With your journey from NZ
We saw the sea rage fierce and wild
When we – flew overhead.
It's sad you fed but twice a day
For four long days of pain
We talk a lot about it
– Drinking cocktails on our plane.

We're awfully brave MPs
Touring the southern seas
Daring disease and mosquitoes too
Determined, we've got a job to do
Though Jojo's pretty tough
He'll tremble at the knees
So hear about our fearless flight
We're awfully brave MPs.

The kind of food you're getting here
We heartily endorse
We've tasted all the dishes
– At the Officer's Mess of course
We're glad the Patriotic Board
Still serves you seasoned sets
With tons of Christmas parcels
And the mould-proof cigarettes.

We're awfully wise MPs
Touring the southern seas
Terribly earnest and dreadfully grim
Telling you sternly: 'You'll soon be in'.
If it's facts you want,
Just ask us what you please
– And then we'll hold a secret session –
We're awfully wise MPs.

We hope you like the 'Kiwi' sheet
Our praises high it shouts
We trust you'll all be tutored
For the next election bouts
You'll want to write the folks about
Our visit when we go
Be sure you don't abuse us
Lest the enemy gets to know.

We're awfully kind MPs
Touring the southern seas
Calmly ignoring your hopes and fears
Telling New Zealand you're bored to tears
We'll send you plenty of beer
From your home across the seas
Expect it in a year or so
We're awfully kind MPs.

We've seen your censorship first-hand
We think it quite essential
You know, of course, that all our mail's
Marked 'Strictly Confidential'.
We're sure you have heaps and heaps of clothes
And nice new shorts we've heard
Too bad you're bored in such fine isles
– salubrious is the word.

We're awfully frank MPs
Touring the southern seas
Bringing the news you've longed to hear
Just hold your breath and cock an ear
You'll be sailing home
Full speed before the breeze
Within the nest – ten years or so
We're awfully frank MPs.

So rule Brittania,
Brittania rule the seas
You may call us what you like –
We're awfully bright MPs.

– with apologies to Walter Nash and others.

The other view

I sigh for the meadowed paddock,
For the pastures rich and green,
For the lowing herd and the bridled horse
And the bowl of richest cream.

I sigh for the gantry'd housetop,
For the neatest garden there,
For the blue cornstalk and the marigold
And the orchid rich and rare.

I sigh for my cosy armchair,
For my paper and my pipe,
For the wind without and the warmth within
And the symphony of life.

I sigh for my wife and children,
For all that they have been,
For the happy laugh and the quickened tear
And the boy I haven't seen.

And so, as I sigh and wonder
Of the things that on me depend,
I thank the God who has given so much
For this simple man to defend.

New Zealand, New Caledonia and the South Pacific War

Ian McGibbon

Traditionally, New Zealand had little connection with New Caledonia, which was regarded as lying within the Australian sphere of influence. For a long time the island, as a French possession, was seen as a possible source of threat. Apart from one brief visit in August 1914 by the New Zealand force heading for German Samoa, New Zealand military forces had little contact with it. All this changed as a result of the Second World War. Japan's invasion of the South Pacific and the United States decision to mount a counter-offensive in the Solomon Islands ensured a new focus on New Caledonia in Wellington. When New Zealand and New Caledonia found themselves part of the American South Pacific Command, with Australia included in a different command area, the way was opened for much closer interaction between them, not least because the US command headquarters was established in Noumea. A New Zealand air force squadron operated from New Caledonia from July 1942 to March 1943. The army established a much bigger presence when it deployed the 17,000-strong 3rd NZ Division to the island from November 1942. New Zealand troops formed part of the island's defences before moving north to the Solomon Islands to operate against the Japanese. The division's base remained at New Caledonia until it was withdrawn to New Zealand in September 1944. Following the war, ties between New Caledonia and New Zealand reverted to their former limited state.

Traditionnellement, la Nouvelle-Zélande a peu de relations avec la Nouvelle-Calédonie, qui est considérée comme appartenant à la sphère d'influence australienne. A l'exception d'une brève visite en août 1914 par une force maritime se rendant aux Samoa, les forces armées néo-zélandaises avaient peu de relations avec l'armée française. Tout changea lorsque l'es Etats-Unis utilisèrent la Nouvelle-Calédonie comme un porte-avion arrière et demandèrent l'intervention à leurs côtés de la Nouvelle-Zélande. L'état-major néo-zélandais établie dans l'île la 3ème division, forte de 17000 hommes, dès novembre 1942. Puis, les troupes néo-zélandaises participèrent à la bataille des Salomon, leur base arrière restant en Nouvelle-Calédonie. La 3è division quitta l'archipel en septembre 1994 et depuis lors, les relations d'essence militaires entre la Nouvelle-Calédonie et la Nouvelle-Zélande se sont fort réduites.

Between November 1942 and February 1943 New Caledonia underwent its second friendly invasion within a year. More than 13,000 New Zealanders arrived in the island in four main drafts. The biggest and last – more than 7,000 men – was conveyed by the US troopship *West Point*, which arrived on New Year's Eve. Not all of the New Zealanders were happy with their lot – two men committed suicide at the time of arrival, and two more died within days from natural causes or food poisoning.[1] The rest adjusted without difficulty to their first experience of a foreign land, and were soon hard at work improving their billets and training for combat.

This commitment to New Caledonia had not been foreseen in New Zealand's pre-war planning. It stemmed from the aggressive actions of Japan in the previous year and took place in a completely different framework to that which traditionally underpinned New Zealand's military activities. Before 1942, the New Zealand armed forces had virtually no contact with New Caledonia. Geographical and strategical influences lay behind this state of affairs. Lying within the confines of the Australian naval station, New Caledonia was seen as part of an Australian sphere of responsibility. New Zealand looked north and north-east – to Fiji, Samoa, the Cook Islands and the French territories in the Society Islands. Strategically, the Southwest Pacific was downgraded by assumptions underlying New

Zealand's defence policy, especially in relation to the British naval base at Singapore. Provided British plans worked, there would be little threat to territories in the Southwest Pacific, and hence little need to prepare for their defence.

Pre-war approach

The first direct New Zealand military contact with New Caledonia occurred unexpectedly in August 1914. At British request New Zealand on 15 August had dispatched a 1,370-man force in two troopships guarded by three weak light cruisers to capture the radio station at Apia. The expedition's initial destination was Suva, where it was to rendezvous with the Australian navy's battlecruiser HMAS *Australia*. But while heading north the ships were diverted to Noumea to await a delayed *Australia*, arriving there on 20 August 1914. Next day the troops were landed to undertake an 8-kilometre route march. Interestingly, among them were two men who would be involved in New Zealand's decision to send troops to New Caledonia in 1942 – Carl Berendsen and Edward Puttick. In 1942 the former was the Prime Minister's chief adviser as head of the Prime Minister's Department, while Puttick held the Army's highest position – General Officer Commanding the New Zealand Military Forces. Puttick described Noumea as 'a straggly kind of place, with one or two large buildings, and a very mixed population' of about 11,000. His chief impression appears to have been the polygot nature of the population.[2] Berendsen's lasting memory was of the spiders, both their size and 'the vividness of the colouring'.[3] Unlike Puttick, he would revisit the island repeatedly in the next war. The convoy departed for Suva on 24 August, delayed one day when one of the ships ran aground.[4]

Apart from this brief, helpful connection in the Great War, New Zealand thoughts about New Caledonia, and other French possessions in the Pacific, had tended to be influenced by a sense that they presented a potential threat to New Zealand's interests. As early as 1852, Governor Grey had proposed sending an expeditionary force to seize Tahiti in the event of an Anglo-French war occurring.[5] When France annexed New Caledonia in the following year, he warned London that the 'ultimate probable object' was to harass the British colonies in the South Pacific and their trade.[6] Several writers in New Zealand later in the nineteenth century outlined scenarios in which New Caledonia was used as a base for operations against New Zealand.[7] Such concerns were not confined to writers. As late as the early 1930s, service officers in Wellington were still considering, albeit at British instigation, the threat presented to New Zealand by French forces in New Caledonia. With New Zealand's defence strategy founded on the Singapore base, the government was primarily concerned with European events which might affect Britain's ability to send its fleet to operate from it in the event of Japan presenting a threat. Although there was no expectation of any imminent clash with France, the ally of the Great War, services plan for contingencies, even unlikely ones. In 1925 a war memorandum arrived in Wellington from the Admiralty in London setting out British plans in the event of hostilities with France. In an echo of Governor Grey, the New Zealand naval authorities (all the senior officers were Royal Navy men on loan) suggested that, in such an eventuality, an expeditionary force should be sent from Auckland to seize Tahiti, which was then undefended.[8] Seven years later, after a revised memorandum had been received, they repeated such advice, suggesting that the denial of the oil tanks there (and at Noumea, which Australia might deal with) would reduce the ability of the French squadron in the Oceania region to operate freely.[9] Adolf Hitler's accession to power soon emphasised the unreality of such contingency planning, and the Admiralty advised that it should be regarded as just a planning exercise[10] – but it was 1938 before the war memorandum was formally rescinded.[11] By this time, of course, Britain and France had once again been pushed closer together by the threat posed by Germany.

As the international situation deteriorated in the 1930s, New Zealand became increasingly worried by the security position in the Southwest Pacific. Defence issues were addressed at a conference of British, New Zealand and Australian authorities held in Wellington in early 1939. As yet, there was no expectation that Japan would invade the region in strength (that would depend on it seizing the Singapore base, which was not considered likely). The main concern was raiders moving south to attack New Zealand or Australian shipping or ports. The conference agreed to establish a line of reconnaissance through which Japanese raiders heading in this direction would have to pass. Australian aircraft operating from Port Moresby and New Zealand aircraft from Suva would bring the area under surveillance, with the New Hebrides as the point of intersection of the two efforts. New Caledonia, lying further south, was not regarded as a primary area of interest, though the conference did discuss such issues as landing and overflight rights in relation to the island.[12] More information was sought from the Governor about resources in New Caledonia – a request he complied with some months after the war began.[13]

New Zealand's war strategy

Despite this new concern about the South Pacific situation, New Zealand's response to the crisis in September 1939 was Europe-focused. As in 1914, its war effort was developed within a British framework. New Zealand's strategy was to ensure that the British Commonwealth was at least not defeated – and the vital theatres in this struggle were obviously not going to be in the Pacific. Despite concerns about Japan's intentions, the government decided to despatch an expeditionary force to Europe. It did so in the expectation that the 2nd New Zealand Expeditionary Force would join the British Expeditionary Force in France – a re-run of the First World War. Initially, however, this force would complete its concentration and training in Egypt rather than winter in the United Kingdom. New Caledonia's response to the crisis was similar; it also planned to send men to fight in France, as it had done in the Great War.[14]

The Allied defeat in Western Europe in May-June 1940 upset these plans. No New Zealand units – or New Caledonians – fought on French soil, though numerous New Zealanders served as part of Royal Air Force squadrons operating in France until June 1940. New Zealand's 2nd Division later took part in the ill-fated Greek campaign, culminating in its evacuation from Crete. It then formed part of the 8th Army (as did Free French forces, in which New Caledonians served) and was involved in the Desert campaign when in December 1941 Japan dramatically transformed the war. New Zealand watched in horror not only as the United States Navy was mauled at Pearl Harbor but also as the British fleet for Singapore was sunk off Malaya and, in due course, the Singapore base itself was lost. In these dire circumstances New Zealand was confronted with a strategic conundrum – should it continue to make its main effort in Europe or bring its troops home to meet the enemy at the gates?

In the event, New Zealand decided to leave the 2nd Division in the Mediterranean theatre. These days this outcome is often depicted as evidence of New Zealand's unwillingness to stand up for itself vis-à-vis the British, in contrast to the assertiveness of Australia, which withdrew two of the three Australian divisions in the Middle East. But in reality the Australian deployment was made at British request, and New Zealand's ability to repatriate its own division was hampered by practical considerations relating to shipping and, not least, the danger presented by strong Japanese naval forces marauding the Indian Ocean after February 1942. New Zealand looked to the United States to fill the gap in the Pacific.[15]

A New Caledonia focus

The catastrophe that befell France in June 1940 immediately impelled New Zealand to take a closer interest in the situation in both New Caledonia and Tahiti. Prime Minister Peter Fraser lost no time in sending messages to the Governors of both French territories, expressing sympathy for their governments and people in 'this tragic hour', applauding the heroism of French resistance and hoping for the continued co-operation of 'our French Allies in New Caledonia'. He offered to supply coal and foodstuffs and any other assistance required.[16] While he addressed both Governors, New Zealand was more interested in Tahiti. The possibility of New Zealand sending a representative to Tahiti was raised in July 1940,[17] and two months later the cruiser HMS *Achilles* was sent to the island in support of the elements that had rallied to the Allies.

In New Caledonia New Zealand was at first just an interested observer. It welcomed evidence that Vichy-appointed administrators were clearly not popular with most of the population, who were keen to continue the fight. There was satisfaction in Wellington when Henri Sautot was appointed as Governor by General de Gaulle and arrived in Noumea to the acclaim of the population. The decision by the people in both New Caledonia and Tahiti to rally to the Free French ensured that the colonies were excluded from aggressive measures planned by the British authorities against French possessions for the contingency of war between the Allies and Vichy France.[18] In New Caledonia's and Tahiti's case, these would no doubt have followed the lines of the Admiralty's war memorandum discussed above. In keeping with its earlier approach, New Zealand was content to leave Australia to take the lead in dealings with the new regime in Noumea. Early in 1941 an Australian military mission proceeded to New Caledonia. Returning to Sydney via New Zealand, it discussed the island's defence problems with New Zealand Army authorities.[19] New Zealand concern about the island's defences was reflected in its decision, soon after these talks, to make available two 6-inch guns for the defence of Noumea. Sent to Australia, they were held there for a time because of uncertainties aroused by Vichy supporters' activities before eventually being installed.[20]

When the war with Japan began, the Free French National Committee in London lost no time in instructing all French civil and military authorities to collaborate to the fullest extent possible with the Allies, including the provision of bases.[21] The recently arrived French High Commissioner to the Pacific, Commandant d'Argenlieu, was given control over all French in the Pacific,[22] a move that would soon lead to friction with Governor Sautot which would eventually lead result in the departure of both from the island. The evolving war situation brought New Caledonia increasingly to the fore as an element in New Zealand's security. Fears were heightened by the arrival of Japanese forces in the Solomon Islands in strength. Once Guadalcanal was in their hands, it seemed only a matter of time before they moved south to capture the New Hebrides and New Caledonia. The New Zealand Chiefs of Staff now regarded the retention of the latter as vital not only for its resources (especially nickel) but also as a defensive bastion. They considered that New Zealand would be free from invasion so long as New Caledonia and

Fiji were not lost. Even so, there was a tendency still to regard New Caledonia as an Australian responsibility. New Zealand was not forthcoming in January 1942 when d'Argenlieu requested it to take some of the Japanese who had been interned after Japan's entry to the war; of the 1200 internees, Australia had agreed to take 600.[23]

New Zealand drew comfort from reassuring indications that the Americans were alive to the significance of New Caledonia. News was received from Washington that the British and American Chiefs of Staff had agreed to the United States furnishing forces for New Caledonia as soon as possible. The troops – a force of about 22,000 men was envisaged – would be provided from a convoy leaving the United States for Australia in the second half of January 1942. A final decision would be made when the convoy reached Australia. No hint of this decision was to be given to the Free French authorities in Noumea, who were to be informed just before the force landed.[24] Understandably, in the absence of this information and in light of the Japanese advance, the French administrators in Noumea became increasingly agitated. The danger of invasion seemed to have been elevated by the existence of three airfields on the island, which had been upgraded by the New Caledonians at Allied behest. When the New Zealand Chief of the Air Staff, Air Commodore Robert Goddard, visited Noumea in early 1942, d'Argenlieu threatened to destroy the airfields if no assurance were received of immediate reinforcement. The High Commissioner pleaded for some aircraft, even civil, to allow him to search out approaching Japanese.[25] Both Australia and New Zealand, conscious of the importance of the airfields with the American force in the offing, sought to avert d'Argenlieu's dire threat. Australia sent a Catalina flying boat to New Caledonia for a few weeks, while New Zealand's Minister in Washington, Walter Nash, secured from the American authorities a promise to send six Catalinas, which had recently arrived in Brisbane.[26] These aircraft, with American crews, were operating in New Caledonia within a week.[27]

New Caledonian fears were allayed on 12 March 1942 when a 17,000-man force under General Patch arrived. With the consent of the Governor, Patch assumed command of Noumea's defences. A small Australian detachment which had been in New Caledonia since

December 1941 was now sent to the New Hebrides.[28] The American advent was very timely, for it coincided with a heightened sense of threat. The American air commander was expecting trouble at any minute, and fearful that his forces would not be organised properly in time to deal with it.[29] In fact, it would be two months before the Japanese began planning in earnest to invade New Caledonia, a force of 5,500 men being earmarked for the task. Within weeks, however, Japanese defeat at Midway would put an end to such plans.[30]

American influence

With the Americans ensconced in New Caledonia, New Zealand interest in the island could be expected to decline. That this was not the case stemmed from two major influences. These were the framework of operations established by the Americans and the American decision to mount a campaign in the Solomon Islands.

In April 1942 the United States established two commands in the Pacific theatre – the South West Pacific and the Pacific, commanded by General Douglas MacArthur and Admiral Chester Nimitz respectively.[31] This arrangement, which came into effect on 8 May, had important implications for New Zealand, not least because all its forces except those for the land defence of New Zealand came under Nimitz's command. It found itself part of the South Pacific area, an element of Nimitz's vast command, whereas Australia was part of the South West Pacific command. New Zealand protested against this separation from Australia to no avail. That New Caledonia was also part of the South Pacific Command under Vice Admiral R.L. Ghormley, who arrived in Auckland on 21 May 1942 and assumed command on 19 June, not only took Australia out of the New Caledonia picture but also opened the way to New Zealand-New Caledonian interaction on a much great scale than hitherto. With American troops landing in New Zealand in June 1942, both were in a similar position as American base areas.

New Caledonia's location assumed greater significance as a result of the American decision to mount an offensive against Japanese forces in the Solomon Islands. U.S Marines from New Zealand and the United States would be landed on Guadalcanal on 7 August. In preparation for the operation, Ghormley transferred his headquarters to Noumea on 1 August. Although temporary, this change of location became permanent as the Solomons campaign dragged on longer than expected. It ensured a close New Zealand focus on New Caledonia. Eventually, in April 1943, the New Zealand Chiefs of Staff installed Colonel C.W. Salmon in Noumea to serve as their representative at the South Pacific Command HQ.[32]

American decisions led to the first New Zealand commitment of forces in the island. New Zealand was asked to send six RNZAF Vincents from Fiji to New Caledonia to undertake anti-submarine patrols. Unconvinced that the Vincents were suitable for operations in which hostile action was possible, the New Zealand air authorities substituted Hudson bombers. Two were sent from Fiji, and others later from New Zealand, along with ground staff and personnel. From these elements a squadron – 9 General Reconnaissance Squadron – was formed in July 1942. By November it had a strength of 36 officers and 245 other ranks.[33]

Attached to Task Group 63.1 and operating from an airfield on the Plaine des Gaiacs, 9 Squadron helped to patrol the seas for 650 kilometres around the island. Its particular task was the daily dawn and dusk anti-submarine patrols around the coast, beginning on 21 July 1942. This activity would continue until March 1943. Although the flights were relatively uneventful, occasional possible submarine sightings kept the airmen on their toes. One of the squadron's Hudsons bombed a possible submarine contact in the pre-dawn of 6 February 1943.[34]

At one stage it seemed that New Zealand might increase its RNZAF presence in New Caledonia. Following a Ghormley suggestion initiated by the New Zealand Chief of the Air Staff, the War Cabinet on 16 September 1942 approved plans to send 1 Aerodrome Construction Squadron to New Caledonia to work on airfields there.[35] But in the event no action was taken on this proposal because the New Zealand unit lacked equipment; it had been lost as a result of Japanese attack on the ship evacuating the unit from Singapore. Eventually the Americans indicated that they had more than enough engineering resources without it.[36] With the departure of 9 Squadron in March 1943, RNZAF involvement in

New Caledonia ended, though aircraft continued to transit through New Caledonian airfields and a flying-boat servicing party would be briefly stationed at Île Nou to deal with transient aircraft after the end of the war to assist with the repatriation of RNZAF personnel and equipment from the forward areas.[37]

Even as New Zealand airmen settled into the routine of operations, the question of ground force involvement in New Caledonia was under active consideration. Before 1942 the New Zealand Army's main effort in the South Pacific had been in Fiji, where from 1940 a force of 8000 men, which eventually became known as the 3rd Division, had been built up. Following the American assumption of responsibility for the defence of the colony and the arrival of relieving American forces, the 3rd Division was pulled back to New Zealand, where it constituted a potential contribution to the American effort being planned in the Solomons.

When he discussed the role of New Zealand forces with the GOC New Zealand forces, Lieutenant-General Sir Edward Puttick, on 28 July 1942, Ghormley indicated that he envisaged the 3rd Division going to Guadalcanal to relieve Marines there as soon as they captured the island, allowing them to undertake further amphibious operations. Ghormley suggested that New Zealand prepare a force – four possible configurations involving from one to three brigades were advanced depending upon manpower and equipment available – for embarkation any time after 25 August.[38] Puttick had to convince the government that such a step would not endanger New Zealand itself. 'I cannot conceive any probability of an invasion of N.Z. at this stage.' He pointed to the significance of New Caledonia for New Zealand security – so long as it and Fiji were held there was no danger unless the Allies suffered a major defeat at sea. Because this latter was always a possibility – the naval forces upon which the Allied effort depended 'could conceivably be removed in a matter of hours', he warned – New Zealand should continue defence preparations at home while sending the force to the Solomons, as requested.[39]

But events did not play out as Ghormley expected. Although the Americans landed on Guadalcanal on 7 August without difficulty, they were soon engaged in a bitter struggle with Japanese forces. Both sides fed more men into the struggle while naval forces clashed with sometimes disastrous consequences for the US Navy. It was shortly after news of one of these clashes that a distracted and irritated Ghormley found himself confronted by a delegation from Wellington led by Peter Fraser and including both Minister of Armed Forces Coordination J.G. Coates and Minister of Defence Frederick Jones – as well as Carl Berendsen, back in Noumea almost twenty-eight years to the day after his visit in 1914. (In his memoirs Berendsen described Noumea as 'a charming little town, a little down-at-heel as such tropical settlements tend to become, but magnificently sited and enjoying a beautiful climate.')[40] The meeting, in the morning of 12 August, did not go well for the New Zealanders, especially after Ghormley accused the Prime Minister of publicly exposing his plans to attack the Solomons before the invasion. They came away without any indication from the Admiral of how he intended to use the troops that New Zealand was willing to send to the combat zone.[41]

It would be two months before a positive indication was received of Ghormley's intentions. On 16 October he requested that a two-brigade force be sent to New Caledonia as soon as transportation could be provided.[42] Since there was still a possibility of Japan attacking the island, the 3rd Division, commanded by the citizen-soldier Major-General Harold Barrowclough, would be deployed to bolster its defences. Given this possible role, Barrowclough insisted that the force must be prepared to fight if necessary. This required it to be brought up to full strength as soon as possible, especially by recovering two of its battalions which were detached in Norfolk Island and Tonga. The War Cabinet quickly agreed to proceed on this basis.[43]

New Zealanders in New Caledonia

The implementation of Operation Kiwi proceeded as smoothly as the difficult transport situation allowed. Shipping was not readily available, and even as late as May 1943 significant units of the 3rd Division remained in New Zealand.[44] An advance party had reached the island on 2 November 1942, and Barrowclough flew to Noumea five days later. He was given the task of defending the northern sector of the island. Almost immediately, however, these defence plans altered, as the Americans finally cleared the Japanese from Guadalcanal and looked to drive north. Their lessening concern regarding possible attack on New Caledonia was reflected in the decision to deploy the 43rd US Division forward into the combat zone. The New Zealanders took over its sector in addition to their own, which meant they were widely dispersed throughout the island.[45]

It was always the New Zealand government's intention that the 3rd Division's sojourn in New Caledonia would be temporary and that it would move forward to undertake active operations against the Japanese.[46] In May 1943 Prime Minister Peter Fraser noted the need to avoid changes that might unduly delay the division's use in an offensive role 'or probably might result in their being used solely as garrison troops'.[47] Consideration was again given to sending Barrowclough's men north. At the same time New Zealand's manpower difficulties and preference to maintain the 2nd NZ Division at full strength, even after the end of the North African campaign in May 1943, also raised the possibility of its disbandment. In this unpropitious climate of uncertainty, Barrowclough had to fight hard to get an operational role for his division, a battle made more difficult by the low priority the Americans accorded to ground forces in terms of their requirements of New Zealand; they rated them after both air and navy in terms of priority. Barely disguising his frustration at the 'shabby treatment' of his division – he was described as 'completely outraged at the turn of events' – Barrowclough struggled to persuade a dubious War Cabinet in Wellington to allow his division to respond to an American request for its services in the combat zone. 'All he asked for was one campaign.'[48] His efforts were rewarded: on 27 June the government agreed that the 3rd Division, organised on a two-brigade basis, should take part in the operations further north from New Caledonia.[49]

This outcome raised the question of where the division's base should be – in New Caledonia or in New Zealand. Barrowclough discussed this matter with the Americans as early as February 1943, when he took it up with the head of the War Plans Staff in Halsey's

HQ. The question had implications for how permanent the facilities created for his division would be, an urgent matter because of the deterioration caused by climatic conditions to supplies that were not properly stored under cover. In the context of rest and recovery between operations, Barrowclough was unhappy with the idea of his division returning to New Zealand on the grounds that it would lose discipline, fitness and fighting efficiency. He preferred to have the base in New Caledonia at least till after the division had completed two tours of duty in the combat zone.[50] By June New Caledonia was seen to offer several other advantages over New Zealand as a base. It was much closer to the scene of the fighting and the New Zealanders were already installed there. An accumulated reserve of ammunition was already on hand. However, the facilities available were less satisfactory than those that could be used in New Zealand. Moreover, having a base in New Caledonia would necessitate double handling of supplies moved forward from New Zealand.[51]

The issue was still not settled in June as the New Zealanders prepared to move forward. Puttick discussed the matter with Admiral Wilkinson, and then contacted Vice-Admiral W.F. Halsey, who had relieved Ghormley as commander of the South Pacific area. Puttick warned that the decision on the location of the New Zealand base would 'vitally affect administrative planning for its maintenance, and will determine the nature and extent of reserve supplies, base installations and base maintenance units'. With Halsey's failure to express an opinion on the base location issue, the base by default remained in New Caledonia.[52] Barrowclough was happy with this outcome. He regarded the time spent by his men on the island 'as most useful in fitting troops for warfare in these hot, muggy climates'. New Caledonia, in his vew, was 'an ideal training ground for tropical warfare', not least because it was free from malaria.[53]

With the base in New Caledonia, several thousand New Zealanders were stationed on the island for nearly two years, not finally returning to New Zealand until September 1944 when the division was withdrawn and later disbanded. They did not find the situation onerous. Relations with the locals were amicable – in contrast to problems that arose between the Americans and New Caledonians. A tendency on the part of the Americans not to pay due regard to the New Caledonians caused friction.[54] Governor Laigret complained in December 1943 that the Americans appeared 'to forget that there is a great difference between being stationed in a friendly country and occupation of an enemy country'. This, he noted, contrasted sharply with the New Zealand approach.[55] New Zealand was fortunate to have officers in New Caledonia who were conscious of the need to tread carefully in dealings with the local inhabitants. Colonel Salmon, the Chiefs of Staff representative, referred in November 1943 to 'our policy of maintaining goodwill with the New Caledonians and other French islands'.[56] Barrowclough, a lawyer by profession, was conscious of the friction that could arise from breaches by New Zealanders of French laws or civil proceedings against them, given that there was no system of martial law in place. 'We are not here as conquerors', he reminded Wellington.[57] He secured French agreement to an arrangement that greatly reduced the potential jurisdictional problems. A committee of four members, two each of French and New Zealanders, considered cases on the basis of natural justice.[58] No significant grievances arose.

This sympathetic and sensitive attitude was replicated in Wellington, as was evident when President Roosevelt raised the possibility of removing New Caledonia from French control after the war.[59] Although ending the French presence in the South Pacific accorded with longheld New Zealand aspirations – in 1913 Prime Minister William Massey had suggested that the British Empire offer France territory in Africa in exchange for its share of the condominium in the New Hebrides and New Caledonia[60] – Fraser's government was unsympathetic. It joined its Australian counterpart in resisting the idea that wartime operations might provide a basis for changes of sovereignty, an approach that angered the Americans. The uncompromising Australasian stance stemmed mainly from a desire to preserve British control of islands occupied by the Americans; consistency demanded that the same concept be applied to French possessions. But Fraser was also an advocate of a moral foreign policy: arbitrarily changing the sovereignty of French territories in the Pacific would be unjust, in his view, to French populations in the Pacific that had willingly joined the Allies and sent men to fight for the United Nations. New Zealand made clear that any attempt to implement Roosevelt's suggestion in relation to New Caledonia would be 'totally unacceptable' to it.[61]

Despite the close involvement with New Caledonia from 1942 to 1944, Prime Minister Fraser did not see any value in establishing closer ties with the island more permanently. He rebuffed a suggestion by the Chief of the Air Staff, Air Vice-Marshal Leonard Isitt, that a consular officer be accredited in Noumea following the withdrawal of the military mission led by Salmon.[62] Nonetheless, the wartime events had changed New Zealand's perception of New Caledonia. In October 1944 the Chiefs of Staff described it as one of three islands or groups that were vital to New Zealand's defence, along with Fiji and Tonga.[63] They urged the importance of New Zealand taking an active interest in its defence. But they also recognised that political problems were likely to complicate any post-war co-operative efforts. They suggested that the New Hebrides would be a more appropriate focus for defence preparations in the region.[64]

Despite these new perceptions of New Caledonia's place in New Zealand's security, the impact of the deployment of 1942-44 on either New Zealand foreign and defence policy or culture eventually proved to be limited. The efforts of the 3rd Division were overshadowed in the public mind by the exploits of the 2nd Division in the Mediterranean, and there was a tendency to regard service in the South Pacific as relatively undemanding, especially given popular misconceptions about conditions in tropical isles. The New Caledonia deployment received relatively little attention in post-war years. Nor did close interest in the defence of the Southwest Pacific long survive the end of the war. Attention in Wellington was drawn increasingly to the confrontation emerging in Europe between the Soviet Union and its erstwhile allies. The South Pacific was quickly overshadowed. With the revival of pre-war naval arrangements, New Caledonia was once again located within an Australian sphere of interest. Old influences reasserted themselves – though the substantial war cemetery at Bourail ensured that New Zealand's presence in New Caledonia would not altogether be forgotten.

Notes

1 GOC 3rd Division (Maj-Gen H. Barrowclough) to Army HQ, 26 Jan 1943, AD12, 28/15/2, Army Department records, Archives New Zealand (ANZ).
2 Lt E. Puttick to 'Jack' [Irene Dignan], 21 Aug 1914, Puttick Papers, 1/4, ANZ.
3 'Reminiscences of an ambassador', Book 1, p. 228, McIntosh Papers, MS-Papers-6759-450, ATL.
4 Ibid., p. 229; Puttick to 'Jack', 26 Aug 1914, Puttick Papers, 1/4.
5 See Ian McGibbon, *The Path to Gallipoli, Defending New Zealand 1840-1915* (GP Books, Wellington, 1991), p. 6.
6 Angus Ross, *New Zealand Aspirations in the Pacific in the Nineteenth Century* (Clarendon Press, Oxford, 1964), p. 50.
7 Garry Clayton, 'Francophobia in New Zealand', in *60 years ago, celebrating the anniversary of diplomatic relations between New Zealand and France* (No publisher cited, Wellington, 2006), p. 51, citing two authors, Artemidorous and Julian Grix, who posited New Caledonia as a base for attacks on New Zealand.
8 Naval Secretary to Admiralty, 9 Nov 1925, N2, 08/11/11, Navy Department records, ANZ.
9 Ibid., Notes by Staff Officer (Intelligence), 'Revised French War Memorandum --- M00486/32 Aug 1932', 12 Oct 1932, Naval Secretary to Secretary of the Admiralty, 25 Nov 1932.
10 Ibid., Secretary of the Admiralty to Naval Secretary, 31 Dec 1934.
11 Ibid., Secretary of the Admiralty to Naval Secretary, 21 Dec 1938.
12 See UK High Commissioner for the Western Pacific to Governor-General of New Zealand, 1 Jun 1939 (copy), AIR1, 118/2/10, Air Department records, ANZ.
13 Ibid., Governor, New Caledonia, to UK High Commissioner for the Western Pacific, 2 Dec 1939 (translated copy).
14 Interview with Governor Laigret, 18 Dec 1943, in O.A. Gillespie, *The Pacific* (War History Branch, Wellington, 1952), App VI, p. 342.
15 On the Mediterranean versus the Pacific issue see Ian McGibbon, *New Zealand and the Second World War, The battles, the people and the legacy* (Hodder Moa Beckett, Auckland, 2004), pp. 104-5.
16 UK High Commission, Wellington, to Secretary of State for Dominion Affairs, No 247, 24 Jun 1940, EA1, 86/19/1, External Affairs Department records, ANZ.
17 Ibid., UK High Commissioner, Wellington, to Prime Minister, 18 Jul 1940.
18 Naval Secretary to Naval Officer in Charge, Auckland, 15 Jun 1941, N2, 08/11/11.
19 Acting Prime Minister, Canberra, to Prime Minister, No 48, 10 Feb 1941,

AIR1, 118/2/10; F.B. Stephens to A.D. McIntosh, 27 Feb 1941, EA1, 86/19/1.

20 Prime Minister to Secretary of State for Dominion Affairs, 22 Mar 1941, CNS Australia to CNS New Zealand, 6 Jun 1941, Admiralty to New Zealand Naval Board, No 505, 7 Sep 1941, N2, 020/14/19, ANZ.

21 Secretary of State for Dominion Affairs to Prime Minister, Wellington, No 487, 11 Dec 1941, AIR1, 118/2/10.

22 Ibid., Secretary of State for Dominion Affairs to Prime Minister, Wellington, No 489, 10 Dec 1941.

23 UK Consul-General, Noumea, to Navy Office, Wellington, 13 Jan 1942, and reply dated 20 Jan 1942, N2, 020/14/19.

24 Ibid., Australian Legation, Washington, to Department of External Affairs, Canberra (copy), 16 Jan 1942.

25 Air HQ, Wellington, to Air Board, Melbourne, No A262, 8 Feb 1942, AIR1, 109/6/6.

26 Ibid., Air Board, Melbourne, to Air HQ, No A696, 10 Feb 1942, NZ Air Attaché, Washington, to RNZAF HQ, No Air1, 19 Feb 1942.

27 See Prime Minister, Canberra, to Prime Minister, Wellington, No 77, 26 Feb 1942, AIR1, 132/2/4.

28 'Extract from Lt-Cdr Beasley's Memo of 16 March 1942', N2, 020/14/19.

29 Memorandum, 'Noumea', 28 Mar 1942, AIR1, 109/6/6.

30 Gillespie, pp. 206-8.

31 NZ Minister, Washington, to Prime Minister, No 112, 2 Apr 1942, EA1, 81/10/4.

32 J.G. Coates to Vice-Admiral W.F. Halsey, 25 Feb 1943, Notes of a Conference in Noumea, 2 Mar 1943, Coates Papers, MS Papers 1785, folder 181, ATL.

33 J.M.S. Ross, *Royal New Zealand Air Force* (War History Branch, Wellington, 1955), pp. 130-1.

34 Ibid., pp. 132-3.

35 Rear-Admiral C.M. Cooke to Goddard, 5 Sep 1942, War Cabinet minute, 16 Sep 1942, AIR1, 130/16/1.

36 See ibid., RDO Auckland to RDO Noumea, 24 Feb 1943.

37 Ross, p. 314.

38 GOC (Lt-Gen Sir Edward Puttick) to Minister of Defence, 31 Jul 1942, AD12, 28/15/1.

39 Ibid., GOC to Minister of Defence, 3 Aug 1942.

40 'Reminiscences of an ambassador', Book 2, p. 401, McIntosh Papers, MS-Papers-6759-458, ATL.

41 Coates, 'Delegation to Noumea', 17 Aug 1942, Coates Papers, MS Papers 1785, folder 181, ATL. Gillespie, p. 74, implies, incorrectly, that the meeting with Ghormley took place on 9 August 'a few hours after' the first naval battle. Berendsen, in his memoirs (Book 2, p.398, MS-Papers-6759-457), seems to have confused the meeting with a later one that he attended with Coates. He states that Ghormley, after reacting 'violently and decisively' to the size of the delegation, allowed only he and Coates to go aboard the ship to meet with him

in what was 'a very tragic interview indeed'.

42 COMOSOPAC to COMOSOPAC (Admin), 16 Oct 1942, AD12, 28/15/1.

43 Ibid., GOC to Minister of Defence, 16 Oct 1942, Assistant CGS to US Naval Attaché, 17 Oct 1942. Prime Minister to NZ Minister, Washington, No 586, 17 Oct 1942, EA1, 86/19/1.

44 GOC 3rd Division to HQ USAFISPA, 6 May 1943, AD12, 28/15/1.

45 GOC 3rd Division to Army HQ, 10 Feb 1943, AD12, 28/15/4.

46 Prime Minister to Prime Minister, Australia, 16 Dec 1942, in Robin Kay (ed.), *The Australia-New Zealand Agreement 1944* (Historical Publications Branch, Wellington, 1972), p. 19.

47 Prime Minister to NZ High Commissioner, Canberra, 15 May 1943, in Kay, p. 26.

48 A.D. McIntosh to C.A. Berendsen, 9, 16 Jun 1943, in Ian McGibbon (ed.), *Undiplomatic Dialogue, Letters Between Carl Berendsen and Alister McIntosh 1943-52* (Auckland University Press, Auckland, 1993), pp. 26-30.

49 War Cabinet minute, 27 Jun 1943, AD12, 28/15/1.

50 Ibid., GOC 3rd Division to Army HQ, 2 Feb 1943.

51 Ibid., GOC, Wellington, to Cmdr, South Pacific, 11 Jun 1943.

52 See ibid., GOC, Wellington, to Cmdr, South Pacific, 11 Jun 1943, and reply, n.d. [received 21 Jul 1943].

53 Barrowclough to Puttick, 21 Oct 1943, Puttick Papers, 5/5.

54 See Governor of Fiji to UK High Commissioner, Wellington, 7 Dec 1942, AD12, 28/15/1.

55 Interview with Governor Laigret, 18 Dec 1943, in Gillespie, p. 343.

56 Salmon to J.T. Paul, 29 Nov 1943, EA1, 81/11/2.

57 GOC 3rd Division to Army HQ, 12 Mar 1943, AD1, 310/1/56.

58 Ibid., Minister of External Affairs to Secretary of State for Dominion Affairs, No 335, 23 Jul 1943.

59 See NZ Minister, Washington, to Minister of External Affairs, 12 Jan 1944, in Kay, p. 174.

60 Prime Minister to Governor of New Zealand, 8 Sep 1913, G26/6, Governor records, ANZ.

61 Notes by New Zealand Representatives on Draft Agenda, 17 Jan 1944, in Kay, p. 105.

62 N. Deschamps (Australian Official Resident, Noumea) to Department of External Affairs, Letter No 2, 24 Aug 1944, ABHS, 950, W4627, 308/4/1 ANZ.

63 Chiefs of Staff, 'Paper. . . on Security in Relation to the South Pacific', 12 Oct 1944, in Kay, p. 219.

64 Ibid.

'Neo' lands in Oceania: New Caledonia and New Zealand[1]

Adrian Muckle

With the stabilisation of the political situation in Kanaky New Caledonia since 1988 and the end to French nuclear testing announced in 1996 there has been a renewed interest in the integration of France's Pacific territories within the region. Focusing on Kanaky New Caledonia's place in the Pacific (rather than on France in the Pacific) and its relations with Aotearoa New Zealand, this paper examines the recent calls for the better regional integration of New Caledonia and considers the extent of New Caledonia and New Zealand's shared colonial heritage, and the potential for research focussed thereon.

Avec la stabilisation de la situation politique de la Kanaky-2 atomique française dans le Pacifique en 1996, il existe à nouveau une reflexion sur l'intégration des territoires français du Pacifique dans la region. Cette contribution portera sur la place de Kanaky-Nouvelle-Calédonie dans le Pacifique (plutôt que sur la place de la France dans le Pacifique) et ses relations avec Aotearoa-Nouvelle-Zélande. Il s'agira de présenter leur héritage colonial commun et les importantes possibilities de recherches croisées qui en découlent.

> New Caledonia, New Zealand's nearest neighbour (ignoring Norfolk and Lord Howe Islands), was settled by Europeans (and others) from the mid-nineteenth century onward, the tangata whenua of both countries wound up at the dirty end of the stick, and the people of European descent in both places are largely ignorant of, and subconsciously guilty about, their colonial past and its effects on the present (Corne 1995, p. 48).

Despite their geographical proximity, the linguistic, economic and political borders established by French and British colonisation have worked to restrain, as well as obscure, relations between Kanaky New Caledonia and Aotearoa New Zealand. Yet, both are linked by more than neo-European names; they share important physical, cultural and historical features and developments arising in each country, from European colonisation and its legacies, have important parallels in the other. As argued by linguist Chris Corne, it is New Caledonia's colonial heritage which makes it 'as much a part of Australasia and the insular Pacific as New Zealand is'. With only a few exceptions, however, there has been little academic discussion of this shared colonial heritage and its implications both for comparative historical studies and for understanding developing bilateral and regional relationships.

As part of an attempt to map some potential research directions and areas involving relations between Kanaky New Caledonia and Aotearoa New Zealand, this paper surveys the shared legacy of European colonisation and colonialism in each country. To what extent can these countries be examined as part of an area of shared colonial and postcolonial experience and interaction?; do they have a common history that has been neglected?; and how important is that history for future relations?[2] This paper is conceived as the beginning of a project rather than an end in itself. A preliminary discussion outlines converging calls for more research devoted to better understandings of the place of each country within the Pacific region. In the main body of the paper I turn to examine the extent of New Caledonia and New Zealand's shared colonial heritage.

In both countries the need to develop and promote better understandings of, and relations with, the rest of the Pacific islands region is evident in both political and research environments. The last five years have seen several calls for the better integration of New Caledonia within Pacific research in the humanities and social sciences. For a 2003 special issue on New Caledonia, the *Journal de la Société des Océanistes* asked contributors to consider 'their vision of New Caledonia and the future of relations between different countries of the Pacific'. At the same time a Paris-based 'Research Group on New Caledonia' cast its research agenda in terms of the need to 'rethink' themes developed in New Caledonia in the light of research conducted elsewhere in the Pacific. At the August 2004 'Symposium on French Research in the Pacific' researchers from around the region were invited to Noumea to share their opinions as to future directions for research. In the social sciences and humanities stream the overwhelming concern was the need to adapt research *to local needs* (for research about New Caledonia to be based in New Caledonia); one of the resolutions expressed was that France should do more to situate its research *in* rather than *on* the Pacific. Also evident was the desire of researchers and students based in New Caledonia to be able to establish contacts that break with local institutional confines. In April 2006, at a series of 'Workshops on Governance and Applied Research' (AGORA) in New Caledonia local participants noted the need for the development of comparative studies on the experiences of other Pacific island countries in a variety of social science domains (e.g., education, customary law and the impact of mining projects).[3] Researchers at the University of New Caledonia have been developing postgraduate courses to focus more on the region. For its part the New Caledonian government has established a Bureau of Regional Co-operation and External Relations to manage its regional, multilateral and bilateral engagements. The 2007 'New Caledonia in New Zealand' cultural season is another initiative of the New Caledonian government, the Provinces and the French Pacific Fund to lift New Caledonia's profile in New Zealand.

While New Caledonia in particular is seldom mentioned by New Zealand-based academics and organisations, the need to develop and promote better understandings of, and relations with, the Pacific islands is very much evident. On the academic front, historian Kerry Howe (2003) has lamented the increasing separation of modern New Zealand and Pacific Islands history writing; and another historian has challenged writers of NZ histories to consider NZ's involvement in the Pacific as part of the national history (Salesa 2005). The Pacific Cooperation Foundation, backed by the NZ government, has been charged with improving New Zealanders' understanding of the Pacific and their region.

These calls and initiatives may be seen as the products of at least two developments: on the one hand, the greater autonomy that New

Caledonia has acquired since the 1998 Nouméa Accord, including the freedom to establish relations with its neighbours and to join the Pacific Islands Forum (as an observer since 1999 and more recently as an associate member);[4] on the other hand, there is the growing awareness in New Zealand of the country's Pacific identity, its growing Pacific communities, as well as the need to bring into focus areas overlooked by national and linguistic frames of reference.

Such projects are all the more important because New Caledonia is largely absent from current debates about the Pacific islands region in Australia and New Zealand. If evoked at all, it is as the exception or as a place that experienced some instability back in the 1980s. In political analyses of the region, the French territories are often set aside as 'a separate category of Pacific country because of the dominant position the French state holds and the overwhelming force it can bring to bear either on externally or internally generated strife' (Hegarty 2004, p. 9). In this way New Caledonia is often marginalised, but, somewhat paradoxically, precisely at a time when the rhetoric of New Caledonian politics and research increasingly evokes the idea of New Caledonia as an emergent and integrated Pacific nation.

In interviews prior to the May 2004 elections, for example, New Caledonian politicians were called upon for their views on New Caledonia's place in the Pacific. France Debien (Rassemblement-UMP) noted that:

> After having been isolated and marginalised, New Caledonia is now fully recognised, even envied, on the regional stage. The [2003] Papeete meeting, presided over by the President of the Republic, Jacques Chirac, with all the French parliamentarians of the Pacific at his side, was a frank recognition of the extent of the integration of France and its territories in our regional environment. We must now go further because henceforth our neighbours respect us both as French people and as Oceanians living in a prosperous, stable country whose republican values of generosity [gift giving] and humanism are now unanimously recognised (*Les Nouvelles Calédoniennes*, 5 May 2004).

François Burck (FCCI) commented that:

> In the Pacific context, New Caledonia is an exception; it's a great

> country at the heart of the South Pacific, it's a francophone country in an anglophone ocean. In this sense its own identity must be reinforced. The image of New Caledonia needs to be affirmed and communications need to be multiplied and facilitated. The emergence of great nations like China may give New Caledonia a considerable boost, it being a staging post for Europe in the Pacific (*Les Nouvelles Calédoniennes*, 27 April 2004).

Common to these and other responses was a belief in New Caledonia's economy as a key to its place or acceptance in the region. According to Yannick Lechevalier (Entente française Nord), New Caledonia 'must be a platform for regional economic development. If we have a little ambition, New Caledonia could occupy an important place among the states that surround us and develop relations that will surely be profitable for us' (*Les Nouvelles Calédoniennes*, 30 April 2004). For Jean-Raymond Postic (Calédonie mon pays), 'Economically it is New Caledonia's vocation to become a small regional power especially if she integrates herself in the Oceanian [Pacific] context' (*Les Nouvelles Calédoniennes*, 30 April 2004). It is also clear that France's resolute presence in the Pacific and New Caledonia's status as part of France cannot be ignored, but this increasing emphasis on New Caledonia itself as an emergent or integrated Pacific/Oceanian nation deserves critical attention, as recent diplomatic overtures also suggest.

Since France came in from the nuclear cold in 1996 and since the signing of the Nouméa Accord in 1998, there has been a warming of relations at a more official level—a courting of New Caledonia by Australia and NZ. Though New Caledonia was nearly absent from the Australian Senate's 2003 report on a 'Pacific Engaged', an Australian parliamentary delegation to New Caledonia in the same year recognised it as a 'regional leader in terms of economic performance and governance' albeit 'assisted greatly by France's substantial financial and other support'. The delegation was 'pleased to see that New Caledonia is assuming a wider role in regional affairs, and that it may be an increasingly important partner for Australia in promoting shared values in the region.' The delegation described New Caledonia as a 'valuable partner' in the development of 'Pacific solutions to Pacific problems'. It 'found senior decision-makers to be well-disposed towards Australia, with many having strong personal and family links'. On the cultural front, the delegation reported that 'The Tjibaou Cultural Centre would be a model worthy of study for any proposed museum of indigenous culture and heritage in Australia.' It was impressed by the centre's aesthetics and Tjibaou's forward-looking vision, expressed in the statement 'To return to tradition is a myth' (Hansard, Senate, 23 June 2004, pp. 24759-61). Identifying these shared values and the groups among whom they are shared should tell us more about the future development of relations between New Caledonia and its neighbours.

In 2005 New Caledonia (as NZ's third largest Pacific export market) was visited by a seventy-strong New Zealand delegation. Its leader, Foreign Minister Phil Goff, noted the greater ability of New Caledonia to make decisions locally as a factor in NZ's changing approach to the French territories and urged that barriers to trade be further reduced. In the context of PICTA, Goff noted that '"we're looking at the integration [into the Pacific region] not only being on a political front but also on a trade front to try and integrate the French territories into trading arrangements in the Pacific"' (*NZ Herald*, 29 March 2005, p. A12). The ministerial visit was criticised, however, for its failure to formally visit or acknowledge the Customary Senate established under the 1998 Nouméa Accord.[5] Some blame was directed towards the French High Commission and the local (New Caledonian) government—both accused of persisting in a refusal 'to ignore France's commitment under the Nouméa Accord "to establish new relations with Kanak in accordance with contemporary realities"'. By far the larger part of criticism, however, went towards the NZ consulate—accused of being more familiar with France than with New Caledonia (Boengkih 2005; Chappell 2006, p. 406). Why this might have been the case is not clear. It was perhaps the absence of clear protocols and the fact that NC has not yet organised to adopt its own country symbols (a process only initiated in 2007); it was perhaps because of the higher priority given to trade and economic relations. Regardless, the incident serves as a reminder of the need for better understanding between the two countries, pointing as it does to a potential grey area of New Zealand's relations with an increasingly autonomous New

Caledonia (albeit still governed by parties opposed to independence) and with France.

There is a real value in considering the ways in which New Caledonia is (and has been) connected with its Pacific neighbours. Such an exercise also has a decolonising potential in that it helps break down the isolation of New Caledonia imposed by French colonisation (cf. Tjibaou 1996, pp. 119-120). For New Zealanders or Australians on the other hand, the value is perhaps that New Caledonia is almost as far as one can get without going very far at all; in the same way that learning another language for new insights or different perspectives on things taken for granted, this distance has the potential to be a good thing if used constructively. To this end, the remainder of this discussion has two objectives. On the one hand I seek to map some of the points of connection—past and present—between New Caledonia and New Zealand. These are not confined to bilateral ties, but include areas in which comparative studies might help inform a broader consideration of Kanaky New Caledonia in the Pacific. On the other hand, I draw attention to the circulation of ideas, models, peoples and the potential for a comparative analysis of colonial projects and their legacies. To what extent does a shared colonial heritage—the legacies of European settlement and colonisation—provide the basis for relations between these two countries, their governments and their peoples? To better bring relations between NC and NZ into focus (and to better consider New Caledonia's place in the Pacific), this paper purposefully sets aside entanglement in questions about France and NZ, France in the Pacific or the "French Pacific" which dominates much of the historical scholarship on this part of the world.

Geology and botany link both countries closely. Relations began at least 80 million years ago, before the landmass of which both were part gradually separated from Gondwana. Botanical research and horticultural magazines reveal the *Ghosts of Gondwana* (Gibbs 2006) and 'Our many cousins' (Williams 2000), including members of the genera *Metrosideros* (such as the Pohutukawa) and *Corynocarpus* (such as the Karaka) (Stevenson 1978; Dawson 2005). Unique flora and fauna, including endangered and flightless birds—the Cagou and the Kiwi—provide both countries with common environmental and conservation challenges (Hay 1984) as well as emblems.

With human colonisation of the Pacific further indirect links were established. Although first settlement began about two thousand years earlier in New Caledonia (*c.*3200 ago) than in New Zealand, both Kanak and Maori share the Austronesian linguistic heritage, and common ancestors in the Lapita people, the first settlers of Remote Oceania.[6] In human cultural terms New Caledonia appears more diverse than New Zealand: it sits in Melanesia rather than Polynesia and twenty-eight indigenous languages are still spoken. Yet, Kanak and Maori patterns of political organisation have much in common, both being characterised by openness, and respect for principles of consensus and consultation. Historian Bronwen Douglas has argued that 'in most respects New Caledonian and Maori leadership were more like each other than either was like the leadership stereotype for the particular culture area within which each was located' (Douglas, 1979: 21). The degree to which this still holds true for modern styles of leadership and political organisation is one potential area of research.

European exploration, trading and annexation of New Zealand by England in 1840 and of New Caledonia by France in 1853 laid the foundations for more direct relations and for the circulation of colonial power, knowledge and experience. European-indigenous encounters in the late-eighteenth century provide the foundations for the building of colonial histories and mythologies in both countries. In New Caledonia, English explorer James Cook's landing near Balade in 1774 and his positive encounter with Kanak has been long contrasted with French explorer Bruny d'Entrecasteaux's negative reaction in 1794 (e.g., Mariotti 1953). For later critics of French colonisation this first encounter with Cook represented a missed opportunity to recognise Kanak as a people (e.g., Dousset, 1970: 27). Jean-Marie Tjibaou, the late Kanak independence movement leader, said that 'Those who will agree, like Cook, to recognise us, to perform custom with us Kanaks, at the limit, if they persevere in their thought processes, they will be able to obtain a Kanak nationality' (Tjibaou, 1996: 201). Settlers and their descendants, though, have regretted a different kind of missed opportunity;

since the late-nineteenth century, they had seen the possibility 'of a colonisation that might have succeeded, had it been English' (Dahlem, 1996: 128).

Comparative studies of how these encounters have been treated, represented, reinterpreted in different traditions of local historical writing would provide excellent insights into shifting, colonial foundation narratives in these two countries and the way they have been inflected by British and French, as well as Kanak and Maori, influences. Historical research need not be the only frame of reference for such comparisons, however. It is relevant to recall how the emergence of Aboriginal history has challenged conventional historical narratives of Australian history and the silences surrounding historical injustices. Examples of this include stories about the arrival of Captain Cook which challenge and subvert European Australian myths about Cook as discoverer and founder by representing him as an invader who imposed unjust law (Attwood 1996: xviii-xxi; cf Attwood 2005). Writers and historians have drawn attention to the other possibilities that existed in the past, to imagined histories, and to a need to 'foreshadow and advance a *post*colonial relationship by offering a postcolonial interpretation of [. . .] historical beginnings', especially moments of first contact (Neumann 1994: 129).

In New Caledonia one example of this kind of imagining is the work of Pierre Gope and Nicolas Kurtovitch (2002). In their play, 'The gods are one-eyed' (*Les dieux sont borgnes*) they explore New Caledonia's past, present and future, and seek to transcend political divisions, using encounters with Cook as a central device (cf. Faessel 2004). After arrival in New Caledonia, their James Cook is transformed into the *akua*, Lono, and eventually killed at the hands of Kanak, not Hawaiians, though the word Kanak is itself derived from the Hawaiian *kanaka* (cf. tangata). In a similar vein, New Zealand artist Michel Tuffery's recent 'First Contact' exhibition reinterprets eighteenth-century encounters involving Cook (or Cookie), Mai and Tupaia in New Zealand through a twenty-first century Polynesian prism (Pataka Museum of Arts and Cultures, Porirua, 26 August-25 November 2007).

Patterns of European annexation, settlement and colonisation provide more traditional points of comparison and connection, as do Maori and Kanak experiences of colonisation. Australian and New Zealand business interests were vital to the establishment of European settlement in New Caledonia. As Tremewan has noted, Roman Catholic missionaries to New Caledonia in 1843 were indebted to Philippe Viard (future Bishop of Wellington) for his knowledge of Maori language which facilitated communication with Kanak of Wallisian ancestry; and in the 1850s Bishop Selwyn brought Loyalty islanders to New Zealand to be trained for the Anglican church's Melanesian mission in the 1850s (Tremewan, this volume). In the 1840s, the sandalwood trade drew New Caledonia into the web of commerce and resource extraction flung out into the Pacific from settlements in Australia and New Zealand. It was at a public meeting in Wellington in 1843 that James Paddon first recruited settlers, including six Maori—a group described in NZ press as 'the most extraordinary and promiscuous set of passengers that ever sailed from a port'—for the establishment of his trading depots first in the New Hebrides and later in New Caledonia (Shineberg, 1967: 98). Little is known about this group, except that some Maori were still at Paddon's stations in New Caledonia in 1854 (Hollyman 1995).

It was Australia rather than New Zealand that provided France with the model for its own attempt at penal settlement and rehabilitation in New Caledonia between 1864 and 1897, but British practice on land matters in New Zealand inspired and comforted French administrators in their alienation of Kanak land (Douglas 1972, p. 369 fn 37). And in the early-twentieth century one colonial inspector cited Frederick Edward Maning's *Old New Zealand* for the insights that it might offer into Kanak conceptions of property rights (Pégourier, 1919, pp. 5-6). NZ historians, increasingly fascinated by Scottish and Irish studies may be intrigued to know that Carton 205 in the French National Archives geographical series on New Caledonia contains a dossier on the New Zealand government's recruitment of Scottish settlers in 1864-1869. What conclusions were drawn? Colonial wars provided another form of shared experience; the largest war between Kanak and settlers in 1878-79 was extensively reported by Australian correspondents. Earlier in the 1860s, a midshipman in the British navy witnessed reprisals on both Kanak and Maori (Kerr 1856-62). If French administrators defended their policies towards Kanak with reference to more dire Australian experiences in Tasmania—a recurring motif in New Caledonian colonial discourse (Muckle 2006, p. 107)—what did New Zealand signify? In times of hardship, settlers sometimes looked towards Australia and NZ as alternative destinations (Papin, 1997, pp. 27 and 104); and in 1909 some went so far as to request annexation by Australia. In 1928, anticipating legislation to protect Maori burial sites or caves, the NZ government sought information about any equivalent French legislation in New Caledonia.[7] From such sketchy details emerges a picture of the circulation and production of colonial knowledge and experience.

Closer examination of the extensive colonial literature relating to European travel in the Pacific islands in the nineteenth and twentieth centuries will certainly reveal more reporting on, and sharing of, colonial experiences. Race, colonial development, and South Pacific security will be important themes. In the late-nineteenth century, dealing with convicts and deportees from NC prompted consternation in New Zealand and inter-government communication (Liava'a, 2001; Marshall, 2001).[8] In the early-twentieth century, concern about the growing number of Japanese settlers in New Caledonia prompted one NZ newspaper to send a journalist there in 1911 (Gordon 1960, p. 35) and the idea of New Caledonia and other Pacific islands to the north as a buffer between New Zealand and Asia eventually reached its height in 1942-44. A postwar example is provided by travel writer Judy Fallon's visit to the Hienghène and Tipindjé valleys; there she encountered a local named Ferron who complained that with the demise of cannibalism and under missionary influence the Kanak had 'lost their zest for life'; what they needed, he claimed, was to be taught 'football' 'as the Maoris were' (Fallon 1952, p. 54). While it is difficult to interpret such comments as anything other than examples of entrenched racism, they also direct us to ask what New Zealanders and New Caledonians talked about when they met: football?, hunting?, farming?, each others' "natives", each others' "colonials"? To what extent has the history and experience of colonisation provided the basis for relations between the two and is this still the case?

It is necessary, though, to be attentive to the different dynamics and asymmetries operating in the two countries, especially those of economy, population and scale which impose real differences on human experiences. While early European settlement schemes for both countries had agrarian ideals in common, colonial experiences differed. The mining of nickel ore (of which New Caledonia has one of the world's largest repositories) rather than agriculture dominated the New Caledonian economy by the end of the nineteenth century and continues to do so. Penal settlement and indentured labour—Javanese, Japanese, Vietnamese and ni-Vanuatu—provided New Caledonia with its manpower, while rural development and free settlement languished. Whereas NZ became a Dominion in 1907 and gained greater autonomy and independence, NC experienced the opposite movement; a tightening of controls by France, and a raising of tariff barriers after 1893 (Buttet 1997, pp. 20-22).

The twentieth century's two world wars drew Australia, NZ and the Pacific islands into international conflicts. Both NZ and NC made significant sacrifices and contributions to the Great War.[9] Commemoration of the Great War in New Caledonia has never been the pillar for the kind of nationalism evident in New Zealand, but recent commemorations have sought to evoke the possibility of a shared history of Kanak and European participation in the Great War as New Caledonians, and to emphasise the ties that still bind New Caledonia to France. According to Boubin-Boyer, emphasising the participation of all ethnic groups in World War One will help the 'Caledonian communities' to 'forge together the common destiny anticipated by the 1998 Noumea Accord' (Boubin-Boyer, 2005). Yet to be examined is the history and local meaning of Anzac day celebrations in New Caledonia.

It was also during the Great War that a minor literary connection was established. Visiting the Zone des Armées, New Zealand-born writer Kathleen Mansfield Beauchamp (aka Katherine Mansfield) began an affair with New Caledonian-born French novelist Francis Carcopino Tusoli (aka Francis Carco, 1886-1958), the son of a Corsican prison warder. The affair 'contributed to' Mansfield's stories, 'An Indiscreet Journey' and 'Je ne parle pas français' (O'Sullivan 1998; cf. Griscelli 1988). Mansfield's portrait of Raoul

Duquette in the latter story is said to be based on Carco:

> My name is Raoul Duquette. I am twenty-six years old and a Parisian, a true Parisian. About my family—it really doesn't matter. I have no family; I don't want any. I never think about my childhood. I've forgotten it (Mansfield 1962, p. 68).

Unlike Mansfield, Carco was reluctant to evoke the terrain of his childhood, the first ten years of which were spent in New Caledonia; the reasons perhaps were personal ('a family of crazies' and a violent father according to one commentary), but it would not be drawing too long a bow to say that it could also have been the taint of the penal heritage.[10] Such reticence would be typical of other New Caledonian-born French citizens who until the late 1980s sought to avoid discussion of this past. In this respect there are significant differences in how people relate to the colonial heritage in these two countries that would be worth exploring.

Of obvious significance to both New Caledonia and New Zealand are the ties established during the second world war when New Caledonia became 'buffer', 'aircraft carrier', 'stepping stone' and 'staging post' for the Allied campaign against Japan. While this second world war saw the linking of the Pacific islands in the minds of the colonial powers as a single theatre requiring new forms of cooperation and laying the foundations for postwar regional organisations, the division of labour within that theatre meant that New Zealand and New Caledonia came within one sphere, leaving Australia and PNG in another. 20,000 NZ troops sent to the Pacific passed through New Caledonia, and several hundred—principally airmen—still lie in the NZ cemetery at Bourail. Notwithstanding the recent publication of *Against the Rising Sun* (oral histories from veterans of that war) and the 'War in Paradise' exhibition (Museum of Wellington City & Sea, August 2007), the extent of New Zealand's wartime presence in New Caledonia remains little known.

What relations and impressions were formed? Did they last? What do they tell us about people from the two countries? What experiences were shared? Did NZ troops in any way identify with French settlers or see any reflection of their own colonial society in 1940s New Caledonia? The titles of the official and unofficial histories of the second NZEF and other publications produced by and for the troops are indicative of an army humour—*Base Wallahs*, *Bonjour*, *The arty AnTiDote*, *Transit Tramp*, *New Caledonia: Know her to Love Her.* ... —but reveal little about how they responded to the local people, if indeed they had the opportunity. However, a closer glance at the unofficial histories (as provided by the 'War in Paradise' exhibition) for evidence of how the New Zealanders saw New Caledonia indicates several recurring topics: landscape, race and Frenchness. Running through these descriptions is the theme of disillusionment or deception and the suggestion that New Caledonia was both foreign and familiar in ways not anticipated.

Misplaced expectations account for some of this deception, as is evident in initial assessments of New Caledonia's west coast: 'Most of us had expected a tropical vista to open before our eyes as we neared land, but there was not a vestige of tropical vegetation to be seen'. Nor did it compare very favourably with the landscape left behind; on the initial approach: 'Hills, always hills. Some thought of the ranges below Cambridge, where the grass was green and soft and the dawn came up with a sparkle over the Waikato valley.' Upon closer inspection, 'only a week away from the Waikato, it looked like a private entrance into Hell. Then the dust cleared and revealed real grass. A few cattle grazed beside a stream' (Gillespie 1947, *Stepping Stones to the Solomons*, p. 36). Later, after months of tedium, men such as W.E. Scott had no regrets leaving this 'Foul isle of the sea' (Scott 2007, p. 15). The Solomons campaign, though, provided the antidote to tropical desire; upon the return:

> The eye was no longer cramped by encompassing trees; the hills by day and the sky by night were wide open to view. ... it was surprising, too, to find the cattle down by the streams, the broad expanses of grass, even reaching beneath the tents the long roads that led somewhere—all these things had something of beauty in them. Even the niauolis were not so repulsive. If NC looked like this, what must NZ be like (Gillespie 1947, *Stepping Stones to the Solomons*, pp. 73-74).

In descriptions and comments on the local inhabitants a not inconsiderable emphasis on evidence of racial diversity and mixing is evident: 'The cosmopolitanism of the East which Nouméa presents to the new arrival is as unexpected as it is colourful; the Javanese women with their doll-like figures; the Tonkinese, their teeth and lips stained by betel-nut chewing and their stocky figures accentuated by their national costume of slacks, all stood in sharp contrast to what the NZers had left behind only a few days earlier' (NZ Army Third Division, *Pacific Pioneers*, pp. 131-2). What further observations were made or conclusions drawn?

A third preoccupation was with clichés and stereotypes of France or Frenchness; wine, women, cheese and the lure of Nouméa as a South Pacific Paris or paradise. Here, too, disillusionment sometimes prevailed: 'All troops had an opportunity of having a quick look at Nouméa and were disappointed. The shops were empty, the streets were dirty. Pretty French girls were conspicuous by their absence and, instead, a motley crowd of NC natives and Javanese patrolled the streets. This was not the "Paris of the Pacific"' (Gillespie 1947, *Pacific Saga*, p. 41). There have been studies of the influence that the Allied troops had on Kanak (e.g., Brown 1995), but what impression did the New Zealanders have on New Caledonians more generally, other than the gendarmerie's complaint that they drove too fast through the villages and refused to obey US military police?

What knowledge was exchanged? What did people—individually and collectively—learn from New Caledonia or about themselves and their country while serving there? As noted by Tryon (this volume), linguist Jim Hollyman's interest in New Caledonia stemmed from his service there during the war. Eric Ojala, an agricultural instructor turned sergeant, contributed an article to the *NZ Journal of Agriculture* detailing New Caledonian farming practices (Ojala 1943). Exploring the possible link between his New Caledonian experience and the development of such practices as tree fodder use is well beyond my expertise, but further studies would do well to consider what impressions lasted and what kinds of connections endured.

After 1944, the future of colonial rule and colonialism emerge more clearly as issues of common interest or concern. US President Roosevelt's opinion (expressed at the Pacific War Council on 12 January 1944) that New Caledonia should be taken off France and possibly handed over to Australia or NZ met vehement opposition from the latter. Statements in the subsequent Australia-NZ agreement (e.g., clause 27, that 'no change in the sovereignty or system or system of control of any of the islands of the Pacific should be effected except as a result of an agreement to which they are parties or in the terms of which they have both concurred) 'flabbergasted' US Secretary of State Cordell Hull who commented that 'this agreement would seem to show that Australia and NZ have their minds on the whole question of territorial settlement in the Pacific, with special reference to New Caledonia and other areas' (Memorandum by the Secretary of State [Cordell Hull] of Conversation with the PM of Australia and the Minister for Australia in the US, in Kay (ed.), p. 276). This support for continued French possession of New Caledonia, in the face of potential US interest, contributed to the breakdown of relations with Roosevelt and the US in the Pacific War Council (see Weeks 1989, note 35; cf. William Roger Louis; cf. Gordon). Related and underlying concerns at this time were security and air links (e.g., the development of commercial aviation); until jet technology developed further New Caledonia was a vital link in trans-Pacific aviation.

For at least one French official, too, the war heralded a potential change in thinking about New Caledonia's relationship with France. Writing in 1944, in light of New Caledonia's 'loyalty to the French community' and its newfound place as a centre of Pacific affairs, Pierre Olivier Lapie (a former Governor of Chad and Director of External Affairs in de Gaulle's wartime cabinet) observed that:

> New Caledonia is also a member of the Pacific community, and perfectly conscious of occupying an advanced position. She is also aware of being *interdependent* not only with the nearby lands but also with those countries which have a share in the security and prosperity of the Pacific (Lapie 1944).

Underlying the statement was an awareness that French settlers in New Caledonia had in the past 'felt some bitterness towards the mother country . . . because it felt that its rightful place in the family of France was withheld' and the realisation that the post-war era would need to see changes in the relationship between France and its colonies. Lapie went on to describe initiatives associated with the Brazzaville conference which he hoped would lead to the establishment of a 'post-war federal constitution of the French Empire'. Such an arrangement, he argued, would allow the maintenance in New Caledonia of French patriotism, a 'community of interests with other nations of the Pacific' and resource exploitation. Furthermore, France 'would give her an entirely free hand in the direction of its local affairs' and 'New Caledonia would of course take advantage of its political liberty to establish friendly treaties with the nations of the South Pacific' (Lapie 1944).

While the kind of autonomy promised by Lapie was shortlived (and was wound back from 1963-1998), in the six decades since 1944, the idea of New Caledonia's interdependence within the region has been inflected in different ways in relation to the question of its future status. Jean-Marie Tjibaou, has been celebrated for 'bringing a relational conception to the practice of politics' and international diplomacy: 'Sovereignty means the right to choose one's partners. For a small country like ours, independence means working out interdependency' (Tjibaou 1996: 179). With the renewed thinking about regionalism associated with development of the Pacific island Forum's 2005 'Pacific Plan', this possibility has been given a new relevance: '. . . future inter-country relationships will need to be closer and more mutually supportive if the region is to avoid decline and international marginalisation. Enhanced regional cooperation and integration, and the sharing of resources of governance, are likely to be features of future developments. New thinking about the relationships between sovereign states may hold the key to future sustainability'. The 'Pacific Plan' itself has been described as 'a vehicle for placing the "big idea" of Pacific inter-dependence squarely at the front of the regional political agenda' (Eminent Persons' Group 2004: 10 and 21).

In the 1950s, relations continued to be invigorated by ties established during the war. Building closer cultural ties with New Zealand and Australia was one of the anticipated functions of the 'Institut Océanien' that French authorities planned in 1946-48 (eventually established as the Institut Français d'Océanie and succeeded by ORSTOM and the IRD).[11] Celebrations for the 1953 centenary of the French occupation of New Caledonia included the opening at Ducos of a clinic for leprosy sufferers donated by the Lepers Trust Board of NZ (*Evening Post*, 24 and 29 Sept. 1953).[12]

A plaque there served as a memorial to New Zealand servicemen who died in New Caledonia, until superseded by the unveiling of the Cross of Sacrifice at the Bourail war cemetery in 1955. The establishment of the South Pacific Commission's headquarters in Nouméa in 1949 brought New Caledonia to the centre of Pacific affairs. Post-war prosperity and air travel encouraged tourism, and cultural exchanges became more frequent; schemes to take students and teachers of the French language to New Caledonia date from at least the 1960s. The NZ consulate-general in Nouméa, opened in 1972, is one of New Zealand's earliest diplomatic missions in the region, and NZ continues to provide New Caledonian students with educational opportunities as a form of development assistance.

For both countries, 1975 was a key date in the revival and renaissance of indigenous culture and protest—it was the year of the Maori Land March in New Zealand and the Melanesia 2000 festival in New Caledonia. The latter event was organised by Jean-Marie Tjibaou, who the following year led a New Caledonian delegation to the second Pacific Arts Festival in Rotorua. Cultural events such as the Pacific Arts festivals and games remain important venues for forging closer ties. One of the missions of the cultural centre named in honour of Tjibaou is 'to promote cultural exchanges, particularly within the South Pacific region'; New Zealand artists and performers have been among those contributing to its success and Tjibaou's call for a 'Pacific new home'. Together with visits by voyaging canoes, notably Te Aurere in 2001 (Putaranui 2001), and performing arts groups, these provide other less well-known links and histories of interaction; they are reminders that European settler society is not always the primary referent in relations between the two countries.

In the 1980s, relations were disrupted by the violent clashes between the opponents and supporters of independence which shook New Caledonia. Excluding tourist promotions, it probably remains the case that New Caledonia is best known to New Zealanders for these "troubles". Newspaper article titles such as 'Our forgotten neighbour' and 'Trouble in Paradise' are indicative of NZ reactions and the extent to which NC had been out of public view. Sensitivities were heightened by the campaigns against French nuclear testing and the Rainbow Warrior bombing (Ouvéa was for a time infamous as the name of the yacht used by some of the bombers rather than as one of the Loyalty islands). While some local whites (or their capital) took flight to the Gold Coast or Auckland, Australian and NZ journalists, writers, photographers and academics rushed to the scene. New Zealand novelist James McNeish told the story of the troubles as *Penelope's Island*, through the eyes of an English botanist married to a local settler.

It would seem obvious that the two countries' conflicted experiences of race relations offer the possibility of mutual insights, as well as points of connection. At first glance such analyses are not obvious, but they are implicit in some research. One example is Australian Alaine Chanter's study of the New Caledonian media in the 1980s which applies an analysis of New Zealand Pakeha discourse—the language of racism—to New Caledonia (Chanter 1996; cf. Wetherell and Potter 1992). Criticism during the 1980s, from Australia and NZ, of ongoing French colonialism or its legacy antagonised some New Caledonians who felt that the pot was calling the kettle black. Defending a neighbourly right to offer advice, Alan Ward (the NZ historian and author of *Land and Politics in New Caledonia*), suggested that the 'moral right' of Australians and New Zealanders to comment on affairs in New Caledonia rested as much on the 1000 graves at Bourail and the 100,000 graves in France as on any claim to superior race relations (Ward 1982, p. 76).[13]

Indépendantistes in turn looked to the Pacific region for support and recognition, and to 'reestablish [and] revive traditional routes' (Tjibaou 1996, pp. 119-120). Although often seen in Melanesian terms, developing links with indigenous activists throughout the Pacific was an important part of the Kanak struggle for recognition of their cause, including the eventual re-inscription of the territory on the UN list of territories awaiting decolonisation in 1986.[14] While language has been, and remains, an important (but not insurmountable) barrier to such links, the last few years also have seen translations into English of major works by Kanak writers; notably the collected speeches and writing of Tjibaou (*Kanaky*, 2005) and collections of short stories and poems by writer and Vice President, Dewe Gorode (*Sharing as Custom Provides*, 2004; *The Kanak Apple Season*, 2004).

In the nearly twenty years since the end of the "troubles" in

1988, cultural renaissance in New Caledonia has taken a more "Caledonian" than "Melanesian" form as non-indigenous groups have turned to consider their identities and place in the Pacific. Again, synergies with developments in NZ are especially evident. There has been an outpouring of history and literature exploring various facets of Kanak, Caledonian and Caldoche identities. Choosing a title which echoed New Zealand historian Michael King's exploration of the ethnicity of non-Maori New Zealanders, *Being Pakeha* (1985), a group of New Caledonians of mainly European heritage wrote *Etre Caldoche aujourd'hui* (Being Caldoche today) in 1994—an assertion of their place in New Caledonia and of the need to be Caldoche (a term used to describe the descendants of mainly European settlers) before becoming New Caledonians. King's *Being Pakeha Now*, an assertion of pakeha right to their own identity and even indigeneity, came five years later in 1999 (cf. Denoon and Mein Smith, p. 396).

This is where my mapping exercise ends. As noted in the preliminary discussion the last decade has seen a warming of relations (political, economic and cultural) between New Caledonia and its various neighbours in the Pacific. An aspect of the growing recognition of New Caledonia within, and as part of, the Pacific islands region is an understanding that it need no longer be isolated by its colonial heritage and the contradictions inherent in its ongoing relations with France and Europe, on the one hand, and its no less ambiguous position in the Pacific—betwixt and between island Melanesia and settler colonial Australia and New Zealand—on the other. Yet, there arguably remains a potential tension between the autonomy being accorded to New Caledonia and France's concern to use its Pacific territories as windows for the French presence. It remains to be seen how much room there is for New Caledonia to express its identity in other terms, and to advance its own interests. So far as history and colonial legacies are concerned, it may be that there are not enough shared experiences to constitute a shared past, let alone a history or histories of NZ and NC. At this early stage, though, it would be premature to reach any definite conclusion. What should be more than evident is that both countries have much to learn from each other as regards their colonial histories and decolonisation processes.

References

Attwood, Bain. 'The Past as Future: Aborigines, Australia and the (dis)course of History', in Attwood, Bain (ed.), *In the Age of Mabo: History, Aborigines and Australia*, St Leonards: Allen and Unwin, 1996, pp. vii–xxxviii.

Boengkih, Sarimin J. 'Le peuple kanak encore marginalisé', posting to *Kanaky Online*, 31 March 2005.

Boubin-Boyer, Sylvette. 'Plus de précisions sur les tirailleurs de Nouvelle-Calédonie. . .', http://goutte.a.goutte.free.fr/rubrique/projets/caledofragile/hist.html. Accessed September 2005.

Boyer, Sylvette. 'La mobilisation dans le Pacifique', in Musée de la Ville de Nouméa (ed.), *1914-1918. Mémoires océaniennes de la Grande Guerre. Chronique calédonienne*, Noumea: Musée de la ville de Nouméa, 1999, 12–15.

Brown, Elizabeth. 'Les Mélanésiens et le temps des américains. L'impact de la présence alliée sur les Mélanésiens de la Nouvelle-Calédonie pendant la Seconde Guerre mondiale'. BA Hons Research Essay, Massey University, 1995.

Buttet, Catherine. 'De la grogne au séparatisme: les Européens en Nouvelle-Calédonie (1907-1909)', *Ultramarines*, 14 (1997): 20–27.

Chanter, Alaine. 'Contested Identity: the Media and Independence in New Caledonia during the 1980s', PhD Thesis, Canberra: Australian National University, 1996.

Chappell, David. 'New Caledonia', *The Contemporary Pacific*, 18:2 (2006): 399–413.

Commonwealth of Australia—Senate Foreign Affairs, Defence and Trade References Committee, *A Pacific Engaged. Australia's relations with PNG and the island states of the south-west Pacific*, Canberra: Senate Printing unit, 2003. Available online: http://www.aph.gov.au/Senate/committee/fadt_ctte/completed_inquiries/2002-04/png/report/index.htm.

Corne, Chris. 'Review of Paul de Dekker (ed.), *Le Peuplement du pacifique et de la Nouvelle-Calédonie*', *Antipodes*, no. 1 (1995): 47–51.

Dahlem, Jacqueline. *Nouvelle-Calédonie, pays kanak: un récit, deux histoires*, Paris: l'Harmattan, 1996.

Dawson, John. 'New Caledonia: A Botanical Mecca' in Glynnis M. Cropp, Noel R. Watts, Roger D.J. Collins and K.R. Howe (eds.), *Pacific Journeys. Essays in Honour of John Dunmore*, Wellington: Victoria University Press, 2005, pp. 216–228.

Denoon, Donald and Philippa Mein-Smith with M. Wyndham. *A History of Australia, NZ and the Pacific*, Oxford: Blackwell, 2000.

Douglas, Bronwen. 'A History of Culture Contact in North-Eastern New Caledonia, 1774-1870', PhD thesis, Australian National University, 1972.

——. 'Rank, Power, Authority: a Reassessment of Traditional Leadership in South Pacific Societies', *Journal of Pacific History*, 14:1 (1979): 2–27.

Dousset, Roselène. *Colonialisme et contradictions. Etude sur les causes socio-historiques de l'Insurrection de 1878 en Nouvelle-Calédonie*, Paris: Mouton & Co., 1970.

Eminent Persons Group. *Pacific Cooperation: Voices of the Region*, The Eminent Persons Group Review of the Pacific Islands Forum, April 2004.

Faessel, Sonia. 'Where Literature is Ahead of Politics: World Fiction is Coming to New Caledonia', *New Pacific Review – La Nouvelle Revue du Pacifique*, 2 (2004): 168–174.

Fallon, Judy. *Pacific Pantomime*, Andrew Melrose Ltd: London and Melbourne, 1952.

Fraenkel, John. 'Power sharing in Fiji and New Caledonia', in Stewart Firth (ed.), *Globalisation and Governance in the Pacific Islands*, Canberra: ANU E Press, 2006, pp. 317–348.

Gibbs, George. *Ghosts of Gondwana: the history of life in New Zealand*, Nelson: Craig Potton, 2006.

Gillespie, Oliver A. *Stepping Stones to the Solomons: the unofficial history of the 29th Battalion with the Second New Zealand Expeditionary Force in the Pacific*, [Wellington]: Reed for the Third Division Histories Committee, 1947.

—— *Pacific Saga: the personal chronicle of the 37th Battalion and its part in the Third Division's campaign*, [Wellington]: Reed for the Third Division Histories Committee, 1947.

Gope, Pierre and Nicolas Kurtovitch. *Les dieux sont borgnes*, Nouméa: Éditions Grain de sable, 2002.

Gordon, Bernard K. *New Zealand Becomes a Pacific Power*, Chicago: University of Chicago Press, 1960.

Gorode, Déwé. *The Kanak Apple Season: selected short fiction of Déwé Gorodé*, Peter Brown (trans.), Canberra: Pandanus Books, 2004.

——. *Sharing as Custom Provides: selected poems of Déwé Gorodé*, Raylene Ramsay and Deborah Walker (trans.), Canberra: Pandanus Books, 2004.

Hay, Rod. 'The cagou: a question of survival', *Forest and Bird*, 15:2 (May 1984).

Hegarty, David. 'Intervention, Regionalism, engagement: New Forms of Security management in the South Pacific', *SSGM Working Paper*, no. 3, 2004.

Hollyman, J. 'Birds and plants as seeds of expansion: Governor Grey (and others) and New Caledonia', *Antipodes*, 2 (1996): 9–11.

——. 'Paddon's Maoris, and others: first contacts between New Zealand and New Caledonia', *Antipodes*, 1 (1995): 18–19.

Howe, Kerry. 'Two Worlds?', *New Zealand Journal of History*, 37:1 (2003): 50–61.

Hutching, Megan, with Ian McGibbon and Alison Parr (eds.). *Against the Rising Sun: New Zealanders Remember the Pacific War*, Auckland: Harper Collins Publishers in association with the Ministry for Culture and Heritage, 2006.

Kay, R. (ed.). *Documents on New Zealand External Relations Volume 1 The Australian-New Zealand Agreement 1944*, Wellington: Historical Publications Branch, 1972.

Kerr, Alexander Robert. 'Letters, 1856-62', ms 7257, National Library of Australia.

King, Michael. *Being Pakeha: an encounter with New Zealand and the Maori renaissance*, Auckland: Hodder and Stoughton, 1985.

——. *Being Pakeha Now: reflections and recollections of a white native*, Auckland: Penguin, 1999.

Lapie, Pierre Olivier. 'The Future of New Caledonia', *Pacific Affairs*, 17:3 (September): 336–340.

Liava'a, Christine. 'French Convicts in New Zealand', *The New Zealand Genealogist*, September/October 2001, pp. 323–325.

Marshall, Lucy. 'French Deportees: Convicts and Communists arrive in Auckland', *The New Zealand Genealogist*, November/December 2001, pp. 396–398.

McNeish, James. *Penelope's Island,* Auckland: Hodder and Stoughton, 1990.

Maning, F.E. *Old New Zealand: Being Incidents of Native Customs and Character in the Old Times by A Pakeha Maori*, London: Smith, Elder, 1863.

Mansfield, Katherine. *Bliss and other stories*, London: Penguin Books, 1962.

Mariotti, Jean. *Nouvelle-Calédonie. Le Livre du Centenaire 1853-1953*, Paris: Horizons de France, 1953.

Mein-Smith, Philippa and Peter Hempenstall. 'Australia and New Zealand: Turning Shared Pasts into a Shared History', *History Compass*, 1 (2003).

Mrgudovic, Nathalie. 'New Caledonia's Struggle for Independence: A Regional Perspective', *New Pacific Review – La Nouvelle Revue du Pacifique*, 2 (2004): 105–124.

Muckle, Adrian. 'Tropes of (mis)understanding—imagining shared destinies in New Caledonia, 1853-1998', *Journal de la Société des Océanistes*, 124-1 (2007): 105–118.

Neumann, Klaus. '"In order to win their friendship": Renegotiating First Contact', *The Contemporary Pacific*, 6:1 (1994): 111–145.

New Zealand Army Third Division (2nd NZEF IP). *Pacific Pioneers: the story of the Engineers of the New Zealand Expeditionary Force in the Pacific*, Oliver A. Gillespie (ed.), [Wellington]: Reed for the Third Division Histories Committee [*c*.1945].

Ojala, E.M. 'Farming in New Caledonia', *New Zealand Journal of Agriculture*, 66:5 (15 May 1943): 295–297.

[Ouvrage Collectif]. *Etre Caldoche aujourd'hui*, Nouméa: Ile de Lumière, 1994.

O'Sullivan, Vincent. 'Katherine Mansfield', in Roger Robinson and Nelson Wattie (eds.), *The Oxford Companion to New Zealand Literature*, Melbourne; Auckland: Oxford University Press, 1998, http://www.bookcouncil.org.nz/writers/mansfieldk.html, accessed 10 October 2006.

Papin, Bernard. *Vie et mort de Ludovic Papin chez les Canaques*, Paris: l'Harmattan, 1997.

Pégourier (l'Inspecteur des Colonies). 'Rapport concernant la vérification du service de M. Fourcade chef du Service des affaires indigènes, Inspection 1919', ts, 106 pp, Carton 97W11, Archives territoriales de la Nouvelle-Calédonie (ATNC).

Putaranui, Ata. 'Te Aurere's unscheduled landfall. . . or was it?', *Tu Mai: offering an indigenous New Zealand perspective*, Feb. 2001: 20–25.

Rutland, Joshua. 'Did the Maori Discover the Greenstone?' *Transactions and Proceedings of the Royal Society of New Zealand*, vol. 30 (1897): 29–32.

Salesa, Damon. 'New Zealand and Samoa: Histories of Forgetting', Pacific Studies Seminar at Victoria University of Wellington, 24 May 2005.

Sankey, Margaret, 'The Franco-Australasian Connection: Historical Studies in French Departments in Australia and New Zealand', *AUMLA*, 100 (November 2003): 73–87.

Scott, William E. *Poèmes calédoniens-Caledonian Poems*, Dominique Lataste (trans.), [Nouméa]: Editions du GRHOC, 2007.

Shineberg, Dorothy. *They Came for Sandalwood: A Study of the Sandalwood Trade in the South-West Pacific, 1830-1865*, [Melbourne]: Melbourne University Press, 1967.

Tjibaou, Jean-Marie. *La Présence Kanak*, Alban Bensa and Eric Wittersheim (eds.), Paris: Éditions Odile Jacob, 1996.

——. *Kanaky*, Helen Fraser and John Trotter (trans.), Alban Bensa and Eric Wittersheim (eds.), Canberra: Pandanus Books, 2005.

Schmidt, H.P. *New Caledonia: Know Her to Love Her. A Documentary Survey of the French Colony with illustrations*, Sydney: George A. Jones Pty. Ltd, 1944.

Stevenson, Greta. 'Botanical evidence linking the New Zealand Maoris with New Caledonia and the New Hebrides', *Nature*, 276 (14 December 1978): 704–705.

Veracini, Lorenzo. 'Negotiating Indigenous Resistance in the South Pacific: Australia, Aotearoa/New Zealand and Kanaky-New Caledonia, Three Cases in Historical Redescription', PhD thesis, Griffith University, 2001.

—— and Adrian Muckle. 'Reflections of Indigenous History *inside* the National Museums of Australia and New Zealand and *outside* of New Caledonia's Centre Culture Jean-Marie Tjibaou.' *Electronic Journal of Australian and New Zealand History* (2002).

Ward, Alan. *Land and Politics in New Caledonia*, Canberra: Department of

Political and Social Change, RSPS, ANU, 1982.

Weeks, Charles J. 'An hour of temptation: American interests in New Caledonia, 1935–1945', *Australian Journal of Politics and History*, 35:2 (1989): 185–200.

Wetherell, Margaret and Jonathon Potter. *Mapping the Language of Racism: discourse and the legitimation of exploitation*, New York: Harvester Wheatsheaf, 1992.

Williams, Trish. 'Our Many Cousins in New Caledonia', *Commercial Horticulture*, October 2000, p. 37.

Wittersheim, Eric. 'Melanesian élites and modern politics in New Caledonia and Vanuatu', SSGM Discussion Paper 1998/3, http://rspas.anu.edu.au/papers/melanesia/discussion_papers/ssgmwittersheim.pdf.

Notes

1 Earlier versions of this paper were presented at 'Stepping Forward 2006—An Interdisciplinary Conference for Emerging Researchers', University of Waikato, 15-17 October 2006; and at the NC-NZ workshop in Bourail and Wellington, April and August 2007. Material from this paper has been used in an essay commissioned by the Museum of Wellington City & Sea for the exhibition 'War in Paradise'. The support provided by the convenors of all three events is gratefully acknowledged.

2 Some of the inspiration for this paper was provided by Philippa Mein-Smith's and Peter Hempenstall's agenda for turning the 'shared pasts' of Australia and NZ into a 'shared history' ('Australia and New Zealand: Turning Shared Pasts into a Shared History', 2003). Their starting point is the question: why is it that these countries 'share various pasts [experiences and similar flags] but neglect their common history'; and what are the 'continuing flows and ties between them'?

3 The author is an associate member of the 'Research Group on New Caledonia' and at the AGORA workshop chaired sessions on development, globalisation and regional integration. For examples of studies that explore New Caledonia's place in the region or develop comparative analyses around New Caledonia, see: Eric Wittersheim's work on links between New Caledonia and Vanuatu (1998), Natalie Mgurdovic's study of Melanesian regional linkages (2004), John Fraenkel's comparisons of New Caledonia and Fiji (2006), Lorenzo Veracini's work on comparative historiography (2001); and Veracini & Muckle's study of national museums in Australia and New Zealand, and the Tjibaou Cultural Centre (2002).

4 Under the post-1998 organic law, New Caledonia and France share responsibility for New Caledonia's regional relations.

5 Representatives of the Senate had been invited by the local (New Caledonian) government to meet with the visiting delegation at the Tjibaou Cultural Centre (an organisation with no constitutional status), but this was considered

inadequate acknowledgement of New Caledonia's 'second institution'.

6 Direct links in pre-colonial times have not been established, but in the nineteenth century there was speculation that familiarity with New Caledonia had led New Zealand's first settlers to search for and discover local greenstone/jade deposits (Rutland 1897, p. 31).
7 Protection des Sepultures maoris 1928, Carton AFF POL 743, CAOM.
8 Two of the four references to New Caledonia in the *Appendices of the Journal of the House of Representatives* between 1854 and 1922 involve matters dealing with convicts.
9 Of the 1010 Kanak "volunteers" and 1234 French citizens (ten and twenty-two per cent of the respective adult male populations) engaged, 359 Kanak and 185 settlers died (Boyer 1999, p. 15). In all 120,000 New Zealanders enlisted, 103,000 served overseas and 18,500 died; this includes the 2227 Maori and 458 Pacific Islanders who served in the NZ Pioneer Battalion and of whom '336 died on active service' (Pugsley 2006, p. 81; NZ History Online—First World War, http://www.nzhistory.net.nz/category/tid/215).
10 Griscelli (1988) notes that Carco, for his part, consistently referred to Mansfield as the 'Australian girl' (l'Australienne) and not as from New Zealand.
11 Carton 34APC1, CAOM.
12 After the celebrations, French minister Noël Henry commented on the need for 'closer trade relations and air and sea communications' between NC and NZ, that the two had 'complementary' economies, and that NC could be of use to NZ if it proceeded with industrialisation (*Evening Post*, 29 Sept. 1953).
13 There are 235 NZ graves at Bourail and the lives of a further 280 missing servicemen are commemorated; a total of 515 (NZ Ministry of Culture and Heritage, http://www.mch.govt.nz/emblems/monuments/cwgc.html, accessed 1 Oct. 2007).
14 Stephen Hoadley has argued that 'NZ's initiatives were crucial to the success of the [reinscription] campaign' (Hoadley 2005, p. 53).

Fluid Partnerships: marine resources and community development in Kanaky/New Caledonia and Aotearoa/New Zealand[1]

Paul D'Arcy

New Caledonia has one of the richest marine environments in Oceania. It is a relatively untapped resource because of alternative sources of revenue for the territory from nickel mining and French Government spending. A comparison of legal and governance criteria across the Pacific suggests there are good grounds for increasing Kanak involvement in the management of near-shore waters. A variety of practical, working regimes are already in place in New Zealand and elsewhere and the Pacific as models for New Caledonia that will return cultural, economic and educational benefits to Kanaks as well as enhancing the sustainable management of New Caledonia's territorial seas for the benefit of all New Caledonians.

La Nouvelle-Calédonie possède l'un des écosystèmes marins les plus riches de l'Océanie. Ces resources marines ont été préservées du fait de la predominance des activités minières et des transferts financiers consequents de la France. Il apparait qu'à l'avenir, l'accroissement de l'implication des Kanak dans l'aménagement des zones littorals s'avère tout-à-fait possible. Les realisations déjà existantes en Nouvelle-Zélande et dans les autres Etats du Pacifique devraient pouvoir servir de modèles pour favoriser l'exploitation rationnelle des zones littorales par les Kanak et permettre un développement durable bénéficiant à toutes les communautés.

Introduction

Contemporary New Caledonia presents an interesting paradox within Oceania in that it has one of the richest marine ecosystems in the Pacific Islands, yet also the least harnessed for indigenous empowerment. This chapter seeks to explain why this is so, and how the enormous potential of New Caledonia's marine resources can be realised for the benefit of the indigenous Kanak population as well as the wider New Caledonian community. A number of practical and tested examples exist elsewhere in Oceania[2] to act as models for how this might best be achieved. Aotearoa/New Zealand figures prominently in these examples. The terms Aotearoa/New Zealand and Kanaky/New Caledonia are used here to acknowledge and designate indigenous cultural, economic or political entities that exist today within modern Western political entities and which also predated the latter. These terms are used here primarily in discussing interactions between governments and indigenous communities. Elsewhere, the terms New Caledonia and New Zealand are used for matters concerning legal and political issues where the governments' relations with indigenous minorities are not key political or legal considerations.

New Caledonia's marine resources

The 1500 kilometre long barrier reef surrounding New Caledonia's main island, Grande Terre, and the Isle of Pines is the second largest in world after the Great Barrier Reef in Queensland. The lagoon system enclosed by this reef is the largest in the world. Many more reefs and lagoons exist beyond this central area around offshore islands, reefs and coral cays within New Caledonia's claimed Exclusive Economic Zone (EEZ) of 1,347,964 square kilometres. While New Caledonia's land area is only 18,575 square kilometres, the area of reef and lagoon within its EEZ is 44,000 square kilometres.[3]

New Caledonia's extensive reefs and lagoons are rich in marine biota. A number of local conditions promote this richness. The reefs and lagoons are located near the centre of coral diversity in the world, while local currents and sea temperatures have left them relatively free from the coral bleaching that has hit Queensland's

Great Barrier Reef and parts of Oceania. A large 200 kilometre diameter counterclockwise current to the southeast of Noumea disseminates larvae and juvenile fish out to sea, beyond the reef, where they can grow in an environment much less populated by predators than the reefs and lagoons they return to as the gyre loops back. Upwelling off the southwest coast of Grande Terre promotes biota concentrations by bringing nutrients up to the sunlit areas of offshore waters in which they are concentrated. The combined result is that New Caledonia's reefs and lagoons are populated by a very diverse and unique marine biota. This diversity is currently calculated at around 15,000 marine species, including 800 species not found elsewhere. This total will almost certainly rise as only a small part of the total reef-lagoon system has been systematically investigated.

In addition, a number of seamounts in New Caledonia's EEZ have mineral potential in cobalt, hydrocarbons and phosphates. A number of potential offshore oil fields have also been identified within the northern, southern and western reefs surrounding Grande Terre, off *Le Grand Passage* zone, and in the Chesterfield-Bellona Plateau area. If these potential mineral reservoirs prove to be realisable resources, then the extraction could damage marine biota in the process.

The contemporary economy

There is limited harvesting of this offshore wealth. The two key components in the current New Caledonian economy are nickel and French government spending. Nickel accounts for 90 per cent of export earnings, which equates to billions of dollars annually. French government spending makes up 20 per cent of New Caledonia's gross domestic product (gdp). Approximately half of this is spent on the public sector, and half on health, education and regional development. Other components of the economy include agriculture, tourism and fishing. Local agriculture and stock rearing supplies around half of New Caledonia's domestic needs, while subsistence agriculture remains an important cultural and economic aspect of life for many Kanak. New Caledonia hosts just over 100,000 visitors per year, although the room to expand this figure is curtailed by limited air access and high local costs.[4]

The marine economy is geared to supplying the local market and exporting shrimp. It is still far below its potential sustainable yield. Only 8 per cent of the New Caledonian population's total protein comes from the sea, compared to around 13 per cent for Oceania in general.[5] In recent years the offshore fishery has produced around 2750 metric tons of fish per year, 130 metric tons of mollusks and crustaceans per year, and 1754 metric tons of aquaculture products per year, especially shrimp.

The wealth of New Caledonia is unevenly distributed. The southern end of Grande Terre contains the capital, Noumea, most of population and most of the wealth. The northern half of Grande Terre and the other islands of the territory have indigenous Kanak majorities and remain relatively under-developed, despite recent funding boosts to these regions as part of the process of reconciliation that arose as a result of the troubled decade of inter-ethnic confrontation in the 1980s. It is the contention of this chapter that the neglected marine resources of these under-developed areas offer a sustainable local asset that economically impoverished locals can play a significant role in managing for the economic, environmental, cultural and educational benefit of local Kanak communities as well as the New Caledonian economy as a whole.

Reasons for this pattern of maritime marginalisation

The first step towards realising the potential of marine resources is seeking to understand why they have been so neglected until now. Geography, history and the political economy of New Caledonia have all played a part. Much of the coral-lagoon complex is away from inhabited shores, so that it remains relatively unknown and unexploited, even today. Exploitation has not been necessary as nickel and French government money pad the economy. The importance of nickel to the economy has seen recent tensions between those emphasising the economic benefits of mining and those questioning whether this should override issues of mining damage to fragile marine ecosystems. Kanaks have been to the forefront in seeking environmental controls on mining, especially at Goro.[6]

The prominent role of Kanak in promoting marine environmental conservation is seemingly at odds with the usual perception of Kanak as a predominantly agricultural people with limited maritime interests. This image was reinforced by Kanak dispossession and removal to predominantly inland reserves in the nineteenth century. There was limited legal recognition of Kanak tenure, especially sea tenure, until the 1990s when the Noumea Accords gave power to local elected governments and recognised pre-existing Kanak ties to territory and indigenous tenure. Yet ambiguity and uncertainty remains. While the preamble to the Noumea Accords mentions the sea as a component of territory, section 1.4 of the Accords specifies Kanak ties to the land only.[7] In part this is the result of limited information on Kanak sea tenure and activities at sea. However, as the next section demonstrates, there is sufficient evidence of Kanak ties to the sea to justify legal recognition and rights according to international legal conventions and legal rulings elsewhere in the Pacific.

Kanak maritime rights and sovereignty

While the historical record of Kanak maritime activities is less substantial than for many other parts of Oceania, comparative data from elsewhere in the Pacific suggests that it is still sufficient for a strong case to be made for conveying greater maritime sovereignty upon Kanak communities. The three legal criteria commonly cited for conferring greater maritime control upon indigenous people are generally present across Oceania.[8] Firstly, indigenous principles and practices of maritime tenure generally aid conservation. Anthropological investigations of contemporary indigenous maritime practices within the Pacific Islands generally confirm this. Secondly, there is clear evidence of continuous use, with recognised, if at times contested, title to maritime spaces by families, clans and other communities. Such tenure was as complex and detailed as land tenure before European and Japanese rule, and often continued through the colonial era as has been amply demonstrated in documents from claims such as those brought before the Waitangi Tribunal in New

Zealand where Māori became one of the most dispossessed colonial peoples in Oceania. While few fisheries extended out beyond current 200 mile EEZs, many extended beyond the 3 to 12 mile limits of recognised European coastal tenure regimes until the 1950s.[9]

The last criterion is that indigenous practices are compatible with government fisheries management practices. This is the case in many parts of the Pacific where conservation and sustainability are key shared principles. Local community control of local near-shore fisheries as practiced by Pacific Islanders has also worked well as a conservation and management principle in parts of the Pacific Rim not controlled by indigenous peoples, such as Japan.[10] Pacific Island and Pacific Rim marine management systems represent a wide variety of workable schemes and contexts that are all concerned with disputed near-shore access rights. Comparative studies of such disputes and their resolution are needed to broaden awareness of options and put local disputes in context. A series of local regimes and interest groups can and do operate under a broad umbrella of national or international principles, such as conservation of endangered ecosystems and species being paramount over sector or community interests, and open, but differentiated access to the foreshore on the basis of historical and cultural factors.[11]

Information on the traditional Kanak maritime economy has been outlined by researcher Arthur Dahl. He documents records of fishing techniques, fish species caught, and traditions on the links made by Kanak peoples between the flowering of certain plants and fruits with the best time to catch certain fish. He notes that only a meagre remnant remains of Kanak ritual, *tapu*, and magical practices that were at the core of their fishing culture.[12] Much information has been lost, but Dahl still produces a sizable body of information demonstrating a significant Kanak connection with their rich near-shore environment. Other sources reveal a deeper and broader Kanak engagement with the sea and the importance of the sea to traditional Kanak culture. A recent book on the influence of the sea on New Caledonia shows how Kanak myths are infused with maritime themes and motifs.[13]

The displacement of indigenous communities from their traditional lands, and denial of access to traditional resources by colonial authorities as occurred in New Caledonia, has not been seen to break these rights if memories or records of the previous link remained. The Waitangi Tribunal's judgments on maritime claims (such as that for Muriwhenua in northern New Zealand) is a good example. The Tribunal's judgment presented a far less substantial body of evidence of traditional fishery practices than that available for Kanaky/New Caledonia, with comparative data from elsewhere in Oceania used to fill gaps in the local record. The Tribunal ruled that local Māori had a substantial claim despite disruptions to their access and practices following European colonisation.[14] Even where traditional evidence is absent, archaeological excavations of coastal fish bone and shell middens elsewhere in Oceania can help fill the gap by tracing fisheries back millennia, with species identification revealing which near-shore and offshore ecosystems were fished. The work of archaeologist Tom Dye in tracing centuries of fishing practices in the Marquesas Islands of French Polynesia using this technique is particularly impressive in this regard.[15]

There is also evidence that Kanak fishing strategies benefit conservation. Despite colonial disruptions to Kanak ties with the sea, Yves Magnier has recently been able to detail how conservation-minded traditional Kanak fishing practices were.[16] More significantly, Conservation International's work with Kanaks on the northeast coast of Grande Terre since 2004 reveals detailed marine lore and conservation practices still in place today. Reef surveys of the same area in which these practices are conducted have revealed a healthy and diverse reef and lagoon biota unaffected by coral bleaching, starfish predation, or coral disease.[17] Taken in combination, this evidence provides a strong case for both the continuity of Kanak maritime knowledge and the conservation benefits of traditional practices. This is especially so when these are conducted in partnership with scientific investigators, combining local knowledge and commitment to local sustainability with the greater resources and information available to national and international maritime scientific bodies.

Using maritime resources to empower Kanak communities

The direction of French government finances in rectifying economic gaps between Kanaks and other residents of New Caledonia since the late 1980s has done much to ease the simmering tensions earlier in the decade that prompted this action. However, much remains to be done. While French government resources will remain the main component of resources directed into the hands of Kanaks, marine resources also have an important role to play, a role that extends beyond economic empowerment and into the realms of enhancing Kanak cultural pride, education, and political reconciliation with other New Caledonians. Although Caldoche also have strong bonds to the sea, the sea is still a less contested resource than the land to use to compensate for Kanak dispossession and marginalisation.[18]

Practice in New Zealand and elsewhere in the Pacific region suggests a two-tiered system of marine resource allocation to Kanak will produce the best results for empowering marginalised regions and groups within New Caledonia while at the same time fostering reconciliation by avoiding unnecessary competition over local resources. This system combines local management of local near-shore marine areas, by people with an interest in preserving it, with the allocation of a percentage of income obtained from exploiting offshore fisheries and other resources (such as oil and seabed minerals). A number of local near-shore management schemes in place around the Pacific were noted in the previous section. All have enhanced conservation and conflict resolution and offer a number of viable and applicable models for the management of near-shore waters in New Caledonia, by either Kanak residents alone as is the case in most of northern Grande Terre and the offshore Islands, or by multiple stakeholders as is more often the case in southern and western Grande Terre.

Experience elsewhere suggests that receiving a percentage of the profits of offshore activities is the best scheme for using this territorial zone to empower Kanaks. Kanaks do not have strong tenure claims to this zone, and allocating a percentage of the profits to groups is particularly useful for those who were relocated or otherwise disrupted in the colonial era or are undergoing urban drift, as the allocation of funds is not tied to territorial affiliation, but rather to identity or more flexible group affiliation.

Direct exploitation of offshore resources by indigenous peoples in Oceania has generally not been successful. Elsewhere in Oceania, island nations still only receive a small fraction of the potential wealth contained in their offshore territorial waters. Modern offshore fishing is both expensive and lucrative. Corporations employ fleets and factory ships, sonar, and spotter planes. A tuna fishing vessel can use $5000 worth of fuel per day. The Pacific tuna fishery produces an estimated billion dollars in value-added sales. Island nations consume little of the catch and probably only receive around five per cent of the market value of the reported catch from fishing license fee agreements. License fees are generally the preferred income option for offshore fisheries of most Pacific Island states, however, following the failure of a number of domestic offshore tuna operations in the face of the huge set-up and operational costs and the economies of scale required. Most Pacific Island nations now look to increase their fishery income through developing inshore fisheries.[19] Kiribati, for example, has raised significant revenue in recent years through developing its inshore artisinal fishery, farming seaweed, and harvesting beche-de-mer, shark fins and reef fish for aquariums. These exports produce significant income for local communities. Pearl cultivation has also been a big success in certain atoll communities, such as the northern Cook Islands.[20]

Maritime access for still politically subordinate Pacific Islanders varies significantly, from politically and economically marginalised Hawaiians, to less politically subordinate and better resourced Māori. Heavy demand for waterfront property and big profits from tourism mean that access to coastal land and power are intimately linked in Hawaii and are in many ways inimical to formal recognition of Hawaiian sovereignty. Traditional Hawaiian near-shore rights are recognised in the legal system, but claimants must prove these in an American court. Meanwhile, state and federal lawyers argue over control of waters further offshore within the 200 mile EEZ.[21] In contrast, New Zealand Māori have a quota of the EEZ fishery set aside for them as part of a policy of compensating and empowering them for past grievances.[22]

Even in Aotearoa/New Zealand however, the minority status of Māori has raised concerns among a number of indigenous commentators that legally empowering principles under the Treaty of Waitangi can and may be eroded.[23] Soon after the Waitangi Tribunal process had been set in place to investigate and recommend compensation for historical grievances, the mood of the *Pākehā* (New Zealanders of European origin) majority began to shift from support to concern that the process should be completed as soon as possible, with a cap placed on the amount of compensation. By the mid-1990s, the incumbent National government was talking about a full and final settlement to truncate the more exhaustive, time-consuming and open-ended process that was occurring. Matters came to a head more recently with debate over Māori rights to the foreshore versus the English tradition of the foreshore as a public good open to all. When the New Zealand Court of Appeal concluded in June 2003 that Māori should be given the opportunity in court to prove their customary ownership of the foreshore and seabed, the Labour-led government announced that it would introduce legislation to ensure Māori could never hold exclusive title to the foreshore and seabed. This pre-emptive government action to prevent due judicial process seems to have been somewhat of an over-reaction, given the reasonable and mutually agreed terms of previous compensation settlements. This action highlights the plight and fragility of gains made by Pacific Islander minorities to reclaim their maritime heritage as peoples of the sea.[24] The terms for near-shore management regimes outlined at the end of the last section as options for New Caledonia anticipate the concerns raised in Aotearoa/New Zealand over this issue. These concerns also highlight the crucial importance of education and the dissemination of information on the mutual benefits, and the multiple and legitimate claims of all stakeholders, in issues of maritime governance regimes to avoid unnecessary conflict brought about by misunderstandings and misrepresentations.

The experience of the Ngai Tahu peoples of New Zealand suggests that while physical assets and territory are important for indigenous identity, converting such terrestrial and maritime assets into liquid assets to invest in education and a variety of business opportunities is the best way to modernise and lead to a significant increase in capital. The organisation of Ngai Tahu might also be a model for Kanak groups to follow because of its flexibility and blend of traditional and modern structures. There are 41,496 Polynesian New Zealanders who classify themselves as Ngai Tahu. They have been recognised as an '*iwi* (tribal) authority' by the government and must be consulted by the government over resource management matters in their legally defined *rohe* (tribal territory). Tribal members are spread across most of New Zealand and beyond, and encompass rural and urban communities. Ngai Tahu is a legally recognised charitable trust for the purposes of governance and the administration of its financial matters, balancing traditional concerns with modern business practices. The board consists of representatives from each of the 18 traditional regional sub-groups comprising Ngai Tahu, but it is headed by a CEO and also employs a chief financial officer. Important decisions are made only after extensive consultation, and much of the *iwi*'s financial status and policy debates are carried on its website to increase access and transparency.[25] Ngai Tahu started with a NZ$30 million Crown Settlement in 1998 and has increased its tribal equity substantially since then, largely through astute financial management and sound investments.

Conclusion

Giving local Kanak communities greater control of near shore waters and a share of the profits from harvests further offshore will never rival French government contributions as an income source, but these will represent significant supplements to existing sources if used and invested astutely. They will also enhance Kanak pride and identity, as income derived from past and present beneficial cultural practices and associations with local maritime territory and ongoing contribution to the sustainable use of local reefs and lagoons. Given the degradation of reefs elsewhere, local reefs will only grow in significance over time as biological resources and tourism assets.

This scheme also has much potential for resolving problems with Kanak alienation and under-achievement in the current New Caledonian education system. There is no reason why an environmental section, allowing community-based exercises researching cultural beliefs and activities, cannot be integrated into junior and senior schools. Local textbooks using local environmental icons like the nautilus shell and dugongs (which are large marine mammals) might be produced locally for high schools and primary schools to teach environmental and cultural lessons. Such textbooks would have wider application in the Pacific because of similar environmental issues across the tropical Pacific. A trial of such an approach, using the locally iconic frigate bird as an environmental symbol to explore and teach conservation issues to primary school children in the Caroline Islands of Micronesia, has been very well received.[26] Linking environmental issues to cultural practices can and should be used in conjunction with Western education to produce students grounded in their particular locality and culture, drawing confidence from their heritage to embrace opportunities in the global world.

The territorial waters of New Caledonia are bountiful and relatively untapped. The closer linking of Kanak development to these waters offers exciting, sustainable and feasible environmental, economic, cultural and educational possibilities that will return dividends to all New Caledonians. Practical working examples of everything proposed here already exist elsewhere. New Zealand and other parts of the Pacific hold lessons for New Caledonia on how best to use its maritime assets for Kanaks and other New Caledonians. Used wisely, the value of this remarkable underwater world will only increase with time.

Notes

1 This paper was completed overseas and would not have been possible without the assistance of my colleagues at the Australian National University, Vicki Luker, Michael Wood and Tao Kong, who forwarded missing references to me. I am also indebted to Sarah Powell of Victoria University of Wellington for her advice on sources for New Caledonian interactions with the sea.

2 The terms Oceania and the Pacific Islands are used interchangeably here for all islands with Pacific Island populations. This area is bound by Rapanui in the southeast, the Marquesas Islands in the central east Pacific, the Hawaiian Islands in the northeast, Saipan in the northwest, the island of New Guinea in the southwest, and Aotearoa/New Zealand in the south.

3 The information on New Caledonia's marine resources in this section derives

from Jean-Marie Auzende et al, 'Marine resources of the Economic Zone of New Caledonia', *Oceanologica Acta*, 22 (6), 1999, 557-566; IFRECOR (French Coral Reef Initiative), 'State of the Environment in New Caledonia', http://www.environment.gouv.fr/ifrecor; P. Bouchet et al, 'Assessing the magnitude of species richness in topical marine environments: exceptionally high numbers of mollusks at a New Caledonian site', *Biological Journal of the Linnean Society*, 75, 2002, 421-436; and Environmental Defense, 'Biodiversity Hotspot Reefs under Threat in Kanaky (New Caledonia)', http://www.environmentaldefense.org//article.cfm?contentid=2529, March 2004.

4 The contemporary economic data outlined here is drawn from the New Caledonian country profiles of the New Zealand Ministry of Foreign Affairs and Trade, at http://www.mfat.govt.nz/Countries/Pacific/New-Caledonia.php; Austrade, at http://www.austrade.gov.au/New-Caledonia-profile/default.aspx; and the Food and Agriculture Organization at http://www.fao.org/fi/fcp/en/NCL/profile.htm

5 On comparative marine protein consumption for New Caledonia and Oceania, see EarthTrends, 'Coastal and Marine Ecosystems – New Caledonia', http://www.earthtrends.wri.org, 2003, 2.

6 On the threat posed to reefs by mining in the Goro region, and Kanak protest action, see Environmental Defense, 'Biodiversity Hotspot Reefs under Threat in Kanaky (New Caledonia)', http://www.environmentaldefense.org//article.cfm?contentid=2529, March 2004.

7 The text of the Noumea Accords is available at http://www.ambafrance-au.org/article.php3?id_article=1058.

8 See, for example R. E. Johannes and J. W. Macfarlane, 'Assessing Customary Marine Tenure Systems in the Context of Marine Resource Management: A Torres Strait example' in K. Ruddle and R. E. Johannes (eds.), *Traditional Marine Resource Management in the Pacific Basin: an anthology* (UNESCO, Jakarta, 1990), 241-261.

9 Good profiles of millennia of fishing practices and ecosystems targeted can be found in A. Anderson (ed.), *Traditional Fishing in the Pacific* (Honolulu, Bernice P. Bishop Museum, Honolulu, 1986), especially B. W. Masse's 'A Millenium of Fishing in the Palau Islands, Micronesia', 85-117.

10 J. C. Cordell, 'Defending Customary Inshore Sea Rights', in K. Ruddle and T. Akimichi (eds.), *Maritime Institutions in the Western Pacific* (National Museum of Ethnology, Osaka, 1984), 301-326.

11 The Great Barrier Reef Marine Park Authority management plans and planning processes are good examples. They involved deep consultation and cooperation with wider and more diverse local communities and interest groups, including indigenous peoples. Information on the plan and consultation process can be found at http://www.gbrmpa.gov.au/corp_site/management/zoning, while further information on specific collaboration with indigenous users of the reef can be found at http://www.environment.gov.au/indigenous/fact-sheets/gbrmpa.html.

12 Arthur Lyon Dahl, 'Traditional Environmental Knowledge and Resource Management in New Caledonia', UNEP ISLAND website, http://www.islands.unep.ch/dtradknc.htm, 1-13.

13 Hélène Colombani, 'Le sybolisme marin dans les mythes mélanésiens de Nouvelle-Calédonie', in Philippe Boyer (ed.), *La Mer: Espace, Perception et Imaginaire dans le Pacifique Sud* (Editions l'Harmattan, Paris, 1997), 35-59.

14 Waitangi Tribunal, Department of Justice, *Report of the Waitangi Tribunal on the Muriwhenua Fishing Claim, Wai-22* (Department of Justice Wellington, 1985), available at http://www.waitangi-tribunal.govt.nz.

15 Tom Dye, 'The Causes and Consequences of a Decline in the Prehistoric Marquesan Fishing Industry', in D. E. Yen and J. M. J. Mummery (eds.), *Pacific Production Systems: approaches to economic prehistory* (Department of Prehistory, RSPAS, Australian National University, Canberra, 1990), 70-84.

16 Yves Magnier, 'Plaisance, nuisance?' in Philippe Boyer (ed.), *La Mer: Espace, Perception et Imaginaire dans le Pacifique Sud* (Editions l'Harmattan, Paris, 1997), 195-208.

17 See for example, Kate Barrett, 'Kanak Traditions Guide Future Conservation' at http://web.conservation.org/xp/frontlines/science/02070701.xml, February 2007, and Sheila A. McKenna, 'CI Survey Reveals an Undersea Paradise', http://web.conservation.org/xp/frontlines/science/03150502.xml. McKenna also edited a Conservation International report on this area of reef – see S. A. McKenna et al (eds.), *Une Évaluation Rapide de la Biodiversité Marine des Récifs Coralliens du Mont Panié, Province Nord, Nouvelle Calédonie* (Conservation International, RAP 42, Washington D.C., 2006).

18 Jan-Claude Mermoud, 'La mer et les Caldoches', in Philippe Boyer (ed.), *La Mer: Espace, Perception et Imaginaire dans le Pacifque Sud* (Editions l'Harmattan, Paris, 1997), 179-193.

19 Despite being published almost twenty years ago, R. Teiwaki, *Management of Marine Resources in Kiribati* (University of the South Pacific, Suva, 1988) is still one of the most comprehensive reviews of maritime policy options in the independent Pacific. On the difficulties of Pacific Island tuna fishing enterprises, see M. Jacobs, 'Spoiled Tuna: a fishing industry gone bad', *Micronesian Counselor*, 40, 2002, 1-15, and P. D'Arcy, 'The role of the tuna fishery in the economy of Federated States of Micronesia', *Pacific Economic Bulletin*, 21 (3), 2006, 75-87, 79.

20 Ron Crocombe, *The South Pacific* (University of the South Pacific, Suva, 2001), 309, and F. R. Thomas, 'Fisheries Development in Kiribati: sustainability issues in a "MIRAB" economy', *Pacific Studies*, 26 (1-2), 2003, 1-36, 14-16.

21 G. Daws and G. Cooper, *Land and Power in Hawaii: the Democratic years* (Benchmark Books, Honolulu, 1985), and A. Murikami, 'Konohiki Fishing Rights and Marine Resources' in M. K. MacKenzie (ed.), *Native Hawaiian Rights Handbook* (Native Hawaiian Legal Corporation, Honolulu, 1991), 173-195, 185-188.

22 P. Moon, 'The Creation of the "Sealord Deal"', *Journal of the Polynesian Society*, 107 (2), 1998, 145-174, and S. Webster, 'Maori Retribalization and Treaty Rights to the New Zealand Fisheries', *The Contemporary Pacific*, 14 (2), 2002, 341-376.

23 For the history, underlying principles, and reports of the Waitangi Tribunal, see http://www.waitangi-tribunal.govt.nz. For background and analysis of the role and influence of the Waitangi Tribunal in New Zealand society and history, see M. King, *Nga Iwi o te Motu: 1000 years of Māori history* (Reed, Auckland, 1997), 87-102.

24 Webster, 'Maori Retribalization', and J. Ruru, 'A Politically Fuelled Tsunami: the foreshore/seabed controversy in Aotearoa Me Te Wai Pounamu/New Zealand', *Journal of the Polynesian Society*, 113, 2004, 57-72, and 'What Could Have Been: the Common Law Doctrine of Native Title in Land Under Water in Australia and Aotearoa/New Zealand', *Monash University Law Review*, 32 (1), 2006, 116-144.

25 See the Ngai Tahu website, http://ngaitahu.iwi.nz, and Te Puni Kokere, *Te Kahui Mangai—Ngai Tahu*, available from http://www.tkm.govt.nz/Iwi.aspx?id=87.

26 This project, the Frigate Bird Project, has been trialed in the Caroline Islands by Bruce Campbell and Steve Winter of the University of Guam. The author is currently working with Campbell and Winter on adjusting the scheme to make it equally suited to other parts of Oceania.

Part Three

The 21st century relationship

Aujourd'hui

De la souveraineté autochtone en Nouvelle-Zélande et Nouvelle Calédonie

François Garde

Lorsque les puissances européennes ont établi leur souveraineté sur ces deux archipels, elles ont d'abord reconnu l'existence d'une forme de souveraineté autochtone. Mais très vite, les réalités de la colonisation ont occulté cette dimension. Ce n'est que dans le dernier quart du XXème siècle que cette question a émergé dans le champ politique. La nostalgie de la souveraineté autochtone s'est d'abord exprimé dans les questions de langue et de culture. La question du partage de la terre est centrale, et se relie à celle du partage du pouvoir politique. La question du partage des mémoires enfin est apparue nécessaire. La souveraineté autochtone apparaît dès lors comme un mythe, mais un mythe vivant et qui produit des effets dans le champ politique.

At the very moment when France and the United Kingdom established their power over these two archipelagos, they recognised the existence of some kind of indigenous sovereignty. But very quickly the realities of colonisation led to this aspect being forgotten. It is only recently, in the last quarter of the twentieth century, that the question of indigenous sovereignty has emerged in the political arena. The nostalgia for indigenous sovereignty was first directed towards questions of language and culture. It soon came to the central question of land, however, itself linked to the sharing of political power. The question of sharing memories at last also seemed necessary. Indigenous sovereignty appears from then on as something of a myth, but a living one, one with real effects on political affairs.

La Nouvelle Calédonie[1] et la Nouvelle Zélande sont habitées par les Kanak, depuis 3000 ans, et les Maoris depuis 800 ap JC. James Cook les a découvertes en 1774 et 1769[2] respectivement. Au XIXème siècle, elles deviennent britannique en 1840 et française en 1853.

Comment la souveraineté des Empires coloniaux s'est-elle établie ? Les causes profondes relèvent de rapports de force militaires, économiques, culturels, religieux.

Le juriste pourtant doit rappeler l'existence de traités conclus avec les peuples autochtones. En effet, au-delà de leur effet utile dans leur espace et dans leur temps, ces textes et ce qu'ils sous-entendent ont été réactivés et après un siècle de mort apparente sont devenus sources de revendication politique voire sources de droit dans la période récente.

Ce mouvement repose sur le paradigme suivant. Les souverainetés autochtones existaient avant l'arrivée des Empires coloniaux, qui les ont nécessairement reconnues en contractant avec elles. Oubliées ou niées, ces souverainetés fondent pourtant la légitimité des demandes présentées sur une base explicitement ethnique, et que le droit positif tente de satisfaire. La souveraineté autochtone, puisqu'elle produit des effets, n'a donc pas entièrement disparu.

A cet égard, la comparaison entre la Nouvelle Zélande et la Nouvelle Calédonie est particulièrement éclairante, dans leurs histoires comme dans leurs projets.

Le passé peut être source de rancœur et alimenter les conflits. Il peut aussi permettre un dépassement et la construction d'une solution. La recherche de la souveraineté autochtone amène à se pencher sur les traités qui l'ont reconnue pour l'effacer aussitôt.

Les Empires britannique et français se sont établis en Nouvelle Zélande et en Nouvelle Calédonie selon les usages établis et reconnus à l'époque. Les traités qui furent passés avec des chefs autochtones restent des textes fondateurs. Malgré leurs ambiguïtés, ils sont redevenus des sources d'inspiration.

Dans ces sociétés plurielles, où coexistent des autochtones et les descendants d'immigrants d'Europe ou d'ailleurs, peut-on, doit-on reconnaître des droits spécifiques aux autochtones sans rien retirer aux autres populations ? Le souvenir de la souveraineté autochtone peut-il être, doit-il être une créance valable et reconnue ? Ainsi posée, la question paraît insoluble. Il faut donc dépasser cette opposition et fonder l'avenir sur le destin commun : passer du bon usage des traités au bon usage du partage.

NZ / NC: Du Bon Usage D'anciens Traites

Des traités fondateurs

En Nouvelle Zélande comme en Nouvelle Calédonie, la prise de possession s'est faite par le moyen de traités conclus avec des chefs autochtones.

Le traité de Waitangi a été signé le 6 février 1840 par le capitaine Hobson, consul britannique, et un groupe de 45 chefs. Quelque 500 autres signatures de chefs furent recueillies ultérieurement, et en mai 1840 Hobson déclare la souveraineté britannique sur l'archipel.

Le 1er janvier 1844, des chefs du Nord de la Nouvelle Calédonie signent un traité reconnaissant la souveraineté de la France.[3] Toutefois le roi Louis Philippe ne donnera pas suite, craignant des complications diplomatiques.

C'est le 24 septembre 1853,[4] à Balade, qu'est conclu un accord avec les chefs et proclamé le rattachement à l'Empire français. La cérémonie est réitérée à l'île des Pins le 29 septembre. Diverses cérémonies d'allégeance de chefs ont lieu sur la Grande Terre en 1854. La prise de possession de Maré et Lifou auront lieu en juin 1864, celle d'Ouvéa un an plus tard.

La procédure est donc identique : la prise de possession s'accompagne de la signature par des chefs d'un document en confirmant la validité et y consentant – ou par la présence de chefs valant approbation. Si l'*instrumentum* est différent, l'idée générale est dans les deux cas celle d'une forme d'approbation par les chefs autochtones. L'ace fondateur n'est pas unilatéral, il est, dans une incertaine mesure, synallagmatique.

De tels traités n'étaient toutefois nullement nécessaires selon le droit international alors en vigueur. La prise de possession de terres nouvelles requerrait seulement une occupation effective[5] et une notification aux autres puissances.

Superflues au plan juridique, ces cérémonies pouvaient susciter la critique. Lorsque Dumont d'Urville prend possession de la terre

Adélie, sur le continent antarctique, en cette même année 1840, il la commente ainsi, dans son récit « Voyage au Pôle Sud : « *Suivant l'ancienne coutume que les Anglais ont conservée précieusement, nous en prîmes possession (. . .) il nous semblait que nous venions d'ajouter une province au territoire français par cette conquête toute pacifique. Si l'abus que l'on fait par ces prises de possession les ont fait regarder souvent comme une chose ridicule et sans valeur, dans ce cas-ci au moins nous nous croyions assez fondés en droit pour maintenir l'ancien usage en faveur de notre pays. Car nous ne dépossédions personne et nos titres étaient incontestables. Nous nous regardâmes donc, de suite, comme étant sur un sol français. Celui-ci aurait du moins l'avantage de ne susciter aucune guerre à notre pays.* » C'est dire assez, a contrario, que prise de possession entraîne trop souvent dépossession, contestation, voire conflit.

Ces traités ont paru utiles voire nécessaires à ceux qui les ont conclus. Ils nous donnent un postulat fondamental : une société politique autochtone existait auparavant et a été effacée pour laisser la place à l'ordre politique et juridique occidental. Pour affirmer ensuite une souveraineté coloniale, ces traités constatent nécessairement une souveraineté autochtone antérieure, dont ils organisent la succession.

Cette souveraineté autochtone a été recouverte par celle des Empires, comme un terrain ancien est recouvert par les laves d'une éruption soudaine qui vient bouleverser le paysage. Même enfoui, ce sol participe à sa façon aux échecs et aux succès des récoltes futures, et il arrive qu'on le recherche pour lui–même.

Des traités ambigus

L'existence même de ces traités inégaux repose au mieux sur une ambiguïté, voire sur un mensonge. Aucun des signataires n'était en mesure ni même dans l'idée de tenir ce qu'il promettait.

Les signataires autochtones étaient radicalement incompétents.

Rationae loci tout d'abord : chefs de tribu, ils s'engageaient pour l'ensemble de leur archipel, sans mandat de leurs pairs. Même si les Anglais comme les Français ont recherché à faire contre-signer les traités par le plus grand nombre de chefs, ils n'ont pas obtenu d'unanimité. Or, comme ni la Nouvelle Zélande ni la Nouvelle Calédonie ne constituaient avant la colonisation une entité politique unifiée ou même coordonnée, le traité signé par certains ne sauraient valoir pour les autres.

Rationae personae également. Les autorités traditionnelles disposaient de certains pouvoirs, dans les limites que repéreront plus tard les ethnologues. Ils n'avaient certainement pas la capacité, tel un duc italien ou un prince allemand du XVIIIème siècle, de disposer seuls de leurs terres et de leurs gens pour l'avenir.

Rationae temporis tout autant. Dans les sociétés du Pacifique, toute parole peut être reprise, tout échange peut être dénoué, tout don suscite un contre-don – parfois jusqu'au vertige comme aux îles Trobriand décrites par Malinowski.[6] Pour les occidentaux, l'abandon de souveraineté est par nature irréversible, et les traités engageaient les générations futures.

Rationae materiae, enfin et surtout. Ce qui était en jeu allait bien au-delà d'une alliance militaire même inégale ou de l'accueil d'étrangers d'au-delà des mers : c'était l'effacement complet d'un ordre social, l'appropriation des terres, l'arrivée de milliers de colons, l'effondrement des cultures et des manières d'être. Quelles que soient les bonnes volontés, il n'y avait pas de mot dans les langues autochtones pour dire, pour penser, pour annoncer cette révolution qui n'avait pas de précédent.

La signature des traités par les autochtones repose dès lors au moins sur un malentendu radical – bien au-delà des éventuels malentendus linguistiques . Il faudrait être historien, ou ethnologue, ou maori, ou kanak, pour dire comment les autochtones ont peu à peu compris ce à quoi ils se trouvaient engagés. Le juriste lui ne peut que constater que les signataires ne parlaient pas de la même chose. En théorie civiliste des contrats, on pourrait constater le vice du consentement . . .

Mais pour les européens, l'ambiguïté n'était pas moindre. Les officiers qui ont négocié et signé étaient peut-être sincères, mais la raison d'Etat et la logique poussaient à l'échec.

Quelle valeur en effet ont ces traités ? Certes, en droit international, *Pacta sunt servanda*. Mais ces traités sont-ils de droit international ? A supposer même, pour le raisonnement, que la réunion *ad hoc* de chefs de tribus maoris[7] ou kanak aient constitué d'éphémères sujets de droit international, de telles chimères ont cessé d'exister précisément par les traités qui les incorporaient aux Empires britannique et français. Au soir du traité, seul le droit colonial s'applique, et va évoluer en fonction de sa propre logique, en oubliant tout des conditions de son apparition. En droit interne en effet, de tels traités n'ont pas de sens, les Empires ne passant pas avec leurs éléments constitutifs de contrats dont ils ne puissent modifier les clauses sous certaines conditions.[8] Et qui pourrait se plaindre du non respect de ces traités, puisque les autorités politiques autochtones qui les ont signé ont changé de statut en devenant sujets des Empires ? En outre, l'idée pseudo-darwinienne du déclin progressif des races inférieures, alors très répandue, suggérait une réponse . . . .

De tels traités, étrangers au droit international comme au droit interne, doivent être regardés comme des déclarations politiques ou des promesses. Leur violation ne peut être sanctionnée, et ne peut trouver de juge.

Sont-ils alors radicalement inutiles et trompeurs ? On doit au moins leur assigner deux effets concrets.

D'une part, ils ont été des traités d'armistice, stabilisant pour un temps les positions. La domination militaire des européens n'était pas absolue, et ces traités permettaient, avec un cynisme parfois involontaire, de gagner du temps. Ce processus fut à l'œuvre par exemple en Algérie, où la France conclut avec l'émir Abd el Kader le traité Desmichels de 1832, confirmé par le traité de la Tafna de 1834. Après la violation de son territoire en 1839, l'émir proclame le djihad et est définitivement vaincu en 1847. De même dans le Far West américain, chaque révolte indienne est suivie d'un traité de paix, dont la violation par les Blancs conduisait à une nouvelle révolte et à un nouveau traité, toujours plus désavantageux.

L'autre effet de tels traités était de conforter le droit d'un Empire à faire flotter son pavillon, dans le contexte de compétition coloniale du XIXème siècle.Le fait d'avoir contracté avec des chefs autochtones donnait à la prise de possession une substance et une réalité plus difficilement contestables. La compétition des missionnaires et des consuls autour de la reine Pomaré à Tahiti montre toute l'importance d'un tel parchemin, pour les chancelleries.

Lorsque les possessions coloniales ne seront plus contestées ni de l'intérieur ni par les autres puissances, alors les traités ayant accompli leur vocation sombrent dans l'oubli, pendant un siècle. Ils n 'intéressent plus que les historiens – mais comme le rappelait Marc Bloch, l'histoire est écrite par les vainqueurs.

Des traités revisités

L'idée qu'avait existé une souveraineté autochtone restait, au mieux, une figure de rhétorique.

En Nouvelle Calédonie, l'idée d'un transfert de souveraineté se retrouve par exemple dans un discours du gouverneur Feillet[9] devant le conseil général en 1897, où il fonde le droit de la France à délimiter les réserves sur « l'abandon que [les chefs] nous font de leurs droits de souveraineté dont la France a hérité. »

En Nouvelle Zélande, le souvenir du traité de Waitangi est toujours resté vivace dans la communauté maorie. Le texte original avait été oublié dans un placard, où il ne sera redécouvert, grignoté par les rats, qu'en 1908. Les chefs pourtant s'y référaient fréquemment, pour en déplorer la violation, notamment la dépossession foncière. Leurs demandes n'ont pas eu d'écho dans le débat politique pendant un siècle, et même après que des maoris ont été élus et ont eu accès à des fonctions publiques. L'idée que le traité puisse être source d'inspiration est expressément récusée par plusieurs décisions de juges néo-zélandais jusque dans les années 1960.

Avec les années 1960 et 1970, les autochtones parviennent à faire entendre leurs voix et leurs demandes spécifiques. N'étant plus majoritaires dans la population, ils vont tirer argument de leur ancienneté historique. Leur qualité de premiers occupants, et le souvenir de la souveraineté perdue doivent leur conférer des droits spécifiques.

Jean-Marie Tjibaou[10] déclare en 1984 : « *En 1853 notre pays a vu flotter à Balade le drapeau tricolore qui a enlevé à Kanaky sa souveraineté* » Il ne réclame pas l'indépendance de la Nouvelle Calédonie, ce qui eut été si j'ose dire une indépendance à la néo-zélandaise, mais l'indépendance de Kanaky : une terre kanak, peuplée de kanak – et de ceux que les kanaks inviteraient à rester.

La parenthèse ouverte en 1853 se refermerait, et la souveraineté confisquée aux kanak eut été à eux seuls restituée. Ce projet politique était proche à certains égards de la situation à Fidji, où les mélanésiens ont plus de droits – politiques et fonciers – que les indo-fidjiens.

En Nouvelle-Zélande, les maoris n'ont jamais envisagé ce type d'option, à raison sans doute de leur part plus faible dans la population et du fait que leur pays constitue un Etat souverain depuis 1907. Ils ont cependant obtenu que soit réactivé le traité de Waitangi, par le Waitangi Treaty Act de 1975 – non comme un souvenir historique, mais comme une source directe de droits et un fondement à leurs demandes foncières.

C'est d'Australie qu'est arrivé le signal le plus fort – alors même que l'Empire britannique n'y a jamais conclu de traité avec les aborigènes et s'est approprié ce continent non sans brutalités à leur égard. Avec l'arrêt Mabo de 1992 puis l'arrêt Wik de 1996, la Cour Suprême a affirmé que les droits fonciers autochtones n'avaient pas disparu avec la prise de possession – sous certaines conditions. Il n'y avait ni terres protégées par un traité comme en Nouvelle Zélande, ni terres de réserves comme en Nouvelle Calédonie. Néanmoins, quelque chose avait survécu des droits antérieurs à la prise de possession, dont les héritiers peuvent se prévaloir devant un juge. Quelque chose qui ressemble à un droit de propriété, non à une souveraineté.

La même approche fut celle du Canada, avec la consécration dans la Constitution fédérale en 1982 des « *droits existants – ancestraux ou issus de traités* » , puis la création du Nunavut en 1999 ; ou celle du Danemark, pour consacrer des droits spécifiques aux Inuits du Groenland.

Les revendications politiques n'ont pas besoin d'être fondées sur l'histoire ou a fortiori sur le droit pour aboutir.[11] Mais elles peuvent y trouver des arguments pour conforter leur rhétorique – quitte à réécrire l'histoire ou à modifier le droit. Rien ne serait plus naïf que de prendre à leur valeur faciale de telles racines historiques ou juridiques : elles n'apparaissent dans le discours politique qu'instrumentalisées. Sous cette réserve, il est frappant de voir en 1998 l'accord de Nouméa, document éminemment politique, se référer aux traités pour les récuser : « *Les traités passés, au cours de l'année 1854 et les années suivantes, avec les autorités coutumières ne constituent pas des accords équilibrés, mais, de fait, des actes unilatéraux.* » Par cette phrase, l'accord de Nouméa récuse la procédure utilisée un siècle et demie plus tôt pour signifier qu'elle ne peut démontrer l'acceptation par les Kanak de la présence des autres communautés.

Le Waitangi Treaty Act de 1975, la Constitution canadienne de 1982, l'arrêt Mabo de 1992, le Préambule de l'accord de Nouméa de 1998 se font écho pour rechercher dans le passé les solutions aux problèmes actuels des autochtones dans des sociétés plurielles. Chacun de ces textes à sa façon reconnaît qu'une injustice a été commise.

NZ / NC: Du Bon Usage Du Partage

Le partage de la terre

Les conflits liés à la terre sont au cœur de toutes les difficultés. En Nouvelle Zélande, les terres reconnues aux Maoris par le traité de Waitangi ont cependant été massivement rognées, par des artifices juridiques, tout au long du XIXème et du premier XXème siècles. En Nouvelle Calédonie, des terres, dites de réserve, ont été très tôt reconnues propriété incessible des tribus – néanmoins ces réserves ont été restreintes par l'administration, et des tribus ont été déplacées hors de leurs terres ancestrales. Ces dépossessions entraînent des révoltes (1845-1848 et 1860-1872 en Nouvelle Zélande ; 1878 et 1917 en Nouvelle Calédonie)

Dès les années 1950, la revendication foncière s'est faite entendre et a amené à des politiques volontaristes de réforme foncière au bénéfice des autochtones.

En Nouvelle Zélande,[12] la grande marche de Whina Cooper en 1975 atteint Wellington pour dénoncer la violation du traité de Waitangi et la dépossession foncière. En posant la question des terres, elle soulevait en filigrane la question de la place des Maoris dans la société néo-zélandaise . Une autre grande marche, en 1984, se termine à Waitangi . En 1975 est mis en place le tribunal du traité de Waitangi, qui malgré son nom n'est pas une juridiction qui dit le droit mais une instance paritaire entre Blancs et Maoris de régulation et de recherche de solutions, qui adresse des recommandations à la Couronne. Les tribus peuvent également négocier directement avec la Couronne et, au terme de processus longs et minutieux qui réexaminent les faits depuis 1840, obtenir des restitutions foncières et des compensations financières. Par la médiation ou par la discussion directe, un processus de règlement est à l'œuvre.

En Nouvelle Calédonie, la réforme foncière a été voulue par l'Etat et a débuté avec le ministre Dijoud en 1978. Une agence foncière, l'ADRAF, est chargée depuis une vingtaine d'années de récupérer les terres publiques ou de racheter les terres aux particuliers et de les restituer gratuitement aux tribus. Ces politiques volontaristes et coûteuses ont permis de régler la plupart des revendications foncières.

Restituer les terres en compensation – ou en souvenir - de la souveraineté perdue est une démarche que l'on retrouve également en Australie ou au Canada. Au-delà des spécificités de chaque pays, elle correspond à une volonté de réparer les dommages de la colonisation. Elle s'est parfois accompagné – en Nouvelle Zélande, au Canada, au Danemark – de l'octroi de fonds spécifiques gérés par les autochtones.

Toutefois, restituer ne suffit pas, encore faut-il déterminer à qui, ce qui peut s'avérer particulièrement complexe en cas de revendications concurrentes ; et déterminer dans quelles conditions légales les autochtones peuvent exploiter ces terres.

En Nouvelle Calédonie a ainsi été créé une personne morale spécifique, le Groupement de Droit Particulier Local (GDPL), qui permet une appropriation collective sur laquelle peuvent se caler les droits ancestraux. L'accord de Nouméa fixe comme objectif la création d'un cadastre coutumier, afin de déterminer avec précision les droits de chacun. Cet exercice n'a pas encore été conduit à son terme. Il a néanmoins permis de ramener la paix, d'indiquer une direction et de rassurer les acteurs économiques.

Toutefois, qui peut dire que les accords conclus et les rétrocessions de terres acceptées règlent à jamais la question ? Peut-on le dire mieux que Jean-Marie Tjibaou lors du XIIème Congrès de l'Union Calédonienne à Lifou en novembre 1981[13] : « *La revendication foncière n'est pas la revendication de parcelles de terres, c'est la reconquête de la patrie kanak (...) c'est une étape vers l'indépendance au cours de laquelle il faut s'attribuer les éléments de souveraineté.* »

Le partage du pouvoir

En filigrane de la question des terres se pose en effet la question du partage du pouvoir. Celle-ci ne se confond pas avec celle de l'indépendance, elle en est même l'antithèse. Si aucune des communautés ne doit être contrainte à l'exil, comment organiser les relations entre elles ? Le principe *One man One vote* propose une réponse. Son application absolue conduit à ne considérer que les individus, non les communautés. Or les autochtones, devenus minoritaires du fait de la colonisation , peuvent ne pas s'en satisfaire. Tel est le cas des Kanak.

La Nouvelle Calédonie a organisé depuis 1984 l'émergence de pouvoirs politiques autochtones, avec la provincialisation. Les Kanak sont majoritaires dans deux provinces sur trois. Les provinces sont dotées de pouvoirs importants et de ressources financières garanties, ce qui leur permet de concevoir des politiques originales. La Province Nord en matière minière, la Province des Iles en matière sociale notamment ont ainsi utilisé avec imagination les outils qu'elles ont reçus. Ces politiques sont décidées par des Kanak, conduites par des Kanak, pour des Kanak. Ces espaces de pouvoir installés loin de Nouméa ne sont pas remis en question.

Au niveau de la Nouvelle Calédonie la représentation des provinces au Congrès et les dotations automatiques vers les Provinces ne sont pas fonction de la démographie, mais de clefs de répartition immuables et volontaristes. Ce rééquilibrage conduit à favoriser, politiquement et budgétairement, les Provinces Nord et Iles, les Provinces où les Kanak sont majoritaires.

D'autre part, seuls les Kanak sont représentés au Sénat coutumier. Les membres de cette assemblée ne sont pas élus, mais désignés selon les usages de la coutume. Le Sénat n'intervient dans le processus normatif, en dialogue avec le Congrès, que pour les textes touchant à l'identité kanak : état des personnes de statut coutumier et terres coutumières. Cette participation à l'élaboration de normes, sans équivalent en droit français, traduit l'idée que les Kanak sont les mieux placés pour adopter les textes à eux destinés. Il s'agit bien d'un partage du pouvoir politique.

A plus long terme et pour permettre l'arrivée d'autochtones dans les lieux de décision, le programme Quatre Cent Cadres a pratiqué la discrimination positive pour favoriser les jeunes Kanak dans leurs études supérieures.

Une partie de l'opinion publique considère que les efforts accomplis envers les autochtones sont scandaleux par principe : le parti One Nation en Australie ou le Front National en Nouvelle Calédonie s'en font les hérauts. Mais aucun parti de gouvernement n'en conteste le bien fondé. Le partage du pouvoir sur une base ethnique ne peut être que marginal, pour ne pas heurter trop frontalement les grands principes d'égalité et de la démocratie. Pour le rendre possible en Nouvelle Calédonie, la France a dû modifier sa Constitution.

Le partage des mémoires

Tous ces efforts resteraient vains si les diverses communautés ne se comprennent pas et refusent de se connaître.

L'une des premières manières d'accepter l'autre est d'entendre sa langue. L'anglais et le français sont respectivement langues dominantes. Les langues vernaculaires sont réfugiées dans les cases, dans les églises, les temples et leurs écoles, et dans la plupart des toponymes.

L'unité de la langue maorie lui a permis de mieux résister que la diversité des langues kanak. Le maori est la seconde langue officielle de la Nouvelle Zélande depuis le Maori Language Act de 1987, et toutes les institutions du pays sont au moins partiellement bilingues. Il existe une Maori Language Week, et sur les sites officiels on peut trouver une liste des cent mots de maori que tout néo-zélandais se doit de connaître. Cet effort, conduit depuis deux décennies, ne conduit pas cependant à un réel biculturalisme, même s'il donne un cachet original au pays. Son équipe de rugby ne s'appelle—elle pas les All Blacks[14], où blancs et maoris dansent ensemble le haka avant chaque match ? En apparence et en droit au moins, la souveraineté linguistique est partagée.

Les langues kanak n'ont pas le même statut, le Conseil

constitutionnel[15] veillant avec une rigueur que l'on peut trouver excessive à défendre le français comme langue de la République.[16] Les langues kanak sont seulement déclarées langues d'enseignement et de culture, ce qui n'a pas de contenu précis.

En matière culturelle aussi, la souveraineté occidentale a du mal à partager son empire. Elle joue parfois avec certains codes ou certains savoirs – le tatouage, la sculpture sur bois . . . - mais pour une stricte fonction décorative. Sur la période la plus récente, certains acteurs culturels tentent d'aller au-delà et de faire vivre une culture maori ou kanak contemporaines. Telle est la fonction du Centre culturel Tjibaou à Nouméa et du musée Te Papa à Wellington , ouverts tous deux en 1998, mais avec une différence notable : le Centre Tjibaou promeut la culture kanak, alors que le musée Te Papa illustre la diversité des cultures vivant en Nouvelle Zélande ; si la culture maorie y tient une place notable, elle n'est pas exclusive.

Toutefois, rien ne sera durable tant que les histoires ne seront pas vécues comme étant les mêmes. Deux grands textes[17] évoquent le passé avec des mots que chacune des communautés peut accepter.

Le 22 mai 1995, la reine Elizabeth II, chef de l'Etat, fait une déclaration par la voix du Premier Ministre de Nouvelle-Zélande et s'adresse à la communauté maorie. Elle affirme que « *l'Etat cherche pour le compte de tous à réparer ces injustices qu'il a reconnues, pour autant que cela soit possible à l'heure actuelle, à commencer le processus de cicatrisation et à entrer dans un nouvel âge de coopération avec les autochtones* »

Le 5 mai 1998, l'accord de Nouméa est signé par le Premier Ministre français et les représentants du RPCR et du FLNKS. Il relit l'histoire de la Nouvelle Calédonie, et reconnaît que « *la colonisation a porté atteinte à la dignité du peuple kanak qu'elle a privé de son identité (. . .) Il convient de faire mémoire de ces moments difficiles, de reconnaître les fautes, de restituer au peuple kanak son identité confisquée, ce qui équivaut pour lui à une reconnaissance de sa souveraineté . . . .* »

Il est pour le moins inhabituel qu'un Etat assume de la sorte officiellement les erreurs commises. Mais ces textes n'ont de sens et de force que parce qu'ils se projettent vers l'avenir. Le texte français va plus loin, en ce qu'au-delà de la réparation des préjudices il déduit de l'analyse des erreurs passées une vision dynamique d'un processus politique. Après avoir évoqué la souveraineté du peuple kanak, il se termine par la description du processus électoral qui pourrait amener à la pleine souveraineté de la Nouvelle Calédonie. La période transitoire d'une vingtaine d'années est définie comme la période de la « *souveraineté partagée* » . Ce texte montre ainsi les quatre étapes d'un processus : souveraineté originelle ; souveraineté confisquée ; souveraineté partagée – et peut-être pleine souveraineté. Mais dans les deux dernières, ce n'est plus la souveraineté kanak dont il est question, mais celle des citoyens néo-calédoniens : l'objectif est » *la refondation d'un contrat social entre toutes les communautés qui vivent en Nouvelle Calédonie, et par un partage de souveraineté avec la France, sur la voie de la pleine souveraineté.* » L'opposition kanak / non kanak est dépassée par l'opposition calédoniens / non-calédoniens.

En une trentaine d'années, Nouvelle Zélande et Nouvelle Calédonie auront parcouru des chemins étonnamment parallèles dans leurs relations aux autochtones.

La Nouvelle Zélande a commencé plus tôt et son évolution s'est faite sans drames. Les avancées en matière foncière et culturelle sont considérables et ont changé la place des Maoris dans la société – et le regard des autres sur eux – et la vision que la Nouvelle-Zélande se fait d'elle-même.

La Nouvelle Calédonie est passé par une histoire douloureuse, où la demande kanak et la revendication pour l'indépendance entraient en résonance. La question foncière est en cours de règlement. La refondation politique a été plus profonde, entraînant un partage réel du pouvoir grâce à la provincialisation. La dimension culturelle reste modeste – à quand un Kanak Language Day à Nouméa ?

Le juriste ne peut aller plus loin : il ne peut que décrire des normes et des procédures. Il appartient aux responsables politiques et aux sociologues de dire si et comment la réalité de la vie a été modifiée – et en quelles mains résident les pouvoirs économique et médiatique.

On doit seulement rappeler l'échelle du temps : moins d'un siècle des découvertes à la prise de possession ; un peu plus d'un siècle entre la prise de possession et l'émergence de la revendication autochtone ;

une trentaine d'années seulement depuis lors.

La demande politique des Maoris et des Kanak est frappée de la même contradiction : la nostalgie d'un temps entre soi, d'avant l'histoire ; mais l'impossibilité d'un retour en arrière. Dès lors, la souveraineté autochtone ne peut être posée comme un objectif absolu. Elle ne peut être que relative et contingente. Ce concept seul permet de pleinement entendre ce que disent les autochtones de Nouvelle Zélande et de Nouvelle Calédonie – et pourquoi ces revendications ont été en partie satisfaites.

La souveraineté autochtone, bien sûr, est un mythe. Mais le juriste lui aussi a besoin de mythes. S'il ne le sait pas, il se condamne à ne rien comprendre au traité de Waitangi ni à l'accord de Nouméa, rien à la Nouvelle Zélande ni à la Nouvelle Calédonie.

Notes

1 Au seuil de ce propos, l'auteur tient à dire sa dette envers Norbert Rouland, notamment son « *Introduction historique au droit* » PUF 1998.

2 . . . . redécouverte dans le cas de la Nouvelle Zélande, aperçue et dénommée par Abel Tasman un siècle plus tôt .

3 « Prise de possession » par Jérôme Geoffroy , in '101 mots pour comprendre l'histoire de la Nouvelle Calédonie' dir F Angleviel. ed Ile de Lumière, Nouméa 1997.

4 François Garde « L'Ancre et la mémoire » Revue juridique politique et économique de Nouvelle Calédonie octobre 2007.

5 La condition d'occupation effective , dont la réalité pouvait donner lieu à contestation, sera supprimée par le traité de Saint Germain de 1920.

6 Bronislaw Malinowski, « Les Argonautes du Pacifique occidental » Gallimard 1990.

7 L'article 1 du traité de Waitangi commence ainsi: « *The chiefs of the Confederation of the United Tribes of New Zealand , and the separate and independent chiefs who have not become members of the Confederation . . .* »

8 En droit administratif français, cette faculté de modifier unilatéralement un contrat se dénomme justement . . . le fait du prince.

9 Cité par Frédéric Angleviel « Le gouverneur et les libertés publiques » in Eric Plisson dir « La loi du 28 Pluviôse an VII deux cents ans après: le préfet et les libertés » Presses Universitaires de Limoges 2002.

10 Cité par Frédéric Angleviel « Brève histoire politique de la Nouvelle Calédonie contemporaine 1945- 2005 » ed du GRHOC 2006 p. 208.

11 Sur la valeur de tels traités , outre l'ouvrage cité en note 1 , toujours de Norbert Roulland « Le droit intertemporel et la question néo-calédonienne » in J Y

Faberon « L'avenir statutaire de la Nouvelle Calédonie » La Documentation Française, 1997.

12 Régis Lafargue: 'Le traité de Waïtangi: le symbole et le droit, de la fondation d'une colonie à la naissance d'une nation', Revue juridique et politique Indépendance et coopération 1999, p. 215 à 244.

13 Voir l'ouvrage de F Angleviel cité en note 10, p. 172.

14 Georges Ayache « Rugby : derrière la mêlée, la politique » Politique Internationale, été 2007.

15 Jean-Yves Faberon: 'Indivisibilité de la République et diversité linguistique du peuple français: la place des langues polynésiennes dans le nouveau statut de la Polynésie française', Revue française de droit constitutionnel 1996, p. 607 à 617.

16 Norbert Rouland « Les politiques juridiques de la France dans le domaine linguistique » RFDC 1998.

17 Voir notre contribution *« Autochtones , mémoire et refondation »* Actes du colloque de Nouméa de Novembre 1999 , sous la direction de Jean-Yves Faberon et Guy Agniel « La souveraineté partagée en Nouvelle-Calédonie et en droit comparé » La Documentation Française 2000.

New Caledonia and New Zealand: Similar Histories, Parallel Destinies, Converging Diplomacies

Michel Pérez

Despite their marked differences in size, population and political status, many parallels can be drawn between New Caledonia and New Zealand, two close neighbours whose similarities in terms of history and diplomacy leave ample room for closer and fruitful co-operation in the near future.

Malgré des différences profondes en termes de superficie, de population et de statut politique, il est également possible d'établir de nombreux parallèles entre la Nouvelle-Calédonie et la Nouvelle-Zélande, deux proches voisins dont les points de convergence en matière historique et diplomatique laissent présager une coopération bien plus étroite et fructueuse dans un avenir proche.

Squaring the diplomatic circle

Speaking of diplomatic relations between New Caledonia and New Zealand appears, at first sight, as an impossible challenge. When it is added that as few references as possible should be made to either France or the United Kingdom, the analysis clearly amounts to squaring the circle. Indeed, difficulties arise on various counts.

First of all, in practically all respects, New Caledonia turns more spontaneously to Australia than to New Zealand for her exchanges, and this orientation is nothing new since it goes back to early colonial times. Whether for tourism, higher education or medical purposes, the number of New Caledonians—from all ethnicities—flying to Sydney or Brisbane exceeds by far those travelling to Auckland.

Imports from Australia represent nearly twice the value of those from New Zealand, though the gap has been narrowing in the past few years. The difference is even more spectacular in relation to exports: New Caledonia sells to Australia roughly eighty to one hundred times more than to New Zealand!

History, too, brings New Caledonia and Australia closer: in both cases colonisation started in the pain of 'convictism', and in neither place was any formal treaty ever signed with the colonised populations regarding the massive arrival of outsiders.

Finally, in the economic field, rich mineral deposits are their major source of income and have, to a large extent, ensured their prosperity. No such parallels could be established with New Zealand, whose wealth rests essentially on farming and whose inhabitants descend, for most of them, from free settlers.

As for diplomacy as such, it seems even harder to find similarities between New Caledonia and New Zealand. How could their external relations be possibly compared? New Zealand is a fully-fledged sovereign State, recognised as such by all countries on the international scene, and she has a complete mastery of her diplomatic affairs. New Caledonia, on the other hand, does enjoy a substantial amount of self-governing powers, but she remains—at least for the time being—an autonomous polity within the French Republic. She is therefore deprived of a national diplomacy, and has no specific embassies or consulates overseas to represent her or assist New Caledonian citizens in need when abroad. Thus, there does not seem to be much to say in principle, and the debate could stop here.

Parallels and Similarities

And yet, things are not so simple and the situation is in fact much more complex, on both the New Caledonian and New Zealand sides. Diplomacy is basically a human—and humanistic—science where two and two do not necessarily make four but can amount, depending on circumstances, to 3.8 or 4.1. In the world of embassies and consulates, perceptions matter just as much as realities and subjectivity plays an important role, thus leading to a wholesome and humbling relativism. Besides, landmarks in time and in space, that is history and geography, but also in the demographic and cultural spheres, are central elements that must needs be taken into account. Now, if diplomacy is taken in the fullest and broadest sense of the term, then numerous and fruitful parallels can be drawn between New Caledonia and New Zealand – hence the title of this chapter.

For better or for worse, geography is destiny, and both New Caledonia and New Zealand are firmly rooted in the same part of the world, in the south-western area of the broad Pacific. In the nineteenth century, some settlers dreamt of weighing anchor and planting the two archipelagos somewhere close to European shores. Unfortunately for them, islands are not ships and cannot be moved around. New Caledonia and New Zealand are close neighbours and it will always be so unless there is a sudden acceleration of the continental drift. There is also some sort of emotional proximity between the two polities. For all their love of the island-continent, and for those they call 'les Pokens', New Caledonians still perceive Australia as a gigantic country, maybe too big for them, and therefore somehow threatening, while New Zealand, with its more modest size, leaves them with a reassuring feeling.

From a historical perspective, the forebears of Kanaks and Maori do not seem to have been much in touch with one another—if at all—in pre-colonial times. Now, diplomacy also has to do with regular contacts and sustained communication. This was to come later, in the late eighteenth and early nineteenth centuries when both archipelagos were first explored, and later colonised, New Zealand by the British and New Caledonia by the French. The two rival and competing European powers—neighbours, too, but at the other end of the world—had very similar colonial objectives. Sometimes, it was missionary zeal that urged them to preach the gospel in the South Seas, but more often than not it was the lure of quick profits through economic exploitation that whetted their appetites. They were also bent on getting rid of their surplus or undesirable population—as free settlers in the first instance, as convicts in the second. It was this commonality of interests that laid the foundations for the first exchanges and ties between the people living in the two areas. It should also be noted that both territories were taken possession of in a very short span of just thirteen years: 1840 for New Zealand,

1853 for New Caledonia.

Some might argue that there exists an obvious historical difference between the two political entities in so far as a formal treaty sanctioned the annexation of New Zealand to Britain, whereas no such thing existed in the case of New Caledonia. Though this is true, Waitangi was an unequal treaty that gave much more to the British than to the Maori. Besides, its translation into the Maori language was deliberately twisted so as to exact the consent of Maori chiefs—or at least a fraction of them—to British sovereignty. But the same causes always producing the same effects, with or without a treaty—namely, colonisation, and more particularly land dispossession—led in both places to wars, rebellions and violent clashes between the two ethnic groups and to a rapid dwindling in the numbers of Maori and Kanaks, who were on the verge of extinction by the end of the nineteenth century.

During the two world wars of the twentieth century, Kanaks and Caldoches, Maori and Pakeha, fought together as comrades-in-arms against common enemies on the battlefields of Europe, the Middle East or the Pacific. Most of them volunteered to go to the front, but others—in particular among Kanaks—were forced to enlist in the colonial armed forces. At all events, there remained many shared memories afterwards and, as they always carry weight, they reinforced the bonds already existing, not only between ethnic communities, but also between the two countries. All human beings are the fruits of History, with a capital H, and when History runs parallel in two nations, it inevitably increases the feeling of belonging and the sense of a common destiny.

In demographic terms, New Caledonia follows exactly the same pattern as Australia and New Zealand. It is a settler colony—one of the rare ones France ever controlled—and if there are differences, they are more in degree than in nature. Nothing resembles more a farmer on the west coast of New Caledonia, in his way of life and vision of the world, than a farmer in Queensland or in New Zealand's Far North. And even in their drawling accents and their broad-brimmed hats, they are virtually undistinguishable! But in the field of demography, New Caledonia undoubtedly stands closer to New Zealand than to Australia. In the island-continent,

Aborigines represent 1.5 per cent of the total population and they stand no chance of ever increasing that percentage significantly. In New Caledonia, Kanaks currently comprise some 38 per cent of the total population, but they are expected to reach the 50 per cent mark roughly around 2025, with all the political consequences such a growth entails. In New Zealand, if Maori and Pacific Islanders are grouped together (and there are cultural grounds for doing so), their proportion is expected to rise from the current 22 per cent to 25 per cent in 2020 and to 30 per cent or so in 2050—a quite sizeable minority, while the percentage of Pakehas will gradually decline. In both New Caledonia and New Zealand, but contrary to Australia, the first inhabitants thus represent a political force that will have to be reckoned with in future.

One last point deserves a few developments in the field of demography. Though it is difficult to assess with rigorous certainty, the extent of intermarriage has always been substantial in both archipelagos, probably exceeding 20 per cent of the total population nowadays. Thousands of Pakeha and Caldoches can claim they have Maori or Kanak ancestors: some assert it with pride, while others still tend to remain discreet about it. But the former group is on the rise, while the latter definitely appears to be on the wane.

Perhaps more important than the mixing of different bloods is the very large mixture of cultures that has taken place in everyday life. Over a century and a half, dozens of Maori or Kanak words and phrases have slipped into the English and French languages, giving them a peculiar linguistic flavour. After a good meal in a New Zealand restaurant, it is not uncommon to hear a Kiwi friend exclaim 'puku nui', while a Caldoche, when afraid or surprised, will spontaneously blurt out 'yossi'. Sports and music have greatly assisted in this blending of diverse cultural approaches. Kanaka concerts always attract large multiethnic groups of youngsters in Noumea, and the All Blacks, when touring overseas, systematically dance a lively haka before they start their rugby matches so as to enhance their specific 'New Zealandness'. The Maori language has enjoyed official status since 1987 and is now taught in many schools. As for the twenty-eight extant Kanak languages, they are no longer threatened with extinction: they are actively promoted by a recently created linguistic academy and a specific department is devoted to the study of four of them at university level. Nothing of the sort can be said about Aboriginal languages in Australia.

External relations in the shade of (post-)colonialism

In colonial times, both Maori and Kanaks were deprived of their most basic human rights and therefore had no say at all in public affairs. Such was not the case with the white settlers who were often influential in shaping the foreign policies pursued by their governors. In this respect, it is worth noting that New Zealand was not lacking in ambition and did her best to expand beyond her natural geographical limits, in particular towards various Polynesian archipelagos that London finally accepted to place under her control. The early colonists were urged on by a desire to forestall European rivals, mostly French and German, but also by the lure of quick financial gain in the new territories where they now had a foothold. But the very same sub-imperialist process can also be observed in little New Caledonia, which lost no time in converting the neighbouring New Hebrides—present-day Vanuatu—into the colony of a colony, for commercial reasons, naturally, but also to thwart, as much as possible, the economic and political schemes of British competitors in the archipelago. Thus both New Zealand and New Caledonia went through the same odd process: from colonised they had turned into colonisers.

This does not mean to say that Noumea and Wellington had complete leeway in their dealings with their neighbours. Far from it, as Paris and London kept in fact the upper hand over their external relations and had a final say. It is thus difficult to speak of an independent New Caledonian or New Zealand diplomacy in those colonial days and these metropolitan controls were to last for decades.

And yet things were going to change in a very progressive way. The end of the second world war brought about a huge movement of decolonisation around the planet and between 1945 and 1963 New Caledonia enjoyed some degree of self-government, in particular in the field of external trade where her most pressing concern was satisfied, namely the right to sign formal agreements with her regional neighbours. This freedom was to be short-lived. In the early 1960s, with the setting up of a nuclear testing centre in French Polynesia and the renewed importance of nickel—New Caledonia's main output—as a major strategic ore, Paris took control again and New Caledonia had no choice but to come back into the fold. It was not before serious political troubles erupted in the mid-1980s and threatened civil peace that France contemplated the possibility of a limited devolution of powers to her distant South Pacific colony.

In the case of New Zealand, changes started earlier and were even more gradual. The 'Land of the Long White Cloud' was granted Dominion status—with substantial powers of self-government—as early as 1907. It was then given separate representation at the Paris Peace Conference that followed the end of the First World War, and later a seat of its own in the League of Nations. However, throughout these years, New Zealand officials were perfectly happy with leaving two outstanding sovereign powers—defence and diplomacy—in the hands of London. And when the Statute of Westminster—which allowed her to be independent in those two particular spheres—was introduced in 1931, it must be believed that she was in no hurry to stand on her own two feet since she adopted it only in 1947, only after the trauma of the second world war and some sixteen years later. As for judicial appeals, in cases where a major point of law was at stake, they went to the Privy Council in London until only very recently, in 2003, when this somewhat anomalous possibility for a sovereign State was finally repealed.

Where to from now?

Nowadays, colonialism is held in contempt and is no longer acceptable, on both political and moral grounds. But in this era of globalisation, the very notion of independence is, at best, relative too, in legal, economic and political terms. The sovereignty of European nations is severely curtailed by the European Commission in Brussels. And in New Zealand not so many people raise objections to having a head of state that resides at the far end of the planet, nor question the design of the present New Zealand flag. As for New Caledonia, she is trying to steer a middle way, conscious that interdependence is the key word in contemporary politics, even more so for small polities.

New Caledonia is not a sovereign State and will not be for some time to come. As such, she has no formal diplomatic corps, contrary to New Zealand, and defence will probably remain for decades the exclusive domain of France. By contrast, Kiwis have long had national armed forces at their own disposal. But the question that immediately springs to mind is whether micro-states can really afford such prestigious—but costly—luxuries.

However, ever since the 1988 Matignon Accords, and even more the 1998 Noumea Accord, were signed with France, New Caledonia has enjoyed very tangible powers of self-government. It is thus mandatory for France to consult New Caledonia on all matters that concern her role and activities in the Pacific region or in relation to the European Union, and New Caledonia can, of her own free will, sign agreements with countries in those two areas, provided they are not inconsistent with France's international obligations. New Caledonian diplomacy, though still in its infancy, is therefore effective and this 'shared sovereignty', as it is called, leaves ample room for fruitful exchanges and efficient collaboration in the most diverse fields.

It is in the best interests of micro-polities like New Caledonia to maintain ties with as many partners as possible, within the Pacific region, of course, but also with Europe and even beyond, if only to lessen their dependence. Here again, the situation does not seem to be very different for New Zealanders who—contrary to their Australian cousins—also try to maintain a balance in their external relations and avoid the restrictive constraints inherent in a close political alignment with only one nation.

Notes

1 Imports from Australia: € 1,698,091 (calendar year 2004), € 1,869,094 (calendar year 2005). Imports from New Zealand: € 914,201 (calendar year 2004), € 1,122,316 (calendar year 2005). Source: Institut de la Statistique et des Études Économiques de la Nouvelle-Calédonie.
2 Exports to Australia: € 703,461 (calendar year 2004), € 626,134 (calendar year 2005). Exports to New Zealand: € 7,399 (calendar year 2004), € 8,473 (calendar year 2005). Source: ibid.
3 With the exception of the tiny island of Norfolk, one of Australia's 'external territories', New Caledonia is actually New Zealand's closest neighbour in the region.
4 This is the New Caledonian nickname for Australians. The word is derived from 'English *spoken*'. Locally, New Zealanders are known as 'les Néos' (from 'Néo-Zélandais').
5 The other two were New France (present-day Quebec) until 1763, and Algeria until 1962.
6 Source: personal compilation from Statistics New Zealand/Tatauranga Aotearoa.
7 Literally, 'big belly' in Maori.
8 A vulgar interjection (literally, the female sex) in Drehu, the language of the island of Lifou in the Loyalty archipelago.
9 The Academy of Kanak Languages was launched in November 2006.

Deux voisins dans la mondialisation : les relations économiques entre la Nouvelle-Zélande et la Nouvelle-Calédonie

Gilles Pestaña

Les relations économiques entre la Nouvelle-Zélande et la Nouvelle-Calédonie sont relativement méconnues et demeurent insignifiantes à l'échelle du monde. La proximité géographique des deux pays est-elle un atout pour leurs relations économiques alors que d'aucuns soulignent l'effacement des distances et la globalisation du commerce ? Le fort déséquilibre qui caractérise les échanges commerciaux entre ces deux pays s'explique par de nombreux facteurs notamment celui de la différence de taille (spatiale, démographique, économique). Néanmoins, les relations commerciales et plus généralement économiques enregistrent une croissance depuis maintenant plusieurs années. L'accroissement de la mobilité et des échanges qui accompagnent le mouvement de mondialisation apparaît nettement comme un moyen de rapprochement entre ces deux partenaires.

The economic relationships between New Zealand and New Caledonia are not clearly defined and remain insignificant on a world scale. Can the proximity of the two countries be considered as an asset at a time of trade globalisation when distance is no longer an obstacle? The uneven volume of trade between the two countries can be explained by numerous factors such as differences in terms of area, demography and economy. Nevertheless, the trade relationships and the economic relationships as a whole have been growing for some years now. Increasing mobility and the growth of exchanges that run parallel with globalisation now pave the way to a productive partnership between the two countries.

Il n'existe pas une définition unifiée de la mondialisation. Peut-il en être vraiment autrement ? C'est la plasticité même de cette notion et son large spectre d'interprétation qui en font son succès. En français, « mondialisation » et « globalisation » ont des significations le plus souvent identiques mais qui peuvent aussi différer. La mondialisation est la traduction de l'anglo-américain *globalization*. Le mot de globalisation, à la fois néologisme et anglicisme, s'utilise régulièrement pour désigner le même phénomène bien qu'il puisse recouvrir un sens plus spécifique chez certains auteurs. En effet, de manière plus précise, la globalisation peut désigner les phénomènes dont l'interaction est réellement planétaire comme c'est le cas aujourd'hui des marchés financiers ou des grands (dés-)équilibres écologiques (*global change*).

La mondialisation correspond à un processus d'échelle mondiale qui conduit à une intégration croissante de toutes les parties du monde selon des modalités assez différentes et à des degrés divers. Entre spécialistes, on discute encore des origines de cette mondialisation au point de distinguer parfois plusieurs mondialisations ou de distinguer plusieurs périodes d'une même mondialisation, du même mouvement. Les causes et les conséquences de ce processus, souvent récursif, peuvent être économiques, politiques, culturelles ou technologiques. Une majorité d'analyses, notamment parmi les plus médiatisées, mettent l'accent sur l'aspect uniquement économique de la mondialisation mais il ne fait pas de doute que d'autres champs, d'ailleurs plus ou moins en interaction avec l'économique, sont affectés par ce phénomène complexe tels les flux migratoires, l'état sanitaire, les technologies, les modes, les savoirs, les idées (Firth 2007). La mondialisation et les discours qui l'accompagnent sont aussi vecteurs de plusieurs représentations et lieux communs. Parmi ceux-ci, une lecture erronée de la mondialisation tend à penser la fin des territoires en raison de l'abolition des distances suite aux spectaculaires progrès des technologies de transport des marchandises, des hommes et des informations.

Cette contribution propose d'examiner les relations économiques entre deux archipels voisins du sud-ouest du Pacifique, la Nouvelle-Calédonie et la Nouvelle-Zélande,[1] à travers la critique de cette idée. Si l'abolition des distances était juste, alors ces deux voisins n'auraient pas un intérêt particulier à échanger. Pour autant, le fait d'être voisins sur la planète garantit-il des échanges optimaux ? Quel modèle alternatif d'organisation peut-on proposer entre d'une part, l'abolition des distances que certains affirment et, d'autre part, la tyrannie des distances qui a marqué l'histoire de l'humanité ?

Une étude analytique des échanges économiques entre la Nouvelle-Zélande et la Nouvelle-Calédonie sera présentée afin de revenir sur ce questionnement plus théorique au terme de cette contribution.[2]

L'asymétrie des échanges : différence d'échelle et de compétitivité

La Nouvelle-Calédonie et la Nouvelle-Zélande ont des PIB par habitant relativement proches et de ce point de vue peuvent être considérés comme deux pays[3] développés ce qui constitue un facteur favorable aux échanges commerciaux. Toutefois, il est probable que les inégalités soient plus fortes en Nouvelle-Calédonie comme semble le montrer l'Indice de Développement Humain de l'ONU, indice qui pour 2002 place l'archipel français à la 32e position mondiale (ISEE, 2006) tandis que la Nouvelle-Zélande se classe 18e sur ce critère.

Des échanges commerciaux profondément déséquilibrés . . .

Les échanges commerciaux entre la Nouvelle-Calédonie et la Nouvelle-Zélande se caractérisent par un profond déséquilibre (Figure n°1). Par exemple lors de l'année 2005, la Nouvelle-Zélande a exporté pour 138 millions de $NZ vers la Nouvelle-Calédonie alors que celle-ci exportait seulement 1 million de $NZ soit environ 140 fois moins !

Il s'agit d'un déséquilibre structurel dans les échanges entre les deux territoires puisque en 1990 et en dollars constants, la Nouvelle-Zélande exportait 49 millions $NZ contre 0,4 millions $NZ en sens inverse soit un rapport de 1 à 125.

Quels facteurs peuvent être invoqués pour expliquer cette asymétrie des échanges ?

Figure n°1 **Évolution des échanges entre la Nouvelle-Calédonie et la Nouvelle-Zélande 1990-2006**
1.000.000 Francs CFP environ 15.000 NZ$ en 2007
Source : Direction Régionale des Douanes et ISEE

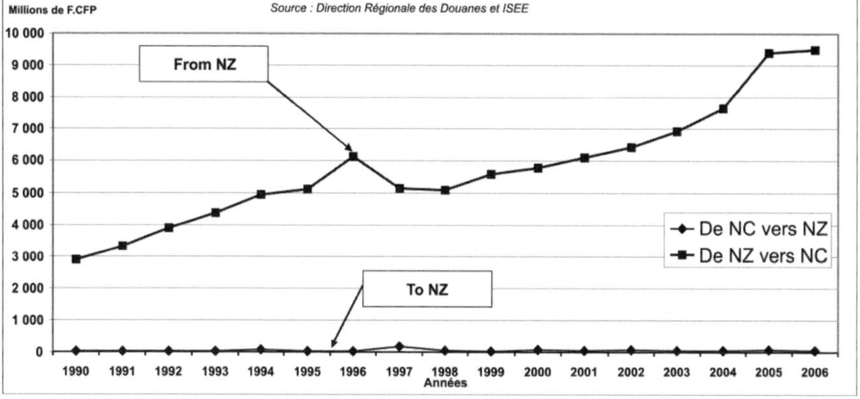

. . . en raison d'une différence d'échelle. . .

Tout d'abord, la différence d'échelle entre les deux territoires constitue une donnée première, incontournable : l'un compte 4.250.000 habitants (2007) l'autre autour de 240.400 habitants (2007), soit un rapport de 1 à 18. Bien qu'il s'agisse de deux archipels, la superficie du territoire néo-zélandais (267.700km^2) est 14 fois plus vaste que celle de la Nouvelle-Calédonie (18.500km^2).

Deuxième raison, la faiblesse des exportations calédoniennes s'explique par une force de production réduite et un marché étroit qui ne permet pas de développer ou de rentabiliser certaines productions. Avec une population assez faible, une faible densité de population (13hab/ km^2 en 2007) et Nouméa comme seule agglomération urbaine réelle, le territoire calédonien ne parvient pas dans un certain nombre de secteurs à atteindre la masse critique qui permettrait le décollage de plusieurs acticités locales.

. . . et d'une économie calédonienne peu compétitive.

A cela s'ajoute, une économie calédonienne très particulière, non compétitive dans une large gamme de productions. Cette économie demeure fortement influencée par le poids de deux secteurs : le secteur public et l'activité minière et métallurgique. Le secteur public pèse pour 22% du PIB (en 2004) et emploie 1/3 des salariés de la Nouvelle-

Calédonie. 37% des recettes du secteur public correspondent aux transferts directs issus de l'État français. L'industrie du nickel constitue une part assez variable de la valeur ajoutée totale du territoire en fonction des cours du métal, cette industrie (mines et métallurgie) pesait près de 9% de la valeur ajoutée en 2003 (IEOM, 2006) mais a dû dépasser les 10% depuis. Par leurs effets induits et indirects ces deux secteurs jouent un rôle moteur dans l'économie. Tandis que l'industrie du nickel est soumise à des soubresauts assez violents à la hausse comme à la baisse, le poids du secteur public est indiscutablement un facteur de stabilité. Le secteur du nickel capte une partie des investissements ainsi qu'une partie de la main-d'œuvre. Les perspectives de croissance de ce marché, notamment en raison de la hausse des prix des matières premières en général et de la construction de deux grandes usines de transformation du minerai de nickel, entraîne la Nouvelle-Calédonie vers une économie de rente par conséquent très peu compétitive sur les autres secteurs. Pour autant, la Nouvelle-Calédonie n'est pas au sens strict concernée par le phénomène de *dutch desease*, ou syndrome hollandais, en raison de la stabilité de sa monnaie (parité fixe avec l'euro[4]) et de la faiblesse du reste du secteur industriel.[5] De même, l'économie calédonienne ne peut être qualifiée d'économie MIRAB[6] (*migrations, remittances, aid and bureaucracy*) étant donné qu'elle ne connaît pas le phénomène migrations-transferts monétaires. La protection des marchés, le poids du secteur public, une législation du travail avec des normes proches des pays développés, un salaire minimum garanti, beaucoup de facteurs expliquent un coût du travail élevé qui, combiné aux importations de nombreuses matières premières, produits alimentaires et équipements, font que la Nouvelle-Calédonie obtient le plus souvent des coûts de production très onéreux. L'indice Big Mac de mai 2006 (IEOM, 2006) illustre parfaitement cette faible compétitivité puisqu'il place la Nouvelle-Calédonie au 5e rang mondial (donc le 5e pays le plus cher du monde selon ce critère) tandis que la Nouvelle-Zélande occupe la 17e place.

En dehors de la rente de localisation que constitue le minerai de nickel, les avantages comparatifs de la Nouvelle-Calédonie sont pratiquement inexistants. 90% des exportations de la Nouvelle-Calédonie dépendent des exportations de produits du nickel. La balance commerciale calédonienne demeure déficitaire avec un taux de couverture qui s'est dégradé : -66 milliards CFP en 2005 soit 61% seulement, dont -38 milliards de francs avec la France et -44 milliards avec l'UE et -9 milliards CFP avec la Nouvelle-Zélande.

Pour expliquer l'asymétrie des échanges entre la Nouvelle-Zélande et la Nouvelle-Calédonie, il faut aussi souligner la compétitivité et les avantages comparatifs de l'économie kiwi dans un certain nombre de secteurs, en particulier dans les produits agricoles et agro-alimentaires.

Des relations économiques modestes mais croissantes

Un commerce bilatéral encore limité mais dans une dynamique positive

Les importations calédoniennes en provenance de Nouvelle-Zélande ont augmenté de 369% sur 20 ans (1987-2006), tandis que les exportations enregistraient une progression sensible mais plus modeste de 81%. Sur les 10 dernières années (1997-2006), la progression des importations néo-zélandaises est moins forte que lors de la décennie précédente (1987-1996) mais continue d'être soutenue alors que les exportations calédoniennes vers l'archipel voisin ont enregistré un repli sensible de -68% sur la période 1997-2006 (Figure n°2).

Figure n°2 **Évolution des importations et exportations de la Nouvelle-Calédonie avec la Nouvelle-Zélande sur les 20 dernières années et les 10 dernières années**

Source : Direction Régionale des Douanes et ISEE

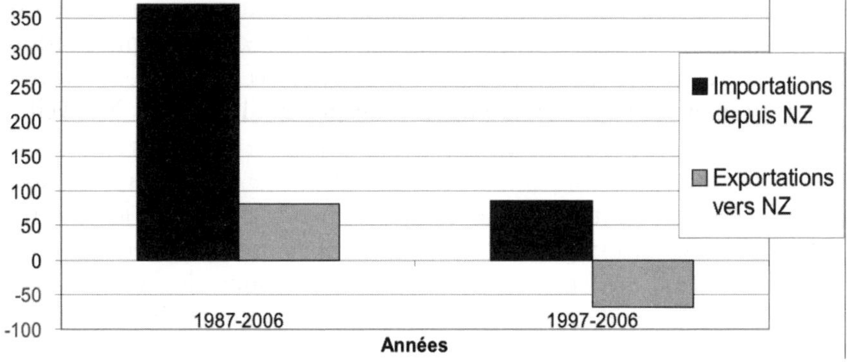

La sortie de la grave crise politique des années 1980 par les accords de Matignon (1988) puis les accords de Nouméa (1998) a permis à l'économie calédonienne de connaître une ère d'expansion économique durant ces vingt années ce qui a été favorable à l'importation stimulée par une consommation soutenue du fait d'un accroissement démographique de 40% sur la même période et d'une élévation sensible du niveau de vie moyen.

Les échanges commerciaux entre les deux pays continuent de se caractériser par une balance commerciale très déséquilibrée avec même, sur les dix dernières années, un essoufflement des exportations calédoniennes en raison d'une faible compétitivité et de l'appréciation du franc CFP lié à l'euro qui a renchéri les productions calédoniennes à l'export (Figure n°3).

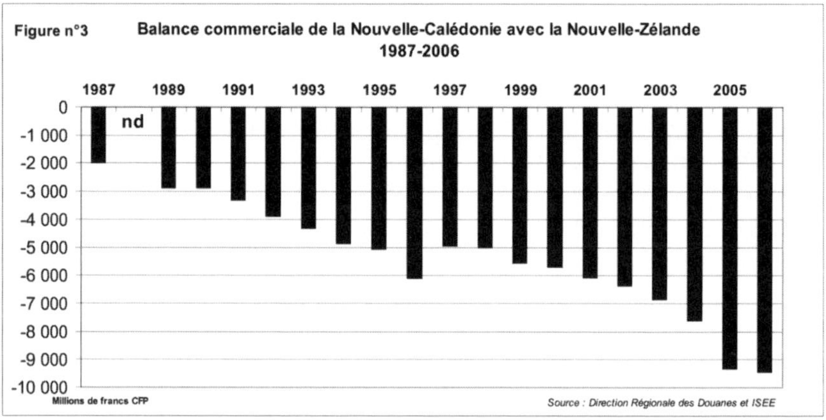

La Nouvelle-Zélande se place comme le sixième fournisseur de la Nouvelle-Calédonie avant les Etats-Unis (3,5%) et le Japon (3%) mais après la France (32% du total des importations en 2006), les autres membres de l'Union Européenne (16%), Singapour (14%), l'Australie (9,5%) et la Chine (5%) qui lui a ravi le rang de 5e fournisseur en 2006. En 2006, la Nouvelle-Zélande comptait donc pour 4,7% des importations calédoniennes mais seulement moins de 0,1% des exportations. Il faut ici rappeler que ces exportations calédoniennes demeurent très largement dominées par les produits du nickel non consommés à ce jour par l'économie néo-zélandaise.

A partir de 2004, la Nouvelle-Calédonie est devenue le 3e client de la Nouvelle-Zélande dans la zone Pacifique après Fidji et la Polynésie Française. En revanche, dans cette même zone Pacifique, la Nouvelle-Calédonie ne se positionne qu'aux 8e ou 9e rangs des pays fournisseurs de la Nouvelle-Zélande. Dans l'ensemble des partenaires économiques de la Nouvelle-Zélande, la Nouvelle-Calédonie est très loin dans la hiérarchie, même comme pays client : dans le dernier rapport de décembre 2006 sur le commerce extérieur de la Nouvelle-Zélande, la Nouvelle-Calédonie se classait au 39e rang des pays clients (0,36% des exportations néo-zélandaises) mais elle se trouvait au-delà de la 50e place parmi les partenaires commerciaux.

Même si le rang médiocre de la Nouvelle-Calédonie doit être relativisé en raison de l'échelle du territoire, les échanges paraissent pourtant insuffisants entre deux archipels voisins. Outre les facteurs déjà évoqués pour expliquer la faiblesse des exportations calédoniennes en direction de l'archipel voisin néo-zélandais, il convient d'ajouter quelques causes supplémentaires.

Tout d'abord, la distance (ou la proximité) culturelle et linguistique compte souvent davantage que la distance géographique. Les deux territoires sont héritiers de deux sphères coloniales, britannique et française, non seulement concurrentes mais aussi deux sphères qui ont proposé des modèles au moins en partie assez différents. La langue n'est pas anecdotique et l'isolat francophone que constitue la Nouvelle-Calédonie dans le Pacifique sud-ouest a toujours constitué un facteur défavorable au développement des relations notamment commerciales entre les deux territoires. Le fait que la Nouvelle-Calédonie soit encore sous tutelle de la France et directement en liaison avec cet État mais aussi avec l'Union Européenne a tendance à limiter l'intégration économique de la Nouvelle-Calédonie dans la zone Asie-Pacifique.

Au-delà des modèles coloniaux et des langues, il faut noter que la Polynésie française, archipel polynésien, entretient des relations économiques et culturelles nettement plus denses avec la Nouvelle-Zélande que la Nouvelle-Calédonie archipel de la Mélanésie. En effet, la Polynésie française bénéficie d'échanges plus soutenus avec la Nouvelle-Zélande puisqu'elle se situe au 33e rang des importateurs de produits néo-zélandais et au 45e rang des partenaires commerciaux de l'archipel néo-zélandais.

On ne peut pas occulter non plus les barrières protectionnistes érigées par la Nouvelle-Calédonie comme freins aux échanges commerciaux et donc aux importations néo-zélandaises. Dans le but de protéger des marchés petits et fragiles ainsi que les entreprises et les emplois qui en dépendent localement, un certain nombre de filières industrielles ou agricoles bénéficient d'un régime de protection efficace. Ces protections commerciales anciennes (taxes, quotas, barrières non-tarifaires) perdurent en raison de l'autonomie de la Nouvelle-Calédonie en matière de commerce extérieur depuis 2000 (art. 22-6 de la loi organique n°99-209 de 1999). Le pays n'est donc pas tenu de suivre les règles commerciales de la France et de l'Union Européenne dont il n'est officiellement qu'un des « territoires associés ». La Nouvelle-Calédonie n'est pas membre de l'Organisation Mondiale du Commerce et n'a donc pas l'obligation d'en appliquer les injonctions.

Bien que la Nouvelle-Zélande et la Nouvelle-Calédonie entretiennent d'excellentes relations commerciales et diplomatiques à ce jour, les deux pays ne sont pas regroupés au sein d'une association commerciale et n'ont pas contracté d'accords commerciaux bilatéraux ce qui ne favorise pas les échanges sans pour autant les en empêcher. Membre de l'Organisation Mondiale du Commerce depuis sa création, la Nouvelle-Zélande appartient également à des associations régionales ou des accords commerciaux régionaux parmi lesquels l'ANZCERTA[7] depuis 1983, l'APEC[8] ou encore le *Trans-Pacific SEP*[9] depuis 2005. Dans l'aire strictement océanienne, la Nouvelle-Zélande est un des membres fondateurs du Forum des îles du Pacifique[10] et participe au *Pacific Agreement on Closer Economic Relations* ou PACER et au SPARTECA,[11] deux accords qui visent à favoriser le commerce dans la zone Océanie et de cette dernière avec l'Australie et la Nouvelle-Zélande. La Nouvelle-Calédonie quant à elle demeure en dehors de ces accords ou associations à visées commerciales. Elle n'est pas non plus intégrée dans le PICTA (*Pacific Island Countries Trade Agreement*) dont l'objet est de favoriser le libre-échange entre nations et territoires de l'Océanie insulaire, Australie et Nouvelle-Zélande exclus. Néanmoins, la Nouvelle-

Calédonie est désormais « membre associé » du Forum des Îles du Pacifique qui est une institution plus politique et diplomatique que commerciale.

Une amélioration récente des relations maritimes et aériennes entre les deux partenaires

Les relations aériennes, pour les individus et quelques marchandises, et les relations maritimes, pour les marchandises, correspondent au poumon des échanges entre deux archipels. Actuellement, Air New Zealand et Air Calédonie international (Aircalin) assurent le trafic aérien régulier entre Nouméa et Auckland. En partenariat pour tous les vols (code partagé), les deux compagnies gèrent quatre rotations par semaine depuis 2002. Aucune autre ville de Nouvelle-Zélande n'est accessible directement depuis la Nouvelle-Calédonie. En 2006, 44.684 passagers ont été embarqués ou débarqués à l'aéroport international de Nouméa-Tontouta sur la ligne Auckland dont 18.000 avaient choisi Air New Zealand. La compagnie néo-zélandaise conserve une place très modeste en Nouvelle-Calédonie puisqu'elle n'assure que moins de 5% du transport de passagers à l'aéroport Nouméa-Tontouta (414.000 passagers en 2006). Les tarifs des titres de transport entre les deux territoires demeurent élevés[12] car ils pâtissent de la situation de monopole d'Aircalin et d'Air New Zealand, de taxe aéroportuaires importantes, et de flux encore limités et avec d'importantes variations saisonnières. Il existe aussi un trafic de fret aérien dans les deux sens en raison d'un vol DHL par semaine : en 2005, 1.200 tonnes de fret furent transportés sur la liaison Nouméa-Auckland.

Le trafic conteneurs en provenance de Nouvelle-Zélande est globalement en progression de 2000 à 2006 : de 2566 conteneurs EVP[13] en 2000 à 3690 EVP en 2006, soit une augmentation de 44% ce qui est révélateur de relations commerciales croissantes (Figure n°4).

En Nouvelle-Calédonie, le trafic maritime avec la Nouvelle-Zélande s'effectue par l'intermédiaire de quatre opérateurs qui assurent en tout plus de 80 escales/an aujourd'hui. Pour la liaison Nouméa/Auckland, la Sofrana assure une escale tous les 15 jours,

Maersk (Moana Services) tous les 14 jours, Bank Line utilise trois navires par mois tandis que le quatrième opérateur PDL (*Pacific Direct Line*) s'occupe d'un navire toute les trois semaines.

Récemment, le 22 juillet 2007, un nouveau porte-conteneur, le Maersk Radford vient de sortir des chantiers navals de Kaoshiung en Chine et assure désormais la liaison Tauranga- Auckland-Nouméa tous les 14 jours (le jeudi) : il opère une boucle Tauranga-Nouméa-Suva-Lautoka. Il s'agit d'un navire rapide (20 nœuds) spécialisé dans les produits frais dont la capacité est 1118 EVP dont 350 EVP frigorifiques. Il peut assurer en 48 heures la livraison de produits frais entre Auckland et Nouméa. Moana Services en est l'agent maritime à Nouméa. Ce type de liaison maritime permet d'envisager dans les mois et années à venir une confirmation d'une croissance des relations commerciales entre la Nouvelle-Calédonie et la Nouvelle-Zélande.

La nature des échanges économiques entre les deux partenaires

La structure des échanges commerciaux et son évolution

La Nouvelle-Zélande constitue un centre stratégique d'approvisionnement en produits alimentaires pour la Nouvelle-Calédonie : viande, produits laitiers, fruits, légumes, sucreries. Il est très fréquent de rencontrer dans les rayonnages des grandes surfaces de Nouméa du bœuf et de l'agneau, des pommes, du lait et d'autres fleurons de l'industrie agro-alimentaire de Nouvelle-Zélande, l'une de ses forces à l'exportation. Les produits alimentaires correspondent au principal poste des importations calédoniennes en provenance de la Nouvelle-Zélande avec de plus une progression sensible ces dernières années, +65% de 2000 à 2005. Les produits alimentaires et les métaux (qui alimentent l'industrie métallurgique calédonienne et le secteur du bâtiment) représentent 60% des importations totales de la Nouvelle-Calédonie en provenance de la Nouvelle-Zélande, il s'agit des deux principaux postes d'importation (Figure n°5).

Les faibles exportations de la Nouvelle-Calédonie en direction de son voisin correspondent essentiellement à des productions agricoles spécifiques (Figure n°6). Il s'agit pour la plupart de productions

Figure n°4 **Nombre de conteneurs EVP débarqués à Nouméa en provenance de NZ (2002-2006)**

Source : Port autonome de la Nouvelle-Calédonie et IEOM

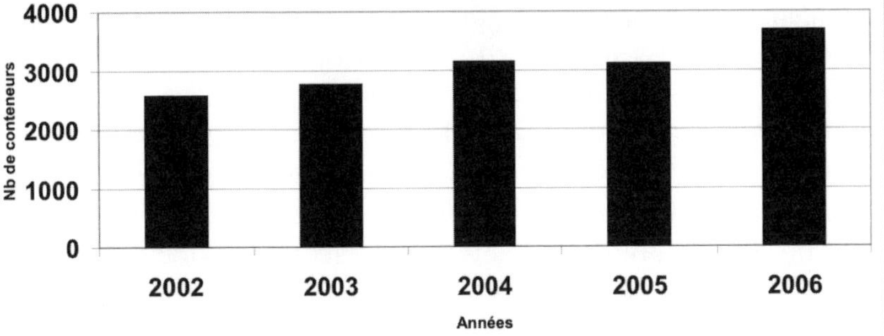

Figure n°5 **Composition des importations en provenance de Nouvelle-Zélande (2005)**

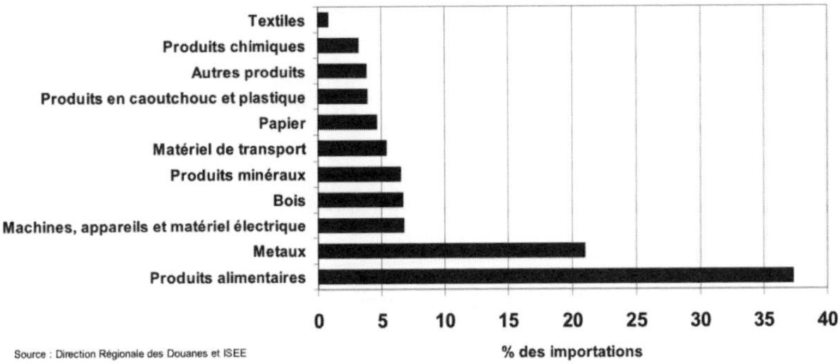

Source : Direction Régionale des Douanes et ISEE

Figure n°6 **Structure des exportations de Nouvelle-Calédonie vers la Nouvelle-Zélande (2005)**

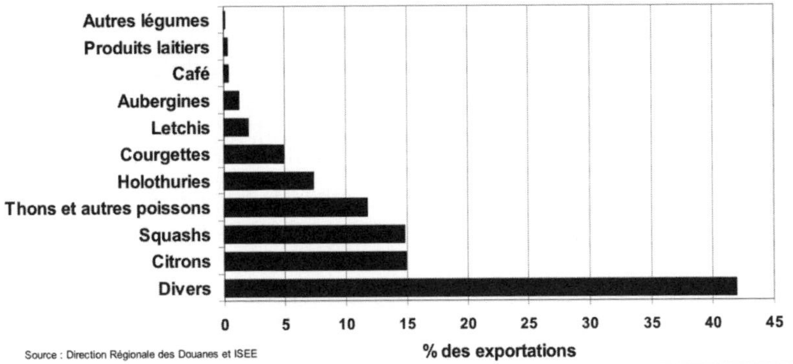

Source : Direction Régionale des Douanes et ISEE

primaires tropicales ou subtropicales faiblement transformées ou simplement conditionnées pour le transport : citrons, holothuries, letchis, café, thon, etc. De ce point de vue, la Nouvelle-Calédonie bénéficie de l'avantage comparatif lié au différentiel de zonalité (tropical/tempérée) même si les proportions de ces exportations demeurent assez anecdotiques en volume et irrégulières.

En effet, d'une année sur l'autre les productions primaires exportées par la Nouvelle-Calédonie varient en proportion mais aussi de nature. Des fenêtres d'opportunité sur le marché néo-zélandais peuvent s'ouvrir pour telle ou telle spéculation comme ce fut le cas pour les pastèques en 1998, les mangues en 2003, les courgettes en 2005, les poivrons récemment. Les coûts de production agricole en Calédonie sont bien trop élevés pour que certaines exportations se pérennisent. Le marché néo-zélandais pour les produits calédoniens correspond à un marché de niches et de « coups » commerciaux. Cela peut expliquer qu'années après années, les opportunités s'usent (ruine des letchis après le cyclone Erika de 2003) et que les exportations calédoniennes, déjà très faibles, s'essoufflent.

Des flux financiers et des partenariats d'entreprises faibles mais croissants

Les flux financiers entre les deux pays demeurent nettement plus difficiles à cerner car les sources disponibles ne précisent pas ce type d'échanges. Même sans sources détaillées sur le sujet, on peut émettre l'hypothèse vraisemblable d'un accroissement des investissements calédoniens en Nouvelle-Zélande et notamment à Auckland. Certains capitaux calédoniens sont désormais investis dans l'immobilier, notamment dans des appartements à Auckland, ou dans l'achat de propriétés. Quelques rares sociétés néo-zélandaises sont présentes sur le sol calédonien notamment dans l'ingénierie minière avec des bureaux à Nouméa. Il existe aussi actuellement un projet d'hôtel en Nouvelle-Calédonie porté par une société néo-zélandaise. Enfin, des sociétés ont des accords dans l'importation de maisons (produits aux normes).

La société néo-zélandaise Bellingham Marine, basée à Auckland, s'est associée à la société calédonienne Kalinowski, un important promoteur de Nouméa, afin de construire la marina de 250 anneaux du quartier de l'Orphelinat, l'une des plus larges du Pacifique en utilisant une technologie innovante d'origine américaine (appelée « *unifloat* »). L'exportation de la squash calédonienne se réalise en relai de celle de Nouvelle-Zélande. Ce marché de contre-saison par rapport à la Nouvelle-Zélande s'organise à travers la société France Calédonie Tropic Export (filiale de l'OCEF[14]) qui est associée au certificateur néo-zélandaise QAS garant de la qualité des squashs calédoniennes pour les acheteurs japonais et néo-zélandais.

Afin de remporter des marchés en Nouvelle-Calédonie, les conseillers en commerce extérieur préconisent aux sociétés néo-zélandaises de s'associer avec des sociétés locales. Ils rappellent en outre qu'un produit qui a reçu suffisamment de valeur ajoutée en Nouvelle-Calédonie peut entrer sans restriction sur le marché européen ce qui représente une opportunité commerciale encore non utilisée par les industriels néo-zélandais.

Une fréquentation touristique asymétrique et marquée par la saisonnalité

Les échanges touristiques ressemblent à ceux de marchandises par leur déséquilibre. Les Néo-Zélandais fréquentent assez peu la Nouvelle-Calédonie puisque seulement 6.930 touristes kiwis sont venus en Nouvelle-Calédonie en 2006, soit 7% du total des touristes reçus. Il s'agit aujourd'hui du quatrième contingent de touristes en Nouvelle-Calédonie, après les Japonais, les Français de la métropole et les Australiens. La part des touristes néo-zélandais stagne puisqu'en 1995 ils représentaient seulement 8% du total des arrivées. En valeur absolue le nombre de touristes de cette origine tend même à diminuer : 7.168 en 1995 avec un maximum en 2000 de 9.576 (Figure n°7). La Nouvelle-Calédonie ne constitue que la 24e ou 25e destination des touristes néo-zélandais et attire seulement 0,37% du total des touristes kiwis (2006). Cette proportion peut-être considérée comme faible ou très faible en raison de la proximité géographique de la Nouvelle-Calédonie et de son potentiel touristique. Toutefois, le coût très élevé de la vie en Nouvelle-Calédonie est sans doute un facteur très limitant mais il ne saurait à lui seul tenir lieu d'explication. En effet, le Vanuatu dont le coût de la vie est plus bas n'accueille que 9.204 touristes néo-zélandais en 2006 soit un volume à peine supérieur. L'échelle de la Nouvelle-Calédonie, déjà invoquée pour la faiblesse du commerce bilatéral, constitue un facteur sans doute recevable de la faiblesse de la fréquentation des touristes néo-zélandais. Un petit pays est *a priori* moins attractif à moins de se spécialiser en un centre de tourisme de masse, tels que les Seychelles, les Maldives ou l'île de Bali. La question de l'adaptation des infrastructures touristiques et en particulier hôtelières se pose aussi. La Nouvelle-Calédonie doit sans doute se spécialiser dans le haut de gamme pour gommer les effets dissuasifs du coût de la vie. Un produit phare attirait des touristes néo-zélandais, il s'agissait du Club Med de Nouméa mais celui-ci a fermé ses portes en 2002 et depuis il n'existe plus de produit d'appel de ce type même si une autre clientèle néo-zélandaise revient. Il existe enfin un tourisme néo-zélandais affinitaire qui correspond à la famille et aux amis des ressortissants kiwis qui vivent en Nouvelle-Calédonie (seulement quelques dizaines). Parmi les facteurs qui freinent la fréquentation touristiques des néo-zélandais, la langue et la méconnaissance de la Nouvelle-Calédonie sont des éléments ayant une influence indiscutable mais difficile à évaluer. Par exemple, une enquête récente montre que 2/3 des australiens pensent que la Nouvelle-Calédonie est à plus de 6 heures d'avion de Sydney. Il est possible qu'un certain nombre de néo-zélandais surestiment l'éloignement de la Nouvelle-Calédonie. Les touristes kiwis partent plus volontiers à Fidji (106.000 touristes kiwis), dans les îles Cook (45.000), à Samoa (31.000) ou à Tonga (15.000), là où existent une proximité culturelle (Polynésie) et un tourisme affinitaire plus important. Enfin, sur une période d'analyse plus longue, la conjoncture politique ou diplomatique a eu un rôle non négligeable dans l'érosion cyclique du nombre de touristes néo-zélandais fréquentant la Nouvelle-Calédonie (Figure n°8).

Le pays du long nuage blanc est la troisième destination touristique des néo-calédoniens avec 11.394 visiteurs en 2006 (ISEE, 2007), nettement après l'Australie (36.000) et la France (30.000). En proportion la Nouvelle-Zélande capte 11% des touristes calédoniens. Ce flux place la Nouvelle-Calédonie à la 25e ou 26e place des arrivées touristiques sur le territoire néo-zélandais, plus

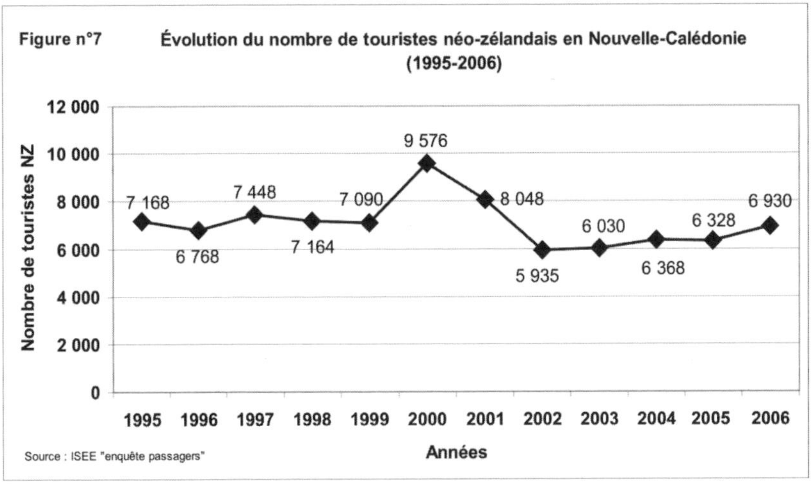
Figure n°7
Évolution du nombre de touristes néo-zélandais en Nouvelle-Calédonie (1995-2006)
Nombre de touristes NZ
12 000
10 000
8 000
6 000
4 000
2 000
0
7 168
6 768
7 448
7 164
7 090
9 576
8 048
5 935
6 030
6 368
6 328
6 930
1995 1996 1997 1998 1999 2000 2001 2002 2003 2004 2005 2006
Source : ISEE "enquête passagers"
Années

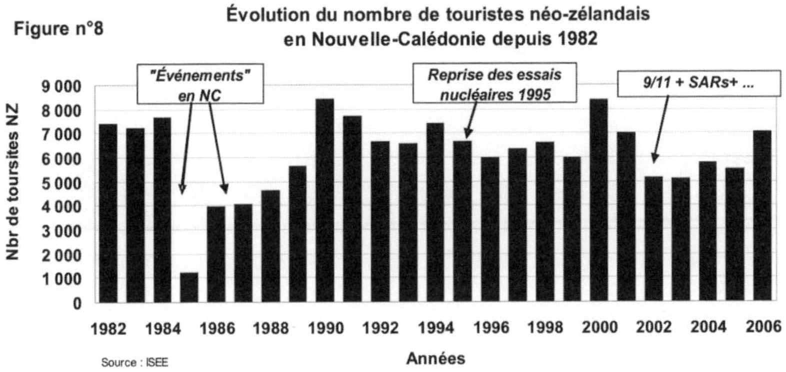
Figure n°8
Évolution du nombre de touristes néo-zélandais en Nouvelle-Calédonie depuis 1982
"Événements" en NC
Reprise des essais nucléaires 1995
9/11 + SARs+ ...
Nbr de touristes NZ
9 000
8 000
7 000
6 000
5 000
4 000
3 000
2 000
1 000
0
1982 1984 1986 1988 1990 1992 1994 1996 1998 2000 2002 2004 2006
Source : ISEE
Années

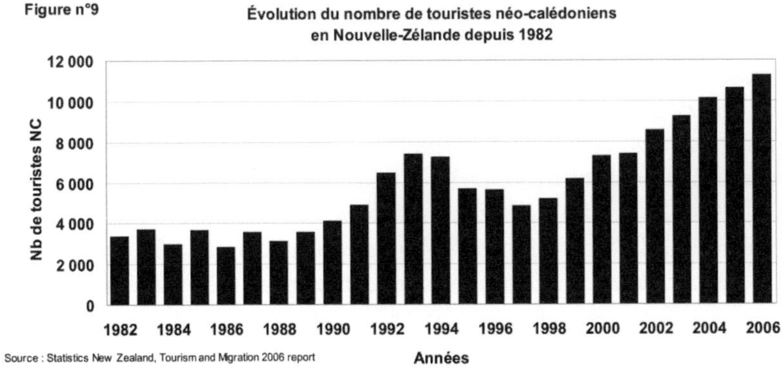
Figure n°9
Évolution du nombre de touristes néo-calédoniens en Nouvelle-Zélande depuis 1982
Nb de touristes NC
12 000
10 000
8 000
6 000
4 000
2 000
0
1982 1984 1986 1988 1990 1992 1994 1996 1998 2000 2002 2004 2006
Source : Statistics New Zealand, Tourism and Migration 2006 report
Années

que le Danemark (10.000) mais moins que la Suède (12.000), ce qui démontre la faiblesse des flux. Pourtant cette destination connaît une croissance soutenue depuis déjà 10 ans (Figure n°9). Selon les données du Tourism and Migration 2006 report (Statistics NZ), le nombre de touristes calédoniens a doublé de 1997 à 2006 : de 4.847 à 11.244. Cette fréquentation touristique connaît des variations saisonnières avec des flux plus élevés en été, les mois de décembre et janvier correspondant aux vacances scolaires dans les deux pays. Inversement, l'hiver est une période vraiment creuse, juin et juillet ayant été les deux mois avec les plus faibles flux de touristes néo-calédoniens en 2006 (Figure n°10). Cette irrégularité sur l'année est plus accentuée que la fréquentation touristique en provenance d'autres archipels du Pacifique et notamment la Polynésie française, Samoa, Tonga, Cook et Fiji.

Figure n°10 Évolution saisonnière des touristes néo-calédoniens en Nouvelle-Zélande en 2006

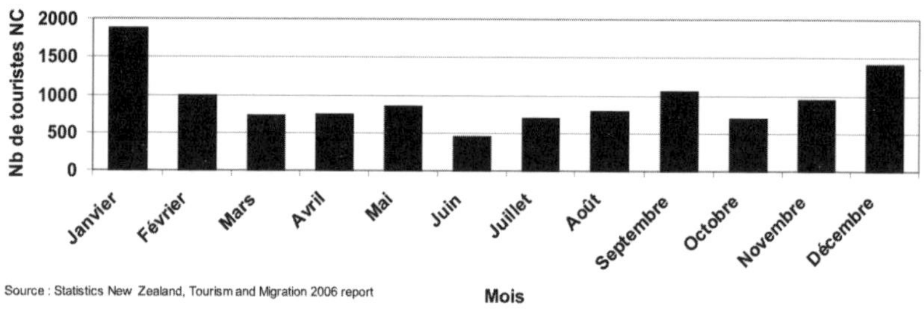

Source : Statistics New Zealand, Tourism and Migration 2006 report

Un rapprochement commercial dans un contexte de mondialisation

Les échanges économiques entre la Nouvelle-Calédonie et la Nouvelle-Zélande sont sans aucun doute favorisés par des niveaux de vie sinon comparables du moins assez proches. Les produits néo-zélandais alimentent un marché à fort pouvoir d'achat en Nouvelle-Calédonie. La proximité géographique constitue à l'évidence un autre facteur favorable puisque si la Calédonie était simplement à l'autre extrémité du Pacifique, nul doute que les échanges avec la

Nouvelle-Zélande seraient sensiblement plus faibles. Cependant cette proximité[15] n'est pas totalement exploitée comme le montrent par exemple les échanges plus denses entre la Nouvelle-Zélande et la Polynésie Française pourtant plus éloignée. En revanche, la différence de taille démographique et économique (population, PIB) joue en défaveur du volume des échanges commerciaux entre les deux partenaires sans compter les particularités des deux économies et notamment la faible compétitivité et les protections commerciales de l'économie calédonienne. Au total, l'examen des relations économiques entre la Nouvelle-Calédonie et la Nouvelle-Zélande incarnent un exemple parmi tant d'autres qui rappelle l'importance de la proximité géographique et donc du facteur de la distance. Aussi, sur un plan plus général, les relations commerciales entre les deux pays s'accordent à un des modèles explicatifs les plus classiques. Afin d'expliquer l'intensité des échanges bilatéraux, le modèle déjà ancien qui demeure relativement pertinent correspond au modèle de gravitation, basé sur l'analogie de la loi de gravitation universelle de Newton, que Roger Brunet préfère nommer plus pragmatiquement modèle d'attraction quand il s'agit d'objets socio-spatiaux (Brunet, 2004). Ce modèle a fait l'objet de multiples perfectionnements par les économistes (Fontagné et al. 2002) mais peut se résumer ici en deux principes élémentaires : les échanges sont favorisés par la proximité géographique d'une part, et par la taille économique d'autre part, soit le principe de distance[16] et celui de masse. Ainsi, en théorie, plus deux pays sont proches, plus leur potentiel d'échange est élevé et plus ils sont « gros » (c'est-à-dire peuplés et/ou ayant un PIB important) et développés (critère du PNB par tête notamment), plus ils ont des chances d'échanger. Il est évident que de nombreux autres facteurs viennent perturber ce modèle mais ce dernier compte tenu de sa simplicité conserve un pouvoir explicatif respectable.

Quels que soient les progrès de la mondialisation et de l'internationalisation des échanges, les distances ne sont toujours pas abolies, autrement dit, elles continuent d'influencer les échanges internationaux d'une manière ou d'une autre. Ce sont le temps et le coût de franchissement des distances qui ont été réduits, d'ailleurs assez inégalement à la surface de la planète. Cette contraction économique de l'espace-temps favorise, entre autres phénomènes, une intégration et une interaction croissantes des espaces économiques et des sociétés. D'ailleurs le renchérissement du pétrole et de l'énergie en général démontre, s'il en était besoin, que la distance à un coût même si l'intensité des échanges n'est pas une fonction linéaire de la distance. Les territoires et les différentiels entre territoires sont au cœur des logiques de production et d'échange aujourd'hui. La mondialisation permet simplement d'élargir le champ d'utilisation des différentiels entre les territoires (aux différentes échelles) et articule par exemple une division internationale du travail et des divisions régionales du travail. Il serait tout aussi faux de penser que les frontières étatiques ne comptent plus. Les économistes comme les géographes mènent des recherches accrues depuis quelques années sur « l'effet frontière » qui loin de disparaître est au contraire désormais reconnu et analysé (Disdier, 2005).

Pour conclure, si l'on peut déplorer que le niveau des échanges économiques entre la Nouvelle-Calédonie et la Nouvelle-Zélande ne soit pas plus élevé, en revanche, il faut constater qu'il progresse assez sensiblement (Figure n°11), précisément en raison de la mondialisation des échanges et de l'accroissement des mobilités. Les importations provenant de Nouvelle-Zélande sont en croissance constante ces

Figure n°11 Évolution annuelle des importations calédoniennes en provenance de la Nouvelle-Zélande 1988-2006

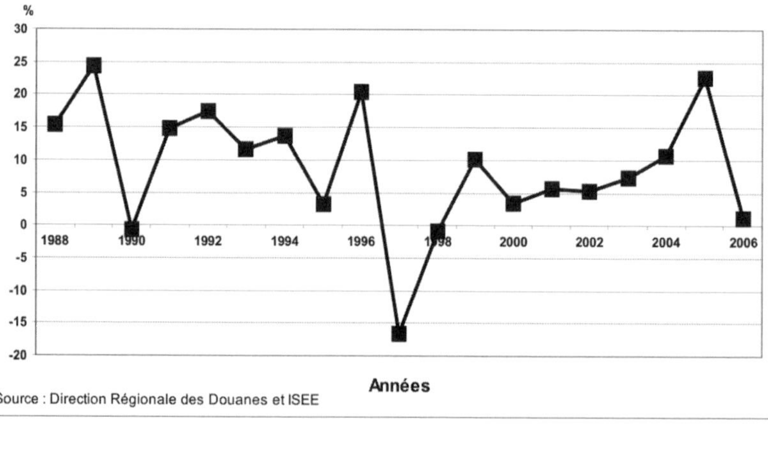

Source : Direction Régionale des Douanes et ISEE

dernières années : elles ont triplé entre 1990 et 2006 pour passer de 3,3% à 4,7% du volume total des importations néo-calédoniennes. Les exportations calédoniennes vers la Nouvelle-Zélande ont elles aussi triplé mais demeurent infimes il est vrai. Ces croissances ont été plus rapides que l'accroissement global des échanges de la Nouvelle-Calédonie pour la même période ce qui démontre le dynamisme du commerce entre les deux pays ces dernières années. Les produits kiwis, notamment alimentaires, bénéficient d'une bonne image de marque en Nouvelle-Calédonie et les préoccupations en matière sanitaire des deux côtés sont à l'origine de coopérations comme la mise en place du protocole phytosanitaire du MAF (Ministry of Agriculture and Forestry) à l'exportation depuis la Nouvelle-Calédonie afin d'obtenir le *phytosanitary certificate*. Les relations commerciales entre la Nouvelle-Zélande et les autorités de la Nouvelle-Calédonie sont au beau fixe de même que les relations politiques.[17] Le nombre de rotations maritimes et aériennes a augmenté de manière sensible ces dernières années. Après plusieurs années d'effritement des flux, les touristes néo-zélandais fréquentent davantage la Nouvelle-Calédonie avec une croissance du nombre de touristes kiwis de 9,5% entre 2005 et 2006 et d'environ de 30% entre 2006 et 2007. Finalement, c'est la mondialisation qui permet aux voisins de se rapprocher.

Bibliographie

Brunet, Roger. *Le développement des territoires. Formes, lois, aménagement.* Éditions de l'aube, 2004. 95p.

Bertram, Geoff. The MIRAB model in the twenty-first century. *Asia Pacific Viewpoint*, 47 (1), 2006. p. 1-13.

Disdier, Anne-Célia. Les mutations de l'économie mondiale. Les frontières comptent-elles encore ? *Les cahiers français,* n°325, Mondialisation et commerce international. La Documentation française, 2005. p. 39-42.

Firth, Stewart. Pacific Islands Trade, Labor, and Security in an Era of Globalization. *The Contemporary Pacific*, volume 19, n°1, 2007, p. 111-135.

Fontagné, Lionel ; Pajot, Michael ; Pasteels, Jean-Michel. Potentiels de commerce entre économies hétérogènes : un petit mode d'emploi des modèles de gravité. *Economie et Prévision.* 2002/1-2, n°152-153, p. 115-139.

Institut de la Statistique et des Études Économiques. *Tableaux de l'économie calédonienne. Édition 2006*. Nouméa : ISEE, 2006. 277p.

Institut de la Statistique et des Études Économiques. *Bilan économique et social 2006*. Nouméa : ISEE, 2006. 48p.

Institut d'Émission d'Outre-Mer. *La Nouvelle-Calédonie en 2006*. Nouméa : IEOM, 2007. 250p.

Leviol, Jean (sous la dir.). *Exporter en Australie Nouvelle-Zélande*. Paris : UbiFrance, 2004. 326p. (coll. L'essentiel d'un marché)

Poirine, Bernard. *Éloignement, insularité et compétitivité dans les petites économies d'outre-mer*. Paris, AFD CEROM. Conférence « économies d'outre-mer », 26 juin 2007. 24p.

Sénat de la République française. *Rapport d'information sur la mission du 7 au 16 février 1997 en Australie et en Nouvelle-Zélande*. Paris : Sénat, 1997. 86p.

Trade New Zealand. *New Caledonia. Country brief*. Wellington : Trade New Zealand, 2002. 11p.

—*Les Nouvelles Calédoniennes*.

<URL: www.info.lnc.nc>

—Mission économique de l'Ambassade de France.

<URL: www.missioneco.org/NouvelleZelande>

—New Zealand Ministry of Foreign Affairs and Trade. Manatū Aorere.

<URL: www.mfat.govt.nz/Countries/Pacific/New-Caledonia.php>

<URL: www.mfat.govt.nz/Trade-and-Economic-Relations/Trade-Agreements/index.php#negotiation>

—Statistics New Zealand.

<URL: www.stats.govt.nz/economy/exports-and-imports/default.htm>

< URL: www.stats.govt.nz/tables/tourism-and-migration-2006.htm >

Notes

1 Notées parfois NC et NZ dans les illustrations.

2 L'auteur tient à remercier l'ADECAL et l'ISEE pour les renseignements et statistiques fournis et en particulier Mme Doriane Sanchez-Le Bris, M. Alain Chung et Mme Anne Rosaire. Les propos exprimés dans cette contribution n'engagent que l'auteur.

3 L'usage veut que l'on puisse parler de pays au sujet de la Nouvelle-Calédonie en raison de son statut inédit dans la République française qui en fait un territoire doté d'une large autonomie et d'un processus pouvant conduire à terme à une indépendance politique complète.

4 Sur la base 1000 francs CFP = 8,38 €.

5 Pour certains auteurs ayant une vision très large du concept, tel B. Poirine (1997) par exemple, les signes d'un syndrome hollandais sont déjà présents

depuis longtemps en Nouvelle-Calédonie de même que dans l'ensemble des départements et collectivités d'outre-mer français.

6 Concept lancé par Geoffrey Bertram et Ray Watters dans un article de 1985 : The MIRAB economy in South Pacific microstates, *Pacific Viewpoint*, 26 (2), p. 497-519.

7 *Australia New-Zealand Closer Economic Relations Trade Agreement*

8 *Asia Pacific Economic Cooperation*

9 *Trans-Pacific Strategic Economic Partnership*) avec Brunei Darussalam, Chili, et Singapour)

10 *Pacific Islands Forum* fondé en 1971, anciennement connu comme le Forum du Pacifique Sud

11 *South Pacific Regional Trade and Economic Co-operation Agreement*

12 Souvent un prix du billet autour de 70.000F CFP, soit 1100 $NZ ou 590E environ

13 Équivalent vingt pieds

14 OCEF : Office de Commercialisation et d'Entreposage Frigorifique.

15 Proximité toute relative en Océanie puisque la Nouvelle-Calédonie est distance d'environ 1800 km du nord de la Nouvelle-Zélande.

16 La distance géographique étant retenue comme proxy du coût du transport (Fontagné et al, 2002).

17 Les échanges amicaux (sportifs, scientifiques, culturels,. . .) et les visites diplomatiques (politiques, commerciales,. . .) entre les deux pays se multiplient ces dernières années. La saison de la Nouvelle-Calédonie en Nouvelle-Zélande en 2007 illustre ce regain de reconnaissance.

Qu'en est-il de l'amour ? Vers un bilan des liaisons interethniques dans les littératures de Kanaky/Nouvelle-Calédonie et d'Aotearoa/Nouvelle-Zélande

Sarah Powell

'Érotiques' mais 'tabous', les rapports intimes noués entre indigènes et Européens ne devaient pas durer. Tel fut, du moins, l'avis répandu dans l'imaginaire populaire à l'époque coloniale. Cet avis, n'a-t-il pourtant pas évolué au cours du XXe *siècle et des premières années du III*[e] *millénaire ? Dans cette étude, nous nous proposons d'explorer l'état des relations amoureuses interethniques à partir d'une sélection de textes fictifs de Kanaky/Nouvelle-Calédonie et d'Aotearoa/Nouvelle-Zélande. Restant attentifs aux rapports de force et aux lois de l'attirance physique en vigueur au sein du couple biculturel, nous nous interrogerons sur l'enjeu de l'acculturation et sur l'importance dévolue à la nécessité de comprendre, voire d'assumer, l'altérité culturelle de son compagnon/ou de sa compagne, pour aboutir à un rapport d'amour durable dans la fiction contemporaine, pour ne pas dire dans la vie hors-textuelle.*

'Erotic' but 'taboo', any intimate relationships developed between natives and Europeans weren't meant to last. Or at least, that was the popular opinion in colonial times. How might this opinion have evolved over the course of the twentieth century and the early years of the third millennium? In this study, we assess the amorous interethnic relationships that feature in a variety of creative texts from Kanaky/New Caledonia and Aotearoa/New Zealand. Conscious of the power relations and laws of physical attraction operating within the bicultural couple, we examine the notion of

acculturation and also the value placed on the need to understand, and even take on, the cultural difference of one's companion in order to establish and sustain a long-lasting and loving relationship in contemporary fiction, if not in real life.

La nuit, peut-elle rencontrer le jour ?
Peut-on s'aimer sans se connaître, sans se comprendre ?
Et quelle est, enfin, la couleur du cœur ?[1]

Posées par des personnages en couples mixtes, ces questions se retrouvent autant dans la fiction de Kanaky/Nouvelle-Calédonie que dans celle d'Aotearoa/Nouvelle-Zélande. En guise de réponse, nous nous proposons de survoler quelques-uns des rapports intimes noués dans ces deux littératures entre sujets européens et indigènes, les deux premiers groupes démographiques de ces deux creusets culturels du Pacifique sud.[2] Plus précisément, nous nous interrogerons sur les conditions dans lesquelles forment, durent et dissoudrent les relations amoureuses interethniques chez différents écrivains de ces deux pays voisins. Aussi, là où d'autres chercheurs tendent à se préoccuper du sort de la progéniture métisse issue de tels couples, nous privilégierons le couple en soi.

Dans les années 1970, deux 'sœurs' océaniennes, l'une māori, l'autre kanak, prennent la plume pour composer des textes mettant en valeur l'identité de leur peuple et plantent ainsi les jalons d'un nouveau champ littéraire dans leurs terres respectives. Coïncidence ou non, c'est une heureuse convergence qui sert à déterminer l'un des paramètres de la présente étude, celui de la périodisation des textes examinés ici. Pour honorer donc le chemin que partagent ces deux auteurs phares de la Nouvelle-Calédonie et de la Nouvelle-Zélande, nous prendrons en compte les premiers écrits de Déwé Gorodé[3] et de Patricia Grace, ainsi que ceux, plus récents, de leurs camarades de lettres. Parmi ces derniers, signalons ceux auxquels nous nous bornerons à nous référer dans ce travail resté en cours de développement : Claudine Jacques, Arlette Peirano, Anne Bihan, Alain Lefèvre, Ismet et Nicolas Kurtovitch pour la Nouvelle-

Calédonie ; Sue McCauley, Alice Tawhai, Paula Morris, Fiona Kidman et Glenn Colquhoun pour la Nouvelle-Zélande. Dans les deux cas, il s'agit d'un mélange d'auteurs *âju-âboro* et *popwaalé*, *tangata whenua* et *pākehā*, autochtones et allochtones, masculins et féminins.

Avant de nous lancer dans notre analyse, il convient de rappeler que dans les deux pays, les peuples indigènes ont vécu une histoire plutôt douloureuse et antagonique avec des colonisateurs européens venus s'imposer aux 'naturels' et spolier leurs terres. Les relations entre les deux groupes étaient donc souvent marquées par le mépris, la répulsion, la violence, la crainte. . . et le désir, fantasme mal refoulé et assumé, tant bien que mal, chez bon nombre des cohabitants. En fait, pour citer le poète Glenn Colquhoun, « There are thousands of love stories between Pakeha and Maori. Sometimes we forget to tell them » (11). Mais si l'on oublie de raconter ces histoires, c'est que cet amour restait 'interdit', 'défendu', 'impossible', 'tabou', voire 'inconcevable' dans l'imaginaire populaire.[4] Pour beaucoup, il le reste encore. Effectivement, Colquhoun, descendant de colons écossais, avoue dans son ouvrage au titre des plus allégoriques, *Jumping Ship* (2004), qu'il ne s'attendait pas du tout à tomber amoureux de la vieille māori surnommée Aunty Rongo. Et en Nouvelle-Calédonie, Morgane la Parisienne et son employé Josué forment un « couple insolite et mal assorti » (195) chez Peirano dans *Kanak blanc* (2001), même si le Mélanésien, albinos, n'est pas aussi noir que ses semblables. Parallèlement, dans *Cœurs barbelés* (1998) de Jacques, Malou et Séry sortent rarement ensemble, la Calédonienne cachant son amour aux siens, l'homme de Lifou se le cachant. Croyant que leurs sentiments envers quelqu'un d'une autre ethnicité sont 'anormaux' ou 'contre-nature', pour reprendre le vocable de Weisz-Bonnaud, ces personnages troublés ressentent communément le besoin de s'expliquer la 'perversité' de leurs pulsions affectives.

Pour beaucoup d'entre eux, les lois de l'attirance s'avèrent physiques, si elles ne sont chromatiques aussi. Ainsi Liz, Pākehā bourgeoise, est-elle fascinée par le « brown velvet » (85) de Tug dans *Other Halves* (1982) ; Séry est séduit par la blondeur de Malou et d'Aurélie dans *Cœurs barbelés* ; et William, protagoniste māori de Tawhai, préfère lui aussi des blondes. Ailleurs, Morgane est sensible au « terrible appel de la chair » (Peirano 74) que Josué fait naître en elle, en dépit des « imperfections » de cet « être si peu engageant » (Peirano 34), et chez Tawhai la narratrice māori de « Pale Flower » (2005) trouve 'irrésistible' la peau, douce comme une pâte à pain saupoudrée d'une fine farine blanche, de l'Européen éponyme à qui elle s'abandonne le corps : « And when he pulled down my pants, I belonged to him without question » (128). En fait, bon nombre des rapports interethniques sont caractérisés par une sensualité très intense, quand ce n'est pas une hypersexualité : Morgane, par exemple, est obsédée par ses relations charnelles avec Josué au point d'être prête à se laisser prendre bestialement (Peirano 74), et si Tug est porté sur la 'baise', ou 'screwing' comme il dit, il est d'autant plus libidineux et nubile qu'il a l'allure d'un primitif.

L'érotique faisant corps avec l'exotique, il n'est pas sans hasard que les liaisons interethniques reposent parfois sur des velléités de dominer le sauvage ou de se faire dominer par le sauvage, à la fin même du XXe siècle. Pour Liz, cette Pākehā bien civilisée, son amant māori est une nymphe qu'elle tend à féminiser, à l'image des hommes indigènes émasculés par les colonisateurs pour mieux les subjuguer. À l'inverse, l'amant kanak de Malou se plaît à s'imposer à sa concubine passive et à en faire une esclave : « C'est ainsi qu'il l'aime, soumise. C'est ainsi qu'il la domine et la méprise tout à la fois » (Jacques, *Cœurs* 218). Et encore, la Parisienne qui se veut « une sauvage née » (128) dans *Kanak blanc*, est tellement 'envoûtée' par son amant mélanésien qu'elle renoncerait, elle aussi, à son indépendance de femme libre pour se faire opprimer par lui : « Il était flagrant, lit-on, qu'elle était sous l'influence totale de cet homme et qu'il aurait presque suffi à Josué d'un claquement de doigts pour qu'elle lui obéisse » (Peirano 240). Les rapports de force traditionnels entre indigènes et européens sont donc renversés dans ces deux derniers cas. Mais si les protagonistes kanak et māori profitent des femmes, les exploitant dans leurs propres intérêts, il ne s'agit pas simplement d'une revanche pour assouvir symboliquement leur ressentiment envers les Blancs, car ils les aiment, même s'ils les aiment mal et tout malgré eux.[5]

L'on peut aussi citer ici le cas chez Gorodé où, dans son roman *L'Épave* (2005), une patronne blanche joue volontairement le rôle d'esclave : 'madame' marche à 4 pattes et mendie des coups de fouet et de martinet, suppliant ses amantes kanak, Éva et Léna, de la battre. Jouant le rôle de geôlières, celles-ci apprécient cette « inversion flatteuse » (137) des rapports de force orthodoxes, mais elles savent que ce n'est là qu'un « jeu passager » qui allait « renvoy[er] très vite les uns, les unes et les autres à leur statut réel de maîtres, de maîtresses et d'esclaves » (137). Ainsi Éva et Léna se méfient-elles des « drôles de petites perversités » de 'madame', car elles connaissent bien « le sadisme dominateur réel de la plupart de leurs patrons et patronnes » (137).

Il est vrai que chez Gorodé les filles et femmes kanak tendent à être encore usées par des Blancs, qu'elles soient 'consentantes' ou non. Dans *Sous les cendres des conques* (1985), par exemple, des popinées 'putes' se saoulent et se perdent avec des 'bidasses' qui, dans la nouvelle éponyme d'*Utê Mûrûnû* (1994), les laissent mourir de maladies sexuellement transmissibles. Et dans *L'Agenda* (1996), le recueil de narrations brèves qui paraît dans le sillage de ce dernier ouvrage, les militaires rejettent encore leurs amantes kanak comme « des vieux torchons » (17). Si, en outre, les femmes kanak refusent d'être « l'animal de plaisir » (Gorodé, *Sous* 40) du blanc et des « troupes de soldats qui [envahissent] la tribu » (Gorodé, *Sous* 33), elles se font violer. Ici il faut néanmoins préciser que ce ne sont pas seulement les personnages européens qui les violent, mais les Kanak aussi. Ceux-ci 'font la chaîne' dans plusieurs poèmes gorodéens, sans parler des viols intra-ethniques presque innombrables dans *L'Épave*. Ailleurs, dans le roman de N. Kurtovitch, des Kanak se joignent même aux Blancs pour le faire ensemble dans une sorte de solidarité interethnique dépravée. Lorsque la jeune protagoniste kanak, Léa, refuse de se laisser toucher par un Européen, un Kanak intervient. . . mais ce n'est pas pour défendre sa 'sœurette'. Il soutient plutôt son ami blanc contre la soi-disant discrimination raciale de la victime, demandant à cette dernière : « C'est parce qu'il est Blanc que tu ne veux pas qu'il t'embrasse ? [. . .] Tu as quelque chose contre les Blancs toi ? » (70).[6] Ce ne sont évidemment pas là des rapports d'amour interethniques, mais des relations sexuelles épisodiques fondées sur la destitution, si ce n'est la force et la coercition. En fait, nous ne rencontrons pas de couples interethniques qui s'aiment dans la durée chez Gorodé – sauf le vieux colon et la grand-mère kanak de Maria qui s'aiment depuis l'enfance mais qui n'osent tout de même pas assumer ouvertement leurs « anciennes et premières amours interdites par l'apartheid colonial » (*Épave* 139). Et à quelques exceptions près, il est rare aussi d'en trouver dans les écrits étudiés ici de nos écrivains māori, Grace et Tawhai.

Est-ce vrai que le pronostic pour tout couple mixte s'annonce toujours-déjà mauvais ? Il sera instructif de s'interroger sur les facteurs jouant un rôle dans la survie ou l'échec des rapports intimes entre indigènes et Européens dans nos textes choisis. Pour commencer, il n'est guère surprenant que dans les relations réussies l'« orgasme commun » métaphorique ne suffise pas (Jacques, *Cœurs* 126). Mais en l'absence d'une culture commune, il n'est pas facile pour les personnages d'ethnicités différentes de se retrouver sur un plan autre que physique. Dans la plupart des rapports le moindrement sérieux – qu'il s'agisse de Kanak et Européens ou de Māori et Pākehā – les êtres fictifs ont de vraies difficultés pour comprendre l'altérité culturelle de leur compagnon/compagne. Dans *Cœurs barbelés*, par exemple, les mondes et les mœurs des amants sont « tellement différents » (134, 177) les uns des autres qu'après huit ans ensemble, ils leur restent pratiquement inconnus et incompréhensibles : « Je te touche, dit Séry à Malou, mais je ne t'atteins pas » (214). De même, dans le premier roman de Grace, *Mutuwhenua* (1978), la protagoniste māori Linda-Ripeka et son mari Graeme sont, elle le reconnaît, « not an arm's length from each other, yet [. . .] so far apart » (152). Ayant peur d'élargir le gouffre culturel qui la sépare déjà de Graeme, Linda ne partage pas avec lui « the deep things of the spirit » (130, *passim*), croyant que « in some things there can be no bridge to understanding » (121). Et dans *Other Halves*, l'on trouve des dialogues de sourds et des malentendus culturels entre Liz et Tug, celui-ci lui reprochant un jour ainsi : « 'It was just a joke. [. . .] If you's a Maori you'd come right back at me. You'd know how to take it' » (88-89). Blessée, son amante répond, « 'But I'm not a Maori. I just get hurt' » (89). Plus tard, quand Liz suggère qu'elle serait « a white Maori » pour aimer un Māori, Tug s'énerve encore : « Don't talk stupid. *You* couldn't be a Maori » (231).

Mais est-il vraiment nécessaire d'assumer la vie et les valeurs culturelles de l'Autre pour le comprendre, pour l'aimer ? Est-il même possible de le faire ? Il convient de considérer maintenant l'importance, et les limites, de l'acculturation pour les personnages en couples mixtes dans nos textes choisis.

Ayant grandi en ville loin des siens et de son *tūrangawaewae*, Tug est déjà plutôt détribalisé. Mais en vivant avec Liz, il a encore l'impression de devenir « a brown Paheka » (231), et de perdre son *Māoritanga* qu'elle ne cherche pas, d'ailleurs, à connaître.[7] Pareillement, le protagoniste indigène de *Kanak blanc* qui vit et travaille en milieu européen perd lui aussi une partie de son identité en s'installant en ménage avec une Européenne (cf. 271). Même si Morgane finit par s'ouvrir quelque peu à la famille kanak de Josué qui l'avait bannie, elle fait relativement peu d'efforts pour connaître la 'kanakitude' et les 'choses profondes' de son époux dont les pouvoirs, par exemple, lui demeurent 'mystérieux'. Dans ces deux cas, ce sont les hommes qui s'acculturent pour leurs femmes. Malou, par contre, va jusqu'à quitter les siens et à s'installer à Lifou, la terre patrie de son amant, où elle apprend sa langue, le drehu, et réussit même à s'intégrer dans son clan. Mais elle a beau devenir une 'sœur' aux yeux des Kanak, cette « femme encanaquée » (196) n'en reste pas moins étrangère pour Séry qui lui reproche de devoir encore tout expliquer à cette descendante de colons n'ayant pas, au fond, la même empreinte génétique culturelle.[8] En Nouvelle-Zélande, Colquhoun pose, lui aussi, beaucoup de questions à son 'amante' indigène mais à la différence de Séry, celle-ci ne s'attend pas à ce que son compagnon européen la comprenne depuis l'intérieur avant de pouvoir l'aimer en retour. Si, par ailleurs, Colquhoun veut que « to be Pakeha now is to be part Maori » (53), il sait qu'il ne comprendra jamais tout. Il aura néanmoins compris avec Linda que « completeness of understanding is not so important when there is love » (Grace, *Mutuwhenua* 121).[9]

L'amour dans ces deux dernières narrations, *Jumping Ship* et *Mutuwhenua*, n'est pas en fait basé sur le désir sexuel,[10] mais sur une tendresse et une amitié sincères qui transcendent la couleur de l''écorce' et les autres différences « that could never be resolved », pour citer encore Linda (Grace, *Mutuwhenua* 152). Il en est de même chez Morris dans *Queen of Beauty* (2002) où John et Mere se rencontrent dans le noir d'une salle de cinéma où toute distinction se perd. Ils se retrouvent alors dans un espace presque virtuel, en parfaite harmonie : « He shone the pictures and she answered back, reading them through the keys of the piano and making the pictures come alive. Their private conversation, call and response: every gesture, every look, every moment on screen, translated into a song without words » (219). John et Mere n'ont donc pas besoin de se parler, de passer par un langage logique et systématisé, pour s'aimer. Leur pas de deux est dansé sur une chanson qu'ils composent ensemble et qui dit tout, comme autant de *Romances sans paroles* mélodiques et raréfiées de Verlaine.

Enfin, ce qui semble compter le plus pour la longévité des couples mixtes étudiés ici n'est pas le degré auquel l'un ou l'autre s'acculture ou s'efforce, comme Malou, de « saisir l'indicible » (163), mais ce sentiment d'affection profonde qui naît à deux, dans une relation d'échange organique nous permettant, pour citer Colquhoun, « to be comfortable in each other's places, to be able to celebrate each other's joys, to be able to bury each other's dead » (53). Les mots de ce 'Pākehā Māori' font écho à ceux de N. Kurtovitch dans *dire le vrai* où le poète calédonien s'adresse éventuellement à Gorodé, la cosignataire de l'ouvrage, en écrivant à la première personne du pluriel : « nous referons infatigables le même chemin/ jusqu'à débusquer l'arrogance/ jusqu'à démasquer l'arbitraire/ révéler à soi l'être véritable/ offrir alors ce qu'il y a de pur/ de silencieux d'attentif et patient/ par l'humilité des sentiers/ à deux parcourus » (13).

Mais à la différence des rapports d'amour interethniques dans nos narrations néo-zélandaises, la plupart d'entre eux se soldent par un échec dans les textes néo-calédoniens étudiés ici. Ce désir de N. Kurtovitch resterait donc plutôt un idéal, même dans son roman de 2006 où l'un des personnages regrette que « nous [soyons] en train de perdre, nous tous, la faculté, l'envie, surtout l'envie de dire à un inconnu : Good night, en toute simplicité. [. . .] C'est quelque chose qui devrait être naturel et simple, de recevoir un geste de sympathie, et pourtant ça m'a percuté comme un baiser, comme un geste d'amour. Tu réalises dans quel vide nous vivons » (95-96). Ce passage chez Nicolas nous donne alors à croire que les choses n'ont pas beaucoup évolué depuis 1992[11] où, dans la pièce tragicomique de son frère Ismet, le rapport entre un Roméo caldoche et une Juliette kanak est voué à l'échec, à l'image de celui de Charley et Ida soixante-quinze ans plus tôt dans la « Pastorale calédonienne » de Georges Baudoux. En plein milieu des événements, les deux amants d'I. Kurtovitch rêvent d'habiter « A colourless country, inhabited by men and women of every colour, who will never, never again. . ./ . . .be strangers to one another » (56). Mais la Juliette déclare avec pessimisme « we'll never be able to do it » (56), et le Roméo se fait tuer peu de temps après. Or, sans tenir en compte *La Nouvelle et sublime histoire de Roméo et Juliette* de Pierre Gope mise en scène dans la Grande Terre en avril 2007, nous serions tentés de conclure avec Séry que « la jolie mosaïque ethnique décrite dans les dépliants touristiques cachait des mondes fermés qui se côtoyaient en lisière sans se comprendre » (Jacques, *Cœurs* 118). Il paraît que les 'sangs se heurtent' encore, comme à l'époque des filles de la Néama, ces métisses qui n'arrivent à fonder un rapport durable ni avec un Blanc, ni avec un Kanak au début du XXe siècle (Bloc 207).

Cependant dans les derniers récits courts de Gorodé, les acteurs paraissent sous forme d'oiseaux, et sous l'effet de l'allégorie, leur ethnicité s'efface quelque peu. De même, dans la pièce de Bihan, *V ou Portraits de famille au couteau de cuisine* (2004), l'appartenance ethnique est minimisée chez les personnages qui sont réduits à des pronoms personnels anonymes et universels, 'Lui' et 'Elle'.[12] Ceci n'est pas sans signifiance car nous constatons une tendance similaire dans la fiction de certains écrivains néo-zélandais. Chez Morris, par exemple, la protagoniste vivant à la Nouvelle-Orléans ne revendique aucune appartenance précise : « 'I'm just a foreigner with a strange accent. Nobody knows what a New Zealander is, let alone a Māori or a Pākehā. So I can be whatever I want to be, I guess, [. . .]. I can be both.' 'Or neither,' said Rob » (229). Mais pour son oncle Tahu, Virginia Ngātea n'en reste pas moins « [an] invisible Māori » (229).

Ailleurs, dans *Small Holes in the Silence* publié par Grace en 2006 et *Festival of Miracles* de Tawhai paru un an plus tôt, il s'avère souvent difficile de déterminer l'ethnicité exacte des personnages néo-zélandais : si, chez un couple, l'identité ethnique de l'un des sujets est déchiffrable, celle de l'autre reste ambiguë, ni spécifiquement māori, ni spécifiquement pākehā. Comment peut-on interpréter ce brouillage délibéré de l'ethnicité d'au moins l'un des composants dans ces couples ? Ce n'est sans doute pas pour éviter le choc ou le « qu'en-dira-t-on » qu'évoquait la mise en scène des couples mixtes dans *Kanak blanc* (211), et ailleurs. Au contraire, nous croyons comprendre qu'à l'heure où écrivent ces nouvellistes en Aotearoa/Nouvelle-Zélande, les rapports d'amour entre indigènes et Européens ne sont plus aussi 'inconcevables' ou 'tabous', et que l'on ne se soucie donc plus parfois d'établir les ethnicités des amants qui sont dorénavant des hommes et des femmes, avant d'être Māori et Pāhekā. Effectivement, cette 'omission' donne lieu à se demander si, dans une certaine mesure, les personnages ont su transcender leurs ethnicités pour se rencontrer tout simplement en tant qu'êtres humains. C'est ce que font, symboliquement, les personnages asexués de Gorodé dans *Le Vol de la parole* en essayant de devenir amis pour se créer ensuite un 'destin commun' où ils parviendront peut-être même à s'aimer un jour. Et c'est ce que disent les « Calédoniens de demain » (54) dans la pièce de Lefèvre publié en 2006 où Fando, un adolescent 'mélanésien', et sa copine 'blanche' Zénobie demandent que les intellectuels, les anthropologues, et les politiciens les laissent s'aimer tout simplement, en s'écriant : « Nous les jeunes c'qu'on veut c'est qu'un homme aime une femme et qu'une femme épouse un homme » (52).

Que l'ethnicité des personnages soit implicite ou explicite, il n'est sans doute pas trop utopique de s'attendre à voir se développer une pléthore de rapports interethniques et métissés dans la fiction de Kanaky/Nouvelle-Calédonie au fur et à mesure que cette nouvelle nation se construit sous les plumes et sur les pas de ses habitants multiculturels, d'ici au référendum sur la souveraineté du pays. Comme ceux noués dans la littérature contemporaine d'Aotearoa/ Nouvelle-Zélande, ces rapports seront encore complexes et ambivalents, ratés ou réussis, mais plus que jamais, ils serviront de passerelles pour aller vers l'autre, imaginaire et réel.[13]

En 1975, Gorodé a terminé un poème doux-amer en disant adieu à la tendresse et à l'affection dans une phrase bilingue à l'assonance plaintive des 'o' anglais et fidjien : « So long, loloma » (*Sous* 127). Aujourd'hui il s'agira de (re)trouver l'humilité et le respect pour l'Autre que prônent les oiseaux gorodéens, et de reprendre cette parole à multiples voix, ici et ailleurs, au-delà des mers et des cultures qui séparent, pour finir sur une note plus optimiste et tout aussi syncrétique : 'bozu love', 'hello aroha', 'kia ora, haere mai l'amour'.[14]

Bibliographie

Baudoux, Georges. « Pastorale calédonienne. » septembre 1917. *Légendes noires des chaînes*. Nouméa : Édition du Messager, 1919.

Bihan, Anne. *V ou Portraits de famille au couteau de cuisine*. Nouméa : Éditions traversées, 2004.

Bloc, Paul. *Les Filles de la Néama*. 1964. Nouméa : S.E.H.N.C, 1998.

Colquhoun, Glenn. *Jumping Ship*. Wellington : Four Winds Press, 2004.

Faessel, Sonia. « Éros aux colonies : fantasmes et pulsions de mort. » *Éros et Thanatos dans le Pacifique Sud*. Sous la direction de Sonia Faessel et Michel Pérez.

Nouméa : C.O.R.A.I.L, 2001. 157-171.

—. « Where Literature is Ahead of Politics : World Fiction is Coming to New Caledonia. » *New Pacific Review – La Nouvelle Revue du Pacifique* 2.1 (2003) : 168-174.

Gorodé, Déwé. *L'Agenda*. Nouméa : Grain de sable, 1996.

—. *L'Épave*. Nouméa : Madrépores, 2005.

—. *Sous les cendres des conques*. Nouméa : Édipop, 1985.

—. *Utê Mûrûnû*. Nouméa : Grain de sable, 1994.

Gorodé, Déwé, & Wéniko Ihagé. *Le Vol de la parole*. Nouméa : Édipop, 2002.

Grace, Patricia. *Mutuwhenua, The Moon Sleeps*. Auckland : Penguin Books, 1986.

—. *Small Holes in the Silence*. Auckland : Penguin Books, 2006.

Gulaan, Edouard Guïnedr Wamejo. Entretien. « Portrait : Gulaan, un album universel. » *Compact News* (Nouméa) 133 (avril 2007) : 16.

Jacques, Claudine. *Les Cœurs barbelés*. Nouméa : Éditions du Niaouli, 1998.

—. « L'Homme qui venait d'ailleurs. » *Ce ne sont que des histoires d'amour*. Nouméa : Éditions du Niaouli, 1997.

Jones, Ewen, & Myreille Pawliez. *Dictionnaire néo-zélandais-français Ï New Zealand-French Dictionnary*. Paris : L'Harmattan, 1998.

Kidman, Fiona. *The Captive Wife*. Auckland : Random House, 2005.

Koea, Shonagh. Interview with Kim Hill. *Saturday Morning.* Radio New Zealand, Wellington. 4 August 2007.

Kurtovitch, Ismet. *A Caledonian Pastoral.* Trans. Roy Benyon. Nouméa : Grain de sable, 2002.

Kurtovitch, Nicolas. *Good Night Friend.* Papeete : Au vent des îles, 2006.

Kurtovitch, Nicolas, & Déwé Gorodé. *dire le vrai.* Nouméa : Grain de sable, 2000.

Lefèvre, Alain. *Calédonie mon amour.* Paris : L'Harmattan, 2005.

McCauley, Sue. *Other Halves.* Auckland : Penguin Books, 1985.

Morris, Paula. *Queen of Beauty.* Auckland : Penguin Books, 2002.

Peirano, Arlette. *Kanak blanc.* Nouméa : Pearl édition, 2001.

Tawhai, Alice. *Festival of Miracles.* Wellington : Huia, 2005.

Weisz-Bonnaud, Monique. « Entre désir et mort : l'échec de la relation métisse dans le roman populaire du Pacifique Sud. » *Éros et Thanatos dans le Pacifique Sud.* Sous la direction de Sonia Faessel et Michel Pérez. Nouméa : C.O.R.A.I.L, 2001. 139-156.

Welsh, Elizabeth. « Review of *The Captive Wife* by Fiona Kidman. » *University of Auckland Graduate Journal of Asia-Pacific Studies* 4.1 (2006) : 114-116.

Remerciements

Parmi tous ceux et celles qui m'ont fait des remarques constructives sur ma communication, je tiens à remercier en particulier Adrian Muckle et Christine Tremewan pour leurs suggestions enrichissantes.

Notes

1 Jacques, *Cœurs* 39 ; Grace, *Mutuwhenua* 136 ; Jacques, *Cœurs* 84.

2 Pour les statistiques démographiques, se rapporter au recensement de 2006 pour la Nouvelle-Zélande (http://www.stats.govt.nz/census/census-outputs/default.htm), et à ceux de 1996 et de 2004 pour la Nouvelle-Calédonie (http://www.isee.nc/recenspop/poplegaltab.html). Les chiffres sur la répartition ethnique dans l'archipel néo-calédonien sont officiels dans le premier document, officieux dans le second (cf. la rubrique « Connaissance d'une langue mélanésienne »).

3 Si le premier recueil de poésie gorodéenne, *Sous les cendres des conques*, ne voit le jour qu'en 1985, les dates de rédaction indiquent qu'un grand nombre des poèmes ont été écrits la décennie précédente.

4 Monique Weisz-Bonnaud constate à juste titre que « Le roman colonial, que ce soit en Australie ou en Nouvelle-Calédonie, fait peu de cas des idylles métisses quand il ne les a pas totalement occultées » (139). Ce sont, renchérit-elle, des unions demeurées « furtives et tenues secrètes » (139). Et dans un article de

référence, Sonia Faessel évoque, elle aussi, l'absence conventionnelle d'érotisme dans les lettres calédoniennes, le clivage ethnique étant « si prégnant que bien des auteurs du XIXe siècle n'envisagent pas une quelconque relation entre la femme canaque et l'Européen » (« Éros » 162). En effet, d'après ses recherches approfondies, cette « étroitesse d'esprit » vis-à-vis de l'éros interethnique ne sera pas vraiment remise en cause avant les années 1980 (« Éros » 169).

5 Cet amour difficile s'avère souvent réciproque, les victimes féminines n'aimant pas moins les hommes qui les assujettissent. Tel est aussi le cas de la protagoniste éponyme de *The Captive Wife* (2005), roman signé Fiona Kidman. Dans cette narration se déroulant au XIXe siècle, l'auteur néo-zéalandais attribue à Betty 'Peti' Guard des symptômes du syndrome de Stockholm selon lequel les otages finissent par tomber amoureux de leurs ravisseurs, en l'occurrence Oaoiti, chef de la tribu Ngāti Ruanui. Kidman attribue alors à son héroïne un amour dévoué devant vaincre toute entrave et tout préjugé racistes répandus à l'époque, dont « the [unnatural] inclination of brown or black men to associate with white women » et vice versa (71, cf. 118, 138). Mais dans sa recension de l'œuvre, Elizabeth Welsh est amenée à remettre en cause l'authenticité des sentiments chez cette *captive wife* dans la mesure où ils risquent de se conformer aux tropes (pseudo-) libéraux et libertins de l'idylle idéalisée entre sauvages et civilisés : « despite Betty's declaration of pure love [for Oaoiti], the reader is left questioning the validity of her claim. Is it true love or simply the throes of dramatic infatuation? Does she also possess the melodrama of her husband, and so romanticize her situation? How sincerely we believe in her love remains questionable » (116). De même, l'on peut se douter avec Faessel de l'amour que ressentirait vraiment l'héroïne allumeuse et exubérante de Louis Thiercelin pour le chef Téâ Bouma dans *Chez les anthropophages, aventures d'une Parisienne à la Nouvelle-Calédonie* (1872), roman se déroulant lui aussi au XIXe siècle. En effet, il devient clair que cette dernière, nullement captive ici, se plaît à romancer sa liaison avec le soi-disant cannibale.

6 Pour citer un autre exemple de la 'solidarité interethnique dépravée' en matière de subjugation sexuelle de femmes mélanésiennes, dans *L'Épave,* la 'gamine' Léna devient « l'objet de tous les fantasmes » (99) d'un trio composé de son 'oncle' kanak et des patrons blancs chez qui il travaille en tant que jardinier. Mais si ce dernier se retrouve en prison pour tentative de chantage contre les Blancs, il s'agit pour lui « des histoires de popwaalé dont il n'avait rien à faire » (99). Autrement dit, le 'tonton' ne s'en voulait pas *a priori* aux Blancs et ne se plaignait pas de partager Léna avec eux, ayant été plutôt content de sa 'solidarité interethnique' avec ces autres prédateurs sexuels.

7 Signifiant 'l'endroit où l'on se tient', *tūrangawaewae* se réfère au « sens de l'identité lié à l'appartenance aux terres ancestrales » ; *Māoritanga* se réfère au patrimoine, à la culture, au mode de vie et aux valeurs māori (voir Jones & Pawliez 612, 327).

8 De même, dans « L'Homme qui venait d'ailleurs », la nouvelle que signe Jacques en 1997, le protagoniste éponyme s'installe à Lifou et fond une famille avec une

femme d'Ouvéa. Mais malgré tous ses efforts pour s'encanaquer, cet homme éprouve de vraies difficultés à renoncer à ses valeurs d'Européen qui marquent la différence intrinsèque entre lui et son épouse. L'on retiendra également le « reverse racism » que subit l'écrivain néo-zélandais Shonagh Koea lorsqu'elle se rend, à l'instar de Malou, au sein de la famille de son mari autochtone (Interview with Kim Hill). Nous retrouvons ici encore ce manque de volonté chez les hôtes d'accepter les différences d'une personne 'venue d'ailleurs' qui ne parviendra jamais à assimiler l'ethnicité de ceux de la terre d''accueil', même si l''étranger' s'efforce de la connaître et de la comprendre.

9 En 2007, Gulaan, chanteur kanak de Maré, ne s'est-il pas fait écho à ce sentiment en déclarant lors de la parution de son deuxième album en solo, *Mon amour* : « L'amour, ça peut aller au-delà de tout » (16).

10 Linda n'est pas l'une de ces filles m°ori qui, dit-elle, « lay about giving some bloke hot sex » (Grace, *Mutuwhenua* 45), selon le cliché répandu dans les livres qu'elle lit. Au contraire, la sexualité dans son rapport avec Graeme passe presque sous silence.

11 La pièce voit le jour en 1992, mais sera rebaptisée *Pastorale calédonienne* pour sa mise en scène en 2000 au Centre culturel Jean-Marie Tjibaou. Mais si l'on change du titre, l'on ne change tout de même pas des éléments du scénario qui seraient, on le sous-entend, toujours aussi pertinents huit ans plus tard. A vrai dire, le dramaturge fait fi de l'unité du temps en situant l'intrigue en 1984, tout en incluant des références qui nous transportent aux années 1950 ainsi qu'à l'époque de la révolte de 1917.

12 Le lecteur trouve des indices lui permettant de décoder l'ethnicité des protagonistes (cf. 13, 38, 40), mais Bihan ne souligne pas moins l'universalité de la condition humaine. Ainsi, lorsque 'Elle' annonce qu'elle a été violée par son père, le professeur Campagnol répond sans compassion : « Ça arrive partout. Dans tous les quartiers. Dans tous les villages. À Paris. À New York. Dans la Corne de l'Afrique. De Nouméa à Mata-Utu. De Papeete à Adélaïde. Partout » (43, cf. 51-53).

13 Si pour Fando et Zénobie « ça a bougé aujourd'hui » (Lefèvre 23), nous retiendrons la sage constatation de Faessel selon laquelle « la littérature peut devancer la politique » (« Where Literature » 174). Autrement dit, les relations interethniques établies dans les textes littéraires peuvent s'avérer 'avant-gardistes' par rapport à celles, réelles, du hors-texte. Gorodé se fait l'écho de ce sentiment atténuant dans *L'Épave* en faisant dire à Lila qu'il « faut pas déconner [. . .] Alors ici, là, en Kanaky, on ferait mieux de chanter encore et encore 'no more apartheid', comme nos frères black d'ailleurs. Parce que tout ça, c'est encore des réalités ici, en Kanaky, au-delà de toutes les poignées de main, de toutes les embrassades et autres bisous-bisous câlins, et de tous les accords signés sur le papier. Ouais, ma sœur, en fait, on est toujours considéré comme des moins que rien, ici, chez nous, en Kanaky » (64-65). Mais nous retiendrons aussi le fait que dans cette même narration Gorodé met en scène ce couple kanak-européen s'étant aimé depuis l'enfance et qui ont des enfants

ensemble, et nous n'oublierons pas non plus son appel à la connaissance et compréhension interculturelles dans *Le Vol de la parole*.

14 'Bozu' signifie 'bonjour' en drehu ; 'aroha' veut dire 'amour, affection, compassion' en māori ; 'kia ora, haere mai' est une salutation māori qui se traduit par 'bonjour, bienvenue' (Jones & Pawliez 31, 278, 221).

Colonisation française et littérature du Pacifique: le cas de la Nouvelle-Zélande

Peter Brown

Ces dernières années ont vu un retour de la réflexion sur le « fait colonial ». Cette réflexion prend une forme particulière dans le roman de Geoff Cush ('Son of France', 2002) dont l'histoire se déroule en 1930 dans une Nouvelle-Zélande fantasmée comme protectorat français. Ce qui peut paraître d'abord comme une idéalisation de la « mission civilisatrice » de la France par rapport à la critique faite de la conception anglaise de la colonisation se transforme en constat de l'échec de tout projet colonial. Le récit fait le portrait d'un fonctionnaire de l'empire, qui croit en la « mission civilisatrice », pour mieux en faire ressortir les malentendus et les contradictions, y compris dans la tentation « rousseauiste » qui hante l'imaginaire européen. Mais le roman met également en cause toute notion de pureté ou d'authenticité culturelles et esquisse, sous une forme défensive, les ironies incontournables de l'héritage colonial.

There has been considerable discussion of the legacy of colonialism in recent years. The novel 'Son of France' (2002) by the New Zealand writer Geoff Cush revisits this question in a particular way. Set in 1930 in New Zealand, presented as a 'French protectorate', the work moves from an apparent idealisation of the French approach to colonisation in contrast to that of the British, to a discovery of the failure of the colonial project in whatever form. The narrative portrays a representative of imperial France who believes in his country's 'mission civilisatrice', only to better show its misunderstandings and contradictions, including the Rousseauist temptation that haunts the European imagination. Yet 'Son of France' also questions notions of cultural purity and authenticity in a defensive exploration of the ironic legacy of colonisation.

A l'époque que l'on dit « post-coloniale » on n'en finit pas de faire le bilan, sinon le procès voire l'apologie du colonialisme. En France, début 2005, la polémique est déclenchée lorsque le Parlement fait voter la loi sur les « aspects positifs » du colonialisme.[1] Destinée à reconnaître la contribution des harkis, ces quelque 200 000 Algériens qui avaient combattu pour la France lors de la guerre d'Algérie (1954-1962), cette loi sera abrogée par le Conseil Constitutionnel l'année suivante.[2] Egalement en 2006, le rapport entre colonisateurs et colonisés est mis en lumière par le film *Indigènes* de Rachid Bouchareb, qui aborde le sujet des soldats de l'empire qui s'étaient battus pour la France Libre lors de la Deuxième guerre. Le lendemain de la sortie de ce film, et sur fond de débat de société concernant les injustices discriminatoires, le Président Jacques Chirac a augmenté les pensions de ces anciens combattants pour que ceux-ci soient dorénavant traités de manière égale aux Français de l'Hexagone.

Dans le Pacifique, la situation et l'héritage de la colonisation européenne ont fait l'objet de beaucoup d'attention ces dernières années. En Nouvelle-Calédonie, la reconnaissance voire la réévaluation du « fait colonial » est la base même de l'Accord de Nouméa (1998), qui est le texte qui établit le cadre constitutionnel et social du « destin commun » censé constituer la Nouvelle-Calédonie de l'avenir. Aux îles Fidji les responsables des coups d'état successifs se sont justifiés au nom du besoin de redresser les déséquilibres dus au colonialisme qui avaient créé une situation où le peuple indigène se trouvait gouverné par des Indiens importés comme travailleurs à l'époque du colonialisme. En Australie, depuis les décisions de la High Court concernant les droits fonciers des Aborigènes (Mabo, 1992 ; Wik, 1996), il y a eu un grand débat échauffé (chiffres et contre-chiffres à l'appui) chez les historiens comme chez les politiciens sur la question de l'impact du colonialisme sur le peuple aborigène.[3] Enfin en Nouvelle-Zélande, le Traité de Waitangi a fait l'objet de nombreuses revendications pour et contre quant aux interprétations contemporaines en termes de droits fonciers et de dédommagements.[4]

C'est dans le contexte néo-zélandais que le roman que Geoff Cush publie en 2002, *Son of France*, suscite un certain nombre de questions clé au sujet de la rencontre entre Européens et populations indigènes, non seulement sur le plan documentaire concernant les dispositifs constitutionnels, le Traité de Waitangi, mais aussi sur le plan philosophique comme spéculation romancée. Ceci est d'autant plus intéressant en ce que ce roman réécrit l'Histoire pour projeter la Nouvelle-Zélande comme colonie française. Son dispositif permet ainsi à l'auteur de s'adonner à une réflexion comparée concernant la valeur respective de la colonisation française et britannique et, plus largement, la nature et la destinée de l'échange interculturel.

Ce roman n'est pas bien entendu la première présentation qui compare les mérites du projet colonial des deux grandes puissances européennes dans le Pacifique ; cette tradition remonte au début de la rivalité franco-anglaise dans la Grande Mer. A témoin, un autre « roman », celui que le navigateur Dumont d'Urville écrit en 1825, intitulé *Les Zélandais. Histoire australienne*, dans laquelle l'auteur fait dire au personnage maori Taniwa (Koroké) les propos suivants sur les Français que celui-ci avait croisés en Australie :

> Ils avaient je ne sais quel air qui me semblait différent des Anglais et leur figure portait une empreinte de douceur, d'intelligence et de bonté tout-à-fait remarquables [. . .] Dès lors j'eus de ces Français l'opinion la plus avantageuse et des hommes qui consentent à quitter leur patrie, à affronter toutes sortes de périls, à essuyer toutes sortes de privations dans l'unique intérêt de la science, ne me parurent pas des hommes d'une nature ordinaire (Dumont, 1825 : 132-133).

Lors d'un voyage ultérieur, Dumont, qui d'habitude n'apprécie guère les missionnaires, renchérit en faisant une nette distinction entre les Anglais et les Français à l'avantage de ceux-ci. Il fait cette exception en raison du travail accompli par les missionnaires français en Nouvelle-Zélande. Bienveillants aux yeux de Dumont, les Français n'auraient alors de problèmes vis-à-vis des « indigènes » qu'en fonction des malentendus ou, pire, du comportement malicieux des Anglais provocateurs :

> Nulle part, peut-être, nos missionnaires n'ont produit plus de bien que sur les rivages de la Nouvelle-Zélande [. . .] Nous avions souvent été frappés des effets fâcheux produits par la rivalité des missions catholiques avec les missions protestantes. [. . .] les ministres protestants chercheraient ainsi à réveiller contre le nom français la haine des indigènes, et ils représentaient constamment nos missionnaires comme étant des envoyés de Satan, des hommes ambitieux, qui viennent les dépouiller de leurs biens, sous le manteau d'une religion immorale. (Dumont, 1842-6 : 186-188).

Deux siècles plus tard, *Son of France* fait des comparaisons entre Anglais et Français dans le contexte colonial des « Mers du Sud » en traitant plus généralement des malentendus et des ironies tragiques du contact colonial, ainsi que de la conquête et de la vengeance dans le Pacifique Sud « français ». En l'occurrence il ne s'agit pas de Tahiti ou de la Nouvelle-Calédonie mais de la . . . Nouvelle-Zélande des années 1930. En effet, dans le roman ce pays est fantasmé comme protectorat français - exception faite du « port libre » britannique de Wellington, « the town where the vanquished had stayed on » (Cush, 2002 : 48).[5]

Son of France présente la crise de valeurs d'un officier français, le lieutenant Robert Verdier, qui d'ardent défenseur du progrès industriel qu'il est au début de l'histoire se transforme, au fil de son aventure en ennemi virulent de toute notion de progrès au fil de son aventure. D'entrée de jeu, la passion que Verdier éprouve pour la vitesse et l'acier, symboles de cette civilisation industrielle – « these machines that are the future » (26) – , est incarnée par la nouvelle voiture Citroën dernier cri, qu'il doit conduire de Wellington jusqu'à New Lyon, la capitale française dans la partie nord de l'île (Auckland transposé en ville française), pour le compte du gouverneur français. Mais il se trouve que le lieutenant Verdier abandonne sous peu cette conception du monde dès lors qu'il entame son voyage initiatique en pénétrant dans le Hinterland des Maori auquel, auxquels, il cherchera petit à petit à s'identifier.

Chemin faisant, le lieutenant fait la connaissance d'une jeune femme maori, Marama, qui devient sa maîtresse le temps d'un bref idylle. Mais le roman montre que le temps n'est pas encore suffisamment mûr pour permettre une vraie rencontre des deux cultures. Le peuple maori, du moins tel qu'il est représenté par un jeune rebelle, Titoko, se libère du joug colonial et de l'endoctrinement religieux pour retrouver sa conscience politique et culturelle et se réapproprier son corps, alors que l'anti-héros européen, quant à lui, se dévêt des signes extérieurs d'homme civilisé pour découvrir l'Autre qui est en lui. Verdier finira ainsi par payer de sa vie son désir de faire partie de la terre des Maori qu'il avait commencé à croire sienne.

Qu'en est-il donc de l'aventure coloniale mise en scène dans ce roman ? Quelles sont les possibilités de l'échange interculturel, tant entre Français et Anglais qu'entre Européens et insulaires, projetées par Cush ? *Son of France* établit plusieurs contrastes entre la conception française et la conception anglaise de « la civilisation » et met en lumière leurs approches respectives de la colonisation et du pouvoir. Les Anglais sont qualifiés de mercantiles, pragmatiques et ennuyeux : « Wellington was either engaged in business or fast asleep » (50). Etant entièrement absorbés par des valeurs commerciales, les Anglais ne portent aucun intérêt aux Maori, peuple qu'ils méconnaissent complètement, jusqu'à les confondre avec des « Indiens ». Dans un dédain total des conditions locales, tant physiques qu'humaines, les Anglais détruisent les forêts natives et étouffent – « imprison under varnish » (98) – la qualité naturelle des choses, en raison de « their loathsome English view of indigenous people » (98). Il se peut que leur cynisme les rende plus aptes à faire de l'argent et à exercer le pouvoir, mais ils sont en faillite morale, situation qu'ils projettent sur les autres. Ainsi, lorsque disparaît la nouvelle Citroën, est-ce l'idéologie du gouverneur français en tant que tel qui détermine sa perception des choses et notamment du rôle qu'auraient pu y jouer les indigènes, perception qui « forbade him to assume that his car had been taken by Maori, just as [celle de l'agent d'assurance anglais] obliged him to assume that it had » (99).

Le Français, Verdier, a beau considérer les Anglais comme des « parasites » (65), c'est précisément ce vide de valeurs humaines qui les rend plus aptes que ne sont les Français à gérer un empire. Ceux-ci sont dépeints d'une part comme étant trop imbus d'un orgueil et d'une confiance excessifs à l'égard de la supposée supériorité naturelle de leur terroir, et d'autre part trop préoccupés par leur

« mission civilisatrice » pour pouvoir s'occuper des nécessités banales impliquées par la tâche impériale qu'ils s'étaient donnée.

Tout au long du roman, les Français sont dépeints comme voulant faire la théorie de leur propre enterprise pour évaluer avec leur propre entreprise et pour évaluer l'impact de celle-ci d'une manière qui est totalement étrangère à celle des Britanniques peu enclins, eux, à philosopher sur leurs actions ou les mérites respectifs de l'Homme Naturel ou l'Homme civilisé. La société britannique se contente aussi de reproduire la mère patrie sans la moindre innovation ou imagination. Il y aurait chez les Anglais un tel manque de projet culturel et de savoir-vivre que, derrière leur raideur, les couches supérieures de la société britannique sont présentées comme des admirateurs secrets des Français, reconnaissant en eux les arbitres suprêmes du goût et des maîtres dans l'art et les plaisirs de la vie : « we English are all French at heart » (69).

Dans ces conditions, on serait enclin à conclure qu'il s'agit de l'idéalisation faite par un Néo-Zélandais contemporain de l'approche française du colonialisme, et notamment concernant les peuples colonisés. La civilisation française est représentée comme voyant une valeur de pérénnité dans la culture indigène qui serait donc digne d'être conservée, que celle-ci soit d'ordre naturel - les forêts vierges des Maori - ou le résultat de l'entreprise humaine comme la vieille cité de Fès au Maroc. Les Français se présentent comme étant capables de compléter la culture indigène en raison de leur goût raffiné aussi bien que de leur prouesse technologique. Et inversement, toujours selon cette perspective anti-Gobineau,[6] cette culture indigène pourrait être ranimée grâce au contact avec des cultures étrangères. A cet égard, les Français auraient une contribution unique à faire à la civilisation universelle, en réunissant les qualités de force et de sensibilité, au contraire des Anglais qui détruisent tout ce qui les précède au nom du seul profit mercantile – ainsi que *Son of France* nous les présente du moins.

Verdier se montre sensible envers d'autres mœurs culturelles et linguistiques. Par exemple, il avait pensé que cela relève de son devoir d'apprendre la langue maori et il recommande au gouverneur français d'en faire de même, allant jusqu'à oser corriger la prononciation de celui-ci, par sens du devoir : « Verdier could not let this grossness pass for a second time. It was desirable that . . . an Englishman should make mistakes that would alienate his people from the People of the Land, but this was not the case with the French Resident. » (102). Car c'est le jugement esthétique, au-delà de tout relativisme culturel, qui motive le Français : pour Verdier, plus encore que d'être seulement fausse, la façon européenne de prononcer les mots maori résonne de manière brutale et barbare.

Il est vrai aussi qu'il y a certains Français qui, semblables en cela aux Anglais, mettent en avant l'exploitation coloniale. Cette démarche est incarnée par le propriétaire de plantations qui a un sens fort des hiérarchies et des topologies raciales. Décrit comme un promoteur de « génocide » (36), celui-ci projette son agression et ses anxiétés sur les indigènes qui selon lui vont essayer de devenir indépendants; ce qui est pire à ses yeux, ils seront assistés en cela par les autorités à Paris qui vont « collude with the rebels and let the colonists go to hell » (33).

Le nouveau gouverneur français présente également ce point de vue, du moins concernant les Maori de l'époque pré-coloniale, qui sont pour lui une race d'êtres inférieurs, indignes du statut d'êtres humains, tout simplement ; de surcroît, ce sont des cannibales, dont l'état barbare les voue à l'extinction, chose qu'aucune mystification « religieuse » ne saurait camoufler : « They have a taste for human blood, the last depravity of a doomed race, dressed up in religious mumbo-jumbo » (23). Vus de cette perspective, les Européens, en se défendant, pourraient donc être les sauveurs, tant sur le plan physique que moral, de ces « starving natives » (23), vestiges d'une race moribonde, en leur apportant les bienfaits de l'industrie occidentale, tout le contraire de l'idée d'un quelconque « contact fatal ».

La tradition française de la « mission civilisatrice » va plus loin encore à travers les références faites au Maréchal Lyautey,[7] présenté comme l'incarnation même de la mission civilisatrice à la française, et à la vision qu'il essayait d'appliquer au Maroc. Dans le roman, cette vision est représentée par le lieutenant Verdier, un admirateur du « great man » (16), sous la commande duquel il avait servi en Afrique du Nord. Or, aux yeux de Verdier, la Nouvelle-Zélande semble être « the ideal realisation » (19) de cette vision, où le colonisateur apporterait aux colonies les valeurs de la civilisation ;

en échange, les colonisés, non corrompus par la décadence des Européens, enrichiraient les Européens de souche : « From these colonies a new breed of Frenchmen would return to the old country, bringing new vigour, new life. » (22).

Mais la référence faite dans le roman à la rebellion marocaine de 1925 fait ressortir, par anticipation, l'échec de l'esprit humaniste français qui s'aveugle devant la vraie nature du colonialisme et donc ne peut pas comprendre les rapports de force entre colonisateurs et colonisés. Comme le déclare un ingénieur français désabusé qui avait travaillé auparavant au Maroc : « Lyautey thought he had more in common with an intelligent Moroccan than with an idiot behind a desk in Paris. And he was *wrong.* » (109).

Cette contradiction est double : d'une part, il s'agit d'une grande attention portée au bien-être de l'Autre, le colonisé ; mais d'autre part, étant donné que l'aventure coloniale s'effectua sans consulter les concernés, elle entraîna inévitablement des conséquences désastreuses, où Lyautey fut pris dans le filet de ses propres contradictions, ne sachant plus de quel côté il se trouvait en fait. Verdier, le soi-disant protégé de son héros Lyautey, refuse cependant de voir cela, et essaie de sauver quelque chose du rêve de son héros, en trouvant refuge et consolation dans le fait que celui-ci passât suffisamment de temps au Maroc pour « build some good roads, some fine towns » (110).

Or, il est intéressant que ce soit un ingénieur (français) qui voit la vanité de cette attitude. Il s'agit d'un réaliste dont le parcours ne laisse aucune place pour des notions romantiques. Il rejette avec force le rêve de Lyautey, taxant celui-ci de simple naïveté :

> No ! The Moroccan Hand thumped the table-top. *We* built the roads and towns. Lyautey dreamed them up, but *we* built them. And we didn't build them for the Arabs. The Arabs went on living in their hovels as they saw fit. We gave them time to discover the benefits of civilisation. But the lesson of the Rif rebellion is that *no* colonisation is acceptable to them. They want it *all* back. And sooner or later [. . .] they'll get it all, they'll get the houses we built for the French (110).

Dans ces conditions, Verdier pose la question de la valeur de l'aventure coloniale, de l'utilité de sa présence en tant que fonctionnaire de l'empire : « If Lyautey failed and Pétain will fail, what can we do? » (110). Question à laquelle l'ingénieur donne la réponse sans équivoque : « Go home! . . .Go home and stay there, before the natives string you up. » (110). Malgré cet avertissement, le désir de voyager, de répandre la bonne nouvelle d'une civilisation vraiment humaniste et compréhensive qui réussit à régénérer le civilisateur lui-même, est trop fort pour Verdier, même après la débâcle marocaine, suite à laquelle il est rapatrié. C'est que la vie aux colonies et le sentiment de contribuer au développement de l'humanité sont autant de drogues trop fortes pour le soldat qui pense pouvoir s'intégrer plus facilement dans une culture étrangère que dans sa propre culture.

Certes, il est vrai que cette aventure coloniale n'est pas sans paradoxe philosophique pour Verdier qui est pris entre des désirs d'objectivité absolue – la perspective universelle – et d'engagement subjectif. Il s'adonne à une lutte intérieure où la loi s'oppose à l'action, où le classicisme s'oppose au romantisme. Malgré lui, il reconnaît alors implicitement l'impossibilité logique de l'universalisme français comme projet impérial de conquête totalisante, et il comprend que l'aboutissement logique en serait l'épuisement. En regardant Akaroa, petite ville pittoresque de l'Ile du Sud (qui fut dans la réalité la ville « française » de la Nouvelle-Zélande), depuis les collines qui entourent la ville, il se demande : « How can I have this view and be inside it ? How can I drink all the water and still swim in it ? Dilemmas of modern life. » (14-15).

Néanmoins, la Nouvelle-Zélande représente pour Verdier une sorte de Maroc plus pure, où ce paradoxe pourrait être résolu. A la différence du Maroc aride et stérile, en Nouvelle-Zélande, la civilisation lui semble avoir atteint son apogée, en synthétisant ville et campagne beaucoup mieux qu'il ne fut jamais possible dans cette Afrique du Nord désertique, chaude comme l'enfer. Le roman présente ainsi la Nouvelle-Zélande comme un cas d'expérimentation pour essayer d'évaluer la valeur et la fiabilité de la perspective française de la « civilisation » et sa « mission » dans un cadre colonial.

Pour Verdier, la version néo-zélandaise de la ville marocaine de Fès est la forêt vierge ; or il croit, naïvement, que les Français ont laissé aux Maori cette nature dans un état pur afin de conserver tout ce qui est ancien. Cela le pousse aussi à croire que les Maori, à la différence des Marocains, ne se révolteront jamais, car pour quelle raison le feraient-ils, étant donné que la largesse française leur aurait déjà donné la plupart du pays : « The cover insurance was plain enough. There was nothing in New Zealand to compare with the menace of Abd El Krim. » (111).

Et pourtant, c'est cette nature même de la Nouvelle-Zélande qui va entraîner la chute de Verdier, au fur et à mesure qu'il pénètre dans la forêt vierge en poursuivant son itinéraire qui va du sud au nord le long de la tranche mince de terre qui représente la présence européenne. Entouré du Hinterland maori, il est de plus en plus désenchanté de sa nouvelle machine qui est censée représenter l'avenir, la Citroën dernier cri, et cela pour deux raisons : la première, c'est qu'il se rend compte qu'il s'est lancé dans une expérience, celle de la vitesse, qui est plutôt quantitative que qualitative, et qui s'avère donc insuffisante : « the problem with speed is that it is never fast enough ». (78) Cela entraîne chez Verdier le sentiment du nihilisme, de l'inutilité, voire de la futilité de toute action. Le deuxième défaut de la voiture concerne l'incapacité de celle-ci à s'adapter aux conditions locales, « sauvages », ce qui amène Verdier à se rendre compte de la vanité de sa culture matérielle : « It had taken a Maori boy from a stone-age village to point out that the triumph of the iron-age is rust » (93). Dans ces conditions, la voiture perd tout intérêt pour le Français, devenant « the artifact of an abandoned life » (180).

Dès lors, Verdier est sujet à de nouveaux sentiments qui demandent de nouveaux types de description, un nouveau langage. En prenant contact avec l'essence de ce nouveau monde, le réalisme classique s'avère incapable de décrire ou même de rendre compte de sa vraie expérience – le code classificatoire et le regard scientifique et désintéressé de ce réalisme ne font qu'en exacerber le caractère inapproprié : « They belonged to a world that had already been described too many times by Maupassant. He could not willingly step back into that world. » (95-96).

En faisant des promenades dans la forêt néo-zélandaise, Verdier essaie de se souvenir du nom des arbres et des arbustes qu'il avait appris à Paris alors qu'il étudiait le volume de La Forgue, *La Flore de la Nouvelle-Zélande*, mais son passé, jusque dans ses réussites intellectuelles, compte pour peu quand il doit faire face à la réalité brute de cette terre qu'il a devant lui : « the reality of the bush was a profusion that drove every classification from his head (130). . .Inner New Zealand was a tangled place, best left to the people who understood it. » (130). Verdier décide alors d'explorer le pays en amont de la rivière au-delà de Jerusalem, village ou campement qui est la dernière implantation des missionnaires, en poursuivant son voyage à cheval après avoir perdu sa voiture. L'ironie en est que la quête de regénération de soi entamée par le Français à travers son exploration du Hinterland néo-zélandais débouche sur la contradiction où il tourne le dos à la « civilisation » afin d'atteindre un absolu d'auto-transcendance - lequel est de conception bien européenne.

Or, Verdier avait tout d'abord critiqué les faux dandies d'inspiration rousseauiste et les bohémiens désenchantés – « bad artists and pseudo-intellectuals » (61) - qui cherchaient à fuir la routine de la société urbaine. « In a country with so much wilderness, there was plenty of scope for that decadence called 'Back to Nature'. Rousseau was a powerful drug, especially to people who had never read him. » (177). Sur le plan philosophique, Verdier avait condamné la conception rousseauiste de l'Homme, tout comme le personnage du missionnaire, le Père Claude, l'avait fait, quoique pour des raisons différentes : « all this Rousseau nonsense [. . .] Where did it come from, this ridiculous idea that man is basically good ? And where will it end ? » (133). Aux yeux de Verdier, le modèle rousseauiste est tout simplement une forme d'exotisme, où le rationalisme cherche encore refuge loin des excès de la civilisation européenne, tout en la transposant et en l'imposant dans des pays lointains et sauvages en une sorte de destruction aveugle et délibérée.

Et pourtant, malgré lui, au fur et à mesure qu'il avance dans sa quête, Verdier se laisse de plus en plus inspirer par une sorte de conscience rousseauiste. Dès lors, par exemple, la véritable œuvre d'art pour lui, c'est celle qu'on trouve à l'état de nature alors que ce qu'apporte l'homme civilisé est considéré comme un supplément artificiel – pire, une sorte de crasse dont il faudrait se débarrasser : « Rousseau had proposed a statue to illustrate the condition of civilised man, the artist's work deformed by a crust of dirt and grit. When Verdier fished, he felt that the crust was beginning to crumble and fall away. » (137-138). La Nouvelle-Zélande serait ainsi la terre de la purification, de la rédemption, à la fois à l'égard de la population indigène et du Français.

Dans ce cadre, Verdier croit que ses yeux sont ouverts pour la première fois et il fait l'expérience du sacré : « This place really is a sanctuary » (144). Dans ce monde présenté comme étant vierge, au ventre accueillant, Verdier imagine que Marama, la Maori qui est professeur de français, lui souhaite la bienvenue et l'invite à rester. A ses yeux, Marama – une sorte de Marie Maori ? – est la représentante de la nature mère, l'*ewiges Weibliches*, qui séduit l'homme en lui promettant un bien-être en profondeur. En fait, Verdier va finalement rencontrer plus qu'il n'imagine dans cette nature, à savoir son autre, qui prendra sa revanche, le Maori rebelle, Titoko. Suite à l'expulsion de celui-ci de la mission de Jerusalem quand il était encore jeune garçon, Titoko avait trouvé refuge dans un lieu caché en amont de la rivière. Pendant des années, ce garçon sauvage s'était adonné au trafic de drogues, où il jouait volontiers le rôle d'« outsider », devenant « something of a comic celebrity around the town » (111). Mais, à la longue, même son propre peuple s'était lassé de son comportement et l'avait chassé du *marae*.

Pour Titoko, qui vit dans l'isolement loin de la société, une péniche ballottée dans une tempête offre du bois précieux pour construire sa cabane. Quoiqu'il rejette d'abord l'idée de fabriquer celle-ci en se servant du « Pakeha junk » (123), son pragmatisme et son opportunisme finissent par l'emporter. Ce qui fait que lui et Verdier deviennent des âmes sœurs au fur et à mesure qu'ils avancent dans leur voyage personnel. En parallèle avec le fait que Verdier « s'encanaquise », Titoko, lui, souhaite se réapproprier son identité maori, jusqu'à l'excès même, craignant toute trace d'influence pakeha. Son rêve ou plutôt son cauchemar de se transformer en homme blanc fait de lui une sorte de double de Verdier, lui qui essaie de se transformer, si non en Maori, du moins en un être « naturel ». Ainsi, Titoko décide de renoncer au cannabis, en dépit de sa dépendance, y compris sur le plan financier, de cette drogue qu'il trafique, vu que celle-ci est une importation de France : « from now on nothing would grow in Titoko's earth that was not native to it » (149). Titoko est donc en passe de devenir un (épigone de) Rousseau, tendance Maori.

Titoko n'est pas pour autant un simple disciple de Rousseau. Il se donne le projet de retourner aux sources, projet qu'il pense pouvoir réaliser grâce à la douleur qu'il subit en se faisant tattouer à la manière Moko de la tête jusqu'aux pieds. Ce désir de faire l'expérience de la douleur, Titoko ne l'imagine que comme attribut maori, mais en fait il s'agit plus de son éducation chrétienne qu'à la découverte tardive de valeurs et de traditions indigènes. Titoko va donc à la recherche d'un artiste moko « authentique », mais il découvre, à sa grande déception, que celui qui est le meilleur dans le genre exerce son art à des fins touristiques.

L'ironie de cette histoire, c'est que si Witi, l'artiste maori qui fera le travail que Titoko lui demande, a pu conserver une conception « pure » des méthodes traditionnelles, c'est en raison de l'influence de sa clientèle parisienne ; celle-ci, à la recherche de l'exotisme, insiste à ce que l'artiste reste purement indigène et authentique. L'artiste lui-même aurait bien voulu se libérer de ce moule pour aller dans une nouvelle direction relevant plus de la création contemporaine, mais son marchand d'art français ne lui permettait pas de le faire – pour des raisons purement commerciales : « The strength of native art is tradition. I assure you that if you abandon the old designs your moko-mokai will simply stop selling. » (154). C'est-à-dire que la « tradition » en tant que « pureté » peut se révéler une force conservatrice, une autre forme d'exotisme assorti d'intérêt commercial, d'ailleurs. Même Picasso, le chef de file de l'avant-garde européen de l'époque, que Titoko rencontre par hasard un jour dans la galerie d'un marchand de tableaux à Paris, met l'artiste maori en garde contre toute expérimentation ; ceci est en partie - mais seulement en partie - par intérêt personnel, car Picasso a peur de la concurrence que peut occasionner un vrai « primitif » : « Experiment ? Witi, old boy, you must never do it. If you experiment I would not know where to begin ! » (155).[8]

Verdier, quant à lui, s'en va à travers la campagne, pénétrant dans « le cœur des lumières » ; il change de rythme et de mode de vie – « the slower he walked, the further away from the mission he ended up » (176). Il espionne la cabane de circonstance qui a été fabriquée par Titoko, alors que lui, Verdier, croit qu'elle a été fabriquée par un Européen ignorant des coutumes maori ; en conséquence, Verdier se méfie de cette construction qui pourrait être un précédent ou un signe avant-coureur du déclin à venir :

This hut might mark the beginning of a surreptitious French invasion of the Park – anarchists and eccentrics evading their responsibilities in the city, spoiling the paradise that imperialists and businessmen had respectfully preserved. [. . .] Urbanites from New Lyon succumbing to the ultimate folly of nostalgia for the Maori way of life, lacking whanau and whakapapa, utterly unsuited for the discomforts of the whare, taking refuge in striking poses, dragging boats to the tops of hills and living in them (177-78).

Car, d'une part, les supposés « urbanites » qui se seraient embarqués dans une « ultimate folly » ne sont en fait autre que le seul Maori, Titoko, qui a rejeté la civilisation européenne en s'engageant dans une mission pour ranimer la culture et le mode de vie maori, afin d'y chercher son salut. D'autre part, le comportement de Verdier est, malgré lui, d'inspiration rousseauiste (bien qu'il soit fort possible que lui non plus n'ait pas lu les textes de Rousseau). Il connaît la nostalgie, « nostalgia for the Maori way of life », ayant manifestement abandonné la « mission civilisatrice » des Français tel qu'il l'avait héritée de Lyautey. S'il persiste à pénétrer de plus en plus profondément au cœur du pays, c'est plus par besoin personnel que dans le but de contribuer au « développement » des Maori.

Mais c'est cela justement la contradiction de Verdier, voire celle du texte : le soldat a renoncé à la mission « civilisatrice » de Lyautey afin de sauver ce qu'il y a de mieux dans la culture indigène ; de même qu'il avait déjà rejeté l'approche coloniale « fasciste » (14) de Pétain – celle de l'exploitation, qui est représentée dans le texte par le mari de son ex-maîtresse Juliet ; de même qu'il avait rejeté les Rousseauistes naïfs qui fuient leurs responsabilités à la recherche d'une nouvelle vie de bohème.

Mais qu'en est-il alors du rousseauisme à proprement parler ? Qu'en serait-il, s'il s'agissait d'un projet de renouveler la civilisation à travers une certaine « naturalisation » de celle-ci – ce qui représente l'autre moitié du projet de Lyautey et qui semble être poursuivi ici par Verdier ? Celui-ci se sent complètement à l'aise et en sécurité dans le décor néo-zélandais, à la différence de la situation qui prévalait au Maroc quand il était évident que la population locale était déterminée à repousser les forces françaises d'occupation – et par la violence, s'il le fallait : « Here the situation was reversed. He was working for the right of native peoples, on his way to tell a Frenchman to tear down the house he had built on Maori land. » (178). Or, la réalité de cette situation, c'est qu'il ne s'agit pas du tout d'un Français, mais de Titoko, le rebelle maori, et dans une scène extraordinaire, après s'être trompé dans sa vision des choses, Verdier fait la connaissance de celui qui occupe en effet la cabane. Le Français avait d'abord cru qu'il avait affaire à une œuvre d'art représentant une sentinelle dont il n'avait jamais pu voir la pareille dans les musées de Paris. Cette vision lui donne l'impression d'être très privilégié, car « [f]ew connoisseurs of carving ever saw them in their forest world » (181), dans leur cadre naturel et « authentique ». Ne pouvant se débarrasser de sa sensibilité européenne, malgré lui, il se donne même la mission d'être le protecteur voire le sauveur de l'art et de la culture maori, jusqu'à ce qu'il soit dépassé par la réalité crue de la situation : à cet « artéfact » : « 'Trust me', he whispered. He wanted to reassure the sentinel that if it would come back to the world with him he would be its protector. » (181). Mais c'est précisément à ce instant-là que ce « carving » s'anime pour lui écraser la tête.

Verdier devient alors le prisonnier de Titoko qui avait considéré le Français comme un intrus dans son espace maori. Mais, comme nous l'avons vu, cet acte « d'invasion » de la part du Français est pleine d'ironie : c'est la conséquence de l'outrage ressenti par Verdier qui pense que c'est un Européen d'inspiration rousseauiste qui, dans ce site naturel pur, avait construit sa cabane de style européen. Mais ce fut le soi-disant guerrier maori lui-même qui l'avait fait, après avoir volé le bois dont il avait besoin en démantelant la péniche à la dérive et suite à la consommation de grandes quantités d'absinthe à l'état « pur » qu'il avait volé dans la Citroën de Verdier. La « statue » Titoko s'élance alors et coupe l'oreille à Verdier (un Van Gogh pour un Gauguin ?) avant de la faire cuire dans le but de l'ingérer. Mais au lieu de cela il vomit vite cette oreille, prenant pitié de sa proie qui, *in extremis*, lui rend service à son tour, en apprenant à son bourreau comment il faut préparer l'absinthe.

Titoko transforme alors en figure de Christ l'athée Verdier, lui qui s'est débarrassé de son rationalisme sans pour autant atteindre aucune transcendance : « the beaten head with its long hair and three-day beard looked like the painting of the crucifixion that hung in the church at Jerusalem. » (188). Ceci se passe après la crise spirituelle que subit Titoko lui-même : une fois qu'il vomit l'oreille bouillie de Verdier, il cherche le sens de son geste, le sens de sa vie, dans la Bible, la Bible Maori, car il trouve que sa haine et son désir de revanche sont incapables de rendre compte de son dégoût de soi. Tout en continuant à rejeter l'enseignement banal qu'il avait entendu pendant toute sa vie et qui ne s'appliquait manifestement pas à lui, il trouve un passage de la Bible où Jésus semble perdu dans ce monde ici-bas. Ceci mène à une sorte d'état d' « illumination » (189) pour le non-rationaliste Titoko : « See, I got it all wrong. . .I thought, you put pain in, you get cruelty out. . .But it doesn't work like that. What you get is pity. You put pain in, you get sympathy out. My face hurts. I share my pain-killer with you. Simple. Suffering of Jesus » (188). Le rebelle Titoko découvre alors la valeur de Jésus pour la première fois de sa vie, et il est sincère en faisant des prières « for the Pakeha to be healed » (199), pour sauver la vie de ce Français qu'il vient de crucifier. Pour sa part, Verdier croit qu'en faisant don de sa propre personne - « a gift of himself » (198) - à Titoko, il va porter la politique de son héros, Lyautey, jusqu'à son aboutissement logique ; mais il s'agit là d'une contradiction menant à une *reductio ad absurdum.* Car c'est le rationaliste républicain, Verdier, qui joue le rôle du *Jésus doloroso*, rôle qui lui est confié par le païen rebelle, Titoko, en une sorte de cérémonie chrétienne macabre, car, tout comme les saisons, le calendrier chrétien est renversé aux Antipodes, cette crucifixion ayant lieu à Noël.

Or, l'amante de Verdier, Marama, qui est également l'ex-petite amie de Titoko, connaît l'expérience inverse. Elle fait le même reproche à Titoko que Verdier avait fait quand il s'était imaginé que c'est un Européen qui avait commis le sacrilège de construire une cabane de style européen sur terre maori. Marama, elle, regrette ce qu'elle voit également comme un manque de pureté, et elle se croit obligée de renverser la situation. Elle, qui avait été auparavant comblée dans la présence de ce Français, son amant, désire maintenant prendre sa revanche contre lui : « in the model of the Hashishiin women in Morocco who smoked to give themselves courage, to purify their minds, to lift out of pity, into logic, to invoke duties, to make themselves mad enough not to care. . .Marama smoked and rolled another and sucked it in and held her breath to force the ancient spirit of cruelty through their veins. » (197).

Ce ménage à trois dominé par des malentendus et des trahisons comporte une complication supplémentaire : dans sa tentative de retrouver son identité en tant que Maori, Marama dénonce (à tort) son amant Verdier auprès de Titoko, accusant le Français de l'avoir violée. Ce geste de fausse conscience est encore pire, en ce sens qu'elle invoque « the People and the Land » contre Verdier, lui qui faisait de son mieux pour promouvoir justement ceux-ci : « Didn't they teach you about the Maori ? You can't divide the People of the Land any more than you can divide the land. » (200). Tout comme Titoko, Marama sait pertinemment que son accusation est injuste ; que c'est même lui, Titoko, qui l'avait le premier déflorée, pour ne pas dire violée quand elle avait seulement neuf ans, dans un geste qui affirmait sa volonté d'homme violent tout en défiant l'enseignement de l'Eglise. En fait, c'est avec ce même Verdier quelques années plus tard, lui qui n'est que le deuxième homme dans sa vie, qu'elle s'était vraiment découverte comme femme. L'ironie supplémentaire en est que Verdier a horreur de toute exploitation sexuelle des femmes aux mains des Européens colonisateurs du Pacifique, d'autant plus qu'il reconnaît en lui le potentiel de commettre de tels actes : « the sexuality of concealment and colonisation, still Gauguin's sexuality after all. I know all this. Gauguin is alive in me. The fact that I fear him and fight him proves it. » (160).

Or, l'échec de Titoko, qui n'arrive pas à mettre à mort son captif, Verdier, n'est cependant pas dû (simplement) au fait qu'il sait que Marama ment concernant ce qui lui serait arrivé aux mains du Français. Le refus de Titoko de tuer Verdier est surtout une fonction du fait que l'idée de Titoko de perpétrer des actes de violence rituelle et « pure » rencontre sa propre humanité face à la souffrance de son semblable. C'est la pitié et le dégoût de soi, et non pas la violence gratuite « anoblissante » qui s'emparent de lui pour le rendre à la fois piteux et grand.

Verdier, quant à lui, croyait avoir trouvé l'harmonie et la paix dans l'amour et l'acte d'amour avec une femme maori, laquelle travaillait d'ailleurs comme professeur de français ; qui plus est, il l'avait à tort imaginée dans sa nouvelle Passion comme une sorte de Marie-Madeleine venue lui apporter secours. Mais c'est cette même amante qui tue le Français en succombant tout d'un coup au sens du devoir, ou de l'obstination, afin d'extirper toute trace du Pakeha qui avait pénétré sur sa terre et dans sa culture : « Do you remember the day you arrived ? The people gathered around you as if you were a god. [. . .] You thought you had found the place to put your little fantasy into practice. Little Rousseau. Little du Fresne. Little Verdier. She laughed softly. » (199).

Cependant – ironie ultime du roman –, alors que Marama a pu manger le cœur de l'homme français, cannabilisant ainsi le corps qui avait fait partie de leur union tant réelle que symbolique, elle n'en gardera pas moins une trace de l'homme européen de passage, et cela de manière permanente, et pour l'avenir des indigènes, son peuple dont elle veut restaurer la pureté, à travers l'enfant métis qu'elle porte et dont elle accouchera à Pâques dans le nouveau Jérusalem – l'enfant grâce à qui, pour citer les derniers mots du roman, les Européens vont être dorénavant une partie constituante de l'identité maori, « in whose being the French had secured their place on the Land. » (213).

Quelle leçon tirer de cette histoire de Geoff Cush ? Ne s'agit-il que de la susceptibilité d'un *Pakeha* qui rentre dans son pays natal après avoir passé de longues années à l'étranger et qui réagit aux transformations profondes qui sont survenues à son pays qui est passé dans l'espace de vingt ans d'une colonie anglaise vers une identité biculturelle fortement ancrée dans le Pacifique ?[9] Certes, Cush projette la civilisation européenne « au mieux », non pas anglaise mais française ; et pourtant, cette aventure coloniale se révèle un échec, non seulement parce qu'elle se heurte contre la résistance indigène qui la repousse, mais aussi parce que ses contradictions internes la rendent tout simplement insoutenable.

Mais le résultat de cette interaction entre Européens et populations indigènes n'est pas neutre dans ses effets, étant donnée qu'elle transforme, et pour toujours, colonisateurs et colonisés, y compris sur le plan biologique. Selon la perspective de *Son of France*, toute notion de pureté, que ce soit d'un côté ou de l'autre, serait qualifiée de trompeuse sinon de fausse, dans la mesure où elle prétendrait retrouver le passé « authentique » pour le projeter dans l'avenir. Geoff Cush semble nous indiquer qu'il faudrait forger un *modus operandi* afin de faire face à l'héritage concret du colonialisme et de l'interaction entre colonisés et colonisateurs pour mieux faire face à l'avenir, problématique qui reste manifestement des plus actuelles.

Bibliographie

Bouchareb, Rachid. *Indigènes*, film français, marocain, algérien, belge, 2006.

Brunt, Peter. 'The Temptation of Brother Anatomy: Decolonization and the Tattooing of Tony Formison', in *Tatoo. Bodies, Art, and Exchange in the Pacific and the West.* Nicholas Thomas, Anna Cole and Bronwen Douglas (eds.). Durham: Duke University Press, 2005, pp. 123-144.

Cush, Geoff. *Son of France*, Auckland: Vintage, 2002.

Dumont d'Urville, Jules-Sébastien-César. [1825]. *Les Zélandais: histoire Australienne,* transcrit par Carol A. Legge. TS. Wellington: National Library of New Zealand/Te Puna Matauranga o Aoteroa.

—. 1842-6. *Voyage au pôle sud et dans l' Océanie sur les corvettes l' Astrolabe et la Zélée exécuté par ordre du roi pendant les années 1837-1838-1839-1840 sous le commandement de M. J. Dumont-d' Urville, publié par ordonnnance de sa Majesté sous la direction supérieure de M. Jacquinot. Histoire du voyage.* 10 vols. Paris : Gide, vol. 9.

Gobineau, Joseph Comte de. *Essai sur l'inégalité des races humaines.* Paris : Gallimard, 1983.

Nikora, Linda Waimarie, Rua, Mohi and Te Awekotuku, Ngahuia. 'Wearing Moko: Maori Facial Marking in Today's World', in *Tatoo. Bodies, Art, and Exchange in the Pacific and the West.* Nicholas Thomas, Anna Cole and Bronwen Douglas (eds.). Durham: Duke University Press, 2005, pp. 191-203.

Reynolds, Henry. *An indelible stain? : the of genocide in Australia's history.* Sydney : Penguin, 2001.

Thomas, Nicholas, Cole, Anna and Douglas, Bronwen (eds.). *Tatoo. Bodies, Art, and Exchange in the Pacific and the West.* Durham: Duke University Press, 2005.

Walker, Ranginui. *Ka whawha tonu matou. Struggle without End.* Auckland : Penguin, 2004.

Windschuttle, Kevin. 'The myth of frontier massacres in Australian history. Part I. The invention of massacre stories'. *Quadrant*, October 2000.

Notes

1 Loi du 23 février 2005, dont le 2e aliéna, article 4 évoquait les « aspects positifs de la présence française d'outre-mer ».

2 Le Président Jacques Chirac avait déjà appelé à ce que cet article soit supprimé, mais il fallait que le Conseil Constitutionnel l'ait déclassé d'abord, ce qu'il a fait début 2006.

3 Voir par exemple, le débat entre Keith Windschuttle (2000) et Henry Reynolds (2000 ; 2001), entre autres.

4 Voir, par example, Ranginui Walker (2004). L'ex-leader du Nationalist Party, Don Brash, a, quant à lui, parlé du « Treaty of Waitangi Grievance Indemnity ».

5 Toute citation ultérieure de *Son of France* sera suivie, entre guillemets, du seul numéro de la page du roman.

6 Joseph Comte de Gobineau, penseur du XIXe siècle, disait dans son *Essai sur l'inégalité des races humaines* : 'Les civilisations se sont développées en fonction de leur appartenance à une race. Il y a trois races humaines : la noire, la jaune et la blanche. Les races humaines sont inégales. La noire est la plus humble et gît au bas de l'échelle. . .'.

7 Louis-Hubert Lyautey (1854-1934), militaire français, ministre de la guerre pendant la Première guerre mondiale, dont la carrière s'est surtout associée à la présence française au Maroc et à la « mission civilisatrice de celle-ci.

8 Il est intéressant de noter que Nicholas Thomas conteste justement cette représentation du modernisme européen : 'it is odd that so singular a form of "primitive art" as tattooing should not have attracted the attention of the early twentieth-century modernists who notoriously gained inspiration from African and Oceanic arts' (Thomas, 2005 : 27). Voir également, dans le même volume, le texte de Nikora, Linda Waimarie, Rua, Mohi and Te Awekotuku, Ngahuia. 'Wearing Moko: Maori Facial Marking in Today's World', 191-203.

9 'The country went (to put it crudely) from a largely monocultural, Eurocentric, protectionist welfare state, dependent on British markets and British cultural ideals (the historian James Belich sums up the national super-ego of the period in the phrase "Better Britons") to a post-colonial, bi-cultural and multicultural nation dominated by neo-liberal economics and the global marketplace, and eager to redefine its culture and its identity as uniquely Pacific and Polynesian' (Brunt, 2005: 124).

Contributors

Frédéric Angleviel est professeur des universités en histoire contemporaine à l'université de la Nouvelle-Calédonie. Il a soutenu une thèse nouveau régime d'histoire contemporaine sur Wallis et Futuna en 1989 et une Hdr sur l'historiographie de la Nouvelle-Calédonie en 2002. Certifié dès 1985, il fut professeur d'histoire à l'école normale de Nouvelle-Calédonie de 1987 à 1990 puis directeur du CTRDP de Nouvelle-Calédonie (1991-1994). Il a publié cinq ouvrages, dont une *Brève histoire politique de la Nouvelle-Calédonie contemporaine* (2006), et une cinquantaine d'articles, dont 9 articles en anglais et 3 en italien.

Favorable au travail d'équipe, il co-dirigea en 1992 le manuel d'histoire de la Nouvelle-Calédonie CM et en 1999 un ouvrage portant sur Wallis-et-Futuna. En 2004, il a coordonné un numéro spécial du *Journal of Pacific Studies* (Suva), en 2006 les actes de la 16è Pacific history Association conference et en 2008 les mélanges dédiés au Pr. Jean Martin. Editeur, il a créé en 1997 la collection *101 mots pour comprendre* aux éditions nouméennes île de lumière, (8 titres). A L'Harmattan la collection *Portes océanes* compte 4 titres. Depuis 2003, il est expert au niveau national pour le Ministère de la Recherche à la MSTP puis à la DGRI.

Frédéric Angleviel is professor in contemporary history at the University of New Caledonia and editor of the annual journal *Annales d'histoire calédonienne*. His 1989 doctoral thesis on the religious history of Wallis and Futuna was published in 1994, and in 2002 he completed his second French thesis (HDR) on New Caledonia's historiography (published in 2003). His research interests include perceptions of Christianity in Oceania, identity and migrations, historical sources, and, especially in recent years, the politics and governance of New Caledonia.

Sylvette Boubin-Boyer a soutenu une thèse de doctorat d'histoire à l'Université de Nouvelle-Calédonie en 2001 : « *De la Première*

Guerre mondiale en Océanie – Les guerres de tous les Calédoniens » (publication Septentrion, 2003). Elle est membre de l'équipe d'accueil et Institut des mondes Océanien et Australasien (IMOA-UNC), du Groupe de recherches en histoire de l'Océanie contemporaine (GROHC-UNC), de la Société d'Études Historiques de la Nouvelle-Calédonie (SEHNC) et du CRID 14-18. Elle est également présidente et responsable de la publication de l'Association des professeurs d'histoire géographie de Nouvelle-Calédonie (APHGNC), vice-présidente du Cercle du musée de la Ville de Nouméa, responsable de la cellule éducative et conseillère scientifique au musée de la Ville de Nouméa. Elle a participé à plusieurs colloques internationaux en Australie, France et Nouvelle-Calédonie. Elle a contribué, depuis 1992, à l'élaboration des programmes et de cinq manuels d'histoire adaptée à la Nouvelle-Calédonie et est coauteur d'une douzaine d'ouvrages historiques, consacrés au Chemin des Dames, à l'Océanie française et la Nouvelle-Calédonie. Elle a également publié des articles dans des revues historiques à vocation locale et régionale (*Mwa Véé*, *Annales d'histoire calédonienne*, *bulletin de la SEHNC*, *bulletin de l'APHGNC*, *bulletin de l'association des professeurs d'histoire géographie de Polynésie française*), nationale (*Ultramarines*) et internationale (*Forts & Works* – Nouvelle-Zélande). Enfin, Sylvette Boubin-Boyer vient de diriger l'ouvrage collectif, *Révoltes, conflits et guerres mondiales en Nouvelle-Calédonie et sa region* (2 tomes), publié aux éditions L'Harmattan, Paris, février-mars 2008.

Sylvette Boubin-Boyer received her PhD in History at the University of New Caledonia in 2001. It was entitled 'De la Première Guerre mondiale en Océanie – Les guerres de tous les Calédoniens' (Septentrion, Villeneuve d'Asq, 2003). She is a member of the 'Welcome Committee' and the Institute of Oceanic and Australasian Worlds (IMOA-UNC); of the Research Group in Contemporary Oceanic History (GROHC-UNC); of the New Caledonian Historical Studies Society (SEHNC); and of the CRID 14-18. She is also President (and responsible for publications) of the Association of History and Geography teachers in New Caledonia (APHGNC); Vice-President of the 'Circle of the Museum of the City of Nouméa'; and responsible for the educative unit, and scientific advisor, to the

Museum of the City of Nouméa. She has participated in several international congresses in Australia, France and New Caledonia. Since 1992, she has contributed to the development of five history handbooks and other programmes adapted to New Caledonia. She is also co-author of a dozen of historical works, dealing with the Chemin des Dames, French Oceania, and New Caledonia. She has also published articles in a variety of local, regional, national and international historical reviews. She has just completed supervising a collective work, *Révoltes, conflits et guerres mondiales en Nouvelle-Calédonie et sa region* (two volumes), published in 2008 in Paris by l'Harmattan.

Peter Brown is Reader in the School of Language Studies at the Australian National University. His interests include francophone culture and literature, in particular that of New Caledonia, with works including: *The Kanak Apple Season*; *Living Heritage. Kanak Culture Today* (ed.); and several articles on biennial francophone summit meetings.

Peter Brown, Maître de conférences (Reader) à la School of Language Studies de l'Australian National University, Canberra, s'intéresse depuis de nombreuses années aux littératures « émergeantes » en Océanie, en particulier en Nouvelle-Calédonie, de même qu'à la francophonie culturelle et institutionnelle: *The Kanak Apple Season* ; *Living Heritage. Kanak Culture Today* (ed.); rapports sur plusieurs Sommets de la Francophonie.

Paul D'Arcy is a fellow in the Australian National University's Division of Pacific and Asian History. He has an M.A. in Pacific history from the University of Otago and a PhD from the Australian National University. He researches and teaches Pacific and environmental history, as well as conflict resolution and development in the Asia Pacific region. He published *The People of the Sea: environment, identity and history in Oceania* in 2006. His second book, *Peoples of the Pacific: The History of Oceania to 1870*, will be published by Ashgate in 2008.

Paul D'Arcy est maître de conférences dans le département d'histoire de l'Université Nationale d'Australie. Il a obtenu un M.A. en histoire du Pacifique à l'université d'Otago et un PhD à l'ANU. Il poursuit ses recherches sur l'histoire environnementale du Pacifiquetout en étudiant la résolution des conflits en Océanie et les problèmes de développement dans la région Asie-Pacifique. Il a publié : « *The people of the Sea* » en 2006. Son second livre : « *Peoples of the Pacific* » sera publié par Ashgate en 2008.

Yannick Essertel, Docteur en histoire, Enseigne l'histoire des Mondes extra-européens au Centre universitaire de Bourg-en-Bresse (Lyon III). Il est membre du GRIEM (Groupe de recherches interdisciplinaires sur les écritures missionnaires) et membre du CREDIC (Centre de Recherche et d'étude d'Inculturation du Christianisme). Spécialiste de la mission, il a notamment publié *L'Aventure missionnaire lyonnaise de 1815 à 1962* au CERF en 2001; *Mgr Jean-Baptiste Pompallier, apôtre des Maoris en Nouvelle-Zélande de 1838 à 1868*, in Les écritures de la mission dans l'outre-mer insulaire, Dir. Claire Laux, Brepols, 2007; et divers articles dans des revues spécialisées.

Yannick Essertel, Doctor of history, teaches in the world history programme at the University Centre of Bourg-en-Bresse (Lyon III). He is a member of GRIEM (Group of cross-curricular research on missionary writings) and a member of CREDIC (Centre of Research and study of the inculturation of Christianity). As a specialist in missionary activity, he has published, among other works, *L'aventure missionnaire lyonnaise de 1815 à 1962*, at CERF in 2001; *Mgr Jean-Baptiste Pompallier, apôtre des Maoris en Nouvelle-Zélande de 1838 à 1868*, in the writings of the mission in overseas insular territories, Dir. Claire Laux, Brepols, 2007; as well as other articles in various specialist reviews.

François Garde, sous-préfet puis magistrat administratif, a été notamment secrétaire général adjoint de la Nouvelle Calédonie (1991-1993), conseiller chargé des affaires juridiques et de la Nouvelle Calédonie auprès du ministre de l'outre-mer (1998-1999), administrateur supérieur des terres australes et antarctiques françaises (2000-2005). Il est l'auteur des « *Institutions de la Nouvelle Calédonie* « (2000), et d'une vingtaine d'articles sur les relations du droit français et des réalités de la Nouvelle Calédonie.

François Garde, a senior civil servant, and now administrative first judge, was Deputy High Commissioner in New Caledonia (1991-1993) , Legal Advisor to the Minister for Overseas Affairs (1998-1999), and High Commissioner for the French Sub-Antarctic Islands and the Antarctic (2000-2005). In 2000 he published *The Institutions of New Caledonia* and he has written numerous articles on relationships between French law and New Caledonian realities.

Christian Huetz de Lemps, professeur de géographie tropicale à l'Université de Paris IV Sorbonne, a travaillé à la fois sur la spécificité des îles tropicales, la diversité de leurs sociétés dans le Pacifique, l'océan Indien et la Caraïbe et sur l'histoire des découvertes et de l'exploration maritime. Il a créé et dirigé le Centre de Recherches sur les espaces tropicaux à l'Université Michel de Montaigne de Bordeaux et s'occupe aujourd'hui de l'équipe Pacifique au sein du laboratoire PRODIG-CNRS.

Christian Huetz de Lemps, now Emeritus Professor of tropical geography at the University of Paris IV Sorbonne, and former chairman of the departments of geography in Michel de Montaigne-Bordeaux III and Paris IV Sorbonne Universities, has conducted research into the distinctive identity of tropical islands, including the diversity of their societies in the Pacific, the Indian Ocean and the Caribbean, as well as the history of maritime exploration and discovery. He founded and directed the Tropical Research Centre at Bordeaux III University, and is now a member of the Pacific research team of Prodig-CNRS laboratory in Paris.

Dominique Lataste was born in 1950 in France. She has a PhD in Anthropology from INALCO (Institut National des Langues et Civilisations Orientales, located in Paris) and has been a French teacher. She is co-author (with Fania Toa) of *Living customs in Uvea*

(*Vivre la Coutume à Wallis*), a book about everyday life in Wallis Island. She has lived in different parts of the world, but mostly in the Pacific, and especially on Wallis Island. She is now retired, living in Noumea, New Caledonia.

Dominique Lataste est née en 1950, en France. Elle a un doctorat en anthropologie obtenu à l'INALCO et a enseigné comme professeur de français. Elle est co-auteur avec Epifania Toa de « *Vivre la coutume à Wallis* », un ouvrage qui traite de la vie quotidienne à Wallis. Elle a vécu dans différents pays mais surtout dans le Pacifique et en particulier à Wallis. Retraitée, elle vit maintenant tant à Nouméa qu'à Brisbane.

Stephen Levine is a Professor of Political Science at Victoria University of Wellington and was the founding Head of the university's School of History, Philosophy, Political Science and International Relations. He has written extensively about political and security issues in the Pacific, and has also taught undergraduate and graduate courses on Pacific islands governance and international relations. Professor Levine has served several terms as editor of *Political Science* and in 2005 he was appointed founding co-editor of the Royal Society of New Zealand's new social science journal, *Kotuitui* ('Interweavings' in Maori). His work on Pacific Islands politics and the Asia-Pacific region has appeared in various journals, among them *The Contemporary Pacific*, *Pacific Studies*, *Commonwealth and Comparative Politics*, *The Australian Journal of Political Science* and the bilingual *Revue Juridique Polynésienne*, and Professor Levine has been responsible since 1995 for the annual review of Pacific Islands affairs published in *The Annual Register.*

Stephen Levine est professeur de sciences politiques à l'Université Victoria de Wellington et il a été le fondateur du département d'histoire, de philosophie, des sciences politiques et des relations internationales. Il a publié de nombreux écrits sur la politique et la sécurité dans le Pacifique et a également donné des cours sur les institutions ainsi que les relations internationales dans le Pacifique. Le professeur Levine a été l'éditeur durant plusieurs années de la revue « Political sciences » et il fut co-fondateur en 2005 de la revue « Kotuitui », publiée par la Royal Society of New Zealand. Il a publié de nombreuses études sur la région Asie-Pacifique, en particulier dans les journaux scientifiques suivants : *Contemporary Pacific*, *Pacific Studies*, *Revue juridique polynésienne*. Depuis 1995, il est en charge de la parution de la rubrique concernant le Pacifique dans le *Annual Register.*

Ian McGibbon (D Litt, Victoria University of Wellington) is the General Editor (War History) in the Ministry for Culture and Heritage. He edited the *Oxford Companion to New Zealand Military History* (2000) and is the author of numerous works on New Zealand defence and foreign policy. His publications include the two-volume official history *New Zealand and the Korean War* (1992, 1996), *New Zealand and the Second World War* (2004) and guidebooks to the New Zealand battlefields at Gallipoli and on the Western Front. In 1997 he was appointed an ONZM [Officer of the New Zealand Order of Merit] for services to historical research.

Ian McGibbon, docteur de l'université Victoria, est l'éditeur général des études portant sur l'histoire militaire au ministère de la culture et du patrimoine. En 2000, il a édité le *Oxford Companion to New Zealand Military History* et il est l'auteur de nombreuses publications sur la défense et les affaires étrangères de la Nouvelle-Zélande. Il a rédigé les deux volumes de l'histoire officielle de l'armée néo-zélandaise durant la guerre de Corée. En 1997, il a reçu le titre d'officier de l'ordre du mérite néo-zélandais (ONZM) pour services rendus à l'histoire.

Adrian Muckle (PhD, Australian National University) is a lecturer in the History Programme at Victoria University of Wellington. He teaches Pacific history and has a specialist interest in New Caledonia. He is currently revising a study of the war that occurred in the north of New Caledonia in 1917–18 and is researching the political internment of Kanak between 1887 and 1946 under the colonial *indigénat* regulations.

Adrian Muckle (PhD, Australian National University) enseigne l'histoire du Pacifique dans le Programme d'histoire à l'Université de Victoria à Wellington. Son champs de recherche spécialiste est l'histoire de la Nouvelle-Calédonie. Il écrit actuellement une monographie sur la guerre qui eut lieu dans le nord de Nouvelle-Calédonie en 1917–18, et il prépare une étude sur l'internement politique des Kanak sous l'indigénat entre 1887 et 1946.

Michel Pérez est maître de conférences à l'Université de la Nouvelle-Calédonie et directeur des études à l'Institut de Formation des Maîtres du Pacifique. Il enseigne essentiellement l'histoire sociale et politique du monde anglophone. Ses recherches portent sur la politique intérieure et régionale de l'Australie, avec un intérêt croissant pour les relations internationales de Canberra et son rôle dans la mondialisation.

Michel Pérez is a Senior Lecturer at the University of New Caledonia and Academic Supervisor at the local Teachers' Training College. He teaches mostly social and political history in the English-speaking world. His research focuses on Australia's domestic and regional policies, with increasing attention paid to Canberra's foreign relations and global positioning.

Gilles Pestaña est maître de conférences en géographie à l'Université de la Nouvelle-Calédonie après avoir été enseignant-chercheur à l'université de Limoges de 1997 à 2001. Ses enseignements portent notamment sur l'approche systémique, les espaces urbains ou encore la géographie de la mondialisation. Collaborateur de l'équipe de recherche PRODIG, Unité Mixte de Recherche CNRS de Paris il est aussi membre du Centre des Nouvelles Études sur le Pacifique (CNEP), un laboratoire de l'UNC. Après une thèse sur le thème des « mutations sociales et dynamiques des systèmes ruraux au Fouta-Djalon (République de Guinée) », il mène depuis 2003 ses recherches sur la Nouvelle-Calédonie et sur le Pacifique sur les thèmes des politiques publiques de développement rural et durable, de l'habitat spontané et l'épistémologie de la géographie. Il a collaboré par ses articles à plusieurs ouvrages récents sur le

Pacifique et participe à un programme de l'Agence Nationale de la Recherche sur la production des politiques publiques de développement rural et durable, leur contexte de production et leurs modalités de mise en œuvre.

Gilles Pestaña is senior lecturer in geography at the University of New Caledonia, after having been a lecturer at the University of Limoges from 1997 to 2001. His teaching includes the systems approach, urban space and the geography of globalisation. He is a participant in the research team PRODIG, Unité Mixte de Recherche CNRS in Paris, and he is also a member of the Centre for New Pacific Studies (CNEP), a laboratory of the University of New Caledonia. After completing a doctorate on 'social change and rural systems evolution in Fuuta-Jaloo (Republic of Guinea)' he has been conducting his research since 2003 on New Caledonia and the Pacific, focusing on public policies for rural and sustainable development, informal settlements and the epistemology of geography. More recently he has published articles and books on the Pacific and is participating in a programme of the National Agency for Research (ANR) dealing with the implementation of public policies for rural and sustainable development.

Sarah Powell has written a doctoral thesis on literature from Kanaky/New Caledonia in the French Programme at Victoria University of Wellington where she teaches a variety of courses, including modules on creative writing from the francophone Pacific and on perceptions of the South Seas during the Enlightenment. In addition to publishing several articles on Déwé Gorodé and Claudine Jacques, she has also translated into English a number of short literary texts from Kanaky/New Caledonia.

Sarah Powell fait partie de la section française à l'Université Victoria de Wellington où elle a écrit une thèse doctorale sur la littérature de Kanaky/Nouvelle-Calédonie. Vacataire, elle est chargée de cours divers, se spécialisant dans l'écriture du Pacifique francophone et dans la perception des Mers du Sud au siècle des Lumières. Auteure de plusieurs articles sur Déwé Gorodé et Claudine Jacques, elle a également traduit vers l'anglais de nombreux textes littéraires de Kanaky/New Calédonie.

Peter Tremewan has been working for some years on the relations between France and New Zealand in the nineteenth century. French settlers, whalers, scientists, writers and missionaries have been the subject of his publications as well as of research essays, theses and publications written by his postgraduate students in the French Department of the School of Languages and Cultures at the University of Canterbury. He is the author of *French Akaroa* (1990), about the failed attempt to declare French sovereignty over southern New Zealand, a project that resulted instead merely in the implantation of a small group of French settlers on Banks Peninsula.

Peter Tremewan travaille sur les relations entre la France et la Nouvelle-Zélande au XIXe siècle. Lui et ses étudiants à l'université de Canterbury ont écrit sur les baleiniers, marins, savants, écrivains, missionnaires et colons français qui sont venus en Nouvelle-Zélande. Son livre *French Akaroa* (1990) décrit la tentative française d'annexer l'île du Sud de la Nouvelle-Zélande en 1840: les Français arrivent trop tard et ne créent que le village français d'Akaroa; la France est obligé de tourner ses yeux vers les Marquises et Tahiti, où le capitaine Lavaud, commissaire du Roi à Akaroa, devra se rendre pour être gouverneur.

Darrell Tryon is Professor of Linguistics at the Research School of Pacific and Asian Studies, The Australian National University, His continuing involvement with New Caledonia, its languages and cultures, dates back more than forty years. He was co-editor (with Stephen Wurm and Peter Mühlhäusler) of and a major contributor to the *Atlas of Languages of Intercultural Communication in the Pacific, Asia and the Americas* (1995) and co-author (with Jean-Michel Charpentier) of *Pacific Pidgins and Creoles* (2004). He is currently involved in a major research project on New Caledonian French.

Darrell Tryon est professeur de linguistiques à la « research school » concernant la zone Asie-Pacifique à l'ANU. La part active et soutenue qu'il a prix dans les recherches sur la Nouvelle-Calédonie, tant au niveau de ses langues que de ses cultures, remonte à plus de quarante ans. Il a été co-éditeur de *l'Atlas of languages of Intercultural Communication in the Pacific, Asia and the Americas* (1995) et co-auteur de *Pacific Pidgins and Creoles* (2004). Il a actuellement entrepris une étude sur les différents français parlés en Nouvelle-Calédonie.